PREALGEBRA
JOURNEY INTO A MATHEMATICAL WORLD

Preliminary Edition

JAMES M. SULLIVAN
Massachusetts Bay Community College

PRENTICE HALL, Upper Saddle River, New Jersey 07458

Library of Congress Cataloging-in-Publication Data

Sullivan, James (James M.)
  Prealgebra: Journey into a mathematical world / James Sullivan.—Preliminary ed.
  p.cm.
  Includes bibliographical references and index.
  ISBN: 0-13-958646-6
  1. Mathematics. I. Title
QA39.3 .S85 2002
510—dc21   2001052087

Executive Acquisitions Editor: *Karin E. Wagner*
Editor in Chief, Developmental Math: *Christine B. Hoag*
Editor in Chief, Development: *Carol Trueheart*
Project Manager: *Elaine Page*
Assistant Managing Editor/Production Editor: *Bayani Mendoza de Leon*
Vice-President/Director of Production and Manufacturing: *David W.Riccardi*
Executive Managing Editor: *Kathleen Schiaparelli*
Senior Managing Editor: *Linda Mihatov Behrens*
Executive Marketing Manager: *Eilish Collins Main*
Manufacturing Buyer: *Alan Fischer*
Manufacturing Manager: *Trudy Pisciotti*
Editorial Assistant: *Christina Simoneau*
Art Director: *Jayne Conte*
Cover Designer: *Bruce Kenselaar*

© 2002 by **PRENTICE HALL, INC.**
Upper Saddle River, New Jersey 07458

Printed in the United States of America

10 9 8 7 6 5 4 3 2 1

ISBN: 0-13-958646-6

Pearson Education Ltd., *London*
Pearson Education Australia Pty., Limited, *Sydney*
Pearson Education Singapore, Pte. Ltd
Pearson Education North Asia Ltd., *Hong Kong*
Pearson Education Canada,Ltd., *Toronto*
Pearson Education de Mexico, S.A.de C.V.
Pearson Education —Japan, *Tokyo*
Pearson Education Malaysia, Pte.Ltd.

Table of Contents

Preface to Instructors

Success is a Journey, not a Destination

–Ben Sweetland

This book was written as an alternative to the traditional Prealgebra or Basic Mathematics book and to help students begin building the mathematical foundation needed to function in the 21st century. In today's world, students must achieve a minimum level of mathematical literacy if they hope to succeed in other college courses, have a variety of career choices, and develop the critical-thinking skills necessary for effective citizenship.

In the spirit of the NCTM and AMATYC standards, and the MAA's report on Quantitative Reasoning for College Graduates, this book addresses the need for students to:

- Develop problem-solving strategies while working on meaningful problems of interest.
- Become involved in building simple mathematical models of real world problems.
- Support their mathematical work with logical reasoning.
- Make connections with how mathematics is used in other disciplines.
- Read, write, and speak the language of mathematics with understanding.
- Use technology as a tool to help understand mathematical ideas and solve real life problems.
- Develop confidence in their ability to do and understand any mathematics that they may encounter at school, home, or work.

The core of the material includes basic ideas of number sense, symbolism and algebra, geometry, function, discrete mathematics, probability, and statistics. The material is intended for adult students who place into either a course in Prealgebra or Basic Mathematics.

This book is a starting point for underprepared students to begin their journey into a mathematical world. It is only a beginning, but beginnings are important times. The student will have the opportunity to learn all the topics traditionally taught at this developmental level. However, much of the learning will occur through guided activities called Discovery Adventures. These adventures put the student into real and thought-provoking situations where mathematical ideas naturally arise. The student is guided through these adventures with many questions that lead to active involvement in constructing their own learning. The student is then given feedback on the concepts and procedures present in the activity. The explanations provide a balance between understanding the ideas and learning the procedures.

All the concepts and skills needed to move on to a course in Introductory Algebra will be covered, and more. The coverage will be such that students will get lots of practice mastering each topic by working on in-depth, context-driven activities. These activities are constructed so that the student gains an intuitive understanding of how mathematics works and how it can be applied to the world around them.

While it is assumed that all students will have access to a scientific calculator, some activities will ask the student to put their calculator aside. Some exercises will require them to use it, but most will not mention it at all. The problems are designed to give the student a conceptual understanding of basic mathematics, practice learning routine procedures, and the ability to apply the concepts and procedures to everyday life. The calculator is just a tool, like pencil and paper that is used in the problem solving process. Part of the learning is deciding which tool is most appropriate for different tasks.

On a more personal note, teaching our Basic Math Studies course at Massachusetts Bay Community College has always been a challenge because I could never find any published material that presented Basic Mathematics or Prealgebra as an interesting and useful subject to study. I wanted a text that allowed the student to discover the beauty and power of math in an environment that was comfortable and challenging. It was time to stop complaining about the lack of material and instead dive into creating a book that would motivate students by putting them into real life situations that involve active hands-on learning.

The material has been developed, written, and class tested by the author while teaching numerous sections of Basic Math Studies to a very diverse group of students including many ESL students. There has been constant feedback from the students that has prompted many changes to allow the text to be as user friendly as possible.

I deeply believe in this work and I am committed to seeing positive change occur. I have the confidence to promote this material because I have seen it work! All my students were interviewed at midterm and during the last week of classes. The main purpose of the interview was to review a portfolio of the student's work and to let them do some self-assessment on what they felt they had learned. The interviews validated what I had observed in and out of the classroom. The students were working hard, learning mathematics, and enjoying the experience.

In concluding this preface, let me say that this book was written for the student to enjoy. The idea being that, one can work hard, think creatively, and have fun, all at the same time. It is hoped that the students and instructors will find the material rich in flavor, challenging in content, and fun to use.

I would like to thank the many developmental math instructors who reviewed this book: James Barr, *Laramie County Community College*; Celeste Carter, *Richland College*; Elizabeth Chu, *Suffolk Community College*; Margaret Crider, *Tomball College*; Irene Doo, *Austin Community College*; Rebecca Easley, *Rose State College*; Sharon Edgmon, *Bakersfield College*; Grace Foster, *Beaufort County Community College*; Terry Fung, *Kean University*; Roberta Lacefield, *Waycross College*; Rowan Lindley, *Westchester Community College*; Debra Pharo, *Northwestern Michigan College*; Barbara Sausen, *Fresno City College*; Michael Scroggins, *Lewis & Clark Community College*; Gwen Terwilliger, *University of Toledo*; Sam Tinsley, *Richland College*; Elaine M. Werner, *University of the Pacific*; and Tom Williams, *Rowan-Cabarrus Community College*.

James Sullivan
Massachusetts Bay Community College

Preface to Students

Tell me and I'll forget. Show me and I may not remember. Involve me, and I'll understand.

– Native American saying

While this text will tell you about mathematics and show you the process of doing mathematics, its main purpose is to involve you in doing mathematics. To tell and show must be part of any learning materials, but a student of mathematics does not take ownership of knowledge until he/she is actively involved in creating their own learning. This text will put you into different problem situations and guide you to discover the concepts that will help build your mathematical power. As you gain math power, you will have the confidence to face a world where more and more jobs require mathematical thinking. Thoughtful use of this power will give you the ability to solve math-related problems at home, school, and work. You will gain a vision that allows you to see that mathematics is everywhere and the more mathematical power you develop, the better you will understand and function in the real world.

Many students are apprehensive about starting a mathematics class. Perhaps it has been many years since you have taken any formal mathematics, or maybe you have never seen the reason or relevancy of studying math, or possibly you just never really understood it the first time around. This material was written for you, the student, to be actively involved with in a comfortable environment. You will be challenged to think critically about solving real problems and be asked to express your ideas and results in writing.

The text will take you on a journey into a mathematical world through different discovery adventures. These adventures are intended to be enjoyable problems that will simultaneously challenge, interest and entertain you. While not all problems will meet this expectation for each individual student, it is hoped that the overall effect will be an experience that is useful and fun to take part in. Learning mathematics does not have to be a dreadful chore that students endure to graduate. It can be an exciting exploration that all students look forward to.

Try to start these materials with an open mind and positive outlook. This is an experience that might be different from what you're used to seeing in a mathematics class. Regardless, you need to be actively involved with each problem situation to learn, through discovery, the concepts and procedures of basic mathematics.

Chapter 1

Problem Solving and Number Sense

Section 1.1 Problem Solving in the Real World
Section 1.2 Estimation, Numerical Reasoning, and Mental Arithmetic
Section 1.3 Exponents and Order of Operations

Why should you learn mathematics? When will you use this stuff? The answers to these questions involve solving problems in the context of real and interesting situations. In this chapter, you will begin to develop strategies for solving problems. You will have to read, think, calculate, and write conclusions to problems called Discovery Adventures. These adventures are guided investigations, meaning that you are led along the path to discovery with some information and many questions.

Another goal of this chapter is to help you acquire number sense. This is the ability to perform arithmetic operations, estimate answers, analyze numerical information, reason with numbers in context, and make conclusions based on your work.

The final goal of this chapter is to understand how to apply the concepts of exponent and order of operations. Have fun as you begin your journey into a mathematical world!

Section 1.1 Problem Solving in the Real World

Math Talk

In this section you will encounter words and phrases such as **"real-life," "real-world," "application," "problem," "activity,"** and **"exercise."** These words can take on different meanings in a mathematics textbook than in popular culture. For example, "real-life" and "real-world" can mean what really happens in a person's life and in the world. As you work through this textbook, the phrases "real-life" and "real-world" are used to describe situations that could occur in the world around us. The *real* does not necessarily mean that the situation has actually occurred, only that it is based on events that could happen and are often familiar to us.

If you try to start your car and the engine will not turn over because you left the lights on, then you have a problem. A solution might involve finding someone to jump-start your battery. In this book, you will have problem situations that require mathematical thinking and mathematical skills to find an acceptable solution. Many of these problems are called *applications* because you apply or use mathematical ideas to help find acceptable answers.

The word *activity* can mean you are engaged in a physical or mental action that helps accomplish some task. In a mathematical activity, you apply (use) math concepts to complete a task. The word *activity* is often synonymous with the word *exercise*. In everyday language, *exercise* can mean something you perform as practice or training, such as going to the gym for an aerobic workout. In this text, *exercise* refers to a problem that a student will solve using mathematical reasoning. You are training yourself to use mathematics as a vehicle for solving problems at work, home, and in other classes at school. The hope is that you will be a more valuable employee, a more informed citizen, and a better student. While some mathematical exercises you perform will practice a specific skill, usually the skill will be done as part of an application or an interesting problem that makes use of mathematics. We can engage in physical exercise to feel fit and stay healthy. We can engage in mathematical exercise to feel competent at dealing with situations that involve numerical information and to stay mentally sharp. The word "suppose" will often precede an activity or exercise so that you can imagine yourself in a particular situation when there is a problem to be solved.

Most of these words are related. For example, you might be asked to complete an exercise in which you actively investigate a real-life application of a mathematical concept. That might seem confusing now, but as you solve problems within this book, you will become more comfortable with the language of mathematics.

Brush Up on Solving Money Problems

Money calculations rely on being able to add, subtract, multiply, and divide in dollars and cents. You can write a whole dollar amount as $17 or $17.00. You can write 50 cents as $0.50 as well as $.50 or simply, 50¢. When working with dollars and cents, decimals are always rounded to the nearest hundredths place (two places to the right of the decimal point).

Practice:

1) What is $18.45 added to $12.32?

2) What is $12.32 subtracted from $18.45?

3) What is $1.09 multiplied by 12?

4) What is $152.35 divided by 6, rounded to the nearest cent?

Answers: 1) $30.77, 2) $6.13, 3) $13.08, 4) $25.39

One of the fundamental reasons for studying mathematics is to improve your ability to solve problems. Many problem situations use numerical information and can be expressed in mathematical terms. It is our goal in this section to introduce a five-step problem solving process and begin to develop different mathematical strategies for tackling each problem.

Discovery Adventure 1: Bite-Size Bagels for Breakfast

It is traditional in your early morning math class for one student to bring a breakfast snack to share with the whole class. Bruno's bakery sells bite-size bagels in boxes of 15, 40, and 60. You have ten dollars of spending money that must last the week and you want to know what you can purchase at Bruno's.

a. What questions do you need to think about before buying any bite-size bagels from Bruno's?

_____

_____

_____

_____

Suppose you obtain the following information about Bruno's bakery and your class:
- One box of 15 bite-size bagels costs $2.49 including tax.
- One box of 40 bite-size bagels costs $3.79 including tax.
- One box of 60 bite-size bagels costs $4.19 including tax.
- There are 28 students registered for your math class.
- On average, 2 students are absent from any class meeting.
- On average, each student eats 3 bite-size bagels.

b. How many boxes of each size should you buy for everyone while keeping cost to a minimum? Show all work and then justify your answer in complete sentences.

_____

_____

_____

c. Explain why part *b* is often called an open-ended question with more than one right answer.

_____

_____

_____

d. What is the maximum number of bite-size bagels that can be bought for $8.00? Show all work and justify your answer in complete sentences.

_____

_____

_____

e. How many correct answers are there to part *d*? How is this question different from part *b*? Explain.

_____

_____

_____

_____

Feedback

Each of our lives is filled with problems that require us to **analyze** a situation mathematically, and to find the best course of action to solve it. Since the best course of action can be different for each individual, many problems have no single right answer. These are known as open-ended problems, and the world is full of them. Usually a group of individuals can agree upon a list of viable solutions that the majority of the affected people can live with. Our task is to figure out those action plans that seem most reasonable for solving the problem and then to decide which is the best plan for all concerned. Here are some facts about Discovery Adventure 1 that you might have arrived at:

- Students to feed, $28 - 2 = 26$.

- Bite-size bagels needed, assuming each person eats three, $3 \cdot 26 = 78$

- Possible box combinations that add up to about 78 bite-size bagels,

  one box of $15 +$ one box of $60 = 75$ bite-size bagels
  $$\$2.49 + \$4.19 = \$6.68$$

  one box of $40 +$ one box of $60 = 100$ bite-size bagels
  $$\$3.79 + \$4.19 = \$7.98$$

  two boxes of $40 = 80$ bite-size bagels
  $$2 \cdot \$3.79 = \$7.58$$

  two boxes of $15 +$ one box of $60 = 90$ bite-size bagels
  $$2 \cdot \$2.49 + \$4.19 = \$9.17$$

Since there is no combination that equals 78 exactly, do we skip buying bite-size bagels? Do we just take the total closest to 78? Do we look for a combination that gives us more than 78, so that everyone can have at least 3 bite-size bagels? How much are we willing to spend? Is there a good deal that will give us at least 78 bite-size bagels and keep the price at a minimum? Two boxes of 40 cost only $7.58 and give the class 2 extra bagels. However, for 40¢ more we can get one box of 40 and one box of 60 which equals 100 bite-size bagels. That's 22 extra bagels! But would the students want the extras and do we care if they go to waste?

By placing an $8.00 restriction and asking you to maximize your purchase, we have narrowed the problem to one choice. It can be shown through trial and error (or guess and test) that the combination of 1 box of 40 and 1 box of 60 will give the most (100) bite-size bagels for the money and leave 2¢ change.

****

Even when there is just one right answer to a problem, there are often many ways to arrive at that answer, and each different way can provide insight into what is going on in the problem situation.

In the real world, there are usually many paths that lead to the solution. The beauty of mathematics is that the journey can be different for each of us; yet we all can arrive at the same place.

The real world is full of messy problems with no perfect answers, and most of these involve numbers and mathematics, if we look hard enough. One of our goals is to see more of the world through mathematical eyes. This vision will give us the power to solve complex problems and show us the beauty of living in a mathematical world.

Let's investigate a new situation that involves solving a problem with a specific goal. Your task is to help figure out what needs to be done to accomplish that goal.

Discovery Adventure 2: The Wedding Tuxedo

A good friend named Gerry is getting married in 10 weeks. Gerry's dad just bought a new tuxedo for himself and gave Gerry the old one he got married in. Gerry has confided to you that the tuxedo will never fit unless he loses 20 pounds and wearing it will mean a lot to his father.

a. What weekly goal should Gerry set up to help him lose the weight in a constant manner over time? Express your answer in a complete sentence.

_____

_____

Gerry now needs a game plan. Currently, he consumes around 2500 calories per day and his weight is not changing. You explain to him that he can lose body fat by either decreasing the number of calories taken in through eating or by increasing his physical activity through exercise. Gerry says he is so busy planning the wedding that increasing his exercise is impossible.

b. If the general rule of thumb is one pound of body fat equals 3,500 calories, then find the number of calories he needs to give up per week. Show the calculation and state the answer in words using a complete sentence.

Calculation:

_____

_____

c. How many calories per day is this? Show the calculation and state the answer in words using a complete sentence.

Calculation:

_____

_____

d. How many calories must Gerry give up over the next 10 weeks? Show the calculation and state the answer in words using a complete sentence.

Calculation:

_____

_____

e. How many calories can Gerry have each day? Show the calculation and state the answer in words using a complete sentence.

Calculation:

_____

_____

Feedback

Let's look at an organized way to solve a problem that requires mathematical thinking. Here are five steps you can follow in developing a problem-solving method.

I.   Read for understanding

This means to read and reread the problem until you are familiar with the problem situation and know what you are looking for. Write down what you are trying to find and any given information that will help in the problem-solving process.

II.   Plan a strategy

Develop a game plan on how to approach the problem. If you are unsure what to do, be willing to experiment with different strategies. Some of the strategies to consider are listed below. Don't be afraid to ask for help from your instructor, classmates, friends, and relatives.

Visual Strategies:	• Draw a Picture • Make a Graph
Numerical Strategies:	• Guess and Test (or Trial and Error if you prefer) • Create a Table • Look for Patterns • Perform arithmetic operations
Algebraic Strategies:	• Use an Unknown • Create an Equation • Find a Formula

III.   Implement a strategy

Put into action any strategy that has been developed such as completing a table, drawing a picture with labels, or performing a calculation. Be actively engaged in performing the mathematical work that is necessary to finding possible answers. Make sure you clearly show all your work in an organized manner.

IV.   Check and analyze your results

First ask yourself if your results seem reasonable and make sense in terms of the problem situation. Check your answer(s) by making sure all mathematical work was done correctly.

V.   Make conclusions and summarize them in writing

> The results you obtain should be expressed in words using complete sentences. You need to make it clear to your audience what you have found and what conclusions you have reached.

Let's use the five-step method just described, to solve a slightly different version of Discovery Adventure 2: The Wedding Tuxedo.

Discovery Adventure 3: The Wedding Tuxedo, Revisited

Suppose Gerry is 30 years old and wants to lose 20 pounds as soon as possible. He currently weighs 200 pounds, consumes 2500 calories a day with no change in weight, and is willing to cut his caloric intake to 2000 calories a day until his goal is reached. He is aware of the fact that one pound of fat equals 3500 calories. If his wedding date, May 30, is 70 days away, does he have enough time to reach his goal?

I. Write what is known (or given) and what you are looking for (or trying to find).

GIVEN: _____

_____

_____

_____

FIND: _____

_____

II. Develop a plan by listing any mathematical calculations that are necessary in solving the problem.

_____

_____

_____

III. Perform the calculations and show all your work in an organized manner.

IV. Look over your work and check your answer. Do your results seem reasonable? Explain in writing using complete sentences.

_____

_____

V. Summarize your findings by writing a brief conclusion. Be sure to include your advice to Gerry based on the work you did above.

_____

_____

_____

_____

_____

_____

Feedback

When you list what is given, include only the information that will help you find what you are looking for. In the tuxedo problem, Gerry must find out how many days are needed to lose 20 pounds. Here is a list of items that appear to be useful facts.

- Gerry's goal is to lose 20 pounds.

- He currently consumes 2500 calories per day.

- There is no change in weight while consuming 2500 calories per day.

- He is willing to change his consumption to 2000 calories per day.

- One pound of fat is equivalent to 3500 calories.

- He has 70 days to reach his goal.

Take note that not every bit of information must be used in solving the problem. In the real world, you rarely have problem situations that give you just enough information to solve the problem. You must decide what is important and what can be ignored. Often, you will have to do some research to find all the information needed to arrive at a reasonable conclusion.

Planning your strategy in the tuxedo problem involved three calculations. Below we have listed the planning and the implementation of the plan.

- Find the amount of calories Gerry will cut from his diet by subtracting the new calories per day from the current calories per day.

$$2500 - 2000 = 500 \text{ calories per day}$$

- Find the number of days to lose 1 pound by dividing the calories he cuts from his diet into the calories equal to 1 pound of body fat.

$$\frac{3500}{500} = 7 \text{ days for one pound}$$

- Find the number of days needed to lose 20 pounds by multiplying 20 times the days needed to lose one pound.

$$20 \cdot 7 = 140 \text{ days to lose 20 pounds}$$

The results from the previous calculations seem reasonable because Gerry only cut enough calories to lose one pound per week. Gerry is not going to fit into his tuxedo in time for the wedding based on the given information. What advice would you give to Gerry?

Although this five-step process does not have to be rigidly followed, it forms a good basis to begin our journey into problem solving in the world around us.

In the Study Skill feature on the next page, you will review how to read a table.

Study Skill: How to Read a Table or Spreadsheet

An efficient way to organize and represent numerical information is to use a table or spreadsheet. Tables have rows of cells listed horizontally (across) and columns of cells listed vertically (down). Each cell can be uniquely labeled by expressing its row and column. For example, the highlighted cell R2C3, shaded in the table below, represents the information contained in the area where the second row and third column intersect.

	Column 1	Column 2	Column 3	Column 4	Column 5
Row 1	R1C1	R1C2	R1C3	R1C4	R1C5
Row 2	R2C1	R2C2	R2C3	R2C4	R2C5
Row 3	R3C1	R3C2	R3C3	R3C4	R3C5
Row 4	R4C1	R4C2	R4C3	R4C4	R4C5
Row 5	R5C1	R5C2	R5C3	R5C4	R5C5

In the table below, observe the information on the cost of having a child enroll in a preschool/daycare called Discovery Childcare Center. To interpret the information in the table, notice that the first row and first column have labels that describe the remaining cells of data. For example, if you want to enroll a child in the toddler program for five days, the cost of $169 would be contained in cell R3C2 (across row 3, down column 2).

Discovery Childcare Center

Program	5 Days	4 Days	3 Days	2 Days
Infants	$197	$168	$143	$118
Toddlers	$169	$143	$118	$92
Preschool	$129	$115	$103	$90
Kindergarten	$137	N/A	N/A	N/A

Reading tables is more than just looking up information. Often it will be helpful to interpret the data. For example, do you see any patterns in the data that give you insight into how each number was derived and what, if any significance they could have in your life? Here are some items you might have noted.

- Enrolling a child for 5 days gives the most value for the money, or the cheapest cost per day.
- The Preschool program is the least expensive, no matter how many days of childcare are needed.
- Since N/A means "not applicable," you can only enroll a child in the kindergarten program for 5 days.

Some exercises at the end of this section involve finding an average. If you are rusty on this topic, read the following feature to brush up on finding averages and then try the Practice exercises. Otherwise, go directly to the Section Exercises to enjoy more adventures in problem solving.

Brush Up on Finding Averages

To take the average of 4 numbers, you would add the four numbers together and then divide that sum by 4. For example, Elaine ran in four 10-kilometer road races during the last few months with finishing times of 52, 49, 55, and 54 minutes. What was her average finishing time for these four races?

$$\frac{52 + 49 + 55 + 54}{4} = \frac{210}{4} = 52.5 \text{ or about 53 minutes}$$

To generalize, the average of n values, where n is the number of values, is the sum of the n values divided by n.

Practice:

1) If Brad received a 95%, 88%, and 92% on his last 3 tests, then what is his average for these 3 tests? Round to the nearest percent.

2) Suppose a local weather service recorded the temperatures in degrees Fahrenheit for each day of the past week as 45°, 42°, 54°, 55°, 42°, 44°, 46°. What was the average temperature for the past week? Round to the nearest degree.

3) Suppose you work 4 evenings per week at a local restaurant as a member of the wait staff. During the four nights last week, your take-home pay was as follows: $120, $92, $160, and $116. What was the average daily take-home pay during this week?

Answers: 1) 92%, 2) 47°F, 3) $122

> **Section Exercises: 1.1**

1. Let's define a complete introduction between two people as a verbal exchange of names along with a handshake. The name exchange and handshake will occur only once between any two individuals. For example, Susan to Jim and Jim to Susan is considered to be one introduction.

   a. Find out the number of students in your math class and record it here.

   b. If you are alone, how many complete introductions are possible?

   c. When Lewis met Clark for the first time, how many complete introductions occurred?

   d. Using 3 people, how many complete introductions are possible?

   e. Using 4 people, how many complete introductions are possible?

   f. Do you see any pattern developing? Explain.

   _____

   _____

   g. Come up with a strategy for finding how many complete introductions occur in your whole class if every one of the students performs an introduction with each of the others? In other words, if each student meets everyone else once, how many complete introductions will occur? Consider using one or more of the strategies mentioned earlier as you plan. Then implement the strategy, showing all work below.

h. Check your work and summarize your results in writing using complete sentences.

_____

_____

_____

_____

2. Suppose your instructor has five equally weighted exams before the final. Currently, Jim has taken four exams with scores of 89, 97, 86, 83. What must Jim score on the 5th exam to go into the final with an *A* average (90-100)?

3. Most portrait studios offer copies of your favorite portrait(s) in different sizes and quantities that you can purchase individually, in special packages, or a combination of package and individual. Here is one studio's price list.

Deluxe Package	Standard Package	Individual Prices
1 - 10 x 13	2 - 8 x 10	10 x 13 @ $12
2 - 8 x 10	2 - 5 x 7	8 x 10 @ $8
2 - 5 x 7	16 - wallet	5 x 7 @ $4
12 - wallet	Cost $30	Wallet @ $1
Cost $35		

a. Suppose a loved one wants you to get one 10 x 13, two 8 x 10's, three 5 x 7's and 15 wallet-size pictures. What is the best combination of package and/or individual items?

b. Suppose you want to spend $50.00 and get the most for your money. Knowing that you need 16 wallet-size pictures and only one 10 x 13, what is your best purchase plan? Show all work and explain your answer in complete sentences.

_____

_____

_____

4. A driver's reaction time in applying a vehicle's brakes is the time it takes the driver's foot to move from the gas pedal to the brake pedal. An average driver's reaction time can vary from 1½ to 2 seconds.

a. Suppose you are driving a vehicle at 60 mph, which translates to 88 feet per second. What would be a safe amount of distance to leave between your vehicle and another vehicle in front of you? Show all work and use complete sentences to explain your answer.

_____

_____

_____

b. Suppose a vehicle is going 85 mph, which translates to 140 feet per second, with another vehicle traveling at about the same speed, one car's length in front. If the brake lights of the vehicle in front come on, how far will the car behind travel before its driver reacts? Show all work and use complete sentences to explain your answer.

_____

_____

_____

c. A vehicle's headlights illuminate about 300-400 feet. Suppose a car is traveling at night going 85 mph on a poorly lit highway, and the driver spots a deer down the road. Use this situation to explain why speeding at night is even more dangerous than during the day.

_____

_____

_____

d. What do you think is the biggest factor in causing highway fatalities? Explain.

_____

_____

_____

5. Let's return to Discovery Adventure 2 and Gerry's weight loss situation. It has been two weeks into his diet and you are there for his first official weigh-in. Before Gerry steps on the scale, he confesses that late every evening he raided the refrigerator for a bowl of ice cream. He tells you how every meal was weighed out to keep him exactly at 1500 calories. But after retiring to bed he would dream of luscious bowls of ice cream and wake up with a craving. You check the freezer and find a quart of ice cream. The label reads that each serving is 240 calories. Gerry approaches the scale and kicks off his shoes, saying his feet are sore from the ballroom dancing lessons. You smile, remembering the crash course he takes 3 nights a week and knowing that each vigorous dancing lesson should burn about 200 calories.

a. How far behind is Gerry in his diet schedule?

b. Assuming no more ice cream is eaten, how many more dancing lessons does Gerry need to get back on pace with the weight loss plan?

c. If the ice cream continues to be a nightly ritual and the dancing lessons stop now, then how many days more than 70 would he need to lose the weight?

6. The owners of Funland Park have 12 trampolines that are rented to the public. One 10-minute session costs $3.75 to the consumer. The park is open from 10:00 a.m. to 10:00 p.m.

    a. What is the maximum amount of money that one consumer can spend in an hour renting trampolines just for her/his own use?

    b. What is the maximum amount of income the owners can make in one hour from renting the trampolines?

    c. What is the maximum amount of income the owners can make in a 7-day week from renting the trampolines?

7. Funland Park also has batting cages where you use a bat to hit baseballs or softballs that are pitched from a pitching machine. To operate the device, you deposit a token in a slot and get ready to swing at a pitched ball. One token provides you with a 10-pitch session of batting practice. The prices for buying tokens are listed below.

Number of Tokens	Price	Price per Token
1	$1.50	
4	$5.00	
10	$10.00	
22	$20.00	

    a. To better understand the price schedule, fill in the third column to find out how the cost of each token depends on the number purchased.

    b. If you were the owner of Funland Park, which of the following options would you prefer? Show all work and explain your answer using complete sentences.

- 22 customers each buying 1 token.
- 7 customers each buying 4 tokens.
- 3 customers each buying 10 tokens.
- 1 customer buying 22 tokens.

c. Suppose you have $18 to spend on tokens, what is the maximum number of tokens you can buy?

d. If you want the opportunity to swing at 90 pitched balls, then what is the most economical way to purchase tokens?

8. Suppose Funland Park has a miniature golf course that charges $5.00 for each adult and $3.50 for any child 12 years old and under. On a certain day, the golf course made $3000 in revenue and had 750 customers (adults and children) play miniature golf.

a. Construct a trial-and-error table with the given headings and use a guess and test strategy.

Number of Adults	Number of Children	Revenue Calculation	Revenue ($)	Conclusion
50	700	$5 \bullet 50 + 3.5 \bullet 700$	2700	too low

b. What is the breakdown for adults and children that totals 750 and makes $3000 for Funland Park? How did you find this out?

_____

_____

_____

c. Suppose the golf course changes its price policy so that all customers (adults and children) are charged the same price of $5.00. After one week it is calculated that the average daily attendance has decreased to 700, but revenue has increased to $3500. How could this happen?

_____

_____

_____

_____

_____

9. Suppose there are fifteen people where you work, including yourself, and it's your turn to buy coffee for all the employees. If each cup of coffee cost $1.29 and you have $20 to spend, do you have enough money to buy coffee for everyone? Show all work and state your answer in a complete sentence that explains either how much change you will get back or the amount of money you are short.

_____

_____

10. Suppose an outdoor concert drew 12,000 people who left behind 9 tons of garbage. What was the average amount of garbage (in pounds) left by each person at the concert? *Hint*: One ton equals 2,000 pounds. Show all work and state your answer in a complete sentence.

_____

_____

11. At the end of the semester, a math class decides to buy a $100 gift for their instructor. If all 22 students make an equal contribution, then what will each student need to contribute?

Section 1.2 Estimation, Numerical Reasoning, and Mental Arithmetic

Math Talk

Suppose you are at a sport event, concert, or theater with a group of people. You agree to go to the concession stand and buy food and drink for the 5 people in your party and yourself. The gentleman working behind the concession stand comes back with your order and says, "You had 6 drinks at $1.75 each, 4 hot dogs at $2.50 each, 2 hamburgers at $3.00 each, 3 chips at $1.65 each, 4 candy bars at $3.00 each, and 2 popcorns at $1.75 each. That'll be $135.75 please." You respond, "That total seems a little high." The concession worker gives you a dirty look and says, "Look pal, you do the arithmetic and prove I'm wrong." You respond, "All right, let's see, 6 times $1.75 equals…plus 4 times $2.50 equals…"

Does it matter whether you can keep track of the **exact** results? What type of mental arithmetic is important, and when do you reach for your calculator?

One very important type of mental (in your head) calculation is the ability to **estimate**. For our purposes, estimation is when an **approximate** answer is obtained without the aid of pencil and paper, calculator, almanac, or an exact source.

> An **estimate** can be a quick and/or rough calculation used to obtain an answer that is close to the true value, but not necessarily exact.

In the situation above, you could have taken each price, except the hamburgers and candy bars, and rounded up to the nearest dollar. Then you could approximate:

6 drinks at $2	4 hot dogs at $3
3 chips at $2	2 hamburgers at $3
2 popcorns at $2	4 candy bars at $3
11 items at $2	10 items at $3

The calculation to estimate the total cost becomes $2 \cdot 11 + 3 \cdot 10 = 22 + 30 = \$52$.

The estimate of $52 is far below the price of $135.75, being demanded by the concession worker, and we rounded up the price of many items to the nearest dollar so even $52 is high!

As a second example, suppose someone asks you the population of your hometown. You probably know the amount to the nearest 10,000 people, maybe even to the nearest 1000, but it is doubtful that you know the exact population. Even the town census will not be able to count everyone!

21

Suppose you are reading a newspaper and notice the following headlines.

- Top Woman Basketball Player Earns Over 2 Million Dollars Per Year

- New Year's Eve Crowd of 75,000 Watch Fireworks Display

- Doctor Writes 341 Prescriptions Over Last 6 Months

- Holiday Road Race Attracts 1019 Runners

- Lots O'Money Lottery Jackpot Tops 80 Million

- Police Raid Captures 27 Drug Dealers

- New Sports Arena To Hold 17 Thousand Fans

Which of these headlines do you think are approximate values and which are exact?

****

In this section, we will explore the importance of thinking about numbers without doing exact calculations. So put aside your calculator for awhile, it's time to estimate.

Discovery Adventure 1: Digits

For each expression, estimate the number of digits in the solution. Explain your thinking.
A **digit** is one of the whole numbers from 0 to 9. So, 4320 has 4 digits: 4, 3, 2, and 0. Part *a* is already done and may be used as a model. Do not use a calculator or pencil and paper. Instead try to answer by estimating. After completing all the problems, then you may check your work with a calculator.

a. 186 + 792   Number of digits: __3__

Explanation: *Since 792 is less than 800 and 186 is less than 200, and 800 + 200 = 1000, then*

186 + 792 is less than 1000. Hence the sum has 3 digits.

b. 62 + 992   Number of digits: _____

_____

_____

_____

c. $1353 - 402$ Number of digits: _____

d. $2165 - 220$ Number of digits: _____

e. $12 \cdot 3160$ Number of digits: _____

f. $6 \cdot 788$ Number of digits: _____

g. $2538 \div 5$ Number of digits: _____

h. $31205 \div 15$ Number of digits: _____

_____

_____

_____

Feedback

The problems in Discovery Adventure 1 force you to think about what is close but not exact. More friendly numbers can be calculated in your head. For example, in part *b*, the number 992 is only 8 units away from the number 1000, so adding 62 must give you a sum over 1000 and puts the result in the 4-digit category. In part *e*, the number 12 is close to the friendly number 10. Ten is friendly because multiplying it by another number, such as 3160, adds a zero to that number giving 31,600, which puts the number in the 5-digit category. You could also reason that the difference between 10 and 12 is 2, and multiplying 2 times 3160 gives a product close to 6000. Taken together, 31,600 plus 6000 is going to keep you in the 5-digit category.

****

In the next Discovery Adventure, you will use **numerical reasoning** (logical thinking about numbers) to compare two expressions with the goal of finding out whether one expression is greater than, less than, or equal to the other expression.

Discovery Adventure 2: Logically Speaking

Decide if < (less than), > (greater than), or = (equal) would produce a true sentence. First, think through the problem by carefully considering the numbers and operations involved. Be sure to justify your reasoning in words. Part *a* can be used as an example. Do not use a calculator or pencil and paper. Just estimate. After completing all the problems, you may check your work with a calculator.

a. $261 + 425 + 839$ __<__ $312 + 507 + 898$

Reasoning: <u>Since each number to the left is smaller than the number in the same position to</u>

<u> the right, the sum on the left is less than the sum on the right.</u>

b. $537 + 764 + 311$ _____ $537 + 764 + 313$

_____

_____

_____

c. $950 + 950 + 950 + 950 + 950$ _____ $6 \cdot 950$

_____

_____

_____

d. $63 + 64 + 65$ _____ $64 \cdot 3$

_____

_____

_____

e. $12 \cdot 41$ _____ $12 \cdot 40$

_____

_____

_____

f. $270 \div 10$ _____ $270 \div 7$

_____

_____

_____

g. $2583 \div 48$ _____ $2573 \div 48$

_____

_____

_____

h. $35 \cdot 2 \cdot 37$ _____ $2 \cdot 37 \cdot 35$

_____

_____

_____

i. $676 + 243 + 21 + 150$ _____ $243 + 150 + 676 + 21$

_____

_____

_____

Feedback

Estimation techniques can help you feel more comfortable with numbers and build up your number sense. The last two Discovery Adventures had you think about numbers with the goal of beginning to develop strategies that make it easier to work with numbers. Any number connections you made (and continue to make throughout this book) will allow you to gain confidence in your ability to make intelligent decisions when dealing with number problems. Let's continue our investigation of numbers and their use in the real world.

The number 675 is written, *six hundred seventy-five* and can be expressed as:

Six hundreds plus seven tens plus five ones, or

$6 \cdot 100 + 7 \cdot 10 + 5 \cdot 1$

The words *hundreds, tens*, and *ones* tell us the **place value** of each digit (6, 7, and 5). So the value of any number depends on the placement of each digit, where the ten possible digits are: 0, 1, 2, 3, 4, 5, 6, 7, 8, and 9. Therefore, we can take the same three digits and rearrange the order to obtain a different number. For example,

567 is written *five hundred sixty-seven* but means,

5 hundreds plus 6 tens plus 7 ones, or

$5 \cdot 100 + 6 \cdot 10 + 7 \cdot 1$

If you get confused, just think of money. $567 can be thought of as the sum of 5 one hundred-dollar bills, 6 ten-dollar bills, and 7 one-dollar bills.

****

In the following Discovery Adventure, you will take a close look at how the words: *digit, place value,* and *rounding* are used in the context of a problem.

Discovery Adventure 3: Great American Sweepstakes

Suppose you receive a letter from *The Great American Sweepstakes* that says, "Mr. John B. Gullible is the winner of $21,352,675 if…"

a. Write this amount in words as it might appear on a check.

_____

_____

b. Place each digit of the number 21,352,675 in the proper position in the place value chart below.

Ten-Millions	Millions	Hundred-Thousands	Ten-Thousands	Thousands	Hundreds	Tens	Ones
							•

c. We can express 21,352,675 as the sum of all its digits using the following sentence.

Two ten millions plus one million plus three hundred thousands plus five ten thousands plus 2 thousands plus six hundreds plus seven tens plus 5 ones.

Translate the sentence above into a mathematical expression by using the proper digits and the symbols for multiplication (·) and addition (+). Place your expression below.

d. Complete the following table by rounding 21,352,675 to each of the place values given in the table below. The first column has been completed and may be used as an example.

Round to the nearest Hundred	Round to the nearest Thousand	Round to the nearest Ten-thousand	Round to the nearest Hundred-thousand	Round to the nearest Million
21,352,700				

Feedback

The rule of thumb for rounding says to look at the first digit to the right of the digit you want to round to. If this digit is 5,6,7,8, or 9 then increase the digit you want to round to by one and use zeros to fill up all the remaining digits to the right. Otherwise, a digit of 0, 1, 2, 3, or 4 tells you to keep the digit the same, and use zeros to fill up all the remaining digits to the right.

Often when data are gathered in tables will a rounded number such as 21,400,000 be represented as 21.4 million.

A place value chart helps us write numbers in the system called base 10. This system assumes that the first number to the left of the decimal point gives the number of ones or units, the second number gives the number of tens, the third number gives the number of hundreds, and so on. Thus, in a number like 735, the 3 digits give meaning to the number by their position,

7 represents 7 hundreds
3 represents 3 tens
5 represents 5 ones

Therefore, 735 stands for the sum of 7 hundreds, 3 tens, and 5 ones. As a mathematical expression, using the operations of multiplication and addition,

$7 \cdot 100 + 3 \cdot 10 + 5 \cdot 1$

$700 + 30 + 5$

As you observe the digit(s) of a number from right to left, each place value is 10 times greater than the previous one to the right. Also, if you look from left to right, each place value divided by 10 gives the next place value to the right. For example, the number, 965,724 has place values shown below.

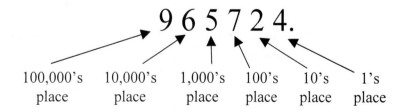

965724.

100,000's   10,000's   1,000's   100's   10's   1's
place   place   place   place   place   place

In general, as you move one place to the left, multiply by 10 to get the next place value. And, as you move one place to the right, divide by 10 to get the next place value. For example,

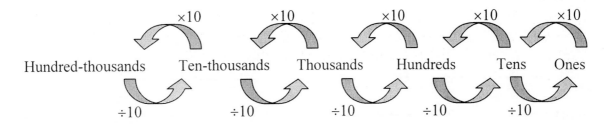

Let's now move on to the Section Exercises where you can explore new problems and practice what you have learned in this section.

Section Exercises: 1.2

1. Each day there are thousands of people infected with the HIV virus. The following table gives estimates on this worldwide health epidemic.

Cumulative HIV Infections Worldwide, 1980 – 1995.

Year	Millions of People	Year	Millions of People
1980	0.2	1990	13.0
1981	0.6	1991	15.5
1982	1.1	1992	18.5
1983	1.8	1993	21.9
1984	2.7	1994	25.9
1985	3.9	1995	30.6
1986	5.3		
1987	6.9		
1988	8.7		
1989	10.7		

(*Source*: Global AIDS Policy Coalition, Harvard School of Public Health *1995 data)

a. Notice that the table heading states, "Cumulative HIV Infections Worldwide." What does the word "cumulative" mean in this situation? Answer in a complete sentence.

_____

_____

b. Find the difference between the total number of infections up to the end of 1995 and the total number of infections up to the end of 1994. Explain what this difference tells us about HIV infections.

_____

_____

_____

c. Express 4.7 million using seven place values.

_____ , _____ _____ _____ , _____ _____ _____

d. If 4.7 million people contracted HIV in 1995, then how many people does 0.7 million represent in thousands?

e. About how many people contracted HIV each day of 1995? Show the calculation needed, and round your answer to the nearest thousand.

f. From 1990 - 1995, Thailand spent about 9 billion dollars on health care and lost worker productivity due to the HIV/AIDS epidemic. Write 9 billion in expanded form (using a digit for each place value).

g. How many millions are in 1 billion?

h. How many zero digits are needed to write out 1 billion?

i. How many zero digits are needed to write out 1 million?

j. What is the difference between 1 million and 1 billion? Answer in a complete sentence.

_____

_____

_____

2. In 1993 the average factory worker's pay was $25,317, while the average CEO's (Chief Executive Officer) pay was $3,772,000. (*Source*: Folbre and The Center for Population Economics, "*The New Field Guide To The U.S. Economy.*")

   a. Round the factory worker's pay to the nearest hundred.

   b. Round the factory worker's pay to the nearest thousand.

   c. Round the factory worker's pay to the nearest ten thousand.

   d. Round the CEO's pay to the nearest ten thousand.

   e. Round the CEO's pay to the nearest hundred thousand.

   f. Round the CEO's pay to the nearest million.

   g. Suppose you were writing an article comparing the average salaries for factory workers versus CEOs in 1993. If you could present just one rounded figure for each occupation, then what information would you print? Explain using complete sentences.

   _____

   _____

   _____

   _____

3. Many of us are in debt to banks and other institutions for things like a mortgage, car loan, or student loan. However, these debts pale in comparison to the national debt which keeps growing. According to the Treasury Department, the Federal debt (total amount of money the government owes to lenders) grew from $910 billion in 1980 to $4.95 trillion in 1995.

   a. Estimate how much the Federal debt grew during the above time period. Do not use a calculator or pencil and paper. Answer in a complete sentence.

   _____

   _____

b. How many zeros are there in 1 billion dollars? Express 1 billion with all its digits.

c. How many zeros are there in 1 trillion dollars? Express 1 trillion with all its digits.

d. How many billions are contained in 1 trillion, or what would you multiply 1 billion by to increase it to 1 trillion?

e. If there were about 260 million people in the United States in 1995, then how much money would every person in the country have to contribute to pay off the Federal debt at that time? First, estimate your answer, then use a calculator or pencil and paper to check your approximation.

Estimated solution:

Calculated solution:

In problems 4 - 7, estimate the answers to the following problems using mental arithmetic (without pencil and paper or calculator). Then explain your reasoning using complete sentences.

4. Suppose you have a choice of two jobs for part-time work. Big-Job promises you an average of 22 hours each week at a rate of $6.15 an hour, while Little-Job will give you 12 hours of work each week at $9.90 an hour. What are the estimated wages for each job?

_____

_____

_____

5. Your instructor puts in her syllabus that for every hour in class a student should do 2 to 4 hours of work outside of class. How many hours (give a range) of homework can you expect each week in your MWF 9:00 - 9:50 mathematics class?

_____

_____

_____

6. If you drive 20 miles to school each day in about half an hour, then what is a reasonable estimate of your average speed? *Note*: average speed $= \dfrac{\text{distance traveled}}{\text{travel time}}$

_____

_____

_____

7. You stop at the grocery store to pick up a few things for dinner. With only $20 dollars of spending money available, you need to estimate the total cost of the 5 food items you picked up. In your shopping cart, the following prices are observed: $1.25, $4.95, $3.59, $8.99, and $1.45. Will your $20 be enough? Do not use paper and pencil or calculator. All work should be done mentally.

_____

_____

_____

To review angles, read the Brush Up feature on the next page before continuing on with Section Exercise # 8 on page 35.

Brush Up on Your Angles

Suppose we have a *point P* which is represented geometrically by a dot and a *line* (or infinite set of points) extending from *P* without end. This line is called a *vector* or ray $\overrightarrow{PA}$, which is denoted by the arrow. If we have two rays that extend from the same endpoint *P* (called the vertex) an *angle* $\angle APB$ is formed. See the figure below.

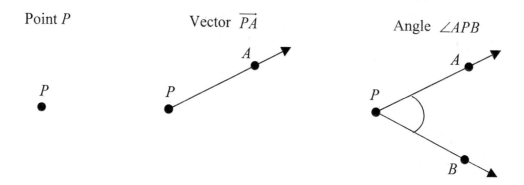

When two *perpendicular* lines or vectors meet, they form a *right angle*, which measures 90° (90 degrees). Rotating the vector one complete revolution is 360° (360 degrees). This means rotating a vector counterclockwise around a point until you trace a complete circle.

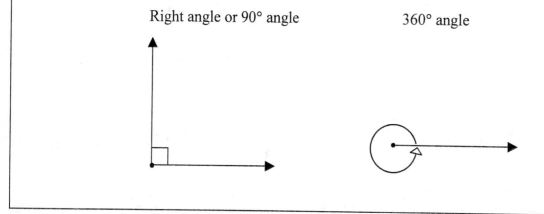

Armed with a refreshed understanding of angles, rays and lines, you may proceed with Section Exercise #8 on the next page.

8. Estimate the degree measure for the six angles given below. This is the amount of rotation required to superimpose one vector on the other. Then explain the mathematical reasoning used to obtain your estimate.

a.

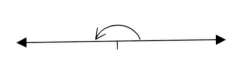

b.

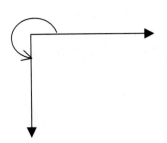

c.

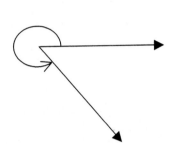

d.

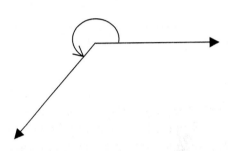

e.

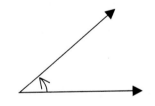

f.

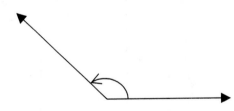

a. _____

b. _____

c. _____

d. _____

e. _____

f. _____

9. Suppose each small square is one square unit and we wish to estimate the area of the geometric object contained inside the large square. Use the small square units to approximate the area of the circle in part *a* and the area of the triangle in part *b*.

a.

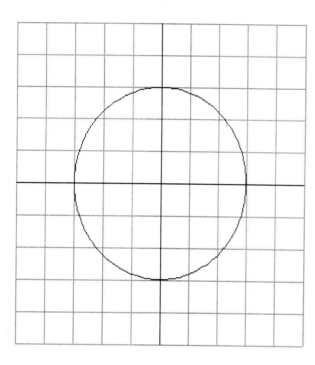

b.

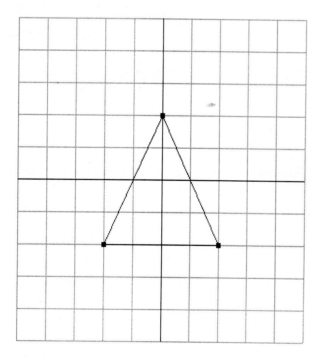

10. During a thunderstorm, you may have noticed that the lightning bolt precedes the sound of thunder by a few seconds. The lightning bolt heats the air around it with such intensity that shock waves form. The shock waves travel through the air as sound waves, which we call thunder. Light travels so fast that we see the lightning immediately. However, since sound travels slower than light, we hear the thunder a few seconds later even though they both occur simultaneously. You can estimate the distance from your position to where lightning hits by counting the number of seconds that pass between the time when you first see the lightning and the time you hear the thunder. Take this time in seconds and divide it by 3 to get the approximate distance in kilometers.

a. If you see a flash of lightning and are able to count three seconds before hearing the thunder, about how far away should lightning hit (in kilometers)?

b. What is the speed in kilometers per second at which the sound of thunder travels to reach your ears? (Recall that speed = distance ÷ time). Explain your answer.

c. Make a statement that compares the speed of light to the speed of sound in the context of this problem situation.

_____

_____

_____

d. Suppose you are out on a golf course with a friend and a thunderstorm is close by. As you watch the lightning and listen for the thunder, the time gap between seeing the lightning and hearing the thunder begins to shrink. What does this mean, and what should you do?

_____

_____

_____

e. Explain what type of data (numerical information) you would have to collect to convince a friend that the lightning from the storm is moving away from you?

_____

_____

_____

Section 1.3 Exponents, Factors, and the Order of Operations

Math Talk

In media you often see or hear the term **exponential growth** refer to a population that is growing very fast. But exactly how fast is exponential growth? The answer depends on something called the growth factor, which tells you how the population increases from one time period to the next. For example, according to *The World Almanac*, by mid-1999 close to 200 million people around the world were using the Internet, and it is estimated that use will double every 9 to 12 months. Here the time period is 9 to 12 months, and the growth factor is 2 because doubling means that the population is 2 times the previous amount.

If the local deer population were tripling every year, then the growth factor would be 3. In other words, after each year passes, there are 3 times as many deer as in the previous year.

If you hear someone say that his or her technology stock grew fourfold over the last 6 months, then it means that over the past 6 months, the value of the stock has increased to 4 times its previous value.

The situations above are all examples of exponential growth. When a population grows exponentially, it is increasing, faster and faster. The rate of increase is slow at the beginning but speeds up with time.

****

Let's take a look at what it means for a number to be a **factor** of a given number. When we write the number 4 as $2 \cdot 2$ (2 times 2), two is called a factor of 4. In this case, the factor 2 occurs twice in the multiplication process. The **identity** here is

$$4 = 2 \cdot 2$$

In other words, 4 is just another way to say $2 \cdot 2$, and $2 \cdot 2$ is just another way to say 4. The form we use depends on the situation.

The number 12 can be written in factored form as $3 \cdot 4$, where 3 and 4 are factors of 12, and 12 is the **product** of the multiplication.   The identity is

$$12 = 3 \cdot 4$$

And since $4 = 2 \cdot 2$, a second identity is

$$12 = 3 \cdot 2 \cdot 2$$

The ability to think of numbers and expressions in different but equivalent forms will help simplify many calculations and will allow us to introduce a new compact notation called an **exponent**.

An *exponent* is a convenient notation for repeated multiplication. For example, suppose we start with a single cell creature that doubles every hour, under ideal conditions. If those conditions are present, 1 becomes 2, 2 becomes 4, 4 becomes 8, and so on. We can express this process using repeated multiplication. For example,

After one hour we have 2,

After two hours we have $2 \cdot 2$ or 4,

After three hours we have $2 \cdot 2 \cdot 2$ or 8,

After four hours we have $2 \cdot 2 \cdot 2 \cdot 2$ or 16,

After five hours we get tired of expressing 2 multiplied by itself a certain number of times,

So we say 2^5 to represent 2 multiplied 5 times, $2 \cdot 2 \cdot 2 \cdot 2 \cdot 2$ or 32.

The expression 2^5 reads as "*two to the fifth power.*" This operation of raising a number to a power is called evaluating exponents. The situation of cells doubling is an example of exponential growth. Specifically, the population of cells at any given hour is 2 times the population in the previous hour. This not only means that cells are growing but that the growth itself is increasing. While the growth does not produce large amounts of cells at the beginning, as time increases the cells will grow faster and faster. After 10 hours you have

$$2^{10} = 2 \cdot 2 \cdot 2 \cdot 2 \cdot 2 \cdot 2 \cdot 2 \cdot 2 \cdot 2 \cdot 2 = 1024 \text{ cells.}$$

The exponent above is 10 but we refer to the expression as "*two to the tenth power.*" The number 2 in the expression is called the base.

Therefore, positive exponents show the number of times the base is to be multiplied. For example, four to the third power or four cubed is written as 4^3 and means 4 multiplied 3 times.

$$4^3 = 4 \cdot 4 \cdot 4 = 64$$

More formally we can define an exponent as follows:

An **exponent** is a number written above and to the side of another number called the base. If you represent the exponent by the unknown value p and the base by the unknown value n, then an exponential expression can be symbolized as follows.

$$n^p$$

Here the exponent p indicates the **power** to which the base number n is to be raised.

Study Skill: Drawing Diagrams

Diagrams or pictures can be very helpful in solving problems because they provide a means for seeing what is happening in the problem. Drawing diagrams forces you to read the problem carefully so that you can make the situation come to life on paper. This allows you to better understand the problem, and it is a visual strategy to help you solve the problem. For example, suppose we have a different single cell creature that can split into 5 equal parts every hour, under ideal conditions. See the figures below.

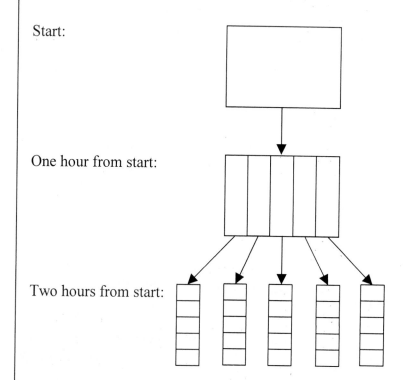

The drawing illustrates that after one hour you have 5 cells and after two hours you have $5 \cdot 5$ or 25 cells. Now you begin to see exponential growth in action. The numbers start to come alive as objects, in this case as cells.

The expression $5 \cdot 5$ can be expressed in exponential notation as 5^2, read as *"five to the second power"* or *"five squared."* Note, since $5^2 = 25$ and $2^5 = 32$, this means that $5^2 \neq 2^5$ (five to the second power is not equal to two to the fifth power).

Next you will go on an adventure to discover what exponents mean and how they are used. Go to the next page and take a journey to St. Ives.

Discovery Adventure 1: Mother Goose Rhyme

It is your turn to read during children's hour at the local library. You have chosen some Mother Goose Rhymes and decide to begin with the following one.

> *As I was going to St. Ives,*
> *I met a man with seven wives,*
> *Each wife had seven sacks,*
> *Each sack had seven cats,*
> *Each cat had seven kits,*
> *Kits, cats, sacks, and wives,*
> *How many were going to St. Ives?*

(*Source*: "The Real Mother Goose," Checkerboard Press)

After reading the rhyme, one of the children raises her hand and asks, "How many things did you (the narrator) meet?"

a. Let's consider this question slowly. Complete the second and third column in the table below by showing the factors needed in the calculation and then the result of performing that calculation. Some of the table has been filled in to get you started.

Number of	Calculation	Result
wives	7	7
sacks	7·7	
cats		
kits		
Total Number ----------- ▷		

b. Express the number of "wives" using exponential notation by placing the number of factors (sevens in the calculation column above) in raised parentheses in the upper right-hand corner next to the number seven.

$$7 = 7^{(\quad)}$$

c. In the same manner as part *b*, express the number of "sacks" using exponential notation.

$$7 \cdot 7 = 7^{(\quad)}$$

d. Express the number of "cats" using exponential notation.

$$7 \cdot 7 \cdot 7 = 7^{(\quad)}$$

e. Express the number of "kits" (kittens) using exponential notation.

$$7 \cdot 7 \cdot 7 \cdot 7 = 7^{(\quad)}$$

f. Express the total number of things in parts *b* through *e* by adding all the exponential expressions together.

$$\underline{\hspace{2cm}} + \underline{\hspace{2cm}} + \underline{\hspace{2cm}} + \underline{\hspace{2cm}} = \underline{\hspace{3cm}}$$

g. Go back and read the rhyme again, then explain how many things were going to St. Ives. Be careful. This is a puzzle that has no right answer! Give the answer that you think is best, and explain your reasoning using complete sentences.

_____

_____

_____

Feedback

If you read the rhyme carefully, it seems that the narrator or author was going to St. Ives and on the journey met a man with seven wives. However, there is no mention of this man going to St. Ives or whether the kits, cats, sacks, and wives were accompanying him on his trip. Based on this reasoning, the answer to the St. Ives puzzle is 1. If the narrator and the man that the narrator met were both going to St. Ives and the man's kits, cats, sacks, and wives were not with him, then the answer would be 2. If the man's kits, cats, sacks, and wives, all totaling $7^1 + 7^2 + 7^3 + 7^4 = 2800$, went to St. Ives with him and the narrator, then there would be 2800 + 2 or 2802 things going to St. Ives. There are many other possible interpretations, but what is important is that you understand the idea of exponents (powers) and that you are able to back up your answer with logical reasoning.

****

Remember when using exponential notation such as 7^n, 7 is called the base, and *n* is called the exponent or power. So an exponential expression will take the following form:

$$base^{exponent}$$

The base is the factor, and the exponent tells you how many times the base is used as a factor. An exponent is often referred to as a *power*.

7^1 is read as "seven to the first power"

7^2 is read as "seven to the second power" or more commonly, "seven squared"

7^3 is read as "seven to the third power" or more commonly, "seven cubed"

7^4 is read as "seven to the fourth power"

7^n is read as "seven to the *n*th power," meaning that there are *n* sevens that are factors.

In the next Discovery Adventure, you will make use of a picture called a tree diagram.

Discovery Adventure 2: Running for President

Suppose you wake up the morning of November 1 and decide to run for President of the Student Government. Your friends think that name recognition and a positive image are keys to winning. You take care of the name recognition by placing signs around campus.   On the next day (Nov. 2), you decide to spread the positive image propaganda by telling your two best friends what a great person you are. They already know that, but since no one else does, you tell each of your friends to use the following day (Nov. 3) to tell two students what a great person you are. Your friends also instruct each of these new people to use the next day to pass the message on to two more people. The process of each person who receives the message telling two new people the next day will continue on everyday up to the election, which will be held on November 11. What is the total number of students that will hear the message by the election?

a.   To begin to visualize this process, complete the following tree diagram up to the fourth day. Each human figure represents one person who knows the message, starting with you on Day 0. List each new day and the number of new messages received on that day. Also, as you finish constructing the tree, feel free to use dots, little circles, or stick figures to represent each new person hearing the message.

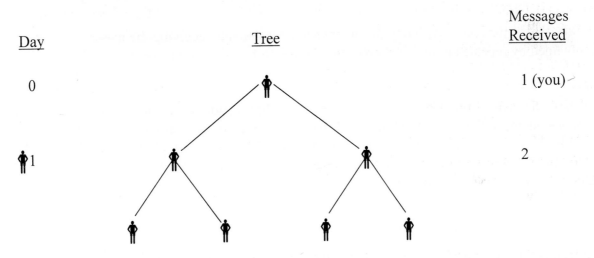

Day	Tree	Messages Received
0		1 (you)
1		2

b. Now use a numerical strategy by organizing data in the table below. Finish what has already been started.

Day	New students receiving message	Total students knowing message
0 (Nov.1)	1 (you)	1
1	2	3
2	4	7
3		
4		
5		
6		
7		
8		
9		
10 (election held)		

c. How many days must pass before at least 1000 students know the message? What is the calendar date on this particular day?

d. Note that at the end of each day the number of new students receiving the message is obtained by repeated multiplication of the same factor. What is this factor?

e. Using the factor from part *d*, show the repeated multiplication needed to obtain the number of new students at the end of the 9th day. First show the factored form with repeated multiplication, and then express the result in exponential form with the factor as the base and the number of times the base is multiplied as the exponent or power.

f. Write out the calculation that shows all the two's (2's) needed to obtain the number of new students receiving the message on the 10th day when the election is to be held.

g. Now use exponential notation to write the product obtained in part *f*.

h. On the *n*th day, how many new students have received the message? *Hint*: Use exponential notation and include the unknown *n*.

i. If the college has 2000 students, how many days must the message continue to be spread before everyone at the college has heard the message?

j. On the day of the election, how many students could have gotten away with telling just one new person the message and still have everyone at the college receive the message?

k. In reality, during the last days before the election, what difficulty will the new message senders encounter? Explain using complete sentences.

_____

_____

_____

_____

_____

Feedback

As the days (1st column) increase by 1, the number of new students (2nd column) who receive the message doubles. The total number of students knowing the message (third column) is the sum of the previous day's total plus the amount of new students receiving the message on the current day. You should also notice that every day's total number is one less than the number of new students receiving the message on the next day.

On Day 10 (Nov. 11), 2047 people could have potentially heard the message, except there are only 2000 students enrolled. So, 47 students on Day 10 would have told the message to only 1 new person.

In reality, it would be impossible to tell all the students the message in this way. For example, at the end of the ninth day, about 1 out of every 2 students has heard the message, and there are about 500 students looking to tell two more people. Since each sender has just one day to pass the message along, finding students to tell would become quite a challenge as the election approached.

****

In the next Discovery Adventure, you will investigate the proper order for completing each operation in an expression that contains more than one operation. For some of the parts, you will need to use a scientific or graphing calculator that follows the order of operations.

▤ Discovery Adventure 3: The Order of Things

Use a calculator that follows the order of operations as a tool to investigate the following problems. Any scientific calculator or graphing calculator should follow the order of operations.

a. Enter $(4+2) \cdot 5$ into your calculator. What is the output?

b. Enter $4+2 \cdot 5$ into your calculator. What is the output?

c. Show the order in which you would perform each operation when simplifying each of the expressions in parts *a* and *b*.

$a.$ $(4+2) \cdot 5$ $b.$ $4+2 \cdot 5$

     Step 1:   Step 1:

     Step 2:   Step 2:

d. How do you decide what operation to perform first in each of the above expressions? Express your answer using complete sentences.

_____

_____

_____

Let's now investigate three new expressions that are similar except for the location of parentheses.

    1) $25+15 \div 5 \cdot 3$ 2) $(25+15) \div 5 \cdot 3$ 3) $25+15 \div (5 \cdot 3)$

e. Enter each of the calculations into your calculator and evaluate the output. Explain the reasons why the outputs are the same or different. Note that many calculator screens express division with a slash / even though the key you press is the traditional division symbol, $\div$.

1)_____

2)_____

3)_____

f. Now evaluate the previous three expressions, step by step, using pencil and paper. For each step, show one operation being performed, and state in words the reason for applying that particular operation at that time.

1) $25 + 15 \div 5 \cdot 3 =$ Step 1: _____

Step 2: _____

Step 3: _____

2) $(25 + 15) \div 5 \cdot 3 =$ Step 1: _____

Step 2: _____

Step 3: _____

3) $25 + 15 \div (5 \cdot 3) =$ Step 1: _____

Step 2: _____

Step 3: _____

Now consider the two new expressions given below.

$$3 \cdot 2^3 \qquad \text{and} \qquad (3 \cdot 2)^3$$

g. Enter each of the calculations into your calculator and evaluate the output. Explain the reasons why the outputs are the same or different.

_____

_____

_____

_____

h. Evaluate the previous two expressions step by step using pencil and paper. For each step, show one operation being performed and state in words the reason for applying that operation at that time.

$3 \cdot 2^3 =$ Step 1: _____

                                                   Step 2: _____

$(3 \cdot 2)^3 =$ Step 1: _____

                                                   Step 2: _____

Feedback

Technological tools, including most calculators, will perform operations in a specific order. In a calculation like $7 + 2 \cdot 3^2 - 12 \div 3$, the calculator will first evaluate the exponential expression 3^2, then it will perform the multiplication and division. Lastly, it will do the addition and subtraction. This sequence of steps is called the **order of operations**, which is the convention that everyone follows, including computers (a calculator is just a handheld computer).

Order of Operations

1. Evaluate whatever is enclosed in grouping symbols first, like parentheses, brackets, braces, and a fraction bar. If you have parentheses contained within parentheses, complete the innermost set of parentheses first and work outward.

2. Exponents or powers are evaluated.

3. Multiply and divide from left to right.

4. Add and subtract from left to right.

Note: If there is more than one operation to be completed within a grouping symbol, then follow the order in steps 2 through 4.

Given an expression such as $7 + 2 \cdot 3^2 - 12 \div 3$, it is helpful to observe the different operations that need to be performed and in what order, before doing any calculations. The expression contains the operations of addition, multiplication, evaluating exponents, subtraction, and division if we read from left to right. However, according to the order of operations, the correct order of calculation is evaluating exponents, multiplication/division, and addition/subtraction.

The parts of the expression separated by a mathematical operation symbol such as + or − are called **terms**. For example,

$$\underbrace{7}_{\substack{\text{first} \\ \text{term}}} + \underbrace{2\cdot 3^2}_{\substack{\text{second} \\ \text{term}}} - \underbrace{12\div 3}_{\substack{\text{third} \\ \text{term}}}$$

The second term $2\cdot 3^2$ is evaluated as $2\cdot 9$ or 18, and the third term $12\div 3$ is 4. Therefore, the expression above simplifies to

$$7+18-4$$

Adding and subtracting from left to right, so that the sum of the first term and second term is 25, minus the third term 4, results in 21. The entire calculation process is shown, step by step, below.

$$7+2\cdot 3^2-12\div 3 = 7+2\cdot 9-12\div 3 \quad \text{Evaluate exponent, } 3^2=9$$
$$= 7+18-4 \qquad\qquad \text{Multiply, } 2\cdot 9=18 \text{ and then divide, } 12\div 3=4$$
$$= 21 \qquad\qquad\quad \text{Add, } 7+18=25 \text{ and then subtract, } 25-4=21$$

If we insert a set of parentheses, then we must evaluate the expression inside the parentheses first. Within the parentheses, we follow the order in steps 2 through 4 of the order of operations given on the preceding page.

$$7+\left(2\cdot 3^2-12\right)\div 3 = 7+\left(2\cdot 9-12\right)\div 3 \quad \text{Evaluate exponent } 3^2=9$$
$$= 7+\left(18-12\right)\div 3 \quad \text{Multiply, } 2\cdot 9=18$$
$$= 7+6\div 3 \qquad\quad \text{Subtract, } 18-12=6$$
$$= 7+2 \qquad\qquad \text{Divide, } 6\div 3=2$$
$$= 9 \qquad\qquad\quad \text{Add, } 7+2=9$$

When given a problem using a fraction bar such as $\dfrac{12+3}{7-4}=\dfrac{15}{3}$, combine the terms in the numerator and denominator before doing the division (symbolized by the fraction bar). When entering such an expression in a calculator, you need to tell the calculator to group $12+3$ and $7-4$ by using two sets of parentheses,

$$\frac{12+3}{7-4}=\left(12+3\right)\div\left(7-4\right)$$

The sum of the two terms in the numerator is 15 and the difference of the two terms in the denominator is 3.

So we have 15 divided by 3 or $\dfrac{15}{3}$. Since 3 divides into 15 evenly, we say the quotient is 5, or

$$\frac{15}{3} = \frac{\overset{1}{\cancel{3}} \cdot 5}{\underset{1}{\cancel{3}}} = 5.$$

Note that 3 and 5 are called *factors* of 15. Since the number 3 is a common factor in the numerator and denominator, it can be divided out to obtain 5 over 1, or 5.

****

In general, adding two terms together results in a *sum*, while multiplying two factors together results in a *product*,

terms   factors

$\bigwedge$ $\bigwedge$

$\underbrace{3+5}$ $\underbrace{3 \cdot 5}$

sum   product

Some students find it helpful to remember the acronym **PEMDAS** (**P**arentheses, **E**xponents, **M**ultiplication, **D**ivision, **A**ddition, and **S**ubtraction) or the phrase *Please Excuse My Dear Aunt Sally*.

Be careful, nothing will replace the experience of lots of practice simplifying numerical expressions. Also be clear that multiplication and division are on the same level, meaning that you do either one as they occur from left to right in the expression. The same is true for addition and subtraction.

Section Exercises: 1.3

1. Suppose someone in your math class decides to spread the rumor that your math instructor drops the lowest test grade. This student tells two friends the rumor at 8 a.m. Monday morning. One hour later, these friends each tell two other friends about the test rumor. After another hour passes, each of these friends tells two other friends the rumor. Suppose the rumor continues to spread in this manner every hour.

    a. Guess how many people have heard the rumor by 4 p.m.? Use any strategy you want to verify your guess.

b. Now organize your information by completing the table below.

Time (hours)	Number of New Friends Hearing Rumor (whole number form)	Number of New Friends Hearing Rumor (exponential form)	Total Knowing Rumor
0	1 (student starting it)	2^0	1
1	2	2^1	3
2	4	2^2	7

c. Look for a pattern to the sequence of numbers in column 3, (exponential form). In general, during the nth hour, how many new people hear the rumor? *Hint*: Think of an exponential expression containing the unknown n.

d. Explain how each hour's total number of people knowing the rumor (last column) can be obtained from the number of new friends hearing the rumor and the previous hour's total number of people knowing the rumor.

_____

_____

_____

e. Look for a pattern to the sequence of numbers in column 4, "total knowing rumor." In general, after the nth hour, what is the total number of people who have heard the rumor? *Hint*: Observe the relationship between the numbers in column 4 and column 2. Then think of an exponential expression containing the unknown n.

2. Try to find the pattern in the following sequence of numbers.

a. Fill in the last missing entry with a value that would continue the pattern in the same fashion.

$$2^4 = 16 \qquad\qquad 3^4 = 81 \qquad\qquad 4^4 = 256$$

$$2^3 = 8 \qquad\qquad 3^3 = 27 \qquad\qquad 4^3 = 64$$

$$2^2 = 4 \qquad\qquad 3^2 = 9 \qquad\qquad 4^2 = 16$$

$$2^1 = 2 \qquad\qquad 3^1 = 3 \qquad\qquad 4^1 = 4$$

$$2^0 = \underline{} \qquad\qquad 3^0 = \underline{} \qquad\qquad 4^0 = \underline{}$$

b. Use complete sentences to express the similarities and differences in the patterns contained in the three sequences given.

_____

_____

_____

_____

3. Make up a new rhyme, similar to the St. Ives rhyme in Discovery Adventure 1, but use the number eight instead of seven. It must end in a question that asks "How many..." and have a solution that makes use of finding the sum of different powers of 8. Be sure to provide a detailed solution below your rhyme.

Title: _____

_____

_____

_____

_____

_____

_____

_____

Solution Process:

4. Use paper and pencil to evaluate the following expressions in an organized, step-by-step manner. Complete one operation at a time and state in words what you did and why. *Optional:* Verify your answer using technology (calculator or computer) that follows the order of operations.

   a. $9 + 5 \cdot 4 \div 10$

   _____

   _____

   _____

   b. $3^2 - 5 + 2^3$

   _____

   _____

   _____

   c. $(20 - 8 \div 2) - 3 \cdot (4^2 \div 8)$

   _____

   _____

   _____

   _____

   _____

   d. $5 \cdot \left[17 - 3 \cdot (4 + 1) \right]$

   _____

   _____

   _____

   _____

5. Suppose you just won a contest and are given the choice of 2 prizes: $100,000 in cash right now or the final result of doubling $1.00 every day for a 3-week period. Which one would you choose? Show all work and use complete sentences to explain the benefits of one choice over the other. *Hint*: Constructing a table might help in organizing your information. Also, consider the work needed to solve Section Exercise #1 on pages 50-51.

_____

_____

_____

_____

6. Given the following five expressions, find two matching pairs that simplify to the same value and explain your reasoning.

$$7+(2\cdot 4) \qquad (7+2)\cdot 4 \qquad 7+2\cdot 4 \qquad 4\cdot (7+2) \qquad 4\cdot 7+2$$

List one matching pair:

_____

_____

List another matching pair:

_____

_____

7. Different placement of parentheses can change the value of an expression. Rewrite the following expression to obtain the results shown for each part below.

$$3 \cdot 2 + 4^2$$

  a. Place parentheses such that the expression simplifies to 54.

  b. Place parentheses such that the expression simplifies to 108.

  c. Place parentheses such that the expression simplifies to 100.

  d. Simplify the given expression, containing no parentheses, by following the order of operations. Perform one operation at each step in the simplification process.

8. Explain why $2^2 = 2 \cdot 2$, but $2^3 \neq 2 \cdot 3$.

  _____

  _____

  _____

  _____

9. Use what you have learned about exponents to show that the following inequality is true. Write your answer using complete sentences. *Hint*: Write the expression left of the "*is not equal to*" symbol in expanded form (a number multiplied by itself a certain number of times). Then write the expression to the right in expanded form to check for equality.

$$3^4 \neq 4^3$$

  _____

  _____   _____

  _____   _____

10. Use the inequality symbols < (is less than) or > (is greater than) between the two exponential expressions so that a true statement results.

a. 8^{10} 9^{10}

b. 5^6 6^5

11. Complete the following table by taking each counting number in the first column and raising it to the power given in columns two through six.

Number	$(number)^1$	$(number)^2$	$(number)^3$	$(number)^4$	$(number)^5$
1					
2					
3					
4					
5					
6					
7					
8					
9					
10					

12. How many zeros are there in 10^7, 10^{10}, 10^{100}? Refer to Section Exercise #11 as needed.

Chapter 1 Summary

Key Terms

Section 1.1

- **Real-life** and **Real-world** are terms used to describe situations that occur in the world around us.
- **Application** – A real-life or real-world problem that "applies" or uses mathematical ideas to help find acceptable answers.
- **Problem** – A situation that requires mathematical thinking and skills to find an acceptable solution.
- **Activity or Exercise** – A task that uses mathematical skills, concepts, and reasoning.
- **Analyze** – To examine a situation in detail.

Section 1.2

- **Exact** – Accurate or correct without any degree of error.
- **Estimate or Approximate** – To make a quick and/or rough calculation to obtain an answer that is close to the true value, but not necessarily exact. To find a solution that is accurate to a specified degree.
- **Digit** – One of the whole numbers from 0 to 9.
- **Numerical Reasoning** – Thinking logically about numbers and drawing conclusions from numerical information.
- **Place Value** – The position of each digit in a number. For example, ones, tens, hundreds are place values; in the number 367, the place value of 3 is hundreds, 6 is tens, and 7 is ones.

Section 1.3

- **Exponential Growth** – Growth that is always increasing and develops from an exponential expression. The rate of increase is slow at the beginning but becomes faster and faster over time.
- **Factor** – A number that exactly divides another number. For example, 20 has factors 1, 2, 4, 5, 10, and 20 because each of these numbers divides into 20 evenly.
- **Identity** – The property of being exactly the same. For example, $4 \cdot 5 = 20$ is an identity because the expression on the left side of the equal sign has the same value as the number on the right side of the equal sign.
- **Product** – The result of multiplying two or more numbers.
- **Exponent or Power**– A convenient notation for repeated multiplication. It is a number written above and to the side of another number called the *base*. For example, the exponent 4 in the expression 3^4 means to multiply 3 (the base) four times.

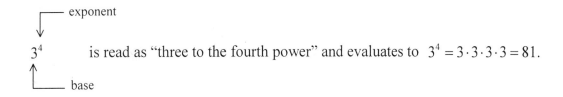

3^4 is read as "three to the fourth power" and evaluates to $3^4 = 3 \cdot 3 \cdot 3 \cdot 3 = 81$.

- **Order of Operations** – A sequence of steps (see below) listing the correct order to perform each operation in an expression.

> **Order of Operations**
>
> 1. Evaluate whatever is enclosed in grouping symbols first, like parentheses, brackets, braces, and a fraction bar. If you have parentheses contained within parentheses, complete the innermost set of parentheses first and work outward.
> 2. Exponents or powers are evaluated.
> 3. Multiply and divide from left to right.
> 4. Add and subtract from left to right.
>
> **Note:** If there is more than one operation to be completed in a grouping symbol, then follow the order in steps 2 through 4.

- **Terms** – Parts of a mathematical expression that are separated by a mathematical operation symbol such as $+$, $-$, $\times$, or $\div$.

****

Questions for Review

1. What is the five-step problem solving process developed in this chapter?

2. List some strategies you might use to solve an application problem.

3. Can you construct, read, and interpret a table of information? For example, suppose the following table is intended to help consumers with pricing when purchasing a certain quantity of widgets (any small, unspecified gadget or device).

a. Complete the fourth column, Total Cost, by adding the data in columns 2 and 3, "Cost" and "Shipping & Handling."

Quantity	Cost	Shipping & Handling	Total Cost
1	$14.50	$5.45	
2	$27.00	$6.50	
3	$40.00	$8.50	
4	$53.00	$9.50	
6	$78.00	$10.50	
12	$158.00	$16.50	

b. If you purchase 6 widgets, how much will you pay for shipping and handling?

c. If you buy 1 widget each month, what will be the total cost over one year?

d. If you make one purchase of 12 widgets, what will be the total cost?

e. How much do you save by buying 12 widgets at one time instead of buying 1 widget each month for one year?

f. If you make one purchase of 12 widgets, what is the cost per widget?
   Hint: Do not include shipping and handling.

4. Do you know how to find an average? For example, find the average in parts *a* and *b* below.

    a. In three strings of bowling, your scores are 162, 175, and 180. What is your average score for these three strings? Round the average to the ones place.

    b. During the past 4 weeks your weekly grocery bill was $136, $152, $145, and $150. What was your average grocery bill during this 4-week time period?

5. What is the difference between finding an *estimated* solution and an *exact* solution? For example, suppose you stop at the grocery store to pick up a few items. Listed below are the items you want to purchase and their actual prices. Suppose you have $10 to spend and want to know quickly if you have enough money to buy all of the items.

- Milk $1.59   • Bread $1.19   • Peanut Butter $4.79   • Jelly $2.09

    a. Explain how you would estimate whether or not you could buy all of the items with $10.

_____

_____

_____

_____

    b. When you go through the checkout, what should be the total cost of your grocery bill?

    c. In this situation, explain the importance of being able to both estimate the answer and find the exact answer.

_____

_____

_____

_____

6. Do you know the meaning of the words *digit* and *place value*? For example, observe the following two numbers and then list the digits of each number, followed by the place value of that digit.

   a. 782   Digits: Place Value:

   b. 12,109   Digits: Place Value:

7. When reading articles in the media, can you tell whether numerical information is approximate or exact? For example, read the two statements below and explain how you know whether the data is approximate (an estimate) or exact.

   a. Study says that women executives make 68¢ for every dollar earned by men in similar positions.

_____

_____

_____

   b. Only 83 women are among the top 2,267 earners listed, as part of the Fortune 500.

_____

_____

_____

8. Evaluate these exponential expressions.

   a. 5^6

   b. 6^5

9. Can you think of a case where switching the placement of the base and exponent in an exponential expression will evaluate to the same answer? If yes, show the identity below.

10. Suppose we start with a single cell creature that triples every hour under ideal conditions.

a. Assuming that ideal conditions are present, set up a tree diagram to illustrate the growth of the cell population over a 2-hour period.

b. Use exponential expressions to show the amount of cells after 1 hour, 2 hours, 3 hours, and 4 hours.

c. Why is this situation a good example of exponential growth?

_____

_____

_____

_____

_____

11. Do you know the order of operations? In each problem below, use the order of operations to explain which method is correct in evaluating each problem.

a.

$$3 + 5 \cdot 4 = 8 \cdot 4$$
$$= 32$$

$$3 + 5 \cdot 4 = 3 + 20$$
$$= 23$$

_____

_____

_____

_____

b.

$$\frac{35 - 9}{5 - 3} = \frac{35}{5} - \frac{9}{3}$$
$$= 7 - 3$$
$$= 4$$

$$\frac{35 - 9}{5 - 3} = \frac{26}{2}$$
$$= 13$$

_____

_____

_____

_____

Chapter 1 Quiz

Use the following problem situation to answer questions #1 – 5.

Suppose you are planning the cost of a ski trip to Powder Mountain with two friends. One of your friends says that a whole-day lift ticket to ski at Powder is $58, and the lodge has a great lunch special for $5.75. You know from past experience that it will cost $20 to fill your vehicle's gas tank and suggest that the gas cost be split 3 ways. Your other friend says that $75 should cover all expenses for each person. You are not so sure and want to find the total cost of the trip.

1. Record what you are trying to find and any given information that seems useful in finding it.

   FIND: _____

   GIVEN: _____

   _____

2. Develop a plan by listing any mathematical calculations that are necessary in solving the problem. Do not compute the results of each calculation yet.

3. Perform the calculations, and show all your work in an organized manner.

4. Check your work and explain whether or not your friend's estimate of $75 is enough for the trip.

   _____

   _____

5. Summarize your findings by writing a brief conclusion. Be sure to express your results using complete sentences.

   _____

   _____

   _____

6. For each problem below, before adding or subtracting, round each number to the specified place value. Then estimate the sum or difference using mental arithmetic.

    a. $7378 + 4786 + 2125$; thousands place

    b. $6377 - 4155$; hundreds place

7. For each multiplication problem below, round each factor to the specified place value. Then estimate the product using mental arithmetic.

    a. $68 \cdot 21$; tens place

    b. $715 \cdot 489$; hundreds place

    c. $2536 \cdot 295$; hundreds place

    d. $83,691 \cdot 1875$; thousands place

8. Suppose you are driving along the highway at an average speed of 65 mph and see a road sign with information that the exit you want to take is 250 miles away. If you want to approximate the amount of time it will take to reach your exit, then what "friendly" numbers would you estimate for average speed and distance?

    Hint: Since $\text{travel time} = \dfrac{\text{distance}}{\text{average speed}}$, use an estimate for average speed and distance that will allow you to divide exactly in your head.

    Distance estimate:

    Average speed estimate:

    Travel time calculation and estimate:

9. Given the exponential expression 2^3, answer the following questions.

    a. Imagine you want to explain the purpose of exponential notation to a friend. Use the words *exponent* and *base* to describe what 2^3 means.

    _____

    _____

    b. Now explain to your friend why $2^3 \neq 3^2$.

    _____

    _____

10. Use the order of operations to simplify the following expressions. Show all work and explain each step in the process.

a. $20 - 10 \div 5$

Explanation:

_____

_____

b. $8 + 4^2$

_____

_____

c. $2 + 3 \cdot (7 - 5)$

_____

_____

d. $\dfrac{8 + 4^2}{2 + 3(7 - 5)}$

_____

_____

Chapter 2

Sets of Numbers and Integer Operations

In Chapter 1, you saw the importance of being able to deal with numerical information in problem solving situations. In this chapter we start to take a close look at different number systems, specifically, whole numbers and integers.

In Section 2.1, you will investigate factoring with whole numbers, explore some basic set theory, discover the elements of prime numbers, and examine the properties of arithmetic and algebra.

In Sections 2.2 and 2.3, you are introduced to negative numbers as a continuation of the whole numbers in the opposite direction. This leads to the set of integers and the understanding of operations with integers. Negative numbers are presented through everyday situations such as balancing a checkbook, temperature scales, revenue versus cost in a business, and upward versus downward force on an object.

Section 2.1 Numbers and Their Properties

Math Talk

In this section you will encounter words such as **set**, **subset**, **finite**, and **infinite**. To continue to build your math vocabulary, let's discuss what these words mean in terms of mathematics and everyday life.

- People often use the word **set** to refer to putting something in place, such as, "I *set* the newspaper on the table." It also means to arrange or put in working order. For example, "The brake was *set* to prevent the car from rolling away." In mathematics, you can think of a set as a class or collection of distinct numbers or objects. For example, the set of numbers on dice are 1, 2, 3, 4, 5, and 6.

- A **subset** is a set of objects that are members of another set. For example, the set of odd numbers on a die (1, 3, and 5) is a subset of the set of all numbers on a die. In mathematics, the word *subclass* has the same meaning as subset. However, in popular culture, one might describe all Labradors as a subclass of all dogs and all redwoods as a subclass of all trees instead of using the word *subset*.

- In our world, a **finite** thing has an end or limit, while an **infinite** thing is endless or without limits. A person's time on this earth is finite, but time itself is infinite. If you are considering buying a new car, someone might say, "there are an infinite amount of choices." In this context, the person means that there are too many choices to consider them all. In math, a set is *finite* if we can count all its members and *infinite* if the members are uncountable, without end. For example, the set of all human beings living on earth is finite. You might think it's uncountable because there are too many people to count, but mathematically there is a limit to the amount of people in the world.

****

Let's begin by looking at some finite and infinite sets. Observe how all the members of a set are enclosed in braces.

The set of counting numbers is an infinite set. $\{\ 1,\ 2,\ 3,\ 4,\ 5,\ \cdots\ \}$

The set of even counting numbers is an infinite set. $\{\ 2,\ 4,\ 6,\ 8,\ 10,\ \cdots\ \}$

The set of even counting numbers less than 10 is an finite set. $\{\ 2,\ 4,\ 6,\ 8\ \}$

The set of odd counting numbers greater than or equal to 5 and less than 11 is an finite set.

$$\{\ 5,\ 7,\ 9\ \}$$

The **natural numbers** are the counting numbers 1, 2, 3, 4, $\cdots$ (the three dots signify that the count continues in this manner without end to infinity). **Factoring** a natural number means to express that number as the product of two or more numbers. For example, there are two different ways to factor the number four:

$$1 \cdot 4 = 4 \text{ and } 2 \cdot 2 = 4,$$

So the **factors** of 4 are 1, 2, and 4.

There are three ways to factor the number 12, using the product of two numbers.

$$\text{Since } 1 \cdot 12 = 12, \ 2 \cdot 6 = 12, \text{ and } 3 \cdot 4 = 12,$$

the factors of 12 are 1, 2, 3, 4, 6, and 12.

Factors of a number can be found by dividing the given number by each natural number. If the division can be done evenly with no remainder, then the **divisor** and **quotient** are factors. For example,

$$\begin{array}{r} 90 \\ 6\overline{)540} \\ \underline{54} \\ 0 \end{array}$$

so the divisor 6 and quotient 90 are factors of the **dividend** 540.

Using division terminology,

$$\text{dividend} \div \text{divisor} = \text{quotient} \quad \text{or} \quad \text{divisor}\overline{)\text{dividend}}^{\text{quotient}}$$

Finding factors of a number can involve trial and error with division. For example, consider the number 20. First, every natural number has the number 1 and itself as factors, so 1 and 20 are two factors. Second, 20 is an even number and all even numbers are *divisible* (can be exactly divided) by 2. Since $20 \div 2$ (20 divided by 2) is 10, the numbers 2 and 10 are two more factors. The next natural number after 2 is 3, but 20 is not divisible by 3. However, after 3 you have 4 and $20 \div 4$ is 5, so 4 and 5 are factors of 20. The natural number 5 follows 4, but since you know already that 5 is a factor, there are not any new factors to be found. Therefore, the six factors of 20 are 1, 2, 4, 5, 10, and 20.

Note that you can find factors in any order. In the example above, you might have known right away that 5 is a factor of 20 because any number that ends in 0 or 5 is divisible by 5. A calculator can be helpful is this process by allowing you to complete many calculations quickly.

The first Discovery Adventure gives you practice with finding the factors of a number.

Discovery Adventure 1: Factors

Now consider the set of natural numbers from 1 to 100 inclusive (including 1 and 100). Your goal is to find the number in this set with the most factors.

a. Find a number greater than 12 and less than 30 that has eight factors. List the number and its eight factors below. *Hint*: A first number is a factor of a second number if the second number divides the first evenly with no remainder.

b. Find a number greater than or equal to 30 and less than 40 that has nine factors. List the nine factors below.

c. Find a number greater than or equal to 40 and less than 50 that has ten factors. List the ten factors below.

d. Find a number greater than or equal to 50 and less than or equal to 60 that has twelve factors. List the twelve factors below.

e. Can you find a number greater than 60 and less than or equal to 100 that has more than twelve factors? If yes, state the number and list its factors. Otherwise list any other numbers that have twelve factors.

f.   Observe the six factors of the number 12, and then examine all the numbers found in parts *a* through *e* that have more than six factors. List these numbers to the right of the number 12 below. Do you see any pattern to this list of numbers with many factors? Use complete sentences to explain the pattern and why you think it occurs.

List of numbers with many factors: 12,   ,   ,   ,   ,   ,   ,   ,   .

_____

_____

_____

_____

Feedback

If we take the set of natural numbers and include zero, the set W of **whole numbers** is obtained.

$$W = \{0, 1, 2, 3, 4, \cdots \}$$

W is the symbol for the set of whole numbers. The members of a set are called **elements**, and they make up a well-defined list of objects. Each element is separated from the next element by a comma, and the whole list is enclosed in braces. **Well-defined** means you can reasonably tell whether or not any given object is contained in the set. Both the set of natural numbers and the set of whole numbers are **infinite sets** because they have no final element.

Discovery Adventure 2: Sets and Whole Numbers

Let's take a look at how you can represent a set using set notation and a number line graph.

a.   Circle any of the following objects that are an element of the set of whole numbers W.

$$3, \text{ elephant, } \frac{1}{2}, 1.25, 123, -2, \text{ Rhododendron, } 1,142,701$$

b.   Write the last object (a number) from the above list in words.

_____

c.   Show how you could represent the whole numbers, $W = \{0, 1, 2, 3, 4, \cdots\}$, on the number line graph below.

0

d. Show how you could represent the whole numbers, 0, 10, 20, 30, ⋯, on the number line graph below.

0

e. Use set notation to display the set of odd natural numbers less than or equal to 7.
Hint: List each element of the set separated by commas and enclosed in braces.

The set described in part *e* is a subset of the larger set of all natural numbers. In other words, every element in the subset is also contained in the set of natural numbers. In addition, the set is a **finite set** because there is a last number, and we can count all of the elements contained in the set. Finally, when a set has no elements, it is called the **empty set** or **null set** and is denoted by ∅ or { }.

f. Use set notation to list all of the elements in the set of whole numbers between 40 and 50 inclusive (including 40 and 50).

g. The set in part *f* is a subset of the whole numbers. Is the set in part *f* finite or infinite? Explain.

_____

_____

h. Use set notation to display the set of whole numbers between 4 and 5.

Discovery Adventure 3: A New Set

Let us define the finite set of six elements shown below and call it *P*.

$$P = \{2,\ 3,\ 5,\ 7,\ 11,\ 13\}$$

a. List all the different ways you can factor 2.

b. List all the different ways you can factor 3.

c. Repeat what you did in parts *a* and *b* for the remaining elements in *P*.

d. Write one or more general statements that are true for all of the elements in the set *P*.

_____

_____

_____

_____

e. All the elements in set *P* are called **prime numbers**. Expand set *P* to contain twelve elements by including the next six consecutive prime numbers after 13.

$P =$

Feedback

A **prime number** is any natural number greater than 1 that can only be factored into the product of one and itself. Equivalently, a prime number is any natural number greater than 1 that is only divisible (capable of being exactly divided) by one and itself. Natural numbers greater than 1 that are not prime numbers are called **composite numbers**. The number 1 is neither prime nor composite. Prime numbers can be considered the basic building blocks of all natural numbers greater than 1, since each of these numbers can be uniquely factored into the product of prime numbers. This fact is known as the **Fundamental Theorem of Arithmetic**.

Fundamental Theorem of Arithmetic

All natural numbers greater than 1 can be written as a product of primes in a unique way.

A set is **closed** under an operation if performing the operation on any two numbers in the set always results in a number from within that set. The set of whole numbers is closed under addition since the sum of any two whole numbers is itself a whole number. For example, 5 and 7 are both whole numbers, and their sum $5 + 7$ is the whole number 12. This is true of any sum where the addends (numbers being added) are whole numbers. So addition is said to be a **closed operation** on the set of whole numbers, or the set of whole numbers is **closed under addition**.

Discovery Adventure 4: Closed Operations

Determine whether or not the remaining operations of subtraction, multiplication, and division are closed on the whole number system. If the operation is closed, state why in words and show a few examples. If the operation is not closed, then show a specific example of the operation applied to two whole numbers in which the result is not a whole number.

a. Is the set of whole numbers closed under subtraction?

_____

_____

Example(s):

b. Is the set of whole numbers closed under multiplication?

_____

_____

Example(s):

c. Is the set of whole numbers closed under division?

_____

_____

Example(s):

Feedback

We have examined two number systems: the set of natural numbers and the set of whole numbers. There are many applications that make use of these number systems. However, we will have to expand beyond them if we want to function in the real world. We have already completed some applications that involve decimal numbers. In Chapter 3, we will study decimal numbers in more detail.

Let's formally introduce the idea of **variable** now. A variable is a symbol, such as the letter a, x, or n, that represents some unknown number(s) from a set of numbers. Variables can be used in an identity such as

$$1 \cdot a = a \qquad \text{or} \qquad 0 + a = a$$

where a represents any number from the set of whole numbers.

The statements above are identities because they are true for all values of the variable a such that

$$
\begin{array}{ccc}
1 \cdot 0 = 0 & & 0 + 0 = 0 \\
1 \cdot 1 = 1 & & 0 + 1 = 1 \\
1 \cdot 2 = 2 & & 0 + 2 = 2 \\
1 \cdot 3 = 3 & \text{or} & 0 + 3 = 3 \\
1 \cdot 4 = 4 & & 0 + 4 = 4 \\
\vdots & & \vdots \\
1 \cdot a = a & & 0 + a = a
\end{array}
$$

Variables can also be used in **conditional equations** to represent unknown quantities. Often it will be your job to find the values for the variable so that the **equation** becomes a true statement. This process is called solving an equation for the variable. For example, suppose you are given the following conditional equations:

$$x + 2 = 5 \qquad \text{and} \qquad 9 - n = 7$$

The equations are called **conditional** because the statement is true for only certain values of the variable. Those values are called the **solution**. Each of the above equations has only one solution or one value that can replace the variable to produce a true statement. Can you find the solutions to these two equations?

For now, let's take a brief look at solving equations using a guess and test strategy. This involves thinking about what value(s) can replace the variable so that the equality holds. You can translate the two equations above into statements with words.

$x + 2 = 5$ means, "The sum of what value and 2 equals 5?"

$9 - n = 7$ means, "The difference of 9 and what value is 7?"

These equations are not very complicated, so you should try to guess and test mentally. This means replacing the variables with numbers that you believe will result in true statements. Since the sum of 3 and 2 equals 5 and the difference of 9 and 2 equals 7, you can state each solution as follows:

$$x = 3 \text{ is the solution to } x + 2 = 5 \text{ because } 3 + 2 = 5 \text{ is true.}$$

$$n = 2 \text{ is a solution of } 9 - n = 7 \text{ because } 9 - 2 = 7 \text{ is true.}$$

Solving equations will be investigated in more detail as you proceed through this textbook. However, the next two Discovery Adventures will explore some of the rules or properties that form the basis of arithmetic and algebra. These adventures will examine how variables are used in identities called *properties*.

Discovery Adventure 5: Addition Properties

Imagine that two groups of students are working separately on the same project at opposite ends of the library. One group consists of three students, and the second group has five students. Since both groups are having trouble finishing their projects, the librarian suggests to each that they combine their knowledge by working together in one large group. It makes no difference whether the group of three joins the group of five or the group of five joins the group of three. In either case, we have a new larger group with eight people. See the figure below which displays that addition is **commutative**, meaning that order is not important when adding.

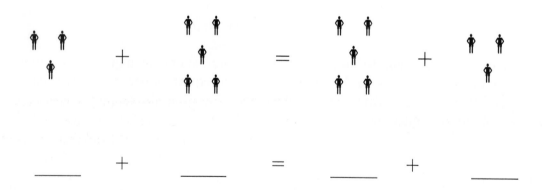

a. In the spaces below the figure, express symbolically the commutative relationship being displayed.

b. The above situation shows that order is not important when adding two numbers. Whether three is added to five or five is added to three, the sum will be eight. Suppose a and b represent any numbers, state a general rule that expresses the **commutative property of addition** in terms of a and b.

Now imagine that there are a group of three students, another group of four students, and a third group of five students. It does not matter if the three-person group combines with the four-person group and then later the five-person group joins in, or if the four-person group combines with the five-person group and then later the three-person group joins in. The combination of the three different groups can occur in any order, and the sum will be the same twelve people.

c. To represent this new relationship visually, on the left side of the equal sign, construct a square that encloses the 3 and 4 groups. Then to the right of the equal sign, construct a square that encloses the 4 and 5 groups.

d. Denote the relationship in part c symbolically by inserting two sets of parentheses in the proper places in the expression below.

$$3 + 4 + 5 = 3 + 4 + 5$$

e. If we let a, b, and c represent any numbers, then state a general rule that expresses the same relationship represented in part d.

Feedback

Parts c, d, and e show that when summing three items (such as groups of people) or terms (such as numbers) it makes no difference how we group the items or terms. This rule is called the **associative property of addition**. The name of the property comes from the fact that no matter how we group (associate) the terms when adding, the sum is always the same. For example, when finding the sum of $3+4+5$, we can add $3+4$ and then add the result to 5, or we can add $4+5$ and then add the result to 3. Symbolically, we use parentheses to group the numbers.

For instance, the example above would appear as,

$$(3+4)+5 = 7+5 = 12 \quad \text{and} \quad 3+(4+5) = 3+9 = 12.$$

Therefore,

$$(3+4)+5 = 3+(4+5).$$

Discovery Adventure 6: Multiplication Properties

Suppose there are fifteen people in a classroom with fifteen chairs. The teacher has arranged the chairs so that the students are sitting in three vertical rows with five people in each row. See the picture below. Three groups of five can be expressed as the product of 3 and 5 and can be represented symbolically as $3 \cdot 5$ ("three times five").

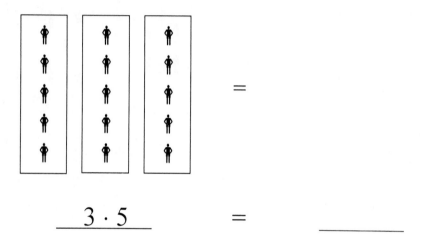

$$\underline{\quad 3 \cdot 5 \quad} \quad = \quad \underline{\qquad\qquad}$$

a. The teacher instructs the class to rearrange the chairs so that the class seating will be in five vertical rows with three people in each row. Show how this new arrangement might look in the space to the right of the picture above.

b. Express the new arrangement of five groups of three in symbolic terms, using the operation of multiplication. Place your expression in the underlined space to the right of the equal sign.

c. Observe the original figure given above part *a* and your newly constructed figure in part *b*. Then use complete sentences to explain any connections you see.

_____

_____

_____

_____

As with addition, when finding the product of three numbers it makes no difference how we group or associate the numbers. For example, when finding the product of $3 \cdot 4 \cdot 5$, we can multiply $3 \cdot 4$ and then multiply the result by 5, or we can multiply $4 \cdot 5$ and then multiply the result by 3. See the figure below. This rule is called the **associative property of multiplication**.

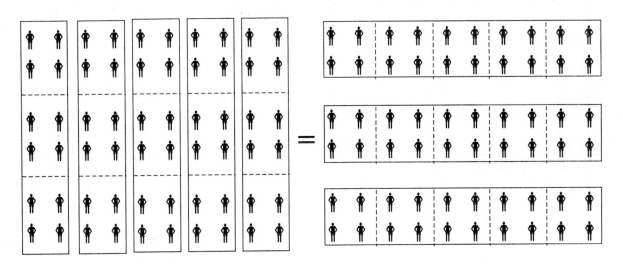

d. Denote the example above in symbolic terms by inserting two sets of parentheses in the proper places in the expression below.

$$3 \cdot 4 \cdot 5 = 3 \cdot 4 \cdot 5$$

e. If we let *a*, *b*, and *c* represent any numbers, then state a general rule that expresses the same associative law represented in part *d*.

Discovery Adventure 7: Best Offer

Suppose your current salary is $25,000 and you are considering two new job offers:
- Company A will double your current salary and then add $5000 to that amount.
- Company B will add $5000 to your current salary and then double that amount.

Which company is offering you the most money? *Hint:* One of the two offers involves the use of parentheses in the expression.

a. Give the entire expression needed to calculate your new salary with Company A. Then complete the calculation in two steps, doing one operation per step. State the operation you are performing to the right of your calculation.

Expression:

Step 1: _____

Step 2: _____

b. Give the entire expression needed to calculate your new salary with Company B. Then complete the calculation in two steps, doing one operation per step. State the operation you are performing to the right of your calculation.

Expression:

Step 1: _____

Step 2: _____

c. Which company's mathematical expression for salary gives you the most money? Explain.

_____

_____

_____

Now suppose several other people receive an offer for the same job as you from Company A and Company B. Since their current salary is unknown to you, consider it to be some dollar amount represented by the variable, s.

d. Construct a table of possible salaries these other people might have and the new amount they would make from Company A and Company B.

Unknown Salary s	Company A's offer	Company B's offer
20,000		
25,000		
30,000		
35,000		
40,000		
45,000		

Note that Company B's offer is always $5,000 more than Company A's offer.

e. Give an expression in terms of the unknown salary s, which can calculate the new salary with Company A. *Hint:* Write an expression using the variable s in place of the salary.

f. Give an expression in terms of the unknown salary s, which can calculate the new salary with Company B.

Feedback

Letting the variable s represent the unknown salary, the variable expression for Company A's offer is $2 \cdot s + 5000$. The offer from Company B can be expressed as $2 \cdot (s + 5000)$. But we know from part d that Company B's offer is always \$5000 more than Company A's offer. So we can add \$5000 to Company A's expression and obtain another variable expression for Company B. For example,

$$2 \cdot s + 5000 + 5000 = 2 \cdot s + 10000$$

This new expression $2 \cdot s + 10000$ must be equivalent to the previous expression $2(s + 5000)$ given for Company B. In symbols, this would appear as

$$2 \cdot (s + 5000) = 2 \cdot s + 10000$$

Note that when the 2 is multiplied by each term inside the parentheses, we obtain the expression to the right of the equal sign,

$$2 \cdot (s + 5000) = 2 \cdot s + 2 \cdot 5000 = 2s + 10000$$

This is an example of the **distributive property for addition**. In general, to multiply a sum (such as $s + 5000$) by a number (such as 2), each term in the sum must be multiplied by that number. The result of 2 being distributed to s and 5000 gives us the expression $2s + 10000$. In this expression, the term $2s$ represents the product of 2 and s or 2 times s, and 10000 represents the product of 2 times 5000.

Letting a, b, and c represent any numbers, the distributive property for addition says

$$a \cdot (b + c) = a \cdot b + a \cdot c \quad \text{and} \quad (b + c) \cdot a = b \cdot a + c \cdot a$$

Note that the second equation above follows from the **commutative property of multiplication,** which states that the order is not important when multiplying two values. In general, if a and b represent any numbers, then $a \cdot b = b \cdot a$.

In summary, we have developed the following rules of arithmetic and algebra.

Properties of Addition and Multiplication

$a + b = b + a$ ⬛ The commutative property of addition

$a + (b + c) = (a + b) + c$ ⬛ The associative property of addition

$a \cdot b = b \cdot a$ ⬛ The commutative property of multiplication

$a \cdot (b \cdot c) = (a \cdot b) \cdot c$ ⬛ The associate property of multiplication

$a \cdot (b + c) = a \cdot b + a \cdot c$ ⬛ The distributive property for addition

---

Section Exercises: 2.1

1. The additive identity is a special number that when added to a quantity results in the same quantity. The multiplicative identity is a special number that when multiplied by a quantity results in the same quantity.

   a. What number is the additive identity?

   b. If a is any number, then give a symbolic rule that represents the additive identity.

   c. What number is the multiplicative identity?

   d. If a is any number, then give a symbolic rule that represents the multiplicative identity.

   e. Fill in each blank with the correct word.

   Subtracting _____ from a quantity gives that same quantity.

   Dividing a quantity by _____ gives that same quantity.

2. The number 4 is a factor of 8 because 4 divides into 8 evenly without a remainder. Complete the following sentences to obtain true statements about factors.

   The number 5 is not a factor of 8 because _____.

   One number is a factor of another number if _____.

3. The number 12 has six factors: 1, 2, 3, 4, 6, and 12. In the pictures below, observe three different arrangements of 12 smiley faces, representing three different ways of factoring 12. To the right of each arrangement, draw another arrangement that shows the commutative property of multiplication visually.

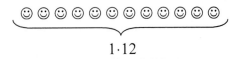

1·12

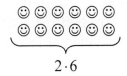

2·6

3·4

4. There are two different ways you can arrange 13 smiley faces into even rows with the same amount of faces.

    a. Draw those two arrangements in the space provided.

    b. Show visually, using uneven rows of smiley faces, why the numbers 2, 3, and 4 do not divide into 13 evenly without a remainder.

   c. Explain why the number 12 is a composite number and the number 13 is a prime number.

_____

_____

_____

5. Every composite number can be expressed as the product of prime numbers, and this unique product is known as the **prime factorization of a number**. For example, to find the prime factorization of 180, we first note that 180 is divisible by 2 because $2 \cdot 90 = 180$. The number 2 is prime. The number 90 is composite since it is divisible by 2, $2 \cdot 45 = 90$. Then, 45 is divisible by the prime number 3 because $3 \cdot 15 = 45$. Finally, 15 is also divisible by 3 because $3 \cdot 5 = 15$. Since 5 is prime, we have the prime factorization of 180 as seen below.

$$
\begin{aligned}
180 &= 2 \cdot 90 && \text{180 is divisible by 2} \\
&= 2 \cdot 2 \cdot 45 && \text{90 is divisible by 2} \\
&= 2 \cdot 2 \cdot 3 \cdot 15 && \text{45 is divisible by 3} \\
&= 2 \cdot 2 \cdot 3 \cdot 3 \cdot 5 && \text{15 is divisible by 3} \\
&= 2^2 \cdot 3^2 \cdot 5 && \text{using exponents}
\end{aligned}
$$

   a. Find the prime factorization of 60. Show all work and explain each step, in the style shown above.

   b. Find the prime factorization of 150. Show all work and explain each step.

6. The classrooms in the Carey building have desks placed in 5 rows, with each row containing 4 desks. Since the college admissions office expects an increase in enrollment, they recommend adding 2 desks to each of the 5 rows.

a. Use the distributive property to demonstrate the number of desks in each class, if we follow the admissions office proposal. *Hint:* The expression should contain parentheses and the numbers 5, 4, and 2.

b. The college president is not sure about the admissions office recommendation. She thinks that anywhere from 1 to 4 desks might have to be added to each of the 5 rows. If we use the variable d to represent the number of desks to be added, give a variable expression that demonstrates the number of desks in each class in terms of d.

c. Suppose we decide to make the number of rows variable (perhaps the rooms can fit anywhere from 4 to 7 rows of desks). Now the situation has classrooms with r rows. Each row will contain 4 desks, and d desks are to be added to each row. Give a variable expression that demonstrates the number of desks in each class in terms of r and d.

7. The numerical expression $2(3+4)$ can be evaluated in two different ways, as seen below.

$$2(3+4) = 2\cdot 3 + 2\cdot 4 \qquad\qquad 2(3+4) = 2(7)$$
$$= 6+8 \qquad\text{or}\qquad = 14$$
$$= 14$$

The first method applies the distributive property by multiplying the term 2 outside the parentheses by each term inside the parentheses and then adding the resulting sum.

The second method follows the order of operations by first completing the sum within the parentheses and then multiplying.

a. Observe the two methods and explain why they produce the same answer.

_____

_____

_____

b. Use the distributive property to rewrite the expression $2(x+4)$ without parentheses.

c. Explain why the following is *incorrect*.

$$2(x+4) = 2(4x)$$
$$= 8x$$

_____

_____

_____

8. Use the distributive property to rewrite the following variable expressions with parentheses. Part *a* has been completed as an example.

a. $5(x+2) = 5 \cdot x + 5 \cdot 2$
$$= 5x + 10$$

b. $7(9+a)$

c. $(t+3) \cdot 8$

d. $4(x+y+z)$

e. $n(6+a+b)$

9. Let's explore whether we can distribute over subtraction similar to the way we have distributed over addition. If *a*, *b*, and *c* represent any numbers, then the distributive property for subtraction says,
$$a \cdot (b-c) = a \cdot b - a \cdot c$$

a. Demonstrate that the distributive property for subtraction holds for $a = 4$, $b = 9$, and $c = 6$. *Hint:* Substitute the given numbers for *a*, *b*, and *c* and show that applying the distributive law gives the same result as applying the order of operations.

b. Demonstrate that the distributive property for subtraction holds for $a = 2$, $b = 7$, and $c = 3$.

c. Why do you think you can distribute over subtraction in the same fashion as addition?

_____

_____

_____

10. A number is divisible by 2 only if 2 divides into it evenly. What type of whole numbers are divisible by 2? Explain your answer using a complete sentence.

_____

_____

11. A number is divisible by 3 if the sum of the digits is divisible by 3.

a. Find a two-digit number that is divisible by 3. Explain.

_____

_____

b. Find a three-digit number that is divisible by 3. Explain.

_____

_____

12. A number is divisible by 4 if its last two digits are numbers that are divisible by 4. Explain whether or not the following numbers are divisible by 4.

a. 116 _____

_____

b. 242 _____

_____

c. 424 _____

_____

d. 508 _____

_____

13. Fill in the blanks to explain the divisibility test for 5.

A number is divisible by 5 if the last digit is either _____ or _____.

Study Skill: Reviewing Concepts

How should you go about reviewing concepts from previous sections and chapters? Reviewing is a process that you should be doing continuously. Everyone needs to look back and go over concepts that were previously covered. Sometimes this will mean just a quick look at some definitions, while other times it will be necessary to rework some problems you have already done. Many concepts are not fully understood without repeated exposure to the same ideas again and again.

The Chapter Summaries are an excellent starting point. Here you can find all the key terms that have been covered in each section, Questions for Review, and a Chapter Quiz. Reviewing the key words can be done quickly and will help strengthen your math vocabulary. The Questions for Review will help you think through the concepts and prompt you to go back to a particular section if they cannot be readily answered. If you need to go back to a particular section, pay special attention to the ideas in the boxes and the words in bold print. This will help you locate the concepts that need to be reviewed.

As reviewing past concepts becomes a regular study habit, you will begin to see a lot more connections between different mathematical concepts. This will help you get the big picture and pull all those loose ideas together. Good luck!

Section 2.2 Addition and Subtraction of Integers

Math Talk

How do you use the words **positive**, **negative**, and **opposite** in everyday language? Let's look at some common ways in which these terms are used.

- If you are **positive** about something, you are definite or certain in your knowledge. A person who has a positive attitude is hopeful, expecting good things.
- If you give a **negative** response to a request, then it is considered a refusal. A person with a negative attitude about something is not likely to be helpful or cooperative.
- People who are **opposites** are considered to be very different. If you and a friend have the opposite opinion, then what you believe is contrary to your friend's belief.

In many situations, positive and negative have opposite meanings. For example, you have math tests at school and medical tests for illness. The results of these tests can be positive or negative. No matter what the test, results that are positive are the opposite (reverse) of results that are negative. If you test negative for an illness, then you do not have that illness. You will be happy with a negative result. However, if your school test has a negative result, then you will not be happy because that means you did poorly.

The police and criminals are on opposite sides of the law. The home team is on the opposite side of the away team. Neighbors live on opposite sides of the fence. It is similar in mathematics where positive and negative are measures in the opposite direction. Positive means having a value greater than 0, while negative is the opposite, a value less than 0. So, if positive numbers are on one side of the fence and negative numbers are on the opposite side, then where is 0?

****

The **positive integers** or natural numbers are 1, 2, 3, 4, $\cdots$. These are counting numbers, a natural part of the world, as concrete as the fingers on our hands. **Zero** is a human invention; the symbol 0 first appeared as a notation to stand for the absence of quantity.

If we use a number line to visualize 0 and the set of positive integers, then any extension of this line to the left of 0 requires a set of values less than 0, called **negative integers**.

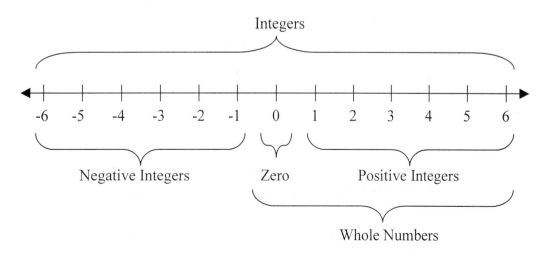

When we include the positive and negative integers and zero, we have the set of **integers** whose members can be symbolized as follows:

$$\{\cdots, \ -3, \ -2, \ -1, \ 0, \ 1, \ 2, \ 3, \ \cdots\}$$

Brush Up on Reading a Number Line

The number line on the previous page shows the integers from –6 (negative 6) up to 6 (positive 6) with a scale of 1 unit. The *scale* is the distance between each little vertical line (or tick mark).

Zero is used as a reference point, where numbers to the right are positive and numbers to the left are negative. Although this number line displays only 12 integers, there are actually an infinite amount of integer values. For example, if you start at zero and begin counting in either direction, there is no end to this sequence of numbers.

Note that the integers occur only at the vertical tick marks. The values between integers will be studied in Chapter 3. You should reference this line often until it becomes a picture that you can visualize in your mind. This will help as you compare different numbers and perform mathematical operations on them.

We will now take a journey through a number of Discovery Adventures that put us into situations where it is necessary to add and subtract integer values.

Discovery Adventure 1: Your Balance of Payments

Money . . . it always seems like you never have enough of it. So you decide that it's time to take a look at your budget. Using last month's bank statement, you decide to construct a table to organize how money is going in (deposit) and out (withdrawal) of your checking account. At the start of the month, you have a balance (current money available), and as time goes by, you write checks to pay bills (a negative transaction which withdraws money) and receive paychecks (a positive transaction which deposits money).

NOTE: All calculations should first be completed mentally or by hand. Afterwards you may check your work with a calculator.

a. Complete the table below by adding to the current balance, a positive number for each deposit and a negative number for each withdrawal. The current balance should increase for each deposit and decrease for each withdrawal. Record each calculation in the fourth column and its sum in the fifth column as a positive or negative balance. Do not complete the end of the month totals in the last row until part *d*. *Hint*: If a withdrawal is greater than the current balance, then your calculation should produce a new balance that is less than 0 or negative.

Transaction	Withdrawal (–) ($)	Deposit (+) ($)	Calculation	Balance ($)
Start of Month				$^+750$
Rent	–600		$^+750 + (–600)$	$^+150$
Auto Loan	–300			
Auto Insurance	–175			
Reg. Paycheck		$^+725$		
Extra Paycheck		$^+225$		
Auto Repair	–575			
Electric	–100			
Telephone	–125			
Cable	–35			
Reg. Paycheck		$^+725$		
Groceries	–310			
TOTALS → End of Month				$^+205$

b. Review the calculations that involved adding a positive and negative number. For example, the first calculation and resulting balance is given as $^+750 + (–600) = {^+150}$. Explain why the balance obtained from these calculations is sometimes positive and sometimes negative.

_____

_____

_____

- When you add positive and negative numbers, what operation actually gets performed?

- When you add positive and negative numbers, what determines the sign (+ or –) of your answer?

- Describe to a friend the process you follow when adding a positive and negative number.

_____

_____

c. Now review the calculations that involved adding two positive numbers or two negative numbers. For example, $-150 + (-175) = -325$.

- While computing the actual calculations, did you add or subtract?

- When adding two positive numbers, what was the sign of the answer?

- When adding two negative numbers, what was the sign of the answer?

- In general, describe to a friend the process you follow when adding two numbers with the same sign. For example, positive plus positive or negative plus negative.

_____

_____

d. Look at the last row in the table, labeled "Totals → End of Month."

- If you add up all the withdrawals, what is the sign of the total? Use complete sentences to explain your reasoning.

_____

_____

- If you add up all the deposits, what is the sign of the total? Use complete sentences to explain your reasoning.

_____

_____

- If you add the total withdrawals and total deposits, what is the sum? How does this value compare with the balance at the end of the month? Explain.

_____

_____

e. Suppose 3 regular paychecks ($725 each) and 1 extra paycheck ($225 from 2nd job) are expected next month. Assuming a $725 paycheck arrives before any bills and there is no extra auto expense, estimate the end balance in the next month's statement. Explain.

_____

_____

Feedback

The acceptance of negative numbers has occurred only during the last two centuries. Prior to this time, most people did not consider negative numbers to be part of reality. If a notice from the bank arrives about being overdrawn because of insufficient funds, I know that I've crossed over into negative territory. I know that if sea level is zero, then above sea level must be positive and below sea level must be negative. I know that if freezing occurs at 0° C, temperatures above 0° C are positive and temperatures below 0° C are negative. I know that velocity is speed with direction, so if forward is the positive direction, then reverse must be the negative (opposite) direction. That's the idea. Negative numbers are part of life.

Sometimes we use other words to represent the concept of negative. For example, if I'm flying in a plane and the plane loses altitude by 2000 ft, then there has been a negative change in height. The word *loses* implies that the plane is 2000 ft. below the height it had been flying at. The navigator could record the change in altitude as –2000 ft, while if the plane increased altitude by 2000 ft, the change would be $^+2000$ ft. When the loss and increase are taken together, the total change in altitude is 0 since the plane is back to flying at the same height. To see this mathematically,

$$-2000 + \left(^+2000\right) = 0$$

It's time for a new Discovery Adventure that will expose you to another situation where positive and negative numbers live.

Discovery Adventure 2: A Change in Altitude

Let's fly the friendly skies of World Air Turbulence (WAT). Suppose your WAT plane is flying at an altitude of 10,000 feet. The weather gets a little rough, and the navigator records the following changes in altitude:

$$-2100 \text{ ft.,} \quad -1725 \text{ ft.,} \quad ^+1875 \text{ ft.,} \quad ^+1500 \text{ ft.,} \quad -450 \text{ ft.}$$

a. Use the five changes above to calculate the total change in altitude. Show all work and explain the purpose of each calculation in terms of the plane flight.

_____

_____

_____

b. What is the plane's new altitude after all these changes occur?

Feedback

Earlier we said that if a plane loses 2000 ft in altitude, followed by an increase in altitude of 2000 ft, then the total change was zero, or

$$-2000 + \left(^+ 2000 \right) = 0$$

$^+2000$ and -2000 are **opposites,** or one is the **additive inverse** of the other.

Recall that the set of whole numbers $W = \{0,\ 1,\ 2,\ 3,\ \cdots\ \}$ is zero along with all the counting numbers. If we include all whole numbers and the opposite of each counting number, we obtain the set of integers (positive and negative counting numbers and zero).

The **set of integers** I can be denoted as,

$$I = \{\ \cdots,\ -3,\ -2,\ -1,\ 0, 1,\ 2,\ 3,\ \cdots\ \}.$$

A nice way to visualize integers is by using points on the number line. Put a dot on the line below at the number 4 and another dot at the opposite of 4.

How far is the point at 4 from 0 on the number line?   _____ units

How far is the point at −4 from 0 on the number line?   _____ units

A number's distance from zero on the number line is known as its **absolute value**. We symbolize absolute value by putting vertical lines around the number. For example,

$$\left|\ 4\ \right| = 4 \text{ is read, "the absolute value of 4 is 4."}$$

$$\left|\ -4\ \right| = 4 \text{ is read, "the absolute value of } -4 \text{ is 4."}$$

Notice that absolute value always produce a result that is greater than or equal to 0. The absolute value of zero is zero, because zero has a zero distance from itself. For example,

$$|0| = 0 \text{ is read as "the absolute value of 0 is 0."}$$

Let's continue to use the number line to explore integer values from a graphical perspective. Take the time to Brush Up on Geometry Terms if necessary, then go to the next Discovery Adventure to learn how to add integers on the number line.

Brush Up on Geometry Terms

A *line* is a straight one-dimensional figure with infinite length but no thickness. Imagine a moving point tracing out a straight path without end. This path is made up of an infinite amount of points extending in opposite directions. Any two points on the line can be used to denote the line. For example, the line *AB*, given below, is denoted as $\overleftrightarrow{AB}$.

A *line segment* is a part of a line with a finite length between two endpoints.

A *ray* or *vector* is a straight line extending from a point in one direction without end.

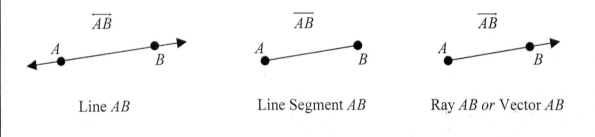

Line *AB*   Line Segment *AB*   Ray *AB or* Vector *AB*

Discovery Adventure 3: Walk This Way

Let us take a walk on the number line (see the figure on the next page) to see how the number line can be used to visualize adding two integers. Any addition will always start at home, which is zero. A positive number indicates that you should walk to the right by the number of units given and a negative number indicates that you should walk to the left by the number of units given. Rays or vectors will show the path of the walk. Suppose we wish to simulate the following sum,

$$^{+}5+\left(-3\right)$$

Guided Walk #1

Our walk will start at home (zero). The positive 5 will tell us to walk 5 units to the right. We simulate the action by drawing a ray starting at 0 and ending at 5. The negative 3 tells us to walk to the left (negative direction) from 5, a total of 3 units. This is simulated by drawing a second ray starting at 5 and ending at 2 (the solution).

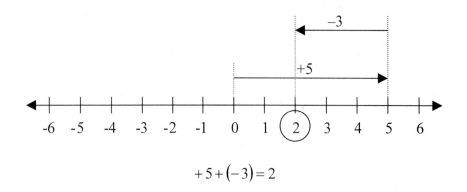

$$+5+(-3)=2$$

The "+" in front of the five, which represents a positive value, is usually omitted, so we can write,

$$5+(-3)=2$$

Guided Walk #2

Let's simulate another walk. This time we will take the sum of –3 and –4, or $-3+(-4)$.

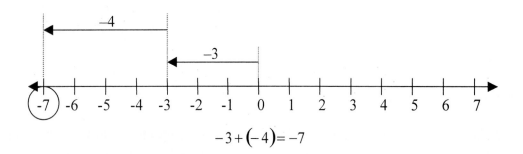

$$-3+(-4)=-7$$

a. It's time to see if you can walk on your own! Add $^{+}6+(-8)$ on the number line below. Be sure to show your path using positive and negative rays or vectors.

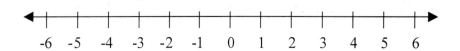

b. For your second walk, simulate adding –4 + 8 using rays or vectors on the number line below.

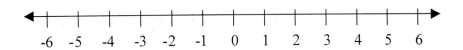

c. Let's take one last walk to feel confident in our ability. Simulate adding $5+(-5)$ using rays or vectors on the number line below.

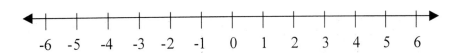

Feedback

On the last simulation you should have found your way home, 0.

$$5+(-5)=0$$

The other two walks would have the following solutions,

$$-4+8=4 \quad \text{and} \quad {}^+6+(-8)=-2.$$

If you ever start to lose the feel for adding positive and negative numbers, just think back to this walking adventure. Start at home (point zero), then move right for a positive number and left for a negative number.

****

To introduce integer subtraction, let's put the concept in financial terms. If a lender cancels a debt that you owe, then the lender has given you a gift. In mathematical terms, this means that if you subtract a negative amount, it is the same as adding a positive amount. Using the variable b to represent any positive, unknown value, we have the following symbolic rule:

$$-(-b) = +b \qquad (b > 0)$$

In words, *subtracting a negative number is the same as adding a positive number.*

Suppose, for example, Uncle Sam decides to forgive your student loan. Then the government has in effect given you a free education. This is certainly adding a positive value to your life. Think of b as the dollar value of the loan. By wiping out what you owe, you can now save that amount for the future.

Specifically, suppose you take out a government loan worth $10,000 to finance your education. The loan is to be paid back in monthly installments after graduation. Upon receiving your diploma, a letter arrives saying that the government wants to give you a gift by canceling your loan debt. This translates to the following symbolic form.

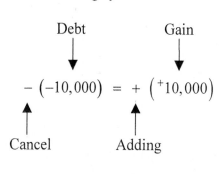

In words, *subtracting negative $10,000 is equivalent to adding a $10,000 gain.*

Now consider a second situation. If the United States government canceled all social security benefits, then many people would have an added burden in their life. Think of b as the dollar value of your Social Security benefit. By taking away your benefit, the government has added a negative value to your income. Suppose your $1000 per month benefit from Social Security is canceled. This translates to the following symbolic form.

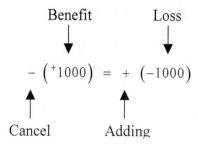

In words, *canceling a $1000 benefit is equivalent to adding a $1000 loss.*

Using the variable b to represent any positive, unknown value, we have the following rule:

$$- (b) \; = \; + (-b) \qquad (b > 0)$$

In words, *subtracting a positive number is the same as adding a negative number.*

In the next Discovery Adventure, you will use a calculator as a tool to help develop a general rule for subtraction of integers. Be sure to look for patterns as you proceed through the adventure.

▣ Discovery Adventure 4: Which Is It, Addition or Subtraction?

In the following problems, use a calculator to investigate subtraction with integers.

a. Enter $7 - 4$ into your calculator. What is the output?

Enter $7 + (-4)$ into your calculator. What is the output?

b. Enter $3 - 5$ into your calculator. What is the output?

Enter $3 + (-5)$ into your calculator. What is the output?

c. Enter $-2 - (-6)$ into your calculator. What is the output?

Enter $-2 + 6$ into your calculator. What is the output?

d. In your own words, what seems to be the rule for subtraction?

_____

_____

e. If a and b are variables that represent any integer, rewrite the following expression using your verbal rule from part *d.*

$$a - b =$$

Feedback

In general, if a and b are integers, then $a - b = a + (-b)$. In words, this means "The difference between a and b equals the sum of a and the opposite of b."

Suppose you have $5 of pocket money and decide to buy $3 of food at the school cafeteria. When you reach the checkout to complete your transaction, here are two ways to look at the process.

- You place a $5 bill on the counter and the checkout person deducts the $3 purchase, leaving you with $2 in change. This could be considered subtraction,

$$5 - 3 = 2$$

- At the register you combine (add) the $5 you own with the $3 you owe for lunch. Owing 3 dollars can be thought of as −3 dollars, so when you combine (add) positive 5 and −3 you end up with positive 2. This can be expressed as addition in the following manner:

$$5 + (-3) = 2$$

In the second case, you interpret subtraction as addition of the opposite. In other words, there is no difference between subtracting an integer and adding its opposite. Therefore, starting with positive 7 and subtracting negative 3, is the same as starting with positive 7 and adding positive 3, or

$$7 - (-3) = 7 + 3 = 10$$

Therefore, the process of starting with an integer and subtracting a second integer from the first is equivalent to taking the first integer and adding the opposite of the second integer.

Here are a few more examples to consider, and then its time for you to practice what you've learned.

    a. $-2 - 6 = -2 + (-6) = -8$

    b. $-3 - (-7) = -3 + 7 = 4$

    c. $5 - 8 = 5 + (-8) = -3$

    d. $-9 - (-3) = -9 + 3 = -6$

> ## Section Exercises: 2.2

1. In a science course, you might study subatomic particles called protons and electrons. Protons have a positive electric charge of 1 unit, and electrons have a negative electric charge of 1 unit. Protons and electrons have equal but opposite charges, so when combined they are neutralized. This means protons and electrons, as a pair, have an electrical charge of 0. Let protons be represented by the symbol © and electrons by the symbol ∟. In this charged particle model, you will pair protons and electrons so that each pair has a charge of 0 or

    (© ∟)   Electric charge of 0 (no charge)

    This is similar to integer arithmetic when you add positive 1 and negative 1 to obtain 0,

    $$1 + (-1) = 0$$

    Suppose a set contains 6 electrons ∟ and 2 protons ©. If we combine protons and electrons into pairs, the total electric charge is –4.

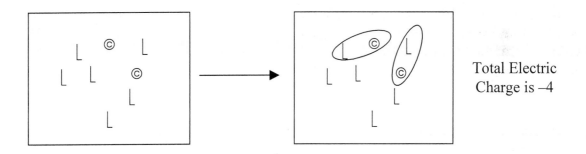

Total Electric
Charge is –4

    This concrete model can be written as a sum: $-6 + (^+2) = -4$ or $-6 + 2 = -4$

    For parts *a* and *b*, determine the total electric charge of the set by pairing protons © and electrons ∟ with circles as in the example above. State the integer sum that each set models.

    a.

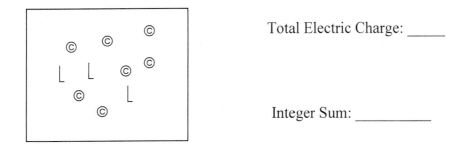

Total Electric Charge: _____

Integer Sum: _____

b.

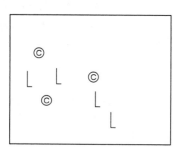

Total Electric Charge: _____

Integer Sum: _____

c. Construct two unique models that will produce a total electric charge of –5.

Integer Sum: _____

Integer Sum: _____

d. Construct two unique models that will produce a total electric charge of $^+3$.

Integer Sum: _____

Integer Sum: _____

2. Suppose you have a set of 5 protons © and want to take away 7 protons. The set needs 2 additional protons for this to happen. One way to accomplish this task is to give the set 2 protons and 2 electrons L, so that you are adding a total charge of 0. You now have enough protons to take 7 away, which will leave 2 electrons, and a set with an electrical charge of –2. This example is a model of doing the integer subtraction, $^+5 - \left(^+7 \right) = -2$.

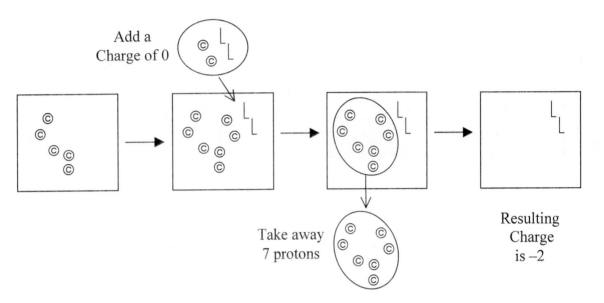

a. Construct a model of the integer subtraction, $^+2 - \left(^-3 \right) = 5$

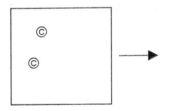

b. Construct a model of the integer subtraction, $^-4 - \left(^-3 \right) = -1$

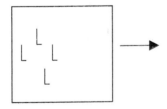

3. In the last exercise, a charged particle example was given as a concrete model of the integer subtraction, $^+5-\left(^+7\right)=-2$. The process can be shown mathematically by the following sequence of steps:

$$^+5-\,^+7=\,^+5+\left(^+2+\,^-2\right)-\,^+7 \quad \text{Add 0 using } \left(^+2+\,^-2\right)=0$$

$$=\left(^+5+\,^+2\right)+\,^-2-\,^+7 \quad \text{Associative Property of Addition}$$

$$=\,^+7+\,^-2-\,^+7 \qquad\qquad \text{Simplify parentheses by adding } ^+5+\,^+2$$

$$=\,^-2+\,^+7-\,^+7 \qquad\qquad \text{Communitive Property of Addition}$$

$$=\,^-2+0 \qquad\qquad\qquad \text{Subtract, } ^+7-\,^+7=0$$

$$=\,^-2 \qquad\qquad\qquad\quad \text{Add}$$

The steps below show a similar procedure being completed on $^+2-\,^-3$. Explain each step.

$$^+2-\,^-3=\,^+2+\left(^+3+\,^-3\right)-\,^-3 \quad \underline{\hspace{9cm}}$$

$$=\left(^+2+\,^+3\right)+\,^-3-\,^-3 \quad \underline{\hspace{9cm}}$$

$$=\,^+5+\,^-3-\,^-3 \quad \underline{\hspace{9cm}}$$

$$=\,^+5+0 \quad \underline{\hspace{9cm}}$$

$$=\,^+5 \quad \underline{\hspace{9cm}}$$

4. Suppose the parking garage at your work has 8 levels. Automobiles enter the garage at ground level, where the car is shown in the picture below. There are 4 levels above the ground level and 3 levels below the ground level. The distance between successive levels is 12 feet.

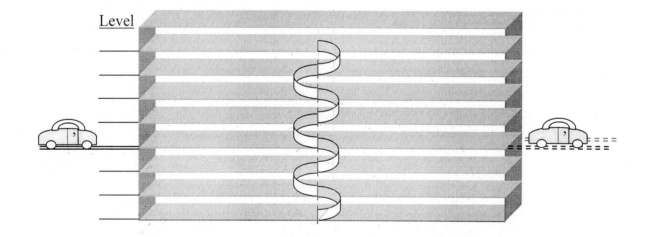

a. The ground level where automobiles enter is level 0. Use integer values to label each level in the picture. Record your results in the spaces to the left of the garage and below the word "Level."

b. On Monday morning you drive into the garage and travel from ground level up to the third level where your company has some reserved spaces. Unfortunately, all the reserved spaces are full, so you travel down to level –1 where there are a few extra spaces available. On the right side of the garage where the car is coming out, draw and label two rays pointing up or down to picture how integers can represent the car's vertical movement within the garage.

c. Use integer addition to show the calculation that represents the car's vertical movement in part b. Then find the solution that represents the level where the car was parked.

d. Use a positive number to represent the amount of feet the car traveled vertically, going up.

e. Use a negative number to represent the amount of feet the car traveled vertically, going down.

f. Use integer subtraction to show the calculation that represents the total vertical distance that the car traveled between levels. Then find the solution.

5. The college that Chris attends requires all incoming freshmen to have a laptop computer for use in class and where they study. Chris decides to start a business renting laptops to other students at the college. She uses most of her savings to buy 20 reconditioned laptops from a wholesaler for $225 per computer. Chris advertises around campus that any student can rent a laptop computer for one semester at a price of $75 per semester, but it must be returned in good condition. Chris expects to run her business during the fall, spring, and summer semesters for each year during the next 2 years.

a. How much will it cost to start Chris's business? Show your work.

b. If Chris is able to rent all 20 laptops for the fall and spring semesters of her first year, what will be her revenue at the end of these two semesters? Show your work.
   Hint: Revenue is the money coming in from the rentals.

c. Calculate the profit after two semesters. Show your work. *Hint: Profit* is the difference between revenue and cost. For example, *Profit = Revenue – Cost*

d. Most businesses have a negative value for profit during the early stages of operation. Use the terms *revenue* and *cost* to explain the status of Chris's business after two semesters.

_____

_____

_____

_____

e. How many laptops must Chris rent during her third semester of business to break even (obtain a profit of $0)? Show all work.

f. Chris's business does break even during the third semester, so she aims to make a profit of $6000 over the next 3 semesters. To reach her goal, what is the new minimum rental price that must be charged for the laptops? *Hint:* She can rent up to 20 laptops per semester.

g. What type of risk is Chris taking if she charges a price greater than $75? Explain using complete sentences.

_____

_____

_____

_____

h. Suppose the increase in price causes a decrease in demand such that Chris is only able to rent 15 computers in each of the last three semesters of running her business. How much is Chris short of her $6000 goal if she uses the rental price from part *f?*

6. Use the idea that subtraction is "addition of the opposite" to rewrite and then compute the following problems. Do not use a calculator except to check your answer.

Problem	Rewrite as Addition of the Opposite	Answer
a. $9 - 5 =$		
b. $9 - (-5) =$		
c. $-9 - 5 =$		
d. $-9 - (-5) =$		

7. A person had the following changes in weight each month over a five-month period:

$$+10 \text{ lbs.}, \quad -5 \text{ lbs.}, \quad -7 \text{ lbs.}, \quad -3 \text{ lbs.}, \quad +4 \text{ lbs.}$$

a. Explain the use of positive and negative symbols in terms of how a person's weight changes.

_____

_____

_____

b. Show the calculations needed to find the total change in weight.

c. How much weight did the person gain? Express this amount as a signed number.

8. Let's watch the action in a youth soccer game between two teams of 4-5 year olds. A child reaches the ball and moves 20 yards in the wrong direction (back toward his own goal). Although the coach likes the way the youth is controlling the ball, he yells at the kid to change direction and move forward. The young athlete spins 180° and heads straight out in the opposite (correct) direction for 17 yards until the ball is taken away by another player. Assuming we measure positive distance toward the opposing team's goal, what is the net gain or loss during this play?

   a. Draw a picture of the problem situation.

   b. Show the calculation needed to find the player's total forward progress (toward the opposing team's goal) and then compute the result as a signed number.

9. In football, the net yards that a player runs are the total yards that the player carries the ball from the line of scrimmage toward the opposing team's goal. Suppose the third string running back is given a chance to run with the ball on two consecutive plays. The first time the player carries the ball he loses 2 yards (he is tackled and down 2 yards behind the line of scrimmage). The next time he carries the ball ends with the player losing 3 more yards. Assume that when a player moves the ball forward (toward the opposing team's goal) from the line of scrimmage, the yards of movement are considered to be positive. However, if he is tackled and down before the line of scrimmage, the yards between the line and where he is down are considered to be negative.

   a. Draw a picture of this situation, showing the movement of the ball during the two plays described above.

    b. Show the calculation needed to find the running back's net yards and then compute the result as a signed number.

    c. If the running back carries the ball one more time during the game and gains 7 yards on the play, then how many net yards will he end up with? Show the calculation and write the solution using a complete sentence.

_____

_____

10. Suppose you start the month with a balance of \$257 in your checking account. During the month, the following changes occurred:

$$-121, \quad -347, \quad 175, \quad -25$$

    a. Show how to add the four changes above. Then state the total gain or loss for the month.

    b. Show the calculation needed to find the ending balance.

    c. Describe what this balance means to your checking account.

_____

_____

_____

_____

11. An airplane was flying at a constant altitude when it encountered turbulence. The following changes in altitude were recorded every five minutes:

$$-1203 \text{ ft.}, \quad -642 \text{ ft.}, \quad +1057 \text{ ft.}, \quad -735 \text{ ft.}, \quad +1528 \text{ ft.}$$

After the last change, the turbulence ended, and the plane resumed flying to another constant altitude. How far above or below the original altitude was the plane after the turbulence stopped? Show all work, and write your answer in a complete sentence.

_____

_____

12. Let's consider an example of measuring a change in quantity by using the following formula:

Change in Quantity = New Value – Old Value

Suppose a group of hikers decide to climb up and down a mountain whose summit is at an elevation of 3252 feet. On the climb up, the hikers stop at a rest camp, which is at an elevation of 1603 feet. They eventually hike up to the summit, rest, then climb down. On the way down, the group stops at the same rest camp as on the climb up.

a. On the climb up from the rest camp to the summit, what is the change in elevation? *Hint*: The new elevation is at the summit, and the old elevation is at the rest camp.

b. On the climb down from the summit to the rest camp, what is the change in elevation?

In parts *c, d,* and *e*, complete the sentence in the context of measuring a change in quantity. Use the words *positive, negative,* or *zero* to complete the sentence.

c. If the quantity increases, then the change is _____.

d. If the quantity decreases, then the change is _____.

e. If the quantity stays constant, then the change is _____.

13. Suppose the outdoor temperature on a particular day drops from a high of 82°F at 1 p.m. to 70°F at 8 p.m.

Two of the following sentences have the same meaning as the sentence above, while the remaining one is not logically correct. Circle the sentence that is flawed. Then explain your reasoning in complete sentences.

- A drop in temperature of 12°F occurred between 1 p.m. and 8 p.m.

- A change in temperature of –12°F occurred between 1 p.m. and 8 p.m.

- A drop in temperature of –12°F occurred between 1 p.m. and 8 p.m.

_____

_____

_____

_____

14. Foreign trade involves nations buying, selling, and exchanging commodities (articles of use or value). Each country will send out (export) and bring in (import) commodities to and from other countries. A country's balance of trade is the difference in the monetary (money) value of its exports and imports. For example, the United States trade balance with another country is calculated using the following formula:

Trade balance = Exports – Imports

In the table below, U.S. trade with selected countries is displayed. You are given the approximate value of exports and imports in millions of dollars. The remainder of the table will be filled in as you work through parts *a* and *b* on the next page.

Country	Exports	Imports	U.S. Trade balance with	Rank of trade balance
China	$14,241.3	$71,168.7	$–56,927.4	
Canada	156,603.4	173,256.1		
Mexico	78,772.5	94,629.0		
Japan	57,831.0	121,845.0		
Germany	26,657.4	49,842.0		

Source: *Office of Trade and Economic Analysis, U.S. Dept. of Commerce*

a. Complete the fourth column using the formula: Trade balance = Exports – Imports. Be sure to express your answer as a signed number in millions of dollars.

b. Complete the last column by ranking each country as #1, 2, 3, 4, or 5 in trade balance by size of deficit. Find the absolute value of each number in column four. The largest result should be ranked #1, second largest #2, and so on.

c. Express the U.S. trade balance with China in dollars instead of millions of dollars. *Hint*: There are six zeros in 1 million dollars, $1,000,000.

d. What would have to occur to produce a positive trade balance with each of these countries? Express your answer using complete sentences.

_____

_____

_____

_____

Section 2.3 Multiplication and Division of Integers

Math Talk

Much of mathematics involves analyzing **patterns**, and these patterns are all around us. There are patterns in numbers, patterns in shapes, patterns of motion and change, patterns of reasoning and communicating, and so on. When a musician sings and plays an instrument, there are patterns in the way the words are sung and the instruments are played. When a painter draws a picture, there are patterns in the shapes and colors of the drawing. When a poet writes a poem, there are patterns in the words and lines. When a mathematician expresses thoughts in symbols, there are patterns to this work as well.

Numerical patterns can be seen in sequences of numbers such as the famous *Fibonacci* numbers given below. Observe this sequence of numbers and try to find a pattern to the way the numbers are listed. Can you list the next three terms?

$$0, \ 1, \ 1, \ 2, \ 3, \ 5, \ 8, \ 13, \ 21, \ 34, \ 55, \ 89, \ \cdots$$

Notice that after the second term, each integer number is the sum of the previous two. What makes this sequence of numbers even more interesting is its occurrence in nature. If you gather some pine cones and count the number of spirals of scales, you will find 8 to the right and 13 to the left—two consecutive Fibonacci numbers. On a pineapple there are 8 spirals to the right, 13 to the left, and 21 vertically—three consecutive Fibonacci numbers. The seeds of a sunflower will form a spiral arrangement in which you can count 55 in one direction and 89 in the other. Why do you think so many objects in nature exhibit patterns of Fibonacci numbers? While research has produced some theories, there have not been any clear answers to this question.

In this section you will get a chance to look at a few of the many patterns that can be created with numbers. By investigating these patterns, you can unlock many of the ideas in this section.

****

Suppose you ask a friend what he knows about multiplication and division of integers. The friend says all he remembers is that minus times minus is plus but doesn't remember why. So do you accept that multiplying a negative number times another negative number equals a positive number? Your friend would really like to know the reasoning behind this rule. This presents you with a mystery that needs to be solved. Let's begin our investigation.

Suppose the variable, a, represents any integer value. Recall that the set of integers can be expressed as

$$\{\cdots, \ -3, \ -2, \ -1, \ 0, \ 1, \ 2, \ 3, \ \cdots\}$$

What is the opposite of a? This depends on what value is assigned to a.

If $a = 2$, the opposite of 2 is -2.

If $a = -3$, the opposite of -3 is $^+3$ or 3.

If $a = 12$, the opposite of 12 is -12.

In math, putting a negative symbol or minus sign in front of a number means to take the opposite of that number. For example,

$-(-1) = {}^+1$ is read as "the opposite of negative one is positive one or just one."

$-\left({}^+5\right) = -5$ is read as "the opposite of positive five is negative five."

In this context, the negative symbol or minus sign outside the parentheses is associated with the word *opposite*. Since it is common practice to drop the plus symbol when denoting a positive value, the two examples above can be written as

$-(-1) = 1$ and $-(5) = -5$.

So what is the opposite of a? Symbolically, we can represent the opposite of a as $-a$.

Discovery Adventure 1: Follow the Pattern

Complete the following list of multiplication problems. Look for patterns as you proceed. Drawing a number line might help you to visualize the pattern that the numbers are following. Do not use a calculator except to check your results!

$$4 \cdot 2 =$$
$$3 \cdot 2 =$$
$$2 \cdot 2 =$$
$$1 \cdot 2 =$$
$$0 \cdot 2 =$$
$$-1 \cdot 2 =$$
$$-2 \cdot 2 =$$
$$-3 \cdot 2 =$$

a. Write in words what you have discovered about multiplying integers.

_____

_____

_____

Repeat the same process on the following list of multiplication problems.

$$3 \cdot 4 =$$
$$3 \cdot 3 =$$
$$3 \cdot 2 =$$
$$3 \cdot 1 =$$
$$3 \cdot 0 =$$
$$3 \cdot (-1) =$$
$$3 \cdot (-2) =$$
$$3 \cdot (-3) =$$

b. What pattern do you observe in the above solutions?

_____

_____

_____

c. In your own words, state a general rule for multiplying integers with different signs (a positive times a negative or a negative times a positive).

_____

_____

Again, repeat the same process on the following list of multiplication problems.

$$3 \cdot (-2) =$$
$$2 \cdot (-2) =$$
$$1 \cdot (-2) =$$
$$0 \cdot (-2) =$$
$$-1 \cdot (-2) =$$
$$-2 \cdot (-2) =$$
$$-3 \cdot (-2) =$$

d.   Observe the last three problems in the list, then write a rule for multiplying integers with the same sign (a positive times a positive or a negative times a negative).

_____

_____

Feedback

In summary, when **multiplying two integer values**, we have the following rules:

- Same signs signal that the product is positive.

$$(-)\cdot(-) = +$$
$$(+)\cdot(+) = +$$

- Different signs signal that the product is negative.

$$(+)\cdot(-) = -$$
$$(-)\cdot(+) = -$$

What will happen if we multiply more than two numbers? Following the order of operations, we can evaluate an expression by multiplying left to right. Observe the following examples.

Evaluate the following expressions:

a. $(-5)(-4)(-7)$

b. $(-6)(-5)(-2)(-9)$

Solution

$$(-5)(-4)(-7) = (^{+}20)(-7)$$
$$\underbrace{\quad}_{+20}$$
$$= -140$$

$$(-6)(-5)(-2)(-9) = \underbrace{(^{+}30)}_{+30}\underbrace{(-2)(-9)}_{-60}$$
$$= (-60)(-9)$$
$$= 540$$

Since the associative property of multiplication allows you to multiply the factors in any order, we did not have to compute each product from left to right. Find the product in the examples above using different orders when multiplying the factors. You should arrive at the same answers as given above.

When you find the product of 3 or more negative numbers, is there a way to figure out the sign of the answer before doing any computation? Observe the examples again.

$$(-5)(-4)(-7) \quad \text{and} \quad (-6)(-5)(-2)(-9)$$

If you can find the sign of the answer just by observation, then you can focus on finding the product of the absolute values of each number. In other words, from the first example you could find the product $5 \cdot 4 \cdot 7$ and then place the sign with the answer.

Since each number in the first example is negative, you could mentally reason that

$$(-)(-) = (+) \quad \text{and then} \quad (+)(-) = (-).$$

Therefore, the answer is negative and $5 \cdot 4 \cdot 7 = 140$, so $(-5)(-4)(-7) = -140$. However, even mentally finding the answer is not the most efficient method when you are finding a product with a lot of factors. So let's investigate a shortcut for dealing with the sign of the answer when finding a product.

Discovery Adventure 2: More Patterns

Investigate the following problem involving multiplication with negative integers. Complete the following table and look for patterns as you proceed.

Input	Output
$(-2) \cdot (-2)$	
$(-2) \cdot (-2) \cdot (-2)$	
$(-2) \cdot (-2) \cdot (-2) \cdot (-2)$	
$(-2) \cdot (-2) \cdot (-2) \cdot (-2) \cdot (-2)$	
$(-2) \cdot (-2) \cdot (-2) \cdot (-2) \cdot (-2) \cdot (-2)$	

a. Write a rule for multiplying two or more negative integers. *Hint:* You should describe two cases.

_____

_____

_____

Construct a new table by rewriting the input column from the previous table using exponential notation. The result written in the output column below should match up with the output column in the previous table. The first row has been completed for you.

Input	Output
$(-2)^2$	4

b. Write a general rule about having a negative number as the base and taking that base to different powers.

_____

_____

c. What pattern do you notice between the number of factors that are negative and the sign of the final result?

_____

_____

_____

Feedback

In general, when multiplying two or more numbers,

- An even number of negative numbers means that the product must be positive.
- An odd number of negative numbers means that the product must be negative.

Also, if you are repeatedly multiplying the same number together, then you can express the calculation using exponential notation.

If the base is negative, then

- An even exponent means that the answer must be positive.
- An odd exponent means that the answer must be negative.

The last two bullets are basically the same as the previous two bullets since evaluating exponents is simply a shorthand notation for repeated multiplication.

Take special care to notice the difference between -2^2 and $(-2)^2$. The first expression says to square 2 and then apply the negative symbol, resulting in -4. For example,

$$-2^2 = -(2 \cdot 2) = -(4) = -4$$

Above, $-(4) = -4$ can be interpreted as "the opposite of positive 4 is -4." In the second expression, $(-2)^2$, square -2 to produce positive 4.

$$(-2)^2 = (-2) \cdot (-2) = 4$$

Discovery Adventure 3: Reciprocal

Division is defined as multiplication by the **reciprocal**, where reciprocal means to interchange the numerator (top) and denominator (bottom). For example,

The reciprocal of 2 or $\dfrac{2}{1}$ is $\dfrac{1}{2}$.

The reciprocal of 3 or $\dfrac{3}{1}$ is $\dfrac{1}{3}$.

The reciprocal of $\dfrac{1}{4}$ is $\dfrac{4}{1}$ or 4.

The reciprocal of $\dfrac{5}{7}$ is $\dfrac{7}{5}$.

a. If n is the numerator and d is the denominator, then what is the reciprocal of $\dfrac{n}{d}$?

It is important to remember that the fraction bar is a symbol for division. We could symbolize 12 divided by 4 as either

$$12 \div 4 \quad \text{or} \quad 12 / 4 \quad \text{or} \quad \dfrac{12}{4}$$

Whichever symbol is used, the operation means to find out the number of 4's that are in 12.

b. Enter $12 \div 4$ into your calculator and write the answer below. Do the same with $12 \cdot \left(\dfrac{1}{4} \right)$.

Explain why you get the same answer. *Hint:* $\dfrac{1}{4}$ times 12 can be interpreted as "What is one-fourth of 12?"

_____

_____

_____

Feedback

Since any division problem can be expressed as multiplication by the reciprocal, all the rules for multiplying positive and negative numbers hold true for division too.

In summary, when **dividing two integer values**, the following statements are true:

- Same signs signal that the quotient is positive.

$$\frac{(-)}{(-)} = + \quad \text{or} \quad (-)/(-) = +$$

$$\frac{(+)}{(+)} = + \quad \text{or} \quad (+)/(+) = +$$

- Different signs signal that the quotient is negative.

$$\frac{(+)}{(-)} = - \quad \text{or} \quad (+)/(-) = -$$

$$\frac{(-)}{(+)} = - \quad \text{or} \quad (-)/(+) = -$$

Section Exercises: 2.3

1. Practice multiplying and dividing the integer numbers below. Do not use your calculator except to check your answers.

    a. $-5 \cdot 6$

    b. $\dfrac{-6}{-2}$

    c. $7 \cdot (-4)$

    d. $10 \div (-5)$

    e. $(-6)(-6)$

    f. $-24/3$

    g. $3(-5)(-6)$

    h. $(-2)(-4)(-3)$

    i. $6(8)(-10)$

    j. $(-5)(-12)(-1)(-9)$

    k. $(-7)(-8)(3)(-2)(0)(-4)$

2. Suppose you have a lever that balances at point F. We can draw the number line on the lever such that 0 is at point F, positive numbers are to the right, and negative numbers are to the left. Assume that if we push down on the lever, the downward force is negative. If we push up on the lever, the upward force is positive. An upward force on a positive position or a downward force on a negative position will move the lever counterclockwise.

    a. Can you describe a situation where the lever will move clockwise?

_____

_____

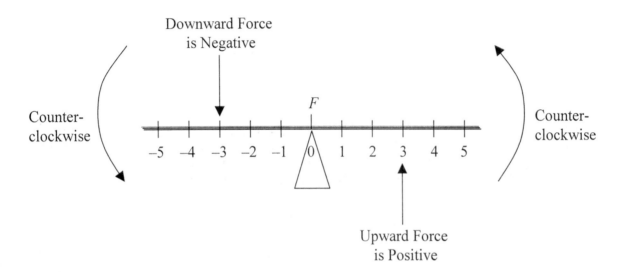

When applying a force at a point, the lever will turn a greater amount the further the force is from point F. The turning tendency equals the product of the force and the position where the force is applied,

$$\text{Turning Tendency} = \text{Force} \cdot \text{Position}$$

For example, applying an upward force of 5 pounds at the point 3, produces a turning tendency of $5 \cdot 3 = 15$ in the counterclockwise direction.

    b. What is the turning tendency when applying a downward force of 5 pounds (force = –5) at the point –3? Explain.

_____

_____

_____

122

c. What is the turning tendency when applying a downward force of 10 pounds (force = −10) at the point 2? Explain.

_____

_____

_____

d. What is the turning tendency when applying an upward force of 2½ pounds (force = +2 ½) at the point −4? Explain.

_____

_____

_____

3. Rewrite each of the following division problems as multiplication by the reciprocal, then calculate the answer. The first row has been completed for you.

Division	Multiplication	Answer
$\dfrac{10}{2}$	$10 \cdot \left(\dfrac{1}{2}\right)$	5
$\dfrac{12}{4}$		
$-15 \div 3$		
$\dfrac{-25}{-5}$		
$16/(-4)$		
$\dfrac{0}{1}$		

4. Generalize the work you did in Section Exercise #3 by rewriting the following expression in terms of multiplication. If a and b are any numbers, except $b \neq 0$,

$$\frac{a}{b} =$$

5. Given the expressions 5^2, -5^2, $(-5)^2$, enter each expression into your calculator and then evaluate the answer. Make sure you use the negative symbol on your calculator instead of the minus sign when entering the last two expressions.

   a. Explain the reason why the outputs are the same or different.

   _____

   _____

   _____

   _____

   b. Now evaluate the same calculations step by step using pencil and paper. State in words what you did and why.

   - 5^2 _____

     _____

   - -5^2 _____

     _____

   - $(-5)^2$ _____

     _____

6. Complete the table below by rewriting each subtraction as addition. Then calculate the solution. *Hint:* The first row shows that subtracting a positive is the same as adding a negative. The second row shows that subtracting a negative is the same as adding a positive.

Subtraction	Addition	Solution
$2-5$	$2+(-5)$	-3
$2-(-5)$	$2+5$	7
$-2-5$		
$-2-(-5)$		
$5-2$		
$5-(-2)$		
$-5-2$		
$-5-(-2)$		
$0-5$		

7. Show that subtraction is the inverse of addition by rewriting the following expression in terms of addition.

    If a and b are any numbers, $a-b=$

8. Complete the following sentences by explaining to a friend how you deal with adding integers.

    a. When adding two integers with different signs, _____

    _____

    _____

    b. When adding two integers with the same signs, _____

    _____

    _____

9. Complete parts *a* and *b* using the rules for adding two integer values.

   a. Pick any two integers with different signs and show how to add them.

   b. Pick any two negative integers and show how to add them.

   c. Repeat parts *a* and *b* until you are able to add without referring to the rules.

10. Complete the following multiplication table, looking for patterns as you work. A few squares have been filled in as an example.

•	−4	−3	−2	−1	0	1	2	3	4
4	−16								
3					0				
2									
1				−1					
0		0							
−1									
−2		6							
−3									
−4									−16

11. Evaluate the following pairs of expressions and record the answers.

   1) $8 + 2 =$
      $2 + 8 =$

   2) $8 \cdot 2 =$
      $2 \cdot 8 =$

   3) $8 - 2 =$
      $2 - 8 =$

   4) $8 \div 2 =$
      $2 \div 8 =$

   a. Which pair(s) produce the same answer?

b. If *a* and *b* are variables that represent any number, such as 8 and 2, can you write two general rules, in terms of *a* and *b*, that demonstrate those operations that can be completed in any order?

_____

_____

c. What are the names of these rules?

_____

d. List the two operations that are not commutative, and explain the relationship that exists when the order is changed.

- The operation of _____ is not commutative.

_____

_____

- The operation of _____ is not commutative.

_____

_____

12. Negative times Negative = Positive

Hopefully the work in this section has convinced you that the above statement is true. However, a more convincing argument involves the distributive property. A proof of why a negative times a positive equals a negative is given below and on the next page. Use a similar approach to show that a negative times a negative equals a positive. In particular, we will show that $\left(^+7\right)\cdot\left(-2\right)=-14$, and then you will prove that $\left(-7\right)\cdot\left(-2\right)=\,^+14$.

Proof:
Given *a*, *b*, and *c* as any real numbers, the distributive property says

$$a\cdot\left(b+c\right)=a\cdot b+a\cdot c$$

or equivalently,

$$a\cdot b+a\cdot c=a\left(b+c\right)$$

Substitute $a=\,^+7$, $b=-2$, and $c=\,^+2$ into the distributive property given above.

$$\left(^{+}7\right)\cdot\left(-2\right)+\left(^{+}7\right)\cdot\left(^{+}2\right)=\,^{+}7\cdot\left[\underbrace{\left(-2\right)+\left(^{+}2\right)}_{0}\right]$$

$$=\,^{+}7\cdot\left(0\right)$$

$$=0$$

Therefore, we have $\left(^{+}7\right)\cdot\left(-2\right)+\left(^{+}7\right)\cdot\left(^{+}2\right)=0$. But we know that $\left(^{+}7\right)\cdot\left(^{+}2\right)=\,^{+}14$, so

$$\left(^{+}7\right)\cdot\left(-2\right)+\underbrace{\left(^{+}7\right)\cdot\left(^{+}2\right)}_{14}=0$$

$$\left(^{+}7\right)\cdot\left(-2\right)+14=0$$

$$\left(^{+}7\right)\cdot\left(-2\right)+14-14=0-14 \qquad \text{subtract 14 from both sides of the equality}$$

$$\left(^{+}7\right)\cdot\left(-2\right)+0=-14 \qquad 14-14=0 \;\; \text{and} \;\; 0-14=-14$$

$$\left(^{+}7\right)\cdot\left(-2\right)=-14$$

The last line is what we were trying to prove.

****

Now it's your turn. Show that $(-7)\cdot(-2)=\left(^{+}14\right)$.

Hint: Follow similar steps as in the previous example, but substitute $a=-7$, $b=\,^{+}2$, and $c=-2$ into the distributive property, $a\cdot b+a\cdot c=a(b+c)$. Also, use the fact we just proved, $\left(^{+}7\right)\cdot(-2)=-14$.

Chapter 2 Summary

Key Terms

Section 2.1

- **Set** – A class or collection of distinct numbers or objects. For example, the set of counting numbers greater than or equal to 1 and less than or equal to 5 is denoted by $\{1,\ 2,\ 3,\ 4,\ 5\}$. Note that each member or *element* is separated from the next element by a comma, and the whole list is enclosed in braces.

- **Subset** – A set of objects that are members of another given set. For example, the natural numbers $\{1,\ 2,\ 3,\ 4,\ \cdots\}$ are a subset of the whole numbers $\{0,\ 1,\ 2,\ 3,\ 4,\ \cdots\}$ because every element in the set of natural numbers is also contained in the set of whole numbers.

- **Finite** and **Finite Set** – A *finite* thing has an end or limit. In a *finite set*, it is possible to count all its members. For example, the set of counting numbers greater than or equal to 1 and less than or equal to 5, or $\{1,\ 2,\ 3,\ 4,\ 5\}$, is finite.

- **Infinite** and **Infinite Set** – An *infinite* thing is endless or without limits. In an *infinite set*, its members are uncountable without end. For example, both the set of natural numbers and the set of whole numbers are infinite sets because they have no final element.

- **Natural Numbers** – Natural numbers are the counting numbers 1, 2, 3, 4, $\cdots$ The three dots signify that the count continues in this manner without end or toward infinity.

- **Factor** and **Factoring** – A *factor* is any number that exactly divides a given number. For example, the number 6 has factors 1, 2, 3, and 6 because each of these numbers can be divided into 6 evenly. *Factoring* means to express a number as the product of two or more numbers. For example, you can factor 6 as $2 \cdot 3$ or $1 \cdot 6$.

- **Divisor** – A number that is to be divided into another number. Also, *divisor* is sometimes used as another word for *factor*.

- **Quotient** – The result of division.

- **Dividend** – A number that is to be divided by another number. For example,

$$\text{dividend} \div \text{divisor} = \text{quotient} \quad \text{or} \quad \text{divisor} \overline{)\text{dividend}}^{\text{quotient}}$$

- **Whole Numbers** – The set of whole numbers includes zero and the set of natural numbers $\{0,\ 1,\ 2,\ 3,\ 4,\ \cdots\}$.

- **Element** – A member of a given set. For example, the number 3 is an element of the set of whole numbers.

- **Well-defined** – A set is *well-defined* if you can reasonably tell whether or not any given object is contained in the set.

- **Empty Set** or **Null Set** – A set with no elements that is denoted by $\varnothing$ or $\{\ \}$.

- **Prime Number** – Any natural number greater than 1 that is only divisible by one and itself. For example, the first ten prime numbers are listed below.

$$\{2,\ 3,\ 5,\ 7,\ 11,\ 13,\ 17,\ 19,\ 23,\ 29,\ \cdots\}$$

- **Composite Number** – Any natural numbers greater than 1 that are not prime numbers. For example, the first ten composite numbers are listed below.

$$\{4,\ 6,\ 8,\ 9,\ 10,\ 12,\ 14,\ 15,\ 16,\ 18,\ \cdots\ \}$$

- **Fundamental Theorem of Arithmetic** – All natural numbers greater than 1 can be written as a product of primes in a unique way.
- **Closed** – A set is *closed* under an operation, if performing the operation on any two numbers in the set always results in a number in that set. For example, the set of whole numbers is *closed under addition* since the sum of any two whole numbers is itself a whole number. So addition is said to be a closed operation on the set of whole numbers, or the set of whole numbers is closed under addition.
- **Variable** – A symbol such as the letter a, x, or n that represents some unknown quantity or number.
- **Conditional Equations** – Equations are *conditional* if the statement is true for only certain values of the variable.
- **Equation** – A formula that expresses the equality of two expressions. Equations can be conditional or identities, which prove true for all values of the variable.
- **Solution** – Those values for the variable that make an equation a true statement.
- **Commutative Property of Addition** – Order is not important when adding two numbers. If a and b represent any numbers, then $a+b=b+a$.
- **Prime Factorization of a Number** – Every composite number can be expressed as the product of prime numbers, and this unique product is known as the *prime factorization*.
- **Associative Property of Addition** – When adding three numbers, it makes no difference how you group the numbers. For example,

$$(3+4)+5=7+5=12 \quad \text{and} \quad 3+(4+5)=3+9=12.$$
$$\text{Therefore, } (3+4)+5=3+(4+5).$$

  In general, if a, b, and c represent any numbers, then $(a+b)+c=a+(b+c)$.

- **Associative Property of Multiplication** – When finding the product of three numbers, it makes no difference how we group or associate the numbers. For example,

$$(3\cdot4)\cdot5=12\cdot5=60 \quad \text{and} \quad 3\cdot(4\cdot5)=3\cdot20=60$$
$$\text{Therefore, } (3\cdot4)\cdot5=3\cdot(4\cdot5)$$

  In general, if a, b, and c represent any numbers, then $(a\cdot b)\cdot c=a\cdot(b\cdot c)$.

- **Distributive Property for Addition** – To multiply a sum by a number, each term in the sum must be multiplied by that number. For example,

$$3\cdot(4+5)=3\cdot4+3\cdot5=12+15=27$$

  In general, if a, b, and c represent any numbers, then

$$a\cdot(b+c)=a\cdot b+a\cdot c \quad \text{and} \quad (b+c)\cdot a=b\cdot a+c\cdot a$$

- **Commutative Property of Multiplication** – Order is not important when multiplying two numbers. If a and b represent any numbers, then $a\cdot b=b\cdot a$.

Section 2.2

- **Positive** and **Positive Integers** – *Positive* means having a value greater than zero. The *positive integers* or natural numbers are 1, 2, 3, 4, $\cdots$ (to infinity).
- **Negative** and **Negative Integers** – *Negative* means the opposite of positive or a value less than zero. The *negative integers* are $\cdots -4, -3, -2, -1$.
- **Zero** – The symbol 0 first appeared as a notation to stand for the absence of quantity.
- **Integers** – A set of numbers that includes all positive and negative integers and zero.
$$\{\cdots, -3, -2, -1, 0, 1, 2, 3, \cdots\}$$
- **Opposite** – The negative integers are *opposites* of the positive integers. For example, –3 and 3 are opposites, or one is the **additive inverse** of the other. In general, if a represents an unknown number, then $-a$ can be interpreted as the *opposite* of a. For example,
$$-(-1) = 1 \quad \text{and} \quad -(5) = -5.$$
- **Absolute Value** – A number's distance from zero on the number line. We symbolize absolute value by putting vertical lines around the number. For example,
$$|-4| = 4 \text{ is read, "the absolute value of } -4 \text{ is } 4".$$

Section 2.3

- **Pattern** – A predictable grouping from a set of numbers or shapes.
- **Multiplying (or Dividing) Two Integer Values** involve the following sign rules:
  - ♦ Same signs signal that the answer is positive.
  - ♦ Different signs signal that the answer is negative
- **Reciprocal** – A fraction made from interchanging the numerator (top) and denominator (bottom) of a fraction. For example, the reciprocal of $\frac{3}{4}$ is $\frac{4}{3}$, and the reciprocal of -4 or $-\frac{4}{1}$ is $-\frac{1}{4}$.

****

Questions for Review

1. Do you know how to find all factors of a given number? For example, find all the factors of the numbers given in parts *a* and *b* below.

   a. 18

   b. 64

2. Can you list elements and name different types of sets and subsets? For example, in each part below, use set notation to list all the elements from the set (described in words). Then state the type of set as either *finite, infinite,* or *empty*. Finally, list a subset of the given set, if possible.

   a. The set of all whole numbers greater than or equal to 1.

      Set: Type: Subset:

   b. The set of natural numbers greater than or equal to 1 and less than 10.

      Set: Type: Subset:

   c. The set of natural numbers less than 1.

      Set: Type: Subset:

3. What does the Fundamental Theorem of Arithmetic tell us about all natural numbers greater than 1?

   _____

   _____

4. Apply the Fundamental Theorem of Arithmetic by finding the prime factorization of the numbers in parts *a* and *b*.

   a. 25   *b.* 180

5. Can you explain when a set is closed under an operation? For example, the set of whole numbers is closed under addition because the sum of any two whole numbers is also a whole number. Answer *True* or *False* to the questions in parts *a*, *b*, and *c*, and then explain your reasoning.

   a. Since 6 and 4 are whole numbers and the result of 6 − 4 is also a whole number, then the set of whole numbers must be closed under subtraction.

   _____

   _____

b. The set of natural numbers is closed under multiplication.

_____

_____

c. The set of whole numbers is not closed under division because any whole number divided by zero is undefined.

_____

_____

6. Can you use the variables *a*, *b*, and *c* to create an equation that represents a property? In each part below, you are given two cases that are examples of a property. State the name of the property and express it in general form using the variables *a*, *b*, and *c*, as needed. For example, $3+5=5+3$ and $7+4=4+7$ are two cases that demonstrate the commutative property of addition, represented in the general form of $a+b=b+a$.

a. $(1+3)+5=1+(3+5)$ and $2+(4+6)=(2+4)+6$

Property Name:

General Form:

b. $4 \cdot 8 = 8 \cdot 4$ and $12 \cdot 3 = 3 \cdot 12$

Property Name:

General Form:

c. $4(2+10) = 4 \cdot 2 + 4 \cdot 10$ and $3(x+7) = 3 \cdot x + 3 \cdot 7$

Property Name:

General Form:

7. Do you know what the *absolute value* means? For example, in parts *a* and *b* you are given a pair of integer values. Use absolute value notation to show which of the two numbers is further from zero on the number line. Explain your reasoning.

   a. −30 or −40

   _____

   _____

   b. −25 or 15

   _____

   _____

8. Observe the pattern below and complete the table accordingly. Then use the information in the table to answer the questions that follow.

3	+	3	=	6
3	+	2	=	
3	+	1	=	
3	+	0	=	
3	+	−1	=	
3	+		=	
3	+		=	
3	+		=	
3	+		=	

   a. Based on the last five expressions, adding integers with different signs can result in an answer that is positive, zero, or negative. How do you determine which of these three results will occur?

   _____

   _____

   b. State a general rule for finding the sum of integers with different signs.

   _____

   _____

9. Observe the pattern below and complete the table accordingly. Then use the information in the table to answer the question.

−3	+	4	=	1
−3	+	3	=	
−3	+	2	=	
−3	+		=	
−3	+		=	
−3	+		=	
−3	+		=	
−3	+		=	
−3	+		=	

Based on the last four rows of this table and the first three rows of the table in problem #8, state a rule for adding integers with the same sign.

_____

_____

10. Observe the pattern below and complete the table accordingly. Then use the information in the table to answer the question.

3	−	0	=	3
3	−	1	=	
3	−	2	=	
3	−	3	=	
3	−		=	
3	−		=	
3	−		=	

What does this table tell you about the result of subtracting two positive numbers?

_____

_____

11. Observe the pattern below and complete the table accordingly. Then use the information in the table to answer the question.

3	–	3	=	0
3	–	2	=	
3	–	1	=	
3	–	0	=	
3	–		=	
3	–		=	
3	–		=	

What do the last three rows tell you about subtracting a negative number from a positive number?

_____

_____

12. Observe the pattern below and complete the table accordingly. Then use the information in the table to answer the question.

3	–	3	=	0
2	–	3	=	
1	–	3	=	
0	–	3	=	
–1	–	3	=	
	–		=	
	–		=	

What do the last three rows tell you about subtracting a positive number from a negative number?

_____

_____

13. Observe the pattern below and complete the table accordingly. Then use the information in the table to answer the question.

−3	−	3	=	−6
−3	−	2	=	
−3	−	1	=	
−3	−	0	=	
−3	−	−1	=	
	−		=	
	−		=	

  a. How are the first three rows of this table similar to the last three rows of the table in Section Exercise #12?

  _____

  _____

  b. How are the last three rows of this table similar to the last three rows of the table in Section Exercise #11?

  _____

  _____

14. Can you write subtraction in terms of addition? For example, follow the pattern in the four problems below, and then complete parts *a* and *b*. Be sure to find the answer after writing the subtraction in terms of addition.

$$7-(-4)=7+4 \qquad 5-8=5+(-8) \qquad -9-(-2)=-9+2 \qquad -6-3=-6+(-3)$$

  a. $-5-(-7)$

  b. $7-9$

15. How do you figure out the sign of the answer when you are multiplying or dividing integer values? For example, complete the following calculations.

  a.

  $7 \cdot 9 =$

  $7 \cdot (-9) =$

  $-7 \cdot 9 =$

  $(-7)(-9) =$

  b.

  $18/6 =$

  $18/(-6) =$

  $-18/6 =$

  $(-18)/(-6) =$

Chapter 2 Quiz

1. How many factors does each of the following classes of numbers have? Answer "one," "two," or "more than two," and then explain your reasoning.

   a. Prime numbers: _____

   _____

   b. Composite numbers: _____

   _____

   c. The number 1: _____

   _____

2. Suppose you are given the identity $4^2 = 2^4$.

   a. Use your knowledge of exponents to show that the above identity is true.

   b. Even though the above equation is true, raising to a power is not commutative. Show an example of a number *a* raised to another number *b*, that is not equal to the number *b* raised to the number *a*. In other words, prove that

   $$a^b \neq b^a.$$

3. Addition and multiplication are commutative operations because the order in which each operation is performed does not matter. For subtraction and division, order is important.

   a. Show an example to demonstrate that subtraction is not a commutative operation.

   b. Show an example to demonstrate that division is not a commutative operation.

138

4. Twin primes are pairs of prime numbers that differ by two. For example, 3 and 5 are twin primes. Find all twin primes that are less than 50. List the twin primes in pairs and separate each pair with a semicolon.

5. Read each sentence below and explain what the positive and negative numbers mean in the sentence.

   a. The highest altitude in North America is the top of Mount McKinley, Alaska at an elevation of 20,320 feet.

      _____

      _____

   b. The lowest altitude in North America is Death Valley, California at an elevation of –282 feet.

      _____

      _____

   c. The current balance in Tom Jones's checking account is –64 dollars.

      _____

      _____

   d. Tom Jones's last bank statement had an ending balance of +240 dollars.

      _____

      _____

6. Refer to Problem #5 above to answer the following questions below.

   a. What is the difference in height between Mount McKinley and Death Valley? First, write out the difference using subtraction with signed numbers, and then give the result.

   b. What is the difference between Jones's current balance and the ending balance from his last statement?

7. Explain two simple methods for adding positive and negative numbers. After each of your explanations, give two examples that apply your method.

   a. In your own words, explain how to add two integers with the same sign.

   _____

   _____

   Example 1:   Example 2:

   b. In your own words, explain how to add two integers with the different signs.

   _____

   _____

   Example 1:   Example 2:

8. Complete the table below by rewriting each subtraction in terms of addition. Then calculate the solution for each row except the last.

Subtraction	Addition	Solution
$3-7$	$3+(-7)$	-4
$3-(-7)$		
$-3-7$		
$-3-(-7)$		
$7-3$		
$7-(-3)$		
$-7-3$		
$-7-(-3)$		
$0-3$		
$a-b$		

9. Evaluate the following expressions.

a. $(2)(-5)(-4)(-3)$

b. $4 \cdot (-5 + 2)$

c. $\dfrac{-60}{-5}$

d. $(-3)^4$

e. -3^4

f. $\dfrac{-4 + 2 + (-7)}{3}$

10. In the following table, you are given the monthly normal temperatures in Fairbanks, Alaska during December, January, and February, the 3 coldest months. The temperatures are in degrees Fahrenheit (°F).

Dec.	Jan.	Feb.
−7	−10	−4

Source: National Climatic Data Center

a. Find the average normal temperature during this 3-month period.

b. Suppose the most recent winter temperatures were colder than normal, averaging -12°F for the same three months. What is the difference between this average and the normal average found in part *a*? State the difference as a signed number, and use a complete sentence to express your answer.

Chapter 3

Rational and Irrational Numbers

Section 3.1 Rational Numbers in Fractional and Decimal Form
Section 3.2 Adding and Subtracting Rational Numbers
Section 3.3 Multiplying and Dividing Rational Numbers
Section 3.4 Numbers That Are Not Rational

It is time to expand your use of numbers by introducing the rational and irrational numbers. Informally, these are numbers that occur between the integer values that you studied in Chapter 2. Some of these numbers like fractions and decimals are commonly used in problem solving, while others like π (Greek letter, Pi) and $\sqrt{2}$ are less well known but still important. Becoming comfortable with these new numbers will allow you to explore more applications in everyday life as you continue your journey into a mathematical world.

In Section 3.1 you will look at many different ways to interpret and represent rational numbers. A rational number will be introduced as both a fraction and as a repeating or terminating decimal. Then you will explore the concept of equivalent fractions using common divisors or factors.

In Section 3.2 you will investigate adding and subtracting rational numbers in fractional and decimal form. Many of the concepts will be explored with the aid of visual models.

Section 3.3 provides problem-solving situations that involve multiplying and dividing rational numbers. You will learn when and how to convert between improper fractions and mixed numbers. Also, rational numbers will be used as the base of exponential expressions.

Finally, in Section 3.4, you will have a chance to discover numbers that are not rational. These irrational numbers will lead us to the Pythagorean theorem and the origins of the number π (Pi).

Section 3.1 Rational Numbers in Fractional and Decimal Form

Math Talk

Let's discuss how the words **rational**, **fraction**, and **decimal** are used in mathematics and popular culture.

In our world, if someone acts *rationally* that person shows good reason or sense. Now the title of this section contains the word "rational," but does this mean you should think of a rational number as a reasonable or sensible number?

The word "ration" comes a little closer to the mathematical meaning of rational. For example, when soldiers receive a "ration of food," they each get a fixed portion or allotment. However, a portion is simply part of a whole. The whole might be a shipment of food to an army where each soldier receives a small part of the whole, his or her ration. So, a part of a whole is one interpretation of a rational number.

In arithmetic, *fraction* and *rational* have the same basic meaning. For example, the fractions $\frac{1}{2}$, $\frac{3}{4}$, and $\frac{1}{3}$ are all rational numbers. If you complete the division indicated by the fraction bar, then a decimal is produced: $\frac{1}{2} = 0.5$, $\frac{3}{4} = 0.75$, and $\frac{1}{3} \approx .33$.

Speaking of $\frac{1}{3}$, can you see one-third of something? Suppose we are talking about a country with about 274 million people (the approximate U.S. population in January 2000). Can you estimate what $\frac{1}{3}$ of that value is? Could you calculate that value exactly? If we want to see the world through mathematical eyes, then we must have a solid understanding of fractions, decimals, and percent.

In this section, you will do the following:

- Discover multiple ways to interpret rational numbers, such as part-whole, quotient, and ratio.

- Investigate different ways to represent a rational number as a fraction, decimal, and percent.

- Explore the idea of a rational number being either a repeating or terminating decimal.

- Develop the concept of equivalent fractions using common divisors or factors.

Let's visualize the meaning of fractions. Look at the fraction board below. Suppose you want to construct a similar but larger board that is made out of cardboard strips with each strip being 1 inch wide. First, we could make a unit strip that is 1 inch wide and 12 inches long and label it 1.

Then we could cut out two 1-inch wide strips and label each of them $\frac{1}{2}$.

How long should each of the $\frac{1}{2}$ strips measure?

How long should each of the $\frac{1}{3}$ strips measure?

How long should each of the $\frac{1}{4}$ strips measure?

How long should each of the $\frac{1}{6}$ strips measure?

Fraction Board

Note that 12 inches remains the original length. You take the fraction and multiply it times 12 each time.

Another way to illustrate the meaning of fractions is to use a number line. Observe the number lines below, then answer the questions that follow. **Note:** The numbers and fractions above and below the same tick mark on the number line are equal to each other.

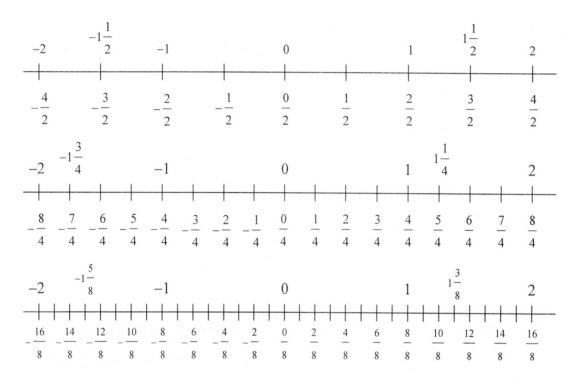

- Referring to the number lines above, list two fractions that have the same value as $\dfrac{1}{2}$, but are written differently.

- List two fractions that have the same value as $-1\dfrac{3}{4}$ but are written differently.

- What are three ways that the value 1 is displayed as a fraction on the number lines?

- What are three ways that the value $-1\dfrac{1}{2}$ is displayed as a fraction on the number lines?

Study Skill: Using Figures to Represent Fractions

One way to visualize fractions is to construct a geometric object such as a rectangle or circle and then divide the object into equal-sized parts or different shapes with equal area.

The concept of fraction is demonstrated by considering how many parts are in the whole unit. The whole unit might be a square that is partitioned into equal-sized triangles (parts). If you shade in some of the triangles, then a fraction is represented by the number of shaded triangles divided by the total number of triangular parts.

For example, the square below has been divided into 4 triangles. If we shade in one of the triangles, then the shaded area is $\frac{1}{4}$ (one fourth) of the total area.

$$\frac{\text{Number of Shaded Parts}}{\text{Total Number of Parts in Whole}} = \frac{1}{4}$$

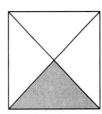

As a second example, let's use a circle to represent 1 whole unit. You can model the fraction $\frac{3}{8}$ by partitioning the circle into 8 equal-sized parts (slices) and shading in 3 of them.

$$\frac{3}{8}$$

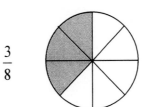

Discovery Adventure 1: A Piece of Pie

It's your turn to have relatives over for the holiday. You promised everyone that you would bake your famous apple pie. However, the weather is so bad that you do not know how many of your 5 relatives will show up. Right now it's just you and your pie, which has been cut into 6 equal-sized pieces (slices).

a. What is the size of each piece in comparison with the whole pie?

b. If you are the only person who shows up, how many pieces do you get?

c. Represent the part of the whole pie you received in fractional form,

$$\frac{\text{number of pieces received}}{\text{total number of pieces in whole pie}} =$$

d. Draw a circle representing your pie. Cut it into 6 equal parts and shade in the parts you received.

e. Before you can eat this wonderful dessert, one of your relatives shows up. What fractional part of the whole do you get if the pie is equally divided between you and your relative?

f. Redraw your 6-piece pie and shade in the number of pieces you will receive.

g. Write the geometric model (shaded pie) as a fraction in the form,

$$\frac{\text{number of pieces received}}{\text{total number of pieces in whole pie}} =$$

h. Now that you know how much you can eat, Uncle Bill walks in. What fractional part of the whole do you get if the pie is equally divided up?

i.   Redraw your 6-piece pie and shade in the number of pieces you will receive.

j.   Write the geometric model (shaded pie) as a fraction in the form,

$$\frac{\text{number of pieces received}}{\text{total number of pieces in whole pie}} =$$

k.   Now your remaining three relatives walk in.   What fractional part of the whole do you get if the pie is equally divided up?

l.   Redraw your 6-piece pie and shade in the number of pieces you will receive.

m. Write the geometric model (shaded pie) as a fraction in the form,

$$\frac{\text{number of pieces received}}{\text{total number of pieces in whole pie}} =$$

Feedback

The pie problem presents the concept of fraction in terms of how many parts are being considered in the whole unit. The whole unit is the 1 circular pie, while the parts are the number of slices received when sharing equally with our friends. The fraction is represented in the form,

$$\frac{\text{Number of parts used}}{\text{Total number of parts in whole}} = \text{ Part of a whole unit}$$

The table below shows the fractional amounts of pie received according to the number of people sharing the whole.

Number of people sharing one pie	Fractional part you can eat
1	$\frac{6}{6} = 1$
2	$\frac{3}{6} = \frac{1}{2}$
3	$\frac{2}{6} = \frac{1}{3}$
6	$\frac{1}{6}$

****

Mathematically speaking, the top number in a fraction is called the **numerator,** and the bottom number is called the **denominator**. A number that can be expressed in fractional form as the quotient of two integers is called a **rational number**. More formally:

> If the variable *a* represents any integer and the variable *b* is any non zero integer,
>
> then the fraction $\frac{a}{b}$ is a *rational number* ($b \neq 0$). $\frac{a}{b}$ ⟶ numerator
>
> $\frac{a}{b}$ ⟶ denominator

Since any integer can be expressed as a quotient with 1 in the denominator, then every integer is also a rational number.

We can say that the set of integers, $\{ \cdots, -3, -2, -1, 0, 1, 2, 3, \cdots \}$ is a subset of the set of rational numbers because every integer is contained within the set of rational numbers.

In the next Discovery Adventure, you will investigate more rational numbers as fractions and compare the numerators and denominators. This type of comparison between two numbers or quantities of the same measure is called a **ratio**.

Discovery Adventure 2: All Stressed Out

When Tom gets stressed, he often reaches for a bag of peanut treats. One day he noticed that the color distribution of the candy was not equal and that the color red was in short supply relative to the other colors. To disprove Tom's theory, you buy 2 bags of peanut treats. You and Tom each take a bag and count the total number of peanut treats inside. Tom counts 24 peanut treats in his bag, and you count 25 in your bag. Now you and Tom each count the number of peanut treats of each different color among the total number in the bag. Tom counts 8 brown, 1 red, 3 green, 6 yellow, 2 orange, and 4 tan. You count 8 brown, 1 red, 2 green, 6 yellow, 3 orange, and 5 tan.

a. For Tom's bag, record the ratio of the number of each color of peanut treats to the total number of peanut treats. Use fractions to express each ratio in the table.

Color	Count	Ratio: $\dfrac{\text{Color count}}{\text{Total in bag}}$
brown	8	$\dfrac{8}{24} = \dfrac{1}{3}$
red		
green		
yellow		
orange		
tan		

b. For your bag, record the ratio of the number of each color of peanut treats to the total number of peanut treats.

Color	Count	Ratio: $\dfrac{\text{Color count}}{\text{Total in bag}}$
brown	8	$\dfrac{8}{25}$
red		
green		
yellow		
orange		
tan		

Feedback

The ratio of 8 brown peanut treats to 25 total peanut treats can be expressed using

fractional notation: $\dfrac{8}{25}$ or 8/25, and colon notation: 8:25.

Note that in Tom's bag, the ratio of 8 brown peanut treats to 24 total peanut treats, $\dfrac{8}{24}$, can be

simplified to $\dfrac{1}{3}$. To **simplify** means to divide out a common divisor or factor from the

numerator and denominator such as

$$\frac{8}{24} = \frac{8 \div 8}{24 \div 8} = \frac{1}{3}$$

To reverse the process, we can multiply the numerator and denominator by 8,

$$\frac{1}{3} = \frac{1 \cdot 8}{3 \cdot 8} = \frac{8}{24}$$

****

The idea that we can multiply the numerator and denominator of a fraction by the same non-zero number and obtain a new, equivalent fraction is called the **Fundamental Principle of Fractions**. In other words, the value of a fraction will not change when multiplying the numerator and the denominator by the same (non-zero) number.

Another way to proceed is to consider $\dfrac{8}{8}$ as a convenient form of 1. Using this fact, we can also

factor the numerator and denominator using a common factor of 8, such that

$$\frac{8}{24} = \frac{1 \cdot 8}{3 \cdot 8} = \frac{1}{3} \cdot \frac{8}{8} = \frac{1}{3} \cdot 1 = \frac{1}{3}$$

Hence, $\dfrac{8}{24}$ and $\dfrac{1}{3}$ are called **equivalent fractions** since they have the same value. Think of

equivalent fractions as different names for the same value.

The numerator 8 and denominator 24 have many common **divisors** or factors such as 2, 4, and 8. Therefore, when **reducing** to an equivalent fraction, we could have divided the top and bottom by 2 or 4, such that

$$\frac{8}{24} = \frac{8 \div 2}{24 \div 2} = \frac{4}{12} \quad \text{or} \quad \frac{8}{24} = \frac{8 \div 4}{24 \div 4} = \frac{2}{6}$$

But, both $\frac{4}{12}$ and $\frac{2}{6}$ have common divisors or factors. In $\frac{4}{12}$ the numerator and denominator have a common divisor of 4, and in $\frac{2}{6}$ the numerator and denominator have a common divisor of 2. Hence, we could continue to reduce them to a simpler form,

$$\frac{4}{12} = \frac{4 \div 4}{12 \div 4} = \frac{1}{3} \quad \text{and} \quad \frac{2}{6} = \frac{2 \div 2}{6 \div 2} = \frac{1}{3}$$

A fraction is simplified to **lowest terms** when the numerator and denominator have no common factor except 1. You might recall that a prime number is a whole number greater than 1 that has no factors other than 1 and itself. We can use this concept to simplify fractions by writing the numerator and denominator as the product of prime numbers.

For example, we can write 8 and 24 as a product of primes using repeated factoring.

Thus, $\frac{8}{24} = \frac{1 \cdot 2 \cdot 2 \cdot 2}{3 \cdot 2 \cdot 2 \cdot 2} = \frac{1}{3} \cdot \frac{2}{2} \cdot \frac{2}{2} \cdot \frac{2}{2} = \frac{1}{3} \cdot 1 \cdot 1 \cdot 1 = \frac{1}{3}$.

In general, every positive integer can be written in exactly one way as the product of its prime factors. Recall that we previously named this the *Fundamental Theorem of Arithmetic.*

The next Discovery Adventure involves using a quotient to share a batch of cookies among friends. Sometimes sharing is easy, but things don't always work out evenly. Let's see why.

Discovery Adventure 3: Fair Share

You arrive early for your math class where you work in small groups solving interesting problems. One person from your group is already there and has brought a bag of 15 cookies to share equally with everyone in the group.

a. If the only two people who show up for class are you and the person who brought the cookies, then how many cookies does each person receive when equal amounts are given to both people?

b. A few minutes before class starts another member of your group shows up. How many cookies do each of you receive when equal amounts are given to all three people?

c. In walks the last member of your group. How many whole cookies do each of you receive when equal amounts are given to all four members of your group?

d. Your group must figure out how many cookies each person would receive if they included more students in the sharing process. Complete the table below to help with this process.

Number of students sharing equally	2	3	4	5	6	7	8
Number of cookies for each student							

e. In the last adventure, the one pie was considered the whole. What is the whole in this case?

f. Looking at the table, do you see any patterns in the number of cookies that each student receives as the group gets larger? Explain using complete sentences.

_____

_____

_____

g. We can generalize the number of cookies each person receives with respect to the number of people in the group. Suppose *n* is the number of students in the group. Write a rule for finding the number of cookies each person receives out of the 15 available.

Feedback

The cookie problem is an example of representing rational numbers as a **quotient**. This means that we *divide* the total number of cookies available by the number of people sharing. For example,

$$\frac{\text{Number of cookies for each student}}{} = \frac{15}{\text{Number of students sharing}}$$

If the number of students sharing is defined as the variable n, then

$$\frac{\text{Number of cookies for each student}}{} = \frac{15}{n}$$

****

In the first three Discovery Adventures, rational numbers are interpreted in different ways using fractions. There is the part-whole relationship where you looked at pieces (parts) of a pie (whole). Then there is the ratio meaning, where you have a comparison of two quantities with the same measure, such as the number of brown peanut treats to the total number of peanut treats. Finally there is the quotient relationship, where you have a number of things (like cookies) divided equally into a number of groups, such as individual students. Speaking of sweets, let's return to the candy from Discovery Adventure 2 and look at other ways to represent rational numbers.

▣ Discovery Adventure 4: From Fractions to Decimals to Percents

On the next page is the table you worked on previously with the addition of two more columns to express the value of each fraction as a decimal and percent. Convert all the fractions to decimals by dividing the numerator by the denominator. Then take the decimal and multiply by 100% to convert to a percent (see below). You will need a calculator when working on this adventure.

$$\frac{8}{25} = 8 \div 25 = 0.32 \qquad 25\overline{)8.00} \qquad 0.32 \cdot 100\% = 32\%$$

$$\begin{array}{r} 0.32 \\ 25\overline{)8.00} \\ \underline{7\,5} \\ 5\,0 \\ \underline{5\,0} \\ 0 \end{array}$$

Color	Count	Ratio: $\dfrac{\text{Color count}}{\text{Total in bag}}$	Decimal	Percent
brown	8	$\dfrac{8}{25}$	0.32	32%
red	1	$\dfrac{1}{25}$		
green	2	$\dfrac{2}{25}$		
yellow	6	$\dfrac{6}{25}$		
orange	3	$\dfrac{3}{25}$		
tan	5	$\dfrac{5}{25}=\dfrac{1}{5}$		

Feedback

All the decimals found in the table above are **terminating decimals**, meaning that the division process produces a finite number of **significant digits** to the right of the decimal.

Enter $\dfrac{3}{11}$ into your calculator. What is the output?

Enter $\dfrac{2}{3}$ into your calculator. What is the output?

The rational numbers $\dfrac{3}{11}$ and $\dfrac{2}{3}$ form **repeating decimals**, meaning that the division process produces numbers to the right of the decimal that continue to repeat without end. Repeating decimals are denoted with a bar over the number(s) that repeat, or three dots meaning that the repeating occurs infinitely.

For example,

$$\frac{3}{11} = 0.2727\cdots \quad \text{or} \quad 0.\overline{27}$$

$$\frac{2}{3} = 0.666\cdots \quad \text{or} \quad 0.\overline{6}$$

Enter $\dfrac{2}{3}$ into your calculator, and compute the answer as a repeating decimal without rounding.

Then multiply the repeating decimal by 100 to obtain the percent equivalent, $66\dfrac{2}{3}\%$.

What you actually see in the calculator is

66.66666667,   but the calculator has rounded to obtain the last digit

and since $\frac{2}{3} = 0.666\cdots$,   we can say $66\frac{2}{3}$

In some applications it will be sufficient to write 67% (rounding to the nearest percent), while at other times you will need to be exact. If a number is rounded, it is important to understand the error involved. In this case, using 67% instead of $66\frac{2}{3}$% means that we are willing to accept an error of $\frac{1}{3}$%. In other words, our estimate of 67% is $\frac{1}{3}$% above the exact value of $66\frac{2}{3}$%.

Now we can express rational numbers in three equivalent forms:

- as the quotient of two integers (a fraction),

- as a terminating or repeating decimal, and

- as a percent.

To get comfortable with rational numbers in all these forms, you need to explore some additional problems in the Section Exercises starting on page 159. If you're rusty on converting between fractions, decimals, and percents, then read the Brush Up feature below.

Brush Up on Converting Between Fractions, Decimals, and Percents

To convert a fraction to a decimal, recall that the fraction bar is a symbol for division.

For example, *one-fourth* means 1 divided by 4, so $\frac{1}{4} = 1 \div 4$ or $4\overline{)1.00}$ with quotient 0.25

$$\begin{array}{r} 0.25 \\ 4\overline{)1.00} \\ \underline{8} \\ 20 \\ \underline{20} \\ 0 \end{array}$$

Two places to the right of the decimal point is the hundredths place, so 0.25 is 25 hundredths or $0.25 = \frac{25}{100}$. Another way to express "divided by 100" is to use the term "percent %." Therefore, "25 hundredths" is the same as "25 divided by 100," which is the same as "25 percent."

$$0.25 = \frac{25}{100} = 25\%$$

As a second example, "three-eighths" means 3 divided by 8, so $\dfrac{3}{8} = 3 \div 8$ or

$$\begin{array}{r} .375 \\ 8\overline{)3.000} \\ \underline{24} \\ 60 \\ \underline{56} \\ 40 \\ \underline{40} \\ 0 \end{array}$$

Therefore, we have $0.375 = \dfrac{37.5}{100} = 37.5\%$.

The diagrams below display conversion "shortcuts" between decimals and percents.

$$0.375 \longrightarrow 0.37.5 \longrightarrow 37.5\%$$

**Convert from Decimal
to Percent**   Move decimal   Insert percent
                     point 2 places   symbol
                     to the *right*

$$5.25\% \longrightarrow .05.25\% \longrightarrow .0525$$

**Convert from Percent
to Decimal**   Move decimal   Drop percent
                     point 2 places   symbol
                     to the *left*

Practice:

1) Express $\dfrac{3}{5}$ as a decimal and a percent.

2) Express $\dfrac{1}{6}$ as a decimal and a percent.

3) Express $\dfrac{5}{8}$ as a decimal and a percent.

Answers: 1) $\dfrac{3}{5} = 0.60 = 60\%$, 2) $\dfrac{1}{6} = 0.1666\cdots \approx 0.167 = 16.7\%$, 3) $\dfrac{5}{8} = 0.625 = 62.5\%$

Section Exercises: 3.1

1. You're playing a computer game where you're trapped in a dungeon, prisoner of the evil Lord Innumeracy. To escape, you will be given four hints, which test your number sense with rational numbers. Read each hint and choose all the fractions that satisfy it. After the fourth hint, you should have just one fraction to choose. This fraction is the key that can open the door to the freedom of rational number literacy. Seven fractions appear below. Begin your quest by going to the first hint in part *a*.

$$\frac{1}{2}, \frac{2}{3}, \frac{3}{7}, \frac{1}{5}, \frac{2}{5}, \frac{5}{4}, \frac{5}{11}$$

   a. Hint 1: List all numbers less than 0.5 to correctly move on. List those values below.

   b. Hint 2: Use the numbers from part *a* that are not equal to 0.4 to continue on. List those values below.

   c. Hint 3: Select the fractions from part *b* that can be written as repeating decimals. List those values below.

   d. Hint 4: Choose the smallest fraction from the remaining fractions in part *c*. The correct choice unlocks the door to a better understanding of rational numbers.

2. Recall Tom's candy table (part *a*) in Discovery Adventure 2: All Stressed Out. Below you will find this previous table with decimal and percent columns added on. Complete the decimal and percent columns. Perform long division, if necessary, to obtain an exact answer (involving a fraction) in the "Percent" column.

Color	Count	Ratio: $\dfrac{\text{Color count}}{\text{Total in bag}}$	Decimal	Percent
brown	8	$\dfrac{8}{24} = \dfrac{1}{3}$	$0.333\cdots$	$33\dfrac{1}{3}\%$
red				
green				
yellow				
orange				
tan				

3. Suppose you have the collection of 9 fractions listed below,

$$\frac{5}{9}, \frac{1}{9}, \frac{6}{13}, \frac{11}{13}, \frac{4}{9}, \frac{10}{12}, \frac{7}{12}, \frac{2}{14}, \frac{8}{14}$$

All these fractions are close to one of these numbers: 0, $\frac{1}{2}$, or 1.

a. What fractions from the list are closer to 0 than the other two numbers above?

b. What fractions from the list are closer to $\frac{1}{2}$ than the other two numbers above?

c. What fractions from the list are closer to 1 than the other two numbers above?

d. Write down a fraction that is closer to 0 than any of the answers you listed in part *a*.

e. Write down a fraction that is even closer to 0 than the one you just listed in part *d*.

f. Write down a fraction that is even closer to 0 than the one you listed in part *e*.

g. Is there one fraction that is nearer to zero than any other fraction? If yes, what is this mystery fraction? If no, why can't 0 be closer to one fraction than any other fraction? Answer using complete sentences.

_____

_____

_____

_____

4. Plot each of the following rational numbers by placing a small dot in the appropriate place on the number line below.

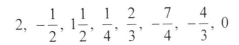

$$2, \ -\frac{1}{2}, \ 1\frac{1}{2}, \ \frac{1}{4}, \ \frac{2}{3}, \ -\frac{7}{4}, \ -\frac{4}{3}, \ 0$$

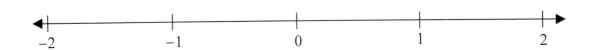

5. In the first week of February the following high temperatures (in degrees Fahrenheit) were reported from Caribou, Maine:

$$-7, \ 2, \ 0, \ -5, \ 1, \ -3, \ -1$$

   a. What was the average daily high temperature for the week? Express your answer in fractional form as the quotient of two integers and as a decimal rounded to the nearest tenth of a degree (one place to the right of the decimal). Note that an average is found by first adding all the values and then dividing the result by the number of values.

   Fraction: Decimal:

   b. If you avoid rounding, do you obtain a terminating decimal or a repeating decimal in part *a*? Record your work and answer below.

6. Construct a fraction board similar to the figure on page 145 by following the directions below:

   1) Cut a strip that is 1 inch wide and 12 inches long and label it 1. This is your unit strip.

   2) Cut two strips, 1 inch wide and 6 $\left(\dfrac{12}{2} = 6\right)$ inches long, and label each strip $\dfrac{1}{2}$.

   3) Cut three strips, 1 inch wide and 4 $\left(\dfrac{12}{3} = 4\right)$ inches long, and label each strip $\dfrac{1}{3}$.

   4) Continue this process until you reach $\dfrac{1}{10}$ on your fraction board. **Note:** Not all denominators divide into 12 evenly, so you will have to do some careful approximating.

7. Compare the pairs of fractions below. Insert the symbol < (less than), > (greater than), or = (equals) between each pair of fractions to make a true statement.

   a. $\dfrac{1}{3}$ $\dfrac{1}{2}$ b. $\dfrac{2}{4}$ $\dfrac{3}{5}$ c. $\dfrac{3}{4}$ $\dfrac{2}{3}$ d. $\dfrac{3}{6}$ $\dfrac{4}{8}$ e. $\dfrac{4}{5}$ $\dfrac{5}{8}$

8. Find two or more fractions that are equivalent to the given number in each part.

   a. $1 =$

   b. $\dfrac{2}{3} =$

   c. $\dfrac{1}{2} =$

9. Recall the Fundamental Principle of Fractions, which states that a fraction's value remains unchanged if we multiply the numerator and denominator by the same nonzero number. For example,

$$\frac{1}{3} = \frac{1 \cdot 2}{3 \cdot 2} = \frac{2}{6}$$

   Suppose you want to compare $\dfrac{3}{5}$ and $\dfrac{5}{8}$ to find out which is larger. Upon examining the fraction boards in Section Exercise #6 and on page 145, you will find that both values measure about the same length. To determine which value is larger, rewrite each fraction so that it contains the same denominator. To find a common denominator, take the product of the given denominators $(5 \cdot 8 = 40)$.

   a. By what number would you multiply the numerator and denominator of $\dfrac{3}{5}$ to get an equivalent fraction with a denominator of 40?

   b. Find the fraction with a denominator of 40, which is equivalent to $\dfrac{3}{5}$. Show all work.

c.   By what number would you multiply the numerator and denominator of $\dfrac{5}{8}$ to get an equivalent fraction with a denominator of 40?

d.   Find the fraction with a denominator of 40, which is equivalent to $\dfrac{5}{8}$. Show all work.

e.   Compare the two fractions with denominators of 40 from parts *b* and *d*. State which fraction is larger and support your answer in writing using complete sentences.

_____

_____

_____

10. Another way to compare fractions is to convert each fraction to a decimal by dividing the numerator by the denominator using long division or a calculator. For example, compare $\dfrac{3}{5}$ and $\dfrac{5}{8}$ by converting the fractions to decimal form.

$\dfrac{3}{5} = 0.600$ or just 0.6

$\dfrac{5}{8} = 0.625$

The tenths digit is the same for both, but the hundredths digit for $\dfrac{5}{8}$ (second digit to the right of the decimal or 2) is greater than the hundredths digit for $\dfrac{3}{5}$ (which is zero). Hence, $\dfrac{5}{8}$ is greater than $\dfrac{3}{5}$ $\left(\dfrac{5}{8} > \dfrac{3}{5}\right)$ as was the case in Section Exercise #9.

• Compare the following three fractions and list them from smallest to largest using less than (<) symbols.

$$\dfrac{4}{9}, \dfrac{3}{7}, \text{ and } \dfrac{5}{12}$$

11. Suppose you pull into a gas station to fill up your gas tank. Even though there are no prices advertised, you go ahead and fill your tank with 8 gallons of regular gas. If the total cost comes to $10, what is the price per gallon that should be advertised?

   a. Express the price per gallon as a ratio (fraction) that compares total price ($10) to number of gallons purchased (8).

$$\text{Price per gallon ratio} = \frac{\text{Total price}}{\text{Number of gallons}} =$$

   b. Find the decimal that is equivalent to the ratio found in part *a* using division (implied by the fraction bar) and express the answer as the price per 1 gallon.

   Price per gallon =

   c. If you return to the same gas station a week later and the price per gallon is unchanged, then how much would it cost to purchase 12 gallons of gas?

Section 3.2 Adding and Subtracting Rational Numbers

Math Talk

"Don't miss this sale, everything is half off!" "Keep running you're almost there, only a quarter of a mile to go!" "Great news, our stock went up by three and seven-eighths of a point!" "What's your secret recipe? "Oh, one-third a cup of this and three-fourths a cup of that." Fractions are such a common part of everyday life that it's important to have a deep understanding of what they mean.

You have learned that a fraction, often called a ratio, is the quotient of two numbers called the numerator and denominator. In the past, we have used the words *dividend* and *divisor* to describe the two numbers or quantities being divided, but it is more common to use the words *numerator* and *denominator* when division is presented in the form of a fraction. For example,

$$\text{Fraction Form:} \quad \frac{\text{Numerator}}{\text{Denominator}} \quad \text{means} \quad \text{Numerator} \div \text{Denominator}$$

To find the *quotient*, divide the numerator by the denominator. So *dividend* and *numerator* have the same meaning, as do *divisor* and *denominator*.

$$\text{Numerator} \div \text{Denominator} = \text{Quotient} \quad \text{or} \quad \text{Dividend} \div \text{Divisor} = \text{Quotient}$$

In this section, you will do the following:

- Discover the concept of adding fractions using a familiar geometric model (round pie).

- Investigate an application and use numerical reasoning to estimate the answer.

- Explore adding and subtracting rational numbers in decimal form using real-life data.

- Visualize adding rational numbers using geometric figures, fraction bars, and the number line.

****

Adding rational numbers in fractional form is straightforward when you have the same denominator. For example, $\frac{1}{5} + \frac{3}{5}$ means the sum of the numerators $(1 + 3 = 4)$ over the denominator, 5.

$$\frac{1}{5} \qquad + \qquad \frac{3}{5} \qquad = \qquad \frac{4}{5}$$

When the denominators are different, you must find a **common denominator**. For example, to add $\dfrac{1}{2} + \dfrac{1}{3}$, we must rewrite each fraction so that they have the same denominator. The pieces from a fraction board make it clear that a common denominator of 6 will help you add these two fractions.

$\frac{1}{2}$			$\frac{1}{3}$	
$\frac{1}{6}$	$\frac{1}{6}$	$\frac{1}{6}$	$\frac{1}{6}$	$\frac{1}{6}$

Therefore,

$$\frac{1}{2} + \frac{1}{3} = \frac{3}{6} + \frac{2}{6} = \frac{5}{6}$$

If you don't have a fraction board to visualize this process, then the simplest way to find a common denominator is to multiply the given denominators. For instance, in the last example, the product of 2 and 3 is 6. Then multiply the numerator and denominator of $\dfrac{1}{2}$ by 3 and the numerator and denominator of $\dfrac{1}{3}$ by 2 to obtain,

$$\frac{1}{2} = \frac{1 \cdot 3}{2 \cdot 3} = \frac{3}{6} \quad \text{and} \quad \frac{1}{3} = \frac{1 \cdot 2}{3 \cdot 2} = \frac{2}{6}$$

Therefore,

$$\frac{1}{2} + \frac{1}{3} = \frac{3}{6} + \frac{2}{6} = \frac{5}{6}$$

Note that $\dfrac{3}{3}$ and $\dfrac{2}{2}$ both equal 1 and multiplying by 1 does not change the value of a fraction, just what it looks like. Now suppose you want to add $\dfrac{1}{4} + \dfrac{3}{8}$. If you proceed as above and find a common denominator by multiplying the given denominators, then you have $4 \cdot 8 = 32$ as the common denominator. However, if you notice that 4 is a factor of 8 ($2 \cdot 4 = 8$), then using 8 as a common denominator is an option.

Look at the fraction board below to visualize how a common denominator of 8 will work. Since 8 is the **least common denominator** (smallest number that 4 and 8 divide into evenly), it will be easier to use than 32. So let's choose 8 as the common denominator knowing that 32 is another option.

$\frac{1}{4}$		$\frac{3}{8}$		
$\frac{1}{8}$	$\frac{1}{8}$	$\frac{1}{8}$	$\frac{1}{8}$	$\frac{1}{8}$

To rewrite $\dfrac{1}{4}$ as an equivalent fraction with a denominator of 8, you must multiply the

numerator and denominator of $\dfrac{1}{4}$ by 2.

$$\frac{1}{4} = \frac{1 \cdot 2}{4 \cdot 2} = \frac{2}{8}$$

You do not need to rewrite $\dfrac{3}{8}$ because it's already in the desired form. So we have,

$$\frac{1}{4} + \frac{3}{8} = \frac{2}{8} + \frac{3}{8} = \frac{5}{8}$$

The last two examples show that a common denominator can always be obtained by multiplying the given denominators, but sometimes you might notice another common denominator that appears to be easier to use. In the example of $\dfrac{1}{2} + \dfrac{1}{3}$, it turns out that multiplying the given denominators gives you the least common denominator, but the second example of $\dfrac{1}{4} + \dfrac{3}{8}$ shows that this is not always the case.

Before moving on, let's see how we could have used a common denominator of 32 to complete the last example, $\dfrac{1}{4} + \dfrac{3}{8}$. Recall that 32 is the product of the denominators 4 and 8. The process then involves multiplying the numerator and denominator of $\dfrac{1}{4}$ by 8 and the numerator and denominator of $\dfrac{3}{8}$ by 4. So we have,

$$\frac{1}{4} = \frac{1 \cdot 8}{4 \cdot 8} = \frac{8}{32} \quad \text{and} \quad \frac{3}{8} = \frac{3 \cdot 4}{8 \cdot 4} = \frac{12}{32}$$

Therefore,

$$\frac{1}{4} + \frac{3}{8} = \frac{8}{32} + \frac{12}{32} = \frac{20}{32}$$

However, $\dfrac{20}{32}$ can be simplified or **reduced** (rewritten with a smaller denominator) to $\dfrac{5}{8}$ if you divide the numerator and denominator by the common factor 4.

$$\frac{20}{32} = \frac{20 \div 4}{32 \div 4} = \frac{5}{8}$$

The first Discovery Adventure will give you a familiar setting in which to visualize adding rational numbers in fractional form. Before you begin discovering more about rational numbers, consider reading the Brush Up feature on Proper versus Improper Fractions and Mixed Numbers. You will need to understand these concepts to feel ready for the next adventure.

Brush Up on Proper versus Improper Fractions and Mixed Numbers

A **proper fraction** is a fraction where the numerator has an absolute value that is less than the denominator. Proper fractions have an absolute value less than one and are the typical fractions you encounter in everyday life. For example, if you have 30 students in your class and 20 of those students are women, then we could say that $\frac{20}{30}$ or $\frac{2}{3}$ of the class are women.

An **improper fraction** is a fraction where the numerator has a greater absolute value than the denominator. Improper fractions have an absolute value greater than 1. For example, if you and a friend split the cost of a dinner check that totals $45, then how much will each of you pay? This can be expressed as an improper fraction because you need to take $45 and divide it by 2.

$$\frac{45}{2} \quad \text{or} \quad 45 \div 2$$

This fraction can be rewritten as a **mixed number** using either one of the following methods.

$$\frac{45}{2} = \frac{44+1}{2} \quad \text{rewrite since 2 divides 44 evenly}$$

$$= \frac{44}{2} + \frac{1}{2} \quad \text{split fraction into two terms}$$

$$= 22 + \frac{1}{2} \quad \text{simplify } 44 \div 2 = 22$$

$$= 22\frac{1}{2} \quad \text{express as mixed number}$$

or

$$\begin{array}{r} 22\,\frac{1}{2} \\ 2\overline{)45} \\ \underline{4} \\ 05 \\ \underline{4} \\ 1 \end{array}$$

If we carry out the division $45 \div 2$ as shown above, we obtain the mixed number $22\frac{1}{2}$.

The name *mixed number* means it has a whole part of 22 and a fractional part of $\frac{1}{2}$.

If you want to change back to an improper fraction, you can reverse the process by multiplying 2 times 22, adding 1, and then dividing the total 45 by 2,

$$\frac{(2 \cdot 22)+1}{2} = \frac{44+1}{2} = \frac{45}{2}$$

Practice:

1) Write $\dfrac{17}{4}$ as a mixed number.

2) Write $8\dfrac{11}{16}$ as an improper fraction.

3) Write $\dfrac{23}{2}$ as a mixed number.

4) Write $26\dfrac{3}{8}$ as an improper fraction.

Answers: 1) $4\dfrac{1}{4}$, 2) $\dfrac{139}{16}$, 3) $11\dfrac{1}{2}$, 4) $\dfrac{211}{8}$

Discovery Adventure 1: I'll Take Apple Pie

Another holiday has arrived and you have been invited to a large gathering at one of your relative's house. The guests have brought four whole pies: one blueberry, two apples, and one pumpkin. When the family starts on dessert, it doesn't take long for the whole blueberry pie and one of the apple pies to disappear. After all have eaten their fill, there are 2 slices of apple and 3 slices of pumpkin left.

a. Draw two circular pies. Label one "apple" and the other "pumpkin." Divide each pie into 6 equal parts, and shade in the parts that represent the remaining pie.

b. Use a fraction to represent the amount of apple pie remaining out of that whole pie. Then do the same with the remaining amount of pumpkin pie. Do not simplify your fractions yet.

Apple fraction:

Pumpkin fraction:

c. Combine the apple fraction with the pumpkin fraction to obtain the total amount of a whole pie left over.

d. How much pie have you and your relatives consumed so far? State your answer in terms of an improper fraction and a mixed number. *Hint:* The numerator of the improper fraction should give you the number of slices consumed, and the mixed number will give you the amount consumed in terms of whole pies.

Improper fraction: Mixed number:

e. Two of your relatives are interested in taking home the leftover pie. How many slices do you have to split two ways? What is the fractional part of one whole pie that is available for one of these relatives? *Hint:* The fraction $\frac{5}{6}$ is equivalent to $\frac{10}{12}$.

_____

_____

f. Is your answer to part e likely to be the way that the two people divide the pie? Why or why not?

_____

_____

g. Just when everything is settled, you turn to leave and drop a slice of apple pie on the floor. Assuming no one wants that piece, what fractional part of one whole pie is now available to divide two ways? Write your answer in simplest form.

h. Suppose that a neighbor from across the street brings over 1 whole pumpkin pie that was leftover from her holiday party. Using your answer from part g, how much pie is now available to split two ways evenly? Write this answer as a mixed number and an improper fraction. Then explain how many slices of pie are left to split among the two relatives.

Feedback

Since each slice is $\frac{1}{6}$ of a whole pie, there are $\frac{2}{6}$ or $\frac{1}{3}$ of an apple pie remaining and $\frac{3}{6}$ or $\frac{1}{2}$ of a pumpkin pie. The sum of these two parts is shown below.

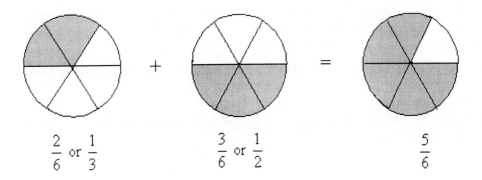

$$\frac{2}{6} \text{ or } \frac{1}{3} \qquad\qquad \frac{3}{6} \text{ or } \frac{1}{2} \qquad\qquad \frac{5}{6}$$

With $\frac{5}{6}$ of one whole pie left, each of the two people interested in leftover pie should receive $\frac{1}{2}$ of $\frac{5}{6}$. The hint in part *e* told you that $\frac{5}{6}$ is the same as $\frac{10}{12}$. Now imagine that you have 1 whole pie that is equally divided into 12 slices instead of 6. Then the fractional value $\frac{10}{12}$ represents 10 slices left out of 12 in a whole pie. Of course now each slice is half the size that it was previously, but you can give each relative 5 slices or $\frac{5}{12}$ of a whole pie.

After one slice of pie falls to the floor, there are $\frac{4}{6}$ or $\frac{2}{3}$ of a whole pie to split 2 ways. When this amount is added to the 1 whole pie leftover from a neighbor's holiday party, we have the following sum,

$$\frac{2}{3} + 1 = 1\frac{2}{3} \quad \text{ or } \quad \frac{5}{3}.$$

If you multiply the numerator and denominator of $\frac{5}{3}$ by 2, the fraction becomes $\frac{10}{6}$.

$$\frac{5}{3} = \frac{5 \cdot 2}{3 \cdot 2} = \frac{10}{6}$$

Each relative can receive 5 slices of pie, where each slice is back to the original size (whole pie is divided into 6 equal pieces). So each relative gets $\frac{5}{6}$ of a whole pie.

****

In the next Discovery Adventure, you will explore how fractions are needed to solve a work problem. This problem provides another opportunity to practice adding fractions in the context of a real-world situation. So read on and discover the power of teamwork!

Discovery Adventure 2: The Power of Teamwork

Sharon and Gerry Sr. have one of their two children help out with the housework every Saturday morning. The children alternate as helpers so that they only have to do housework every other week. The problem is that Rebecca is 16 and can do the list of chores in 3 hours while it takes 13 year old Gerry Jr. 4 hours to finish the same chores. Sharon suggests that the two children work together every week so they can get the job done in less time.

a. If Rebecca is able to complete the chores in 3 hours, what fraction of the chores can she complete in 1 hour?

b. If Gerry Jr. is able to complete the chores in 4 hours, what fraction of the chores can he complete in 1 hour?

c. Working together, what fraction of the chores can Rebecca and Gerry Jr. complete in 1 hour? Show all work including the process of finding a common denominator. Write your answer in simplest form.

d. Estimate how long it will take to complete the whole job (all the chores on the list) with sister and brother working together. *Hint*: To make your estimate, use a common fraction that is close to the answer in part *c*.

e. Why is it helpful to find the fraction of chores that each person could complete in 1 hour?

_____

_____

_____

_____

f. The concept of finding a common denominator can be visualized with a geometric model. Let the whole job (all chores on the list) be represented by a large rectangle. The large rectangle can be split into the appropriate number of parts to represent how long it takes Rebecca to complete the entire job. Shade in the portion of the rectangle to show the part of the job that Rebecca completes in 1 hour working alone.

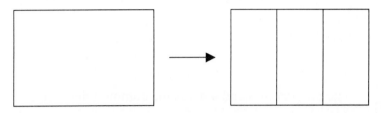

g. Let the same job (all chores on the list) be represented by another large rectangle given below. The large rectangle can be split into the appropriate number of parts to represent how long it takes Gerry Jr. to complete the entire job. Shade in the portion of the rectangle to show the part of the job that Gerry Jr. completes in 1 hour working alone.

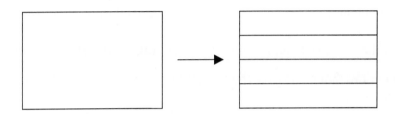

h. If Rebecca and Gerry Jr. work together, then you can add the fractional amount of chores that each completes in 1 hour separately. Show this geometrically by placing your two models from parts *f* and *g* below and find their sum. *Hint*: Split the rectangles for both Rebecca and Gerry Jr. further so that each one has an equal number of parts.

Rebecca   Gerry Jr.   Together

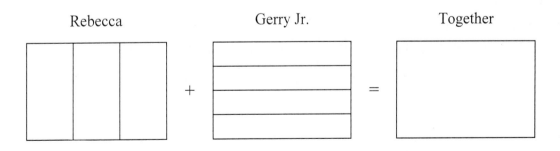

i. What do your answers in part *h* and part *c* have in common?

_____

_____

_____

Feedback

Working alone, Rebecca could complete all the chores in 3 hours. Therefore, she could finish $\frac{1}{3}$ of the job in 1 hour. Since Gerry Jr. could complete all the chores in 4 hours working alone, then he could finish $\frac{1}{4}$ of the job in 1 hour. Working together, brother and sister could complete $\frac{7}{12}$ of the job in 1 hour. The procedure is shown below.

$$\frac{1}{3}+\frac{1}{4}=\frac{1\cdot4}{3\cdot4}+\frac{1\cdot3}{4\cdot3} \qquad \text{The product of 3 and 4 gives the common denominator 12}$$

$$=\frac{4}{12}+\frac{3}{12} \qquad \text{Multiply by } \frac{4}{4}=1 \text{ and } \frac{3}{3}=1 \text{ to obtain equivalent fractions that can be added}$$

$$=\frac{7}{12} \qquad \text{Numerators are added, denominator stays the same}$$

The concept of finding a common denominator can be visualized through a geometric model.

Let the whole job (all the chores) be represented by a **rectangle**. If Rebecca works alone, she can finish $\frac{1}{3}$ of the job in 1 hour. So take the rectangle and divide it into 3 equal parts. The shaded part represents the part of the job that Rebecca completes in an hour.

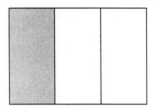

If Gerry Jr. works alone, he can finish $\frac{1}{4}$ of the job in 1 hour. So, divide the rectangle into 4 equal parts. Then shade in the part that he completes in an hour.

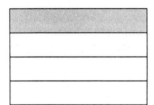

If sister and brother work together, we could add the fractional amount that each completes in 1 hour working separately. For example,

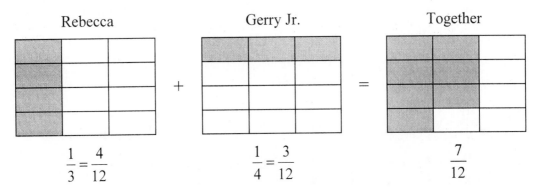

Rebecca $\qquad$ Gerry Jr. $\qquad$ Together

$$\frac{1}{3} = \frac{4}{12} \qquad + \qquad \frac{1}{4} = \frac{3}{12} \qquad = \qquad \frac{7}{12}$$

The value $\frac{7}{12}$ is close to $\frac{6}{12}$ or $\frac{1}{2}$. If the sister-brother team can finish about $\frac{1}{2}$ the job in 1 hour, then the whole job can be completed in about 2 hours.

The first two Discovery Adventures involved adding rational numbers in fractional form. In the next Discovery Adventure, we turn our attention to subtracting rational numbers in fractional form. Here you will use the familiar number line model to help visualize the process. Subtracting fractions is the same as adding since you must find a common denominator.

Discovery Adventure 3:　Subtracting Rational Numbers With a Number Line

The number line below has been divided into eighths. Suppose we want to subtract $\frac{1}{4}$ from $\frac{5}{8}$, or $\frac{5}{8} - \frac{1}{4}$.

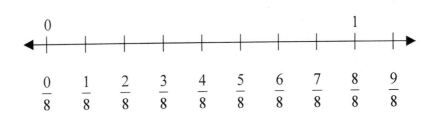

$$\frac{0}{8} \quad \frac{1}{8} \quad \frac{2}{8} \quad \frac{3}{8} \quad \frac{4}{8} \quad \frac{5}{8} \quad \frac{6}{8} \quad \frac{7}{8} \quad \frac{8}{8} \quad \frac{9}{8}$$

a. First write the subtraction as addition of the opposite. *Hint:* Write the first number, change subtraction to addition, and take the opposite of the second number. Do not calculate the answer yet.

$$\frac{5}{8} - \frac{1}{4} =$$

b. On the number line below, start at zero and draw a ray or vector to $\frac{5}{8}$. Label this first vector $\frac{5}{8}$. Then from $\frac{5}{8}$, draw a second vector $\frac{1}{4}$ units in the opposite direction. Circle the number where the second vector ends. This number is the answer.

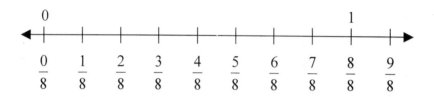

c. Now let's subtract $\frac{1}{2}$ from $\frac{2}{3}$ using rays or vectors. First, divide the number line into intervals of sixths, since both $\frac{1}{2}$ and $\frac{2}{3}$ can be represented in sixths. Make sure you label each slash in terms of sixths.

d. Write $\frac{2}{3}$ minus $\frac{1}{2}$ using equivalent fractions and a least common denominator (LCD) of 6.

$$\frac{2}{3} - \frac{1}{2} =$$

e. Rewrite the subtraction in terms of addition of the opposite with 6 as the LCD and then compute your answer.

f. Similar to part *b*, use rays or vectors on the number line in part *c* to show geometrically how you arrive at the answer in part *e*. Circle the answer on the number line.

Feedback

Subtracting $\dfrac{1}{4}$ from $\dfrac{5}{8}$ is equivalent to adding $-\dfrac{1}{4}$ to $\dfrac{5}{8}$, or

$$\dfrac{5}{8} - \dfrac{1}{4} = \dfrac{5}{8} + \left(-\dfrac{1}{4}\right)$$

Using rays or vectors we have,

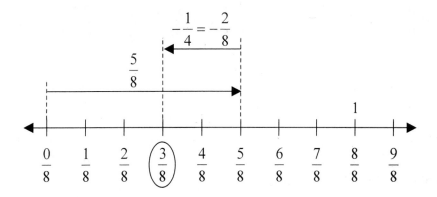

In the second problem, you were asked to subtract $\dfrac{1}{2}$ from $\dfrac{2}{3}$.

$$\dfrac{2}{3} - \dfrac{1}{2} = \dfrac{4}{6} - \dfrac{3}{6} \qquad \dfrac{2\cdot 2}{3\cdot 2} \text{ and } \dfrac{1\cdot 3}{2\cdot 3}$$

$$= \dfrac{4}{6} + \left(-\dfrac{3}{6}\right) \qquad \text{subtraction is addition of the opposite}$$

$$= \dfrac{1}{6} \qquad\qquad \text{simplify}$$

Rays or vectors are used below to show the problem from a geometric viewpoint.

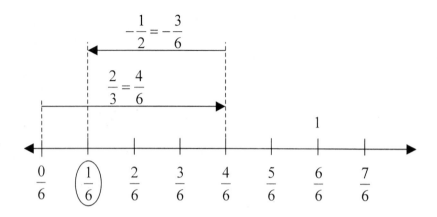

Let's look at one more example before continuing our investigation. We can find the difference of $2 - \dfrac{2}{3}$ numerically (using a common denominator) and geometrically (using a number line):

$$2 - \frac{2}{3} = \frac{2}{1} - \frac{2}{3} \qquad \text{Find a common denominator 3}$$

$$= \frac{6}{3} - \frac{2}{3} \qquad \frac{2 \cdot 3}{1 \cdot 3} = \frac{6}{3}$$

$$= \frac{4}{3} \qquad \text{Subtract numerators and keep a common denominator}$$

$$or \quad = 1\frac{1}{3} \qquad \text{The \textbf{improper fraction} } \frac{4}{3} \text{ can be rewritten as the \textbf{mixed number} } 1\frac{1}{3}$$

Geometrically, we have

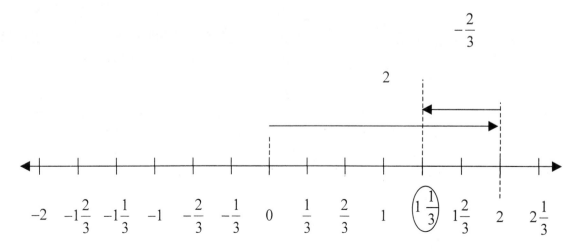

****

In the fourth and final Discovery Adventure for this section, you will investigate another pie problem. The problem involves subtracting rational numbers in fractional form. In particular, you will have the opportunity to work with mixed numbers and improper fractions.

Discovery Adventure 4: The Real Thing

The class is almost over and with all this talk about pie your 4-person group realizes how hungry they are. You suggest going down to the cafeteria knowing that they serve pie by the slice. Upon arriving at the cafeteria you find 3 whole pies with each pie cut up into 8 equal pieces. Your three friends each take one slice while you decide to take two slices.

a. Draw three circles to represent the 3 pies and divide each of them up into 8 equal pieces. Then lightly shade-in the amount of pie that would be left after the group purchased their pie slices.

b. How much pie is left over for other students to buy? Use a mixed number to represent the amount left.

c. After finishing off their pie, the group decides they are still hungry and that each person will get three more slices. Look at the three pies you sketched above and imagine removing 12 more slices. Use a mixed number to represent the 12 slices as a whole number or 1 whole pie plus a fraction of another whole pie. Assume no one else has bought any pie.

d. Go back to the picture you made in part *a*. Mark an "X" on the 12 additional slices your group just bought. The remaining blank pieces represent the amount left over.

e. What fractional part of a whole pie is left over?

f. Write the amount left as the difference between the mixed number in part *b* and the mixed number in part *c*.

(Mixed # left after 1st purchase) – (Mixed # bought during 2nd purchase)

g. If you do not already have a common denominator from part *f*, then as a second step, rewrite the difference using a common denominator for the two fractions.

h. Although the two whole numbers from parts *f* or *g* can be subtracted (2 – 1 = 1), what happens when you try to subtract the two fractional parts $\left(\dfrac{3}{8} - \dfrac{4}{8}\right)$?

_____

_____

i. Since you already know the fractional part of a whole pie that is left over (answer to part *e*), can you explain a way around the problem in part *h*?

_____

_____

_____

Feedback

The numerical process for solving the last adventure is given below.

$$2\frac{3}{8} - 1\frac{1}{2}$$ The LCD for 8 and 2 is 8, so rewrite $\dfrac{1}{2}$ as $\dfrac{4}{8}$

$$= 2\frac{3}{8} - 1\frac{4}{8}$$ Subtract the whole numbers $2 - 1$ to obtain 1 whole pie

$$= 1\frac{3}{8} - \frac{4}{8}$$ Change the mixed number $1\frac{3}{8}$ to an improper fraction $\dfrac{11}{8}$

$$= \frac{11}{8} - \frac{4}{8}$$ Simplify

$$= \frac{7}{8}$$

There are 7 slices left out of 8 or $\frac{7}{8}$ of a whole pie left over.

It can be helpful to keep a visual model of the pies in your mind or on paper while completing your calculations. For example, when converting the mixed number $1\frac{3}{8}$ to the improper fraction $\frac{11}{8}$, the mixed number can be viewed as the sum of 1 whole pie and $\frac{3}{8}$ of a whole pie. Since 1 whole pie has 8 slices, then 1 whole pie can be represented by the fraction $\frac{8}{8}$. This allows you to find the sum, $\frac{8}{8} + \frac{3}{8} = \frac{11}{8}$. Adding the numerators (8 + 3) is like adding 8 slices and 3 slices to obtain 11 slices. So $\frac{11}{8}$ represents having 11 slices out of 8 slices in a whole pie. Finally, subtracting $\frac{4}{8}$ (4 slices out of 8 in a whole pie) from $\frac{11}{8}$ gives you $\frac{7}{8}$ (7 slices out of 8 in a whole pie).

This section has given you a chance to explore the ideas behind adding and subtracting rational numbers in fractional form. The key to this process is an understanding that fractions are combined (added or subtracted) using a common denominator. Finding a common denominator allows you to divide objects (like pies) into an equal number of parts (slices). By having equally sized parts (pieces of pie) you make it easier to add and subtract.

Recall that rational numbers can also be expressed as repeating or terminating decimals. For example, $\frac{1}{3} = 0.333\cdots$ or $0.\overline{3}$ is a repeating decimal, and $\frac{7}{8} = 0.875$ is a terminating decimal. The following exercises will give you the opportunity to add and subtract rational numbers in both fractional and decimal form.

Section Exercises: 3.2

1. The Internet gives any individual the opportunity to check how their stock is performing. Suppose you go on-line and bring up the following data on Bruno Bagel Corporation.

Ticker Symbol	Today's High	Today's Low	Last Price	Prior Close	Change	Trade Time
Bruno	$33\dfrac{1}{2}$	$29\dfrac{5}{16}$	$32\dfrac{13}{16}$	$35\dfrac{5}{8}$	$-3\dfrac{3}{16}$	1:32 p.m.

a. As of 1:32 p.m. this trading day, what is the difference between today's high price per share and today's low price per share? Show your work.

b. The last price represents the price of a share as of 1:32 p.m., and the prior close was the price per share at the close of trading on the previous day. Show how subtracting the prior close price from the last price gives the difference of $-2\dfrac{13}{16}$. Then explain what the negative sign indicates in the "Change" column.

_____

_____

_____

c. If you own 1200 shares of Bruno, then estimate how much your investment lost during the time from the prior closing until 1:32 p.m. today. Do you think this is a cause for concern? Explain.

_____

_____

d. Now observe data from another company that you own stock in. What must the "Last Price" be in order to obtain the "Change" of $+3\frac{3}{4}$?

Ticker Symbol	Last Price	Prior Close	Change	Trade Time
Norwood	?	$16\frac{11}{32}$	$+3\frac{3}{4}$	1:32 p.m.

e. If you own 10,000 shares of Norwood, then estimate how much your investment gained during the time from the prior closing until 1:32 p.m. today. Do you think this is a cause for celebration?

_____

_____

_____

2. The following table compares current welfare programs with a proposed new program called Help-For-Working-Parents (HWP). The new HWP program is based on the idea that health insurance and child care need to be provided for families who only get minimum wage for full-time jobs.

a. Fill in all missing entries for the table below. Complete the last column by finding the difference,

HWP Program – 1994 Program

Costs (in millions of $) For Families *Without* A Parent In Labor Force

	HWP Program	1994 Program	Difference HWP – 1994
Number of Families (millions)	2	4.7	–2.7
AFDC	0	25.3	
Food Stamps	4.9	11.5	
Job training for AFDC clients	0	1	
Housing Assistance	6.9	6	
Medical Care	10.3	24.3	
Child Care	19	13.6	
Cash Fallback	10.8	0	
Total Cost			

b. The difference in number of families is –2.7. What does this number mean in terms of the problem situation? Answer using complete sentences.

_____

_____

c. The difference in Food Stamps is a negative number, while the difference in Housing Assistance is a positive number. What do these two numbers mean when comparing the programs?

_____

_____

_____

d. Repeat the same process in part *a* for the table below.

Costs (in millions of $) For Families *With* A Parent In Labor Force

	HWP Program	1994 Program	Difference HWP – 1994
Number of Families (millions)	5	2.3	2.7
AFDC	22.5	10.3	
Food Stamps	4.7	2.2	
Job training for AFDC clients	7.3	3.4	
Housing Assistance	53.6	10.3	
Medical Care	61.3	12.6	
Child Care	1.5	0.5	
Cash Fallback	4.5	0	
Total Cost			

e. Add the "Total Cost" for each program and enter it in the last row of the table.

	HWP Program	1994 Program	Difference
Total Cost			

f. How much would the proposed HWP welfare program cost the government in new spending?

3. Do people generate more garbage than they used to? According to *The New Field Guide To The U.S. Economy*, in 1960 each person in this country generated on average 2.7 pounds of trash per day, while in 1990 each person generated 4.3 pounds per day. See the figure below for a graphical view and then answer the following questions.

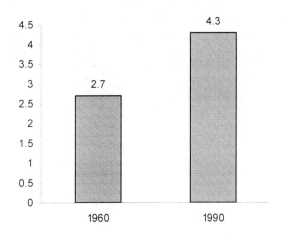

Pounds of solid waste per person, per day, in the U.S.

a. How much more garbage is the average person throwing away in 1990 as compared with 1960? Express your answer as a decimal and a mixed number.

b. After looking at this data, one student pointed out that the reason we have more trash in 1990 is because we have more people in the population. Comment on the validity of this statement, and then explain what the above data and graph are trying to show.

_____

_____

_____

_____

c. Based on the 1990 data, how many pounds of trash does your household throw away each day?

d. How many pounds of trash does your household throw away each week?

e. How many pounds of trash does your household throw away each month?

    f.   How many pounds of trash does your household throw away each year?

4. In this exploration, we will use number lines to approximate the solution to addition problems involving fractions. Estimate the sum of each expression by first finding one of the addends on the number line and then moving a distance equal to the other addend. Place an arrow pointing to the answer as shown in the first example below. Do not use a calculator or any paper and pencil work. Instead approximate using mathematical thinking. Try to think about the size of each fraction in comparison to $\frac{1}{2}$.

$\frac{2}{3}+\frac{1}{2}$

a. $\frac{8}{9}+\frac{3}{4}$

b. $1\frac{3}{8}+\frac{2}{3}$

c. $1\frac{4}{7}+2\frac{5}{9}$

d. $3\frac{1}{3}+1\frac{1}{5}$

5. Suppose you are doing some construction work where you must nail one piece of wood to another. The first piece of wood has $\frac{1}{2}$ inch of thickness to go through to reach the second piece, which has $1\frac{1}{4}$ inch thickness. There are two boxes of nails available: one box has nails that measure $1\frac{5}{8}$ inches long, and the other box has nails of $1\frac{13}{16}$ inches long.

 a. Which nail size do you choose so that the nail does not go all the way through both boards, with the point sticking out?

 b. State how far the point of each nail would go into the second piece of wood if you hammer in both nails with the head pressed next to the first piece of wood?

6. Suppose you are in the middle of taking an exam and have half an hour to finish the last three problems. If you spend a quarter of an hour working on one problem, how much time is left to finish the remaining two questions?

 a. The following statement expresses the problem in writing. Below the words (to the right of the equal sign), state the problem as a subtraction of two fractions.

    Time left = half hour – quarter hour

 b. Since there are 60 minutes in an hour, rewrite the subtraction problem in part a using a common denominator of 60. Then find the solution as a fraction with a denominator of 60.

 c. Observe the answer to part b. What does the value of the numerator and denominator tell us about the problem situation?

 _____

 _____

 _____

187

   d. Suppose you wish to spend an equal amount of time on each of the last two questions. Express the time you should work on each question as a fraction of an hour and as a mixed number in minutes.

7. Kristen's height in bare feet is 5 feet $4\frac{1}{2}$ inches.

   a. If she wears shoes with heels that add $1\frac{3}{4}$ inches to her height, then how tall would she be?

   b. Suppose she has grown $1\frac{1}{4}$ inches in each of the last three years. If Kristen is 13 now, how tall was she at the age of 10 years?

8. Use complete sentences to explain why the following statements CANNOT be true.

   a. $\dfrac{1}{2}+\dfrac{1}{3}=\dfrac{2}{5}$

   _____

   _____

   _____

   b. $\dfrac{5}{6}-\dfrac{3}{4}=\dfrac{2}{2}=1$

   _____

   _____

   _____

    c. $0.5 + 0.5 = 0.10$

_____

_____

_____

    d. $7.28 - .6 = 7.22$

_____

_____

_____

9. Evaluate the following expressions. Express your answer is simplest form or reduce the fraction until 1 is the only number that divides into the numerator and denominator evenly.

    a. $\dfrac{1}{3} + \dfrac{1}{4}$ *b.* $\dfrac{3}{8} + \dfrac{6}{16}$

    c. $\dfrac{7}{2} - \dfrac{2}{7}$ *d.* $\dfrac{7}{9} - \dfrac{5}{6}$

    e. $\dfrac{2}{3} + \dfrac{4}{5}$ *f.* $\dfrac{3}{4} + \dfrac{5}{8}$

    g. $\dfrac{2}{5} + \dfrac{1}{6} + \dfrac{3}{7}$ *h.* $\dfrac{1}{3} - \dfrac{1}{4}$

i. $\dfrac{1}{4} - \dfrac{1}{3}$ *j.* $4\dfrac{2}{3} + 1\dfrac{2}{3}$

k. $2\dfrac{3}{4} + 3\dfrac{1}{6} + \dfrac{1}{12}$ *l.* $6\dfrac{3}{5} - 3\dfrac{2}{5}$

m. $3\dfrac{2}{5} - 6\dfrac{3}{5}$ *n.* $4\dfrac{1}{3} - 2\dfrac{3}{4}$

10. According to Bloomberg News, the average retail price for regular, unleaded gas at self-serve pumps along the East Coast increased from $0.90\dfrac{6}{10}$ on March 8, 1999 to $1.20\dfrac{9}{10}$ on August 23, 1999.

     a. Find the exact price increase over this time interval. Show all work and state your answer using complete sentences.

_____

_____

_____

     b. How would you express the exact price on March 8 and August 23 using the thousandths place instead of the fractional part of a cent?

c. Express the increase in price found in part *a* as a decimal number taken out to the thousandths place.

d. Suppose you filled a 20-gallon tank on each of the given dates, how much more was spent on August 23 as compared with March 8?

11. The following graph shows the cost of home heating oil during the winters of 1996/1997 through 1999/2000. The 1999/2000 cost is projected with the bottom bar representing a warm winter and the bottom and top bars together as being a cold winter.

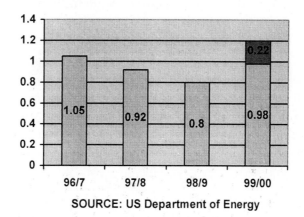

SOURCE: US Department of Energy

a. If the winter of 1999/2000 is cold, what is the projected cost per gallon?

b. Fill in the 1999/2000 cost per gallon from part *a* (a cold winter) in the last row of the second column and the change in cost between each winter in the third column. Express a decrease in cost as a negative change and an increase in cost as a positive change.

Winter Years	Cost	Change in Cost
1996/1997	$1.05	
1997/1998	$0.92	
1998/1999	$0.80	
1999/2000		

   c. Suppose a couple paid $707 to heat their home with oil during the winter of 1998/1999. How many gallons of oil did they use during that winter season?

   d. How much more will the couple in part *c* pay for home heating oil if they use the same amount of oil in 1999/2000 as they did the year before?

- Assuming a warm winter

- Assuming a cold winter

12. Massachusetts Institute of Technology (MIT) had a party to celebrate the start of a $1.5 billion fund-raising campaign. During the dinner, an alumni and former faculty member announced that he would give the institute a gift of $100 million.

   a. The number 100 million is what fractional part of one billion?

   b. If the $100 million gift is the first and only contribution so far, then how much more money must MIT raise to reach the $1.5 billion goal? Give your answer in short form, using a decimal and the word *billion*. Then write the answer in expanded form with the correct number of zeros.

   c. Suppose there were 500 other guests besides the surprise donor at the dinner. How much would each guest have to contribute to reach the goal of $1.5 billion that very evening? Assume that each of the 500 alumni give the same amount.

13. In Discovery Adventure 2, you estimated the time needed for Rebecca and Gerry Jr. to complete the whole job working together. If you attempt to calculate a more accurate answer, it can be shown that the time to complete the job is very close to 1 hour and 43 minutes. Rebecca presented this evidence to her parents claiming that she worked less time when Gerry Jr. and she worked alone every other week. Is she right?

   a. To complete the job alone, Gerry Jr. worked 4 hours but had every other week off. What is the average number of hours per week that he worked over a two-week period?

   b. On average, how much time per week did Gerry Jr. gain or lose by working together with his sister?

c. To complete the job alone, Rebecca worked 3 hours but had every other week off. What is the average number of hours per week that she worked over a two-week period? Express your answer in hours and minutes.

d. On average, how much time per week did Rebecca gain or lose by working together with her brother?

e. Is it more efficient for sister and brother to work together every week or alone every other week? Comment on the pros and cons of each work schedule.

_____

_____

_____

f. Compare the time working on the job together each week with the average time per week when sister and brother are working alone. Do Rebecca and Gerry Jr. put in more hours working together or alone? Explain.

_____

_____

_____

g. When you consider the effects on the whole family, which work plan makes the most sense for everyone involved?

_____

_____

_____

Section 3.3 Multiplying and Dividing Rational Numbers

Math Talk

When people buy items at the deli it is very common to buy a fraction of a pound. For example, you might order $\frac{1}{2}$ pound of turkey, $\frac{3}{4}$ pound of ham, and $\frac{1}{3}$ pound of roast beef. Buying a fraction of a pound means getting less than 1 pound. Now suppose the turkey cost $4.99 per pound, the ham $3.99 per pound, and the roast beef $5.99 per pound. Approximately how much are you going to pay for each item?

Let's estimate the cost of the three meats given above. First, let's round each of the meats to the nearest dollar. Therefore, turkey is $5 per pound, ham is $4 per pound, and roast beef is $6 per pound. The word **per** is used to mean *for each* 1 pound. So if you buy 1 pound of turkey, you pay $5. If you are buying $\frac{1}{2}$ pound, you should pay half of $5 or $2.50. Now you might have done this calculation automatically in your head without really thinking about the operation. Mathematically, the operation is the product of $\frac{1}{2}$ and $5, or equivalently, the quotient of 5 and 2 ($\frac{5}{2} = 2.5$). This means that 5 divided by 2 is the same as 5 times $\frac{1}{2}$.

In general, we say that a first number divided by a second number is equivalent to the first number multiplied by the reciprocal of the second number. Informally, *reciprocal* means to take a fraction and flip it upside down. So the reciprocal of $\frac{2}{1}$ is $\frac{1}{2}$.

Buying 1 pound of ham would cost about $4. Buying $\frac{3}{4}$ of a pound can be calculated as the product of $\frac{3}{4}$ and $4 which equals $3. This calculation can be estimated in your head if you realize that finding one-quarter ($\frac{1}{4}$) of $4 is like dividing $4 into 4 equal parts with each part being $1. Therefore, three-quarters ($\frac{3}{4}$) of $4 must be 3 times $1 or $3.

Can you estimate how much to pay for $\frac{1}{3}$ pound of roast beef? What is the mathematical operation needed to obtain this cost?

In the above context we can associate the word *per* with division. For example, turkey at $5 per pound can be represented symbolically by the following expression,

$$\frac{5 \text{ dollars}}{1 \text{ pound}} \quad \text{or} \quad \frac{\$5}{1 \text{ lb}}$$

Here we are expressing cost per pound as a ratio (fraction). In this sense, there is a relationship between dollars and pounds; specifically, every 5 dollars can buy 1 pound of turkey.

Another word that can imply a mathematical operation is the word **of**. For example, finding $\frac{3}{4}$ of 4 can be represented by $\frac{3}{4} \cdot 4$, and $\frac{1}{4}$ of 4 can be represented by $\frac{1}{4} \cdot 4$. Note that $\frac{1}{4}$ and 4 are reciprocals, and their product is 1.

In this section, you will learn to do the following:

- Discover when to use multiplication and division of rational numbers in real, problem-solving situations.

- Investigate rational numbers as the base of exponential expressions.

- Use a distance, rate, and time model to explore the pattern of change in rational numbers as the numerator stays fixed and the denominator changes by a constant amount.

- Become comfortable in switching back and forth between improper fractions and mixed numbers in the context of real situations.

****

Use the following fraction board to help answer the questions below.

What is $\frac{1}{2}$ of $\frac{1}{2}$?

What is $\frac{1}{2}$ of $\frac{1}{4}$?

What is $\dfrac{1}{4}$ of $\dfrac{1}{2}$?

What is $\dfrac{1}{2}$ of $\dfrac{3}{4}$?

Multiplication is repeated addition. For example, $2 \cdot 3$ means to sum "two of the three's" or "three of the two's,"

$$2 \cdot 3 = 3 + 3 \qquad 2 \cdot 3 = 2 + 2 + 2$$

So, $\dfrac{1}{2} \cdot \dfrac{1}{4}$ stands for "one-half of one-fourth" or "one-fourth of one-half," which in either case is $\dfrac{1}{8}$.

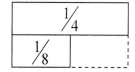 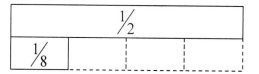

So if $\dfrac{1}{2} \cdot \dfrac{1}{4} = \dfrac{1}{8}$, then $\dfrac{1}{2} \cdot \dfrac{3}{4}$ must be 3 times larger than $\dfrac{1}{8}$ or $\dfrac{3}{8}$.

Therefore, we have found that $\dfrac{1}{2} \cdot \dfrac{1}{4} = \dfrac{1}{8}$ and $\dfrac{1}{2} \cdot \dfrac{3}{4} = \dfrac{3}{8}$. Can you now state a general rule for multiplying two fractions?

Multiplying Fractions

To multiply two fractions, multiply the numerators and multiply the denominators.

As you observe the following examples, note how an improper fraction can be written as a mixed number in the first example, a common factor is divided out of the second example, and a mixed number is changed to an improper fraction in the third example.

Multiply:

- $\dfrac{5}{2}\cdot\dfrac{3}{4}=\dfrac{5\cdot3}{2\cdot4}=\dfrac{15}{8}$ or $1\dfrac{7}{8}$ aside: $8\overline{)15}$ $\begin{array}{r}1\frac{7}{8}\\\underline{8}\\7\end{array}$ or $\dfrac{15}{8}=\dfrac{8+7}{8}=\dfrac{8}{8}+\dfrac{7}{8}=1+\dfrac{7}{8}=1\dfrac{7}{8}$

- $\dfrac{2}{3}\cdot\dfrac{3}{8}=\dfrac{2\cdot3}{3\cdot8}=\dfrac{\overset{1}{2}\cdot\overset{1}{3}}{\underset{1}{3}\cdot\underset{4}{8}}=\dfrac{1}{4}$ or alternatively $\dfrac{2\cdot3}{3\cdot8}=\dfrac{6}{24}=\dfrac{6\div6}{24\div6}=\dfrac{1}{4}$

- $3\dfrac{2}{3}\cdot\dfrac{1}{10}=\dfrac{11}{3}\cdot\dfrac{1}{10}=\dfrac{11\cdot1}{3\cdot10}=\dfrac{11}{30}$ aside: $3\dfrac{2}{3}=\dfrac{3\cdot3+2}{3}=\dfrac{9+2}{3}=\dfrac{11}{3}$

What is half *of* two? This translates mathematically to $\dfrac{1}{2}\cdot2$. By writing 2 as $\dfrac{2}{1}$ and applying the rule for multiplying fractions, we have

$$\dfrac{1}{2}\cdot\dfrac{2}{1}=\dfrac{2}{2}=1.$$

Similarly we have

$$\dfrac{8}{9}\cdot\dfrac{9}{8}=\dfrac{72}{72}=1.$$

These examples imply that a number times its reciprocal equals 1. In other words, the product of a fraction and that fraction flipped over is 1. More formally, we define *reciprocal* as follows:

Reciprocal of a Fractional Expression

The reciprocal of $\dfrac{a}{b}$ is $\dfrac{b}{a}$, where a and b are any number, quantity, or expression. The product of reciprocals is 1.

$$\dfrac{a}{b}\cdot\dfrac{b}{a}=1$$

When asked to find "8 divided by 2", the problem really is "2 times what value is 8", or

$$2\cdot\boxed{}=8.$$

When asked to find "$\dfrac{3}{5}$ divided by $\dfrac{8}{9}$", the problem really is "$\dfrac{8}{9}$ times what value is $\dfrac{3}{5}$", or

$$\dfrac{8}{9}\cdot\boxed{}=\dfrac{3}{5}.$$

To find the correct value to put in the box, we can isolate the box by multiplying both sides by the reciprocal of $\frac{8}{9}$,

$$\frac{9}{8}\cdot\frac{8}{9}\cdot\square=\frac{3}{5}\cdot\frac{9}{8}.$$

Since $\frac{8}{9}\cdot\frac{9}{8}=1$, we have $1\cdot\square=\frac{3}{5}\cdot\frac{9}{8}.$

And 1 times any number is that number, so

$$\square=\frac{3}{5}\cdot\frac{9}{8}=\frac{27}{40}.$$

Therefore, $\frac{3}{5}$ divided by $\frac{8}{9}$ can be found by multiplying $\frac{3}{5}$ by the reciprocal of $\frac{8}{9}$ or $\frac{9}{8}$.

In summary,

$$\frac{3}{5}\div\frac{8}{9}=\frac{3}{5}\cdot\frac{9}{8}=\frac{27}{40} \quad\text{or}\quad \frac{\frac{3}{5}}{\frac{8}{9}}=\frac{3}{5}\cdot\frac{9}{8}=\frac{27}{40}.$$

Can you now state a general rule for dividing two fractions?

Dividing Two Fractions

To divide two fractions, multiply the first fraction by the reciprocal of the second fraction.

Discovery Adventure 1: Baking Dessert

Suppose you want to make a batch of your mother's famous double chocolate peanut butter cookies. You call up Mom who gives you the following "can't miss" recipe.

$1\frac{1}{2}$ cups all purpose flour	1 cup granulated sugar
$\frac{1}{3}$ cup baking Cocoa	1 cup peanut butter
$1\frac{1}{2}$ teaspoons baking powder	$\frac{1}{3}$ cup butter or margarine
$\frac{1}{4}$ teaspoon salt	$1\frac{1}{2}$ teaspoons vanilla extract
2 cups semi-sweet chocolate morsels	2 large eggs

a. If the recipe above makes about $3\frac{1}{2}$ dozen cookies, then explain what you would do to make 7 dozen cookies.

_____

_____

_____

b. Suppose you are having a large party and wanted to make 14 dozen cookies. Calculate the amount of each ingredient you will need. Show each calculation below.

- All purpose flour

- Baking cocoa

- Baking powder

- Salt

- Semi-sweet chocolate morsels

- Granulated sugar

- Peanut butter

- Butter or margarine

- Vanilla extract

- Large eggs

c. Suppose you only have half the amount of certain ingredients required in the original recipe that made $3\frac{1}{2}$ dozen. If you make a batch that is half the size of the original recipe, then how many cookies can you bake? Show all work below.

d. Is there a way to figure out the exact amount of ingredients needed to make 1 dozen cookies? *Hint*: What operation could you perform on the amount of each ingredient to break it up into $3\frac{1}{2}$ equal parts? Use complete sentences to explain your answer.

_____

_____

_____

e. Calculate the amount of the first two ingredients needed to make 1 dozen cookies. Show all work below.

- All purpose flour

- Baking cocoa

f. Based on the two calculations in part *e*, why will it be difficult to make exactly 1 dozen cookies? Use complete sentences to explain your answer.

_____

_____

_____

g. If 1 dozen equals 12 cookies, then how many cookies are there in $3\frac{1}{2}$ dozen?

h. If you use $\dfrac{1}{3}$ of the ingredients in the original recipe for $3\dfrac{1}{2}$ dozen, then how many cookies can you bake? *Hint*: You can find $\dfrac{1}{3}$ of something by dividing it into 3 equal parts.

Feedback

Since the original recipe makes $3\dfrac{1}{2}$ dozen cookies, then you must multiply each ingredient by 2 to make 7 dozen. For example,

$$2 \cdot 3\dfrac{1}{2} = \dfrac{2}{1} \cdot \dfrac{7}{2} \qquad \text{Write 2 as } \dfrac{2}{1} \text{ and change mixed number } 3\dfrac{1}{2} \text{ to } \dfrac{7}{2}$$

$$= \dfrac{14}{2} \qquad \text{Multiply numerators and denominators}$$

$$= 7 \qquad \text{Simplify by dividing out a two, } \dfrac{14 \div 2}{2 \div 2} = \dfrac{7}{1} = 7$$

A second way to look at this is to use a process called *cancellation*, which has you divide out any common factors of the numerator and denominator. For example,

$$2 \cdot 3\dfrac{1}{2} = \dfrac{2}{1} \cdot \dfrac{7}{2} \qquad \text{Write 2 as } \dfrac{2}{1} \text{ and change mixed number } 3\dfrac{1}{2} \text{ to } \dfrac{7}{2}$$

$$= \dfrac{\cancel{2} \cdot 7}{1 \cdot \cancel{2}} \qquad \text{Cancel 2s or divide out the common factor of 2 from the numerator and denominator}$$

$$= 7 \qquad \text{Multiply across the numerator and deominator and simplify}$$

When completing calculations like those above, try to use number sense to do the calculation quickly in your head. For example, think of $3\dfrac{1}{2}$ as $3 + \dfrac{1}{2}$, so you can double (multiply by 2) the whole part 3 to get 6 and double the fraction part $\dfrac{1}{2}$ to get 1. Thus, $6 + 1 = 7$ dozen cookies.

To make 14 dozen cookies, you need to multiply each ingredient by 4. The following two calculations show how to find the amount of all purpose flour and baking cocoa.

$$4 \cdot \left(1\frac{1}{2}\right) = \frac{4}{1} \cdot \frac{3}{2}$$

$$= \frac{\overset{2}{\cancel{4}} \cdot 3}{1 \cdot \cancel{2}}$$

$$= 6 \text{ cups all purpose flour}$$

$$4 \cdot \frac{1}{3} = \frac{4}{1} \cdot \frac{1}{3}$$

$$= \frac{4 \cdot 1}{1 \cdot 3}$$

$$= \frac{4}{3} \text{ or } 1\frac{1}{3} \text{ cups baking cocoa}$$

If you make a batch using $\frac{1}{2}$ the amount of each ingredient, then you can find the product of $\frac{1}{2}$ and $3\frac{1}{2}$ to find how many dozen cookies will result. Then you can multiply this result by 12 because there are 12 cookies in a dozen. For example,

$$\frac{1}{2} \cdot \left(3\frac{1}{2}\right) = \frac{1}{2} \cdot \frac{7}{2}$$

$$= \frac{1 \cdot 7}{2 \cdot 2}$$

$$= \frac{7}{4} \text{ or } 1\frac{3}{4} \text{ dozen cookies}$$

OR

$$\frac{7}{4} \cdot 12 = \frac{7}{4} \cdot \frac{12}{1}$$

$$= \frac{7 \cdot \overset{3}{\cancel{12}}}{\underset{1}{\cancel{4}} \cdot 1}$$

$$= 21 \text{ cookies}$$

To calculate a recipe for one dozen cookies, you need to divide each ingredient by $3\frac{1}{2}$ or $\frac{7}{2}$. For example, to find the amount of all purpose flour and baking cocoa, proceed as follows:

$$\left(1\frac{1}{2}\right) \div \left(3\frac{1}{2}\right) = \frac{3}{2} \div \frac{7}{2}$$

$$= \frac{3}{2} \cdot \frac{2}{7}$$

$$= \frac{3 \cdot \overset{1}{\cancel{2}}}{\underset{1}{\cancel{2}} \cdot 7}$$

$$= \frac{3}{7} \text{ cups all purpose flour}$$

OR

$$\frac{\frac{1}{3}}{\frac{7}{2}} = \frac{1}{3} \cdot \frac{2}{7}$$

$$= \frac{1 \cdot 2}{3 \cdot 7}$$

$$= \frac{2}{21} \text{ cups baking cocoa}$$

The problem is that measuring cups are not available in these fractional amounts. Note that in the calculation of flour we used the traditional division symbol, while in the calculation of baking cocoa we used a fraction bar to represent division. Also, we expressed each mixed number as an improper fraction to complete the calculation.

****

In the next Discovery Adventure, you will investigate a situation that involves repeated multiplication of the same fraction. This presents an opportunity to use an exponential expression when the base is a fraction. You will be asked to use two important problem solving skills: drawing a picture and constructing a table.

Discovery Adventure 2: Follow the Bouncing Ball

Suppose you drop a ball from a height of 4 feet and estimate that each time the ball hits the ground it rebounds (bounces up) to $\frac{2}{3}$ of its previous height.   What is the maximum height of each rebound before the ball drops again?

a.   Start by drawing a picture of the situation above. Include at least 4 rebounds.

b.   Complete the table below by showing the calculation needed to find the height in the second column and then place the result in the last column. Use a mixed number for the height where appropriate.

Rebounds	Calculation	Height (feet)
0		4
1		
2		
3		
4		

c.   After each bounce the new height is calculated by multiplying the previous height by $\frac{2}{3}$.

This means that each new height can be obtained by repeated multiplication of $\frac{2}{3}$. In the table on the next page, show how to represent each calculation using repeated multiplication and exponential notation.

Rebounds	Repeated Multiplication	Exponential Notation	Height
0			4
1	$4 \cdot \dfrac{2}{3}$	$4 \cdot \left(\dfrac{2}{3}\right)^1$	$\dfrac{8}{3} = 2\dfrac{2}{3}$
2	$4 \cdot \dfrac{2}{3} \cdot \dfrac{2}{3}$	$4 \cdot \left(\dfrac{2}{3}\right)^2$	
3			
4			

d. Show the exponential calculation that would be needed to find the height after 8 rebounds and then calculate the answer.

e. If we let the variable n represent the number of rebounds, then what exponential expression symbolizes the height after n rebounds?

Feedback

When you are taking a fraction of something, the word *of* implies the operation of multiplication.

$$\frac{2}{3} \; of \; \text{previous height} \quad \text{means} \quad \frac{2}{3} \cdot (\text{previous height})$$

If we start off at a height of 4 feet, the sequence of bounces could be represented numerically as shown below.

$$\text{First rebound: } \frac{2}{3} \cdot 4 = \frac{8}{3} \text{ feet or } 2\frac{2}{3} \text{ feet}$$

$$\text{Second rebound: } \frac{2}{3} \cdot \frac{8}{3} = \frac{16}{9} \text{ feet or } 1\frac{7}{9} \text{ feet}$$

$$\text{Third rebound: } \frac{2}{3} \cdot \frac{16}{9} = \frac{32}{27} \text{ feet or } 1\frac{5}{27} \text{ feet}$$

$$\text{Fourth rebound: } \frac{2}{3} \cdot \frac{32}{27} = \frac{64}{81} \text{ feet}$$

While repeated multiplication by $\frac{2}{3}$ is fairly straightforward, there is a more compact way to represent the process of repeated multiplication. If we measure the height of the ball after 8 rebounds, we have the following two ways to express this process in symbols:

$$4 \cdot \frac{2}{3} \cdot \frac{2}{3} \cdot \frac{2}{3} \cdot \frac{2}{3} \cdot \frac{2}{3} \cdot \frac{2}{3} \cdot \frac{2}{3} \cdot \frac{2}{3}$$
$$= 4 \cdot \left(\frac{2}{3}\right)^8$$

In general, if the ball rebounds n times, then the height after the nth rebound is given by the exponential expression below.

$$4 \cdot \left(\frac{2}{3}\right)^n$$

****

If the base of an exponential expression is a fraction such as $\left(\frac{2}{3}\right)^3$, then the expression can be evaluated as the quotient of the numerator raised to the third power, 2^3, and the denominator raised to the third power, 3^3. This is demonstrated below.

$$\left(\frac{2}{3}\right)^3 = \frac{2}{3} \cdot \frac{2}{3} \cdot \frac{2}{3} = \frac{2 \cdot 2 \cdot 2}{3 \cdot 3 \cdot 3} = \frac{2^3}{3^3} = \frac{8}{27}$$

When calculating an exponential expression like $4 \cdot \left(\frac{2}{3}\right)^3$ with pencil and paper, remember to follow the order of operations. Evaluate the exponent first, then multiply the result by 4.

$$4 \cdot \left(\frac{2}{3}\right)^3 = 4 \cdot \frac{2^3}{3^3} = \frac{4}{1} \cdot \frac{8}{27} = \frac{32}{27}$$

If a calculator is used, then be sure to insert parentheses in the right places and know the proper calculator key for evaluating exponents. On a scientific calculator, the exponent button might appear as y^x or x^y. On a graphing calculator or computer, the upward arrow symbol or caret ^ is used to raise a number or expression to a power. The base would be entered first, followed by the caret symbol, and then the exponent.

In the next Discovery Adventure, you will use a calculator as a tool to help improve your number sense. Use the calculator to quickly show you the solution to any arithmetic operation, only you can organize the information, look for patterns, and interpret the results.

▦ **Discovery Adventure 3: Products of Counting Numbers and Decimals**

Let's explore the effect of multiplying a natural number by decimals close to 0, $\frac{1}{2}$, and 1. Use your calculator to help complete the following table. Complete the columns by finding the product of the given counting number and the decimal values as shown in the table. Show the operation and solutions in columns 2, 3, and 4. The first row has been completed for you.

Counting Number	Product of Number and 0.05	Product of Number and 0.51	Product of Number and 0.95
20	$20 \cdot 0.05 = 1$	$20 \cdot 0.51 = 10.2$	$20 \cdot 0.95 = 19$
50			
100			
200			
500			
1000			

a. In the second column, you are multiplying each positive integer by a very small number close to 0. Compare the given positive integer in the first column with the product in the second column. Use a complete sentence to explain what happens to a positive integer when multiplied by 0.05.

_____

b. In the third column, you are multiplying each positive integer in the first column by a number very close to $\frac{1}{2}$. Compare the given positive integer in the first column with the product in the third column. Explain what happens to a positive integer when multiplied by 0.51.

_____

c. In the fourth column, you are multiplying each positive integer by a number very close to 1. Compare the given positive integer in the first column with the product in the fourth column. Explain what happens to a positive integer when multiplied by 0.95.

_____

Feedback

Multiplying a natural number by a decimal near 0 results in a product that is very small in comparison to the original number. For example, multiplying a natural number by 0.05 results in a value that is one-twentieth (or 5%) the size of the original number, or

$$0.05 = \frac{5}{100} = \frac{1}{20} = 5\%$$

Multiplying a natural number by a decimal near $\frac{1}{2}$ results in a product that is close to one-half the original number. In particular, multiplying a natural number by 0.51 results in a value that is 51% the size of the original number,

$$0.51 = \frac{51}{100} = 51\%$$

Multiplying a natural number by a number near 1 results in a number that is just a little less than the original number. For example, the product is nineteen-twentieth (or 95%) the size of the original number, or

$$0.95 = \frac{95}{100} = \frac{19}{20} = 95\%$$

In completing Discovery Adventure 3, you continue to build on your number sense. The activity makes use of the calculator as a tool to help you improve your ability to estimate answers and check if the exact calculations are reasonable. For example, if the sales tax on an item that cost $95.95 is 5%, you can estimate the tax by knowing that $0.05 \cdot \$100 = \$5.00$.

If a candidate for political office received 51% of the vote with 1987 people voting, then she should expect that about 1000 people voted for her. If 95% of the 5200 full-time students at your college have at least a part-time job, then there are about 5000 students employed.

This section has presented you with problem situations that allow you to explore the concept of multiplying and dividing rational numbers. The first two Discovery Adventures involve rational numbers in fractional form, while the third Discovery Adventure uses the decimal form.

The Section Exercises will give you a chance to practice what you have learned in the context of real and thought-provoking situations.

Section Exercises: 3.3

1. The trip from Boston to New York City is a distance of 206 miles. Complete the following table to see how the time traveling depends on the car's rate (speed) of travel. The time in hours can be calculated by finding the quotient of distance (in miles) and rate (in miles per hour), $\text{Time} = \dfrac{\text{Distance}}{\text{Rate}}$. Round time to the nearest tenth of an hour.

Rate (mph)	Time (hours)	Change in Time
10	20.6	
20	10.3	$10.3 - 20.6 = -10.3$
30		
40		
50		
60		
70		
80		
90		

a. As the rate increases, what happens to the travel time?

_____

_____

b. Compare the change in travel time between 10, 20, and 30 mph. What general statement can you make about increasing the rate when traveling at slower speeds?

_____

_____

c. Now compare the travel time between 60, 70, 80, and 90 mph. What general statement can you make about increasing the rate when traveling at faster speeds?

_____

_____

d. What does the negative symbol mean for each change in traveling time?

_____

_____

2. Use the following number line as a guide in selecting different rational numbers for variables a, b, c, and d. Make sure that each number you select is in fractional form.

$$-1 \qquad -\frac{1}{2} \qquad 0 \qquad \frac{1}{2} \qquad 1 \qquad 1\frac{1}{2} \qquad 2$$

Pick a number a between $-\frac{1}{2}$ and 0: $a =$ _____

Pick a number b between 0 and $\frac{1}{2}$: $b =$ _____

Pick a number c between $\frac{1}{2}$ and 1: $c =$ _____

Pick a number d between 1 and 2: $d =$ _____

In parts a through h, complete the following sentences by inserting: less than <, greater than >, or equal = in the space above the underline.

a. $b \cdot c$ ____ c

b. $b \cdot d$ ____ d

c. $d \div c$ ____ d

d. $b \div b$ ____ b

e. c ____ c^2

f. $a \cdot b \cdot c$ ____ b

g. a^2 ____ $a \div a$

h. b^3 ____ b^4

3. Answer the following True or False questions based on your knowledge of rational numbers. No calculations are to be done! Circle your answer and explain your reasoning using complete sentences.

a. True or False: $302 \cdot 0.74 > 302$ _____

_____

_____

b. True or False: $5.9 \cdot 0.97 < 6$ _____

_____

_____

c. True or False: $27.1 \cdot 1.04 > 27$ _____

_____

_____

d. True or False: $36 \div 0.5 = 18$ _____

_____

_____

e. True or False: $69.5 \div 1.95 > 69$ _____

_____

_____

f. True or False: $246.3 \div 0.52 > 500$ _____

_____

_____

g. True or False: $76.5 \div 1.3 < 76$ _____

_____

_____

h. True or False: $64 \cdot \dfrac{1}{4} = 16$ _____

_____

_____

i. True or False: $\dfrac{1}{2} \cdot \dfrac{8}{9} > \dfrac{1}{2}$ _____

_____

_____

j. Go back and verify all your answers for *a – i* using a calculator or pencil and paper.

4. In the problems below, estimate each product or quotient. Then place the decimal in the proper place to express the exact answer. By *estimate*, we mean that you should approximate each factor before mentally multiplying them together. Your rough estimate of the product or quotient should tell you where the decimal point belongs in the answer. For example,

$$0.537 \cdot 829.5 = 4454415$$

Since 0.537 is close to 0.5 or $\dfrac{1}{2}$ and 829.5 is near 800, we could figure that $\dfrac{1}{2}$ of 800 is 400, and the decimal would appear four places to the left of the last digit 5,

$$0.537 \cdot 829.5 = 445.4415 .$$

As you complete the following problems, be sure to do all the work in your head without the aid of a calculator or pencil and paper.

a. $6.872 \cdot 3.9 = 268008$

b. $18.91 \cdot 5.025 = 9502275$

c. $9.75 \cdot 252.25 = 24594375$

d. $8.29 \cdot 0.51 \cdot 59.72 = 252490188$

e. $76.34 \div 3.2 = 2385625$

f. $600.708 \div 88.6 = 678$

g. $0.46 \div 0.4 = 115$

h. $73.764 \div 1.08 = 683$

🖩 **5.** Enter each decimal computation from Section Exercise #4 into your calculator. Find the answer, and then round off this result to the stated place value.

   a. Round parts *a*, *b*, and *c* (from Section Ex. #4) to the thousandths place.

   b. Round parts *d* and *e* (from Section Ex. #4) to the hundredths place.

   c. Round parts *f* and *g* (from Section Ex. #4) to the tenths place.

6. The United States uses the Fahrenheit scale to measure temperature, while most other countries use the Celsius scale. The following formula gives the relationship between Fahrenheit and Celsius:

$$F = \frac{9}{5} \cdot C + 32 \, ,$$

where F represents temperature in degrees Fahrenheit and C represents temperature in degrees Celsius. We can use this formula to convert a temperature given in Celsius to its Fahrenheit equivalent. For example, $-5°C$ (negative 5 degrees Celsius) can be substituted into the formula as follows,

$$F = \frac{9}{5} \cdot (-5) + 32$$

$$= \frac{9}{5} \cdot \frac{-5}{1} + 32$$

$$= \frac{9 \cdot -\overset{1}{\cancel{5}}}{\underset{1}{\cancel{5} \cdot 1}} + 32$$

$$= -9 + 32$$

$$= 23°$$

   Use this formula to answer parts *a – d* on the next page.

212

a. Suppose you are traveling to a country where the average high temperature is 30° Celsius during the season you will be going there. What is the temperature in degrees Fahrenheit? What kind of clothes should you pack to feel comfortable walking around the countryside? Show all work and express your answer using complete sentences.

_____

_____

b. On the day you arrive, the actual high temperature turns out to be 32° Celsius. If you call friends in the United States, then what can you report as the high temperature in degrees Fahrenheit? Show how to substitute into the formula, then state the answer, rounded to the nearest degree and using a complete sentence.

_____

_____

c. In the example shown above part _a,_ note that the computation has two steps. First you multiply the Celsius temperature by $\frac{9}{5}$. Then you take the result and add 32 to obtain the Fahrenheit temperature. Convert 95°F to Celsius by following the reverse process of what was just described. Show each step. _Hint:_ The first step in the reverse process should be to subtract 32 from the Fahrenheit temperature, then to divide the result by $\frac{9}{5}$ or equivalently, multiply by $\frac{5}{9}$.

d. State the reverse process completed in part _c_ as a formula that can take a temperature in °F and convert it to a temperature in °C.

7. As of January 2000, *The Hunger Site* on the World Wide Web (www.thehungersite.com) has allowed you to click on a button to make a free donation of food to hungry people around the world. Sponsors of the site pay for each donation, which a person can make once per day. The number of sponsors on any given day can vary with each daily sponsor paying for $\frac{1}{4}$ cup of food per donation.

   a. If there are 4 sponsors for a particular day, then how many cups of food does each donation generate?

   b. If there are 5 sponsors for a particular day, then how many cups of food does each donation generate?

   c. If there are 6 sponsors for a particular day, then how many cups of food does each donation generate?

   d. If a particular day has 5 sponsors and 300,000 donations, then how many cups of food are given to hungry people?

8. The monthly bill from your gas company includes information that compares current usage with usage one year ago. It also compares temperature since this is a factor in how much gas you used.

Usage	Current	Year Ago
Billing Days	27	29
Therms Used	138	157
Avg Daily Usage		
Avg Daily Temp	48	45

   a. Find the average daily usage for the current year's billing period and a similar billing period one year ago. Round your answers to the tenths place, and record the results in the table above.

b. Does the bill indicate any changes in average daily usage? If so, explain possible reasons for the change between this year's billing cycle versus one year ago.

_____

_____

_____

c. The following list shows how the cost of gas is calculated. Do the calculation on each type of charge and record the result in the last column. Then find and enter the total charges for gas in the last row, last column.

Type of Charge (delivery and supplier charges)	Calculation (therms) × (cost per therm)	Charges (dollars)
Customer charge	none	$7.6300
Distribution charge (first 90 therms)	90×0.4000	
Distribution charge (last 48 therms)	48×0.2076	
Distribution adjustment	138×0.0048	
Supplier Charge: Cost of gas	138×0.5567	
Total Charges for Gas		

d. Why are there two rows of calculations for the distribution charge? Explain.

_____

_____

_____

e. The cost of gas at $0.5567 per therm and the distribution adjustment at $0.0048 per therm are the largest and smallest types of charges, respectively. First, explain what these values mean in terms of money. Then describe how each rate affects your total bill.

_____

_____

_____

_____

215

9. Observe the table below, displaying your energy conservation report (part of your electric bill). Complete the last column, giving the amount of kilowatts per day for this year and last year. Round to the nearest kilowatt.

Bill Term	Bill Days	kWh Use	kWh/Day
This Year	33	309	
Last Year	31	582	

a. Explain why rounding the answer is more helpful to the consumer when comparing daily usage. Then make a general statement comparing this year's usage to last year's usage.

_____

_____

_____

b. The table below shows how the cost of electricity is calculated. Complete the table using the following steps:

- Multiply the cost per kWh by the number of kWh used over the 33 days this year to obtain the cost for each service. Enter the cost to the nearest cent in the last column.

- Calculate the total cost of electricity by totaling all the numbers in the last column under cost.

- Be careful when adding the total cost. The fuel adjustment credit (CR) should be considered a negative number since its value is subtracted from the usual service charges.

Services	Cost per kWh	×	kWh Used	=	Cost
Customer Charge					$1.34
Distribution Energy Charge	$0.03556	×	309 kWh	=	
Transition Energy Charge	$0.02000	×	309 kWh	=	
Fuel Adjustment Credit	$0.00400 CR	×	309 kWh	=	−
Energy Conservation Charge	$0.00310	×	309 kWh	=	
Renewable Energy Charge	$0.00100	×	309 kWh	=	
Transmission	$0.00489	×	309 kWh	=	
Generation Service	$0.03500	×	309 kWh	=	
Total Cost of Electricity					

10. Suppose your long distance calling service charges 8¢ per minute plus a 1¢ connection charge for each call. For example, the cost of a call lasting 18:09 (min:sec) would be calculated as shown below. **Note:** Since there are 60 seconds in a minute, $\dfrac{9}{60}$ is the fraction of a minute that is equivalent to 9 seconds.

$$0.08 \cdot \left(18 + \frac{9}{60}\right) + 0.01 = 1.462$$

a. Use the process just described to calculate the dollar amount of each call on your current month's bill, listed below. Round the cost of each call to the thousandths place. Then calculate the total time (min: sec) and amount (cost) for all the itemized calls.

Itemized Calls

number	min:sec	amount
1	18:09	$1.462
2	0:30	
3	0:37	
4	0:20	
5	30:03	
6	50:02	
7	6:13	
8	0:39	
total		

b. Suppose your records indicate that one year ago the monthly telephone bill had itemized calls totaling 85 minutes and costing $6.80. What seems to be the main reason for this year's increase?

_____

_____

_____

Section 3.4 Numbers That Are Not Rational

Math Talk

Let's talk about the words **"irrational," "perfect," "square," "cube,"** and **"root"** as they relate to mathematics and the everyday world.

There are numbers in mathematics that are not rational. In fact, they are called **irrational numbers**. But this does not mean the numbers are unreasonable or strange, although you are not likely to meet one in daily life. The set of irrational numbers does not contain whole numbers, integers, fractions, or decimals. Now after eliminating all these numbers you might wonder what could be left that would be of any use. Even though these numbers are not common, they form an important building block in developing our number sense. What might seem really strange about irrational numbers is that there are more of these numbers than there are rational numbers. Yet both the sets of rational numbers and irrational numbers are infinite.

As you read through this section, you will find that **perfect squares** and **perfect cubes** are special numbers that can be factored into other numbers that are equal. For example, the number 9 is a perfect square of 3 because 3^2 ($3 \cdot 3$) equals 9. The number 8 is not a perfect square because there does not exist a number squared (multiplied by itself) that equals 8. However, the number 8 is a perfect cube because 2^3 ($2 \cdot 2 \cdot 2$) equals 8. What makes these numbers perfect is their ability to be exactly factored into numbers that are equal. Observe the figures below as you contemplate the following questions:

How does a perfect square relate to a plane geometric figure with 4 equal sides?

How does a perfect cube relate to a solid geometric figure with 6 identical square sides?

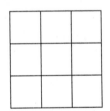

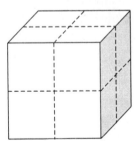

Do you see how the perfect squares 1, 4, 9, 16, and 25 are represented in the figure below?

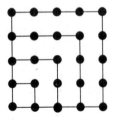

Finding a **root** is the inverse (or reverse process) of raising a number to a power. For example, a second root or square root is the inverse of raising a number to the second power (squaring). In particular, the square root of 9 is 3 because $3^2 = 9$. Also, the third root or cube root is the inverse of raising a number to the third power (cubing). In particular, the cube root of 8 is 2 because $2^3 = 8$. Therefore, perfect squares have exact square roots, and perfect cubes have exact cube roots.

In this section, you will do the following:

- Discover how square roots are used to find the length of the diagonal of a square.

- Investigate a geometric explanation of the Pythagorean theorem.

- Use the Pythagorean theorem to investigate square roots and irrational numbers.

- Explore the origins of π (Pi) through measuring the circumference and diameter of circular objects.

****

We have seen that a *rational number* is a number that can be expressed in fractional form as the ratio or quotient of two integers. In decimal form, a rational number is either a terminating decimal such as $\frac{1}{4} = 0.25$ or a repeating decimal such as $\frac{1}{3} = 0.3333\ldots$ or $0.\overline{3}$. But are there any numbers that cannot be expressed as the ratio or quotient of two integers? Let's investigate by looking at the operation of squaring and its inverse (reverse) operation, the **square root**.

The number 16 is the **square** of 4, written as 4^2. In general, a square is the product of two equal factors such as $4^2 = 4 \cdot 4 = 16$. Square numbers like 1, 4, 9, 16, 25 are called perfect squares of 1, 2, 3, 4, 5 because $1^2 = 1$, $2^2 = 4$, $3^2 = 9$, $4^2 = 16$, $5^2 = 25$, and so on.

The inverse (reverse) operation of squaring is called the *square root*. For example, 4 is the square root of 16, written as $\sqrt{16}$ or $16^{1/2}$. In general, the square root of a number is another number that when multiplied by itself is equal to the original number. Therefore, we say $\sqrt{16} = 4$ because $4^2 = 4 \cdot 4 = 16$.

But what about numbers such as 2 and 3 that are between the square numbers of 1 and 4? Do they have square roots that can be calculated?

Observe the following square roots and think about possible values for the question marks.

$$\sqrt{1} = 1 \qquad\qquad 1^{\frac{1}{2}} = 1$$

$$\sqrt{2} = ? \qquad\qquad 2^{\frac{1}{2}} = ?$$

or equivalently

$$\sqrt{3} = ? \qquad\qquad 3^{\frac{1}{2}} = ?$$

$$\sqrt{4} = 2 \qquad\qquad 4^{\frac{1}{2}} = 2$$

Let's take a specific look at $\sqrt{2}$ or $(2)^{\frac{1}{2}}$ using a **guess and test** procedure. In the table below, you are to *guess* a value between 0 and 1, *test* your guess by squaring the value, and then see how close the result is to the number 2. Continue to refine your guess, getting as close as possible to the number 2.

Guess	Test	Conclusion
1.5	$(1.5)^2 = (1.5) \cdot (1.5) = 2.25$	Too High
1.3	$(1.3)^2 = (1.3) \cdot (1.3) = 1.69$	Too Low

The reason you were asked to estimate the number $\sqrt{2}$ is because there is no exact rational number you can square (multiply by itself) to equal 2. The best you can do is to approximate the answer. Of course, a calculator is a faster tool for grinding out an estimate. If you enter $\sqrt{2}$ (the square root of 2) into a calculator, you will obtain the output,

$$\sqrt{2} \approx 1.414213562$$

The symbol $\approx$ means **approximately equal to**. So your calculator is finding an approximation just like when you were completing the guess and test table above. The big difference is that the calculator can be accurate out to 10 digits in less than a second. Multiplying the decimal 1.414213562 times itself will not give you 2. However, the product will be very close to the number 2. Usually, we do not need to carry out to this many digits and can think of $\sqrt{2}$ as about 1.4.

We cannot find a decimal exactly equal to $\sqrt{2}$ because there is no repeating or terminating decimal that can be squared to produce 2. Numbers like $\sqrt{2}$ that are not rational are said to be *irrational.* More formally, we can define an irrational number as follows.

> Any number that cannot be expressed as the ratio of two integers is a non-terminating and non-repeating decimal called an *irrational number.* In other words, an irrational number is a decimal value that continues endlessly but has no repeating sequence of digits.

Hence, $\sqrt{2}$ is an example of an irrational number, a decimal that never repeats or terminates but also never ends.

$$\sqrt{2} = 1.414213562...$$

The 3 dots after the last digit indicate that the digits keep going on indefinitely without any pattern.

Before working on the next Discovery Adventure, use the Brush Up feature below to review your understanding of right triangles.

Brush Up on Right Triangles

A *right angle* is a 90° angle occurring between two perpendicular lines. For example, in the figure below, the vertical and horizontal lines (sides a and b) are perpendicular and therefore meet at a right angle ($\angle C$) as denoted by the little box.

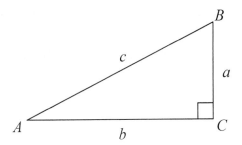

Angle C is a *right angle* (90°)

The sum of angles A, B, and C is 180°

Sides a and b are called *legs*

Side c is called the *hypotenuse*

A *right triangle* is a triangle that has a right angle. In a right triangle, the sides adjacent (or next to) the right angle are often called the legs, and the side opposite the right angle is the hypotenuse.

Discovery Adventure 1: Connecting Tiles to Form a Right Triangle

Suppose you have 3 squares of tiles, and each tile measures 1 square unit in area.

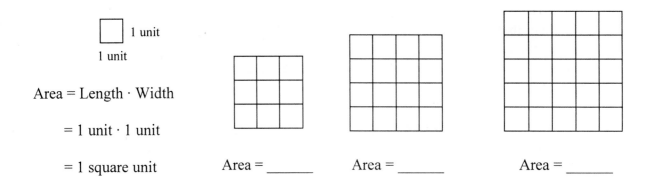

1 unit

1 unit

Area = Length · Width

   = 1 unit · 1 unit

   = 1 square unit

Area = _____   Area = _____   Area = _____

a. Find the area of each of the three squares and record the result in the space provided.

b. Express the area of one of the squares as the sum of the other two, using the whole numbers found in part *a*.

$$\underline{\qquad} = \underline{\qquad} + \underline{\qquad}$$

c. Record the same calculation as part *b*, but express each area in exponential form as a number squared.

$$\underline{\qquad} = \underline{\qquad} + \underline{\qquad}$$

d. Think about how you could arrange the three squares so that they enclose a right triangle (triangle with perpendicular lines that intersect to form a 90° angle.) Then draw a sketch of this figure below. *Hint:* Two of the squares meet at opposite corners and the third needs to be rotated so that two of its corners connect with one corner from each of the other squares.

Here is a geometrical picture of the 3 squares arranged so that a right triangle is formed.

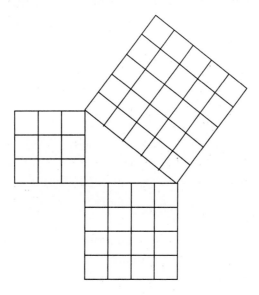

e. If each tile is one square unit, then

• What is the length of the base of the right triangle?

• What is the height of the right triangle?

• What is the length of the side opposite the 90° angle (called the hypotenuse)?

f. In the space below, construct the right triangle from the figure above and label the length of each side as found in part *e*.

g. If you are the foreman for the construction of a building, explain how you can use the above concept to verify that every corner in the building is *square* or 90°?

_____

_____

_____

h. Generalize this situation in the space below. Construct a right triangle where the sides adjacent the right angle are labeled *a* and *b* and the side opposite the 90° angle (hypotenuse) is labeled *c*.

i. Based on previous work, set up a right triangle equation using *a*, *b*, and *c*. *Hint*: Your equation should describe that the hypotenuse squared equals the sum of the squares of the other two sides.

Feedback

A right triangle with hypotenuse *c* and legs *a* and *b* is pictured below.

A right triangle has a 90° angle located at the point where the vertical and horizontal lines intersect.

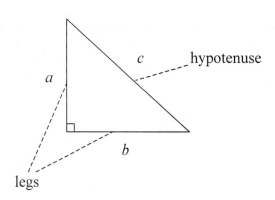

The right triangle equation developed in part *i* of the last adventure is called the **Pythagorean theorem** and is formally defined below.

The **Pythagorean theorem** states that given a right triangle, the hypotenuse squared equals the sum of the squares of the other two sides. If *a* and *b* are the sides adjacent to the right angle (called the legs) and *c* is the side opposite the right angle (called the hypotenuse), then

$$c^2 = a^2 + b^2 \quad \text{or} \quad (hypotenuse)^2 = (leg)^2 + (other\ leg)^2$$

Discovery Adventure 2: The Diagonal of a Square

a. Draw a 1 by 1 unit square on the number line below, so that the base is sitting on the line segment between 0 and 1.

b. Draw a diagonal line from point 0 to the upper right hand corner of your square. Label the diagonal *c*.

c. What is the distance along the base from 0 to 1?

d. Since all sides of a square have the same length, what is the height of the right triangles you have constructed?

e. The right triangles above have two legs, with each leg measuring 1 unit and the hypotenuse (diagonal) having some unknown length, *c*. Use the Pythagorean theorem to fill in the missing entries in the equation below, then try to find the length of *c* by solving the equation.

$$(\quad)^2 = (\quad)^2 + (\quad)^2$$

Feedback

The figure drawn in the last adventure should have been a square with diagonal *c*, such as

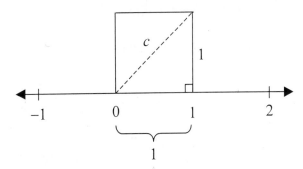

The diagonal splits the square into two right triangles and allows us to apply the Pythagorean theorem to obtain the following equation.

$$c^2 = 1^2 + 1^2$$
$$c^2 = 1 + 1$$
$$c^2 = 2$$

225

The diagonal c can be found by figuring out what value squared is equal to 2. Do you know a positive number taken to the second power that equals 2?

Recall that the inverse of the squaring operation is taking the square root, symbolized by using a *radical* $\sqrt{}$ or raising the number to the $\dfrac{1}{2}$ power, $()^{\frac{1}{2}}$. Therefore, the positive number squared (multiplied by itself) equal to 2 can be expressed by

$$c = \sqrt{2} \quad \text{or} \quad c = (2)^{\frac{1}{2}}$$

This reads as *c equals the square root of 2* and is approximately 1.414 rounded to the thousandths place. Since the inverse of squaring a number is finding the square root of the result,

$$\sqrt{25} = 5 \quad \text{because} \quad 5^2 = 25.$$

In words, the square root of twenty-five is five because five squared is 25.

In Discovery Adventure 3, we will explore the origins of perhaps the most famous irrational number, as represented by the Greek letter π (Pi). This important irrational number appears in many of the geometric formulas that we will study in Chapter 5.

Discovery Adventure 3: A Problem with Pie (Pi)

To begin this adventure you will need the following materials.

Materials:
1) a metric ruler that measures centimeters (cm.), 2) a piece of thread or string that is at least as long as the ruler, and 3) a number of circular objects (tin can, cup, ring, etc.) that the string can fit around.   The string will be used to measure the circumference (distance around a circle).

a. For each circular object, complete the following steps:

1. Record the object you are measuring in the first column of the table.
2. Measure the circumference by wrapping the string around your circular object and marking off one complete wrap-around.
3. Straighten out the string and use your ruler to measure the circumference to the nearest centimeter. Record the result in the second column of the table.
4. Take a metric ruler and measure the diameter (the straight-line distance from one side of the circle, through the center, to the other side) to the nearest centimeter and record the result in third column.
5. Complete the last column by calculating the circumference divided by the diameter. Round your answer to the hundredths place.
6. Repeat the five steps above with at least four other circular objects.

Circular Object	Circumference	Diameter	Circumference / Diameter

b. Explain any pattern you observe in the last column.

_____

_____

_____

c. Suppose one of the objects measures a circumference of 19 cm and a diameter of 6 cm. Explain what happens to the units (centimeters) when you divide centimeter by centimeter in calculating the last column results,

$$\frac{19 \text{ cm}}{6 \text{ cm}}$$

_____

_____

Feedback

The numbers in the last column should be a little over 3, such as 3.1, 3.2, 3.16, 3.14, etc. These values are all approximations to a special irrational number called Pi, which is symbolized by the Greek letter π. If you enter π into your calculator, the following approximation appears as the output,

$$\pi \approx 3.141592654....$$

Again, note the use of the symbolic relation, $\approx$, meaning *approximately equal to* and the three dots which tells us that this number is an endless, non-repeating, non-terminating decimal.

If the circumference is represented by C and the diameter by d, then we can define π using the following equation:

$$\frac{C}{d} = \pi$$

Since the inverse of division is multiplication, we can rewrite this equation in the following format:

$$C = \pi \cdot d$$

Now we will define the largest set of numbers that you will use in this book.

The **real numbers** are the combination of the rational and irrational numbers. Any real number can be graphed as a point on the number line, and each point on the number line can be represented by a real number.

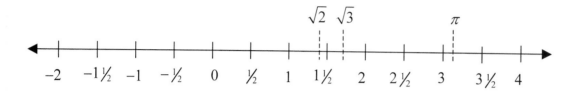

To end this section, we will examine the symbols and rules for *radicals* or *roots*.

A *radical sign*, denoted by the symbol $\sqrt{}$, is placed before a number to indicate that its root is to be extracted. A superscript before or above the radical sign indicates the *order* of the root. For example,

$\sqrt[3]{7}$ symbolizes the third root or cube root of 7.

This superscript is called the **index**. If no superscript appears, then we assume the radical implies the second root or square root. For example,

$\sqrt{3}$ symbolizes the square root of 3.

Another way to symbolize a radical or root is to use a fractional exponent whose denominator indicates the root. For example,

$(7)^{1/3}$ means the third root or cube root of 7, and

$(3)^{1/2}$ means the square root of 3.

In general, if x and y represent any real number and n is a whole number greater than or equal to 2, then

$$x^{1/n} = \sqrt[n]{x}.$$

Finally, the two rules for radicals are given below along with an example of each.

Rules for Radicals: Let the index n be a positive integer and each root be a real number.

Product Rule: $\sqrt[n]{x \cdot y} = \sqrt[n]{x} \cdot \sqrt[n]{y}$ For example, $\sqrt[3]{2} \cdot \sqrt[3]{4} = \sqrt[3]{2 \cdot 4} = \sqrt[3]{8} = 2$

Quotient Rule: $\sqrt[n]{\dfrac{x}{y}} = \dfrac{\sqrt[n]{x}}{\sqrt[n]{y}}$ $(y \neq 0).$ For example, $\sqrt{\dfrac{3}{4}} = \dfrac{\sqrt{3}}{\sqrt{4}} = \dfrac{\sqrt{3}}{2}$

In this section we investigated the set of irrational numbers by looking at such numbers as $\sqrt{2}$ and π. We also defined the set of real numbers as all rational and irrational numbers together. All the other sets of numbers we have studied are subsets of the real numbers. See the figure below to view how all these number sets are interrelated.

Real Numbers

Rational Numbers:
Ratio of two integers,
decimals that repeat or end

$\dfrac{5}{6}$, 0.80, $\dfrac{3}{2}$, $0.\overline{3}$, 57

Irrational Numbers:
Decimals that do not
repeat or end

π, $\sqrt{2}$, 2π, $\sqrt{3}$

Integers:
Positive and negative
counting numbers and zero

$\cdots\ -2,\ -1,\ 0,\ 1,\ 2,\ \cdots$

Non-Integers:
Fractions, decimals
(that repeat or end)
and percents

$\dfrac{3}{4}$, 0.75, 75%

Whole Numbers:
Positive integers and zero

0, 1, 2, 3, $\cdots$

Natural Numbers:
Positive integers

1, 2, 3, $\cdots$

229

Section Exercises: 3.4

1. For each right triangle below, measure all the sides to the nearest millimeter (mm) using a metric ruler. Record your results in the table and compute the remaining columns with the help of your calculator.

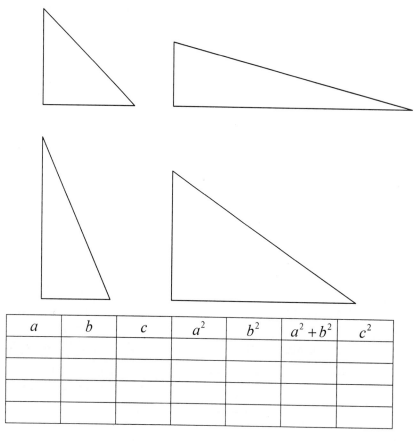

a	b	c	a^2	b^2	$a^2 + b^2$	c^2

a. Explain any patterns you see in the table.

_____

_____

_____

b. If the Pythagorean theorem is true, then should the last two columns be exactly the same? Explain your reasoning.

_____

_____

_____

2. Circle whether the following real numbers are rational or irrational. Explain your reasoning in words using complete sentences.

a. $\frac{2}{3}$, rational or irrational? _____

_____

_____

b. 0.125, rational or irrational? _____

_____

_____

c. $2 \cdot \pi$, rational or irrational? _____

_____

_____

d. $\frac{12}{5}$, rational or irrational? _____

_____

_____

e. $\sqrt{7}$, rational or irrational? _____

_____

_____

f. $5^{\frac{1}{2}}$, rational or irrational? _____

_____

_____

g. $-2\frac{5}{8}$, rational or irrational? _____

_____

_____

h. $\sqrt{64}$, rational or irrational? _____

_____

_____

3. There is an error in each of the following expressions. Point out the error and use mathematical reasoning to explain why there is an error. *Note*: When evaluating numerical expressions using the *order of operations* (shown again below), consider the square root on the same level as exponents or powers. For example, $\sqrt{2} = \left(2\right)^{\frac{1}{2}}$.

Order of Operations
1. Evaluate whatever is enclosed in grouping symbols first, like parentheses, brackets, braces, and a fraction bar.
2. Exponents or powers and square roots are evaluated next.
3. Multiply and divide from left to right.
4. Add and subtract from left to right.

---

a. $\sqrt{2} + \sqrt{2} = \sqrt{4}$

_____

_____

_____

b. $2\sqrt{3} = \sqrt{6}$

_____

_____

_____

c. $\sqrt{16} - \sqrt{9} = \sqrt{7}$

_____

_____

_____

d. $\quad \sqrt{100} - 10 = \sqrt{90}$

_____

_____

_____

4. High Tech Place began with a few small start-up companies but has grown to become a large technology park with a dozen different companies. The only way to access the park from the main highway is to travel 5 miles along Horizontal Way, then make a 90° left turn onto Vertical Line Road and travel 3 miles until the road ends at High Tech Place. A new Access Road has been proposed to relieve heavy traffic and to shorten the commute. Observe the situation and answer the questions below.

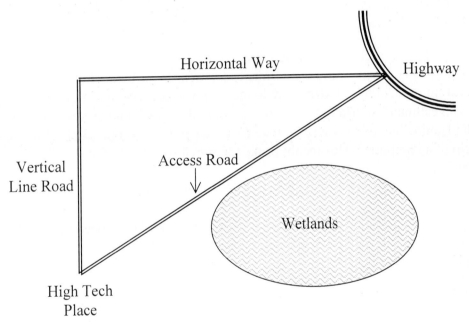

a. Find the length, to the nearest tenth of a mile, of the proposed access road. Show all work.

b. The speed limit along Vertical Line Road and Horizontal Way is 35 mph. The larger access road will have a speed limit of 50 mph. Assuming each vehicle keeps a constant speed, how much travel time will be saved using the Access Road? Show all work and answer in a complete sentence.

_____

_____

    c.   What must the project development team consider before moving ahead with the construction of a new access road?

_____

_____

_____

_____

_____

_____

_____

_____

5. We live in a world full of challenges where most of us can only dream of setting a record for being the best in some event. People continue to set records for being the human who can run the fastest, jump the highest, dance the longest, and so on. There is a race in mathematics to see who can estimate the irrational number π out to the most number of places. In 1989, Gregory and David Chudnovsky were able to carry out π to over a billion decimal places with the help of a computer. This record broke the previous record of 536,870,000 decimal places set by Yasumasa Kaneda in the same year. Kaneda had broken an even earlier record of 530 million set by none other than Gregory and David Chudnovsk.

Assuming computers continue to increase their storage capacity and speed (at which information is processed), will there ever be a final record that cannot be surpassed? Explain using complete sentences.

_____

_____

_____

6. In Discovery Adventure 3, you approximated π by measuring the circumference and diameter of a circle and then calculating their ratio. A more accurate method involves using a formula based on the odd counting numbers. For example,

$$\pi = 4\left(1 - \frac{1}{3} + \frac{1}{5} - \frac{1}{7} + \frac{1}{9} - \ldots\right)$$

Using three terms from the above expression gives the following estimate:

$$4\left(1 - \frac{1}{3} + \frac{1}{5}\right) = \frac{52}{15} \text{ or } 3.4\overline{6}$$

a. Show the steps that are necessary to obtain the previous estimate of $\dfrac{52}{15}$.

b. Use four terms from the formula to obtain another estimate. Show all work.

c. Use five terms from the formula to obtain another estimate. Show all work.

d. Suppose you want to use 100 terms or more, but do not want to complete the work with pencil and paper. How would you proceed in obtaining an estimate of π?

_____

_____

_____

Note: The Chudnovskys set the record by using a formula that is more complicated and efficient than the one given in this exercise.

7. In this problem you will investigate the meaning of the cube root of a number n, symbolized by $\sqrt[3]{n}$. For example, $\sqrt[3]{8}$ means the number whose cube is 8. In other words, suppose 8 is the result of multiplying a number by itself three times. Find that number.

    a. Complete the following table of cube roots.

Input n	Cube Root $\sqrt[3]{n}$	Output
1		
8	$\sqrt[3]{8}$	2
27		
64		
125		

    b. What is the relationship between the input and the output?

_____

_____

_____

    c. Since to cube is the inverse of finding the cube root, let's cube the outputs from part *a* to show that the reverse process gives the original input from part *a*. In other words, enter the outputs from part *a* as inputs to cube. Then verify that cubing results in outputs that correspond to the inputs from part *a*. Recall that cubing is the result of multiplying a number by itself three times or finding the third power of a number.

Input n	Cube n^3	Output
1		
2	2^3	8
3		
4		
5		

d. Let's take the cube root of some unfriendly input values; that is, the cube root of these values are irrational numbers. Complete the table by approximating each cube root to obtain a decimal output rounded to the thousandths place.

Input n	Cube Root $\sqrt[3]{n}$	Output
2	$\sqrt[3]{2}$	1.260
3		
4		
10		
100		
1001		
10000		

e. Why do you think the input for row 7 was chosen to be 1001 instead of 1000?

_____

_____

_____

f. As the input values get larger and larger, explain how the output values increase.

_____

_____

_____

g. If you cube the decimal approximations in the output column, would the result equal the original input value? Explain.

_____

_____

_____

8. In this problem you will explore an alternative notation for square root. Use your calculator to complete the table below. Look for patterns as you proceed and round your output to the hundredths place. *Calculator Note:* You will probably have to put the exponent in parentheses when doing your power calculations, so that the machine knows to take the input to the correct power, $\frac{1}{2}$.

Input n	Raise to ½ Power $n^{1/2}$	Output
1	$1^{1/2}$	1
2	$2^{1/2}$	1.41
3		
4		
5		
6		
7		
8		
9		

a. What is the connection between $n^{1/2}$ and $\sqrt{n}$? Explain using complete sentences.

_____

_____

_____

b. What do you think $n^{1/3}$ symbolizes? Explain in words and state the alternative symbol for this operation.

_____

_____

_____

c. Use your calculator to experiment with the alternative notation for cube root, $n^{1/3}$. Check the results obtained in Section Exercise #7, parts *a* and *d*, on pages 236-237.

9. Find the following positive square roots without using a calculator. Check your work by squaring the result.

$$\sqrt{1} = \underline{\hspace{1cm}} \quad \text{because} \quad (\underline{\hspace{1cm}})^2 = 1$$

$$\sqrt{4} = \underline{\hspace{1cm}} \quad \text{because} \quad (\underline{\hspace{1cm}})^2 = 4$$

$$\sqrt{9} = \underline{\hspace{1cm}} \quad \text{because} \quad (\underline{\hspace{1cm}})^2 = 9$$

a. Based on the results found above, give an estimate (no calculator) of $\sqrt{2}$ and $\sqrt{3}$. Explain your reasoning.

_____

_____

_____

b. Give an estimate (no calculator) of $\sqrt{5}$, $\sqrt{6}$, $\sqrt{7}$, and $\sqrt{8}$. Explain your reasoning.

_____

_____

_____

c. Check your estimates. Record your work in the table below, rounding the output to the hundredths place when necessary.

Input, n	0	1	2	3	4	5	6	7	8	9
Square Root, $\sqrt{n}$	$\sqrt{0}$	$\sqrt{1}$			$\sqrt{4}$					$\sqrt{9}$
Output	0	1			2					3

10. What negative numbers can you square to obtain 1, 4, and 9, respectively?

$$(\underline{\hspace{1cm}})^2 = 1$$

$$(\underline{\hspace{1cm}})^2 = 4$$

$$(\underline{\hspace{1cm}})^2 = 9$$

a. What two values would be possible solutions for the variables x, y, and z, in the equations below?

If $x^2 = 1$, then $x =$ _____ or $x =$ _____

If $x^2 = 4$, then $x =$ _____ or $x =$ _____

If $x^2 = 9$, then $x =$ _____ or $x =$ _____

b. To help solve for the variables in the following equations, use the concept that the inverse of squaring is finding the square root. Observe the model problem below, and then solve the rest in a similar fashion.

Solve:

$a^2 = 2$

$a = \sqrt{2}$ or $a = -\sqrt{2}$

$a = \pm\sqrt{2}$

Check:

$\sqrt{2} \cdot \sqrt{2} = \sqrt{2 \cdot 2} = \sqrt{4} = 2$

$\left(-\sqrt{2}\right) \cdot \left(-\sqrt{2}\right) = \sqrt{2 \cdot 2} = \sqrt{4} = 2$

- $b^2 = 3$

- $c^2 = 5$

- $d^2 = 15$

- $h^2 = 16$

11. In Discovery Adventure 1: Connecting Tiles to Form a Right Triangle, you investigated the Pythagorean theorem using a 3-4-5 right triangle (3-4-5 meaning the length of the hypotenuse is 5 units and the others two sides have lengths of 3 and 4 units). In general, we found that the hypotenuse c squared equals the sum of the squares of the other two sides, a and b, such that,

$$c^2 = a^2 + b^2$$

The triple $a = 3$, $b = 4$, and $c = 5$ gives one possible solution to this equation. Which of the following triples are solutions to the equation above? Answer in a complete sentence and explain your reasoning.

a. The triple $a = 5$, $b = 12$, and $c = 13$

_____

_____

b. The triple $a = 8$, $b = 15$, and $c = 17$

_____

_____

c. The triple $a = 9$, $b = 13$, and $c = 16$

_____

_____

d. The triple $a = 6$, $b = 8$, and $c = 10$

_____

_____

Chapter 3 Summary

Key Terms

Section 3.1

- **Rational** – A value that can be expressed as the ratio of two integers. (see **Fraction** below)
- **Fraction** – A value expressed as the ratio of two integers. For example, given two quantities a and b, the ratio of a to b is a fraction denoted by

$$\frac{a}{b} \text{ or } {}^{a}\!/\!_{b} \text{ or } a/b \quad (b \neq 0).$$

- **Decimal** – A fraction expressed in place-value notation with base 10. A decimal is denoted by a dot, after which digits are placed according to the value to be expressed. For example,

$$0.7 = \frac{7}{10}, \quad 0.75 = \frac{75}{100}, \quad 0.752 = \frac{752}{1000} \quad \text{and} \quad 0.752 = \frac{7}{10} + \frac{5}{100} + \frac{2}{1000}$$

- **Numerator** – In a fraction, the number on the top, above the fraction bar.
- **Denominator** – In a fraction, the number on the bottom, below the fraction bar.
- **Rational Number** – A number that can be expressed in fractional form as the ratio or quotient of two integers.
- **Ratio** – The quotient of two numbers or quantities of the same measure. Comparing two quantities using division is known as *finding their ratio*.
- **Simplify** – To reduce an expression to a simpler form. For example, you *simplify* a fraction by dividing out (canceling) any common factors.
- **Fundamental Principle of Fractions** – The value of a fraction will not change when multiplying the numerator and the denominator by the same (non-zero) number.
- **Equivalent Fractions** – Two fractions that have the same value.
- **Divisors** – All the numbers (also called *factors*) that divide evenly into another number.
- **Reducing** – Simplifying a fraction by dividing out (canceling) any common factors.
- **Lowest Terms** – A fraction is simplified to *lowest terms* when the numerator and denominator have no common factor except 1.
- **Quotient** – One interpretation of rational numbers in which a number of objects are equally divided into a number of groups. For example, in Discovery Adventure 3: Fair Share, we *divide* the total number of cookies (objects) available by the number of people (groups) sharing.
- **Terminating Decimals** – Rational numbers in decimal form that have an end to the digits to the right of the decimal point.
- **Significant Digits** – The digits of a number that express a value to a certain degree of accuracy. For example, the irrational number $\pi = 3.14159...$ can be approximated to 5 significant digits as 3.1416, four significant digits as 3.142, and 3 significant digits as 3.14.
- **Repeating Decimals** – Rational numbers in decimal form that have a pattern of digits that repeat without end to the right of the decimal point.

Section 3.2

- **Common Denominator** – An integer that divides evenly into all the denominators of a group of fractions.
- **Least Common Denominator** – The smallest (least) integer that divides evenly into all the denominators of a group of fractions.
- **Reduced** – Simplified into an equivalent form. A fraction is *reduced* when there are no common factors to divide out of the numerator and denominator.
- **Proper Fraction** – A fraction where the numerator has an absolute value that is less than the denominator. Hence, *proper fractions* have absolute values less than 1.
- **Improper Fraction** – A fraction where the numerator has a greater absolute value than the denominator. Hence, *improper fractions* have absolute values greater than 1.
- **Mixed Number** – A number having an integer part and a fractional part. For example, $2\frac{1}{4}$ has a whole number part 2 and a fractional part $\frac{1}{4}$.
- **Rectangle** – A 4-sided geometric object that has 4 right angles and opposite sides parallel and equal in length. A *square* is a special case of a rectangle with 4 sides of equal length.

Section 3.3

- **Per** – Means "for each" and indicates the operation of division. For example, a vehicle traveling at a speed of 55 miles *per* hour means that the vehicle travels 55 miles for each hour of time. This can be expressed in the form of a fraction where division is implied,

$$55 \text{ miles per 1 hour} \quad \text{or} \quad \frac{55 \text{ miles}}{1 \text{ hour}}$$

- **Of** – In certain contexts, this word implies the operation of multiplication.

  For example, "25% *of* the 200 people answered yes" implies $0.25 \cdot 200$ or $\frac{1}{4} \cdot 200$.

Section 3.4

- **Irrational Numbers** – Any number that cannot be expressed as the ratio of two integers is a non-terminating and non-repeating decimal called an *irrational number*. All real numbers that are not rational must be irrational.
- **Perfect Squares** – A number that is the square of an integer. For example, 1, 4, 9, 16, … are perfect squares because $1^2 = 1$, $2^2 = 4$, $3^2 = 9$, $4^2 = 16$.
- **Perfect Cubes** – A number that is the cube of an integer. For example, 1, 8, 27, 64, … are perfect cubes because $1^3 = 1$, $2^3 = 8$, $3^3 = 27$, $4^3 = 64$.
- **Root** – Finding a *root* is the inverse (reverse process) of raising to a power.
- **Square Root** – The *square root* of a number is another number that when multiplied by itself is equal to the original number. Therefore, we say $\sqrt{36} = 6$ because $6^2 = 6 \cdot 6 = 36$.
- **Square** – To *square* an expression means to raise it to the second power. A *square* is the product of two equal factors such as $7^2 = 7 \cdot 7 = 49$.

- **Guess and Test** – A method for finding the solution to a problem. The procedure involves making a guess at the solution, and then testing how close your guess comes to the desired value. Each new guess is based on the results of the previous guesses. You continue to guess and test until the solution is found or a close approximation is obtained.
- **Approximately Equal To** – Very close (within a desired degree of accuracy) to the exact value.
- **Pythagorean Theorem** – Given a right triangle, the hypotenuse squared equals the sum of the squares of the other two sides. If a and b are the sides adjacent to the right angle (called the legs) and c is the side opposite the right angle (called the hypotenuse), then

$$c^2 = a^2 + b^2 \quad \text{or} \quad \left(hypotenuse\right)^2 = \left(leg\right)^2 + \left(other\ leg\right)^2$$

- **Real Numbers** – The sets of rational and irrational numbers taken together as one set.
- **Index** – A number that indicates the exponent or root. For example, the exponential expression 5^2 has an index of 2, and the radical expression $\sqrt[3]{27}$ has an index of 3.

****

Questions for Review

1. Can you use figures to represent fractions? For example, suppose each rectangle represents a sheet cake that has been divided into an equal number of pieces. Use fractions to represent the shaded part (pieces left) and the unshaded part (pieces taken) from each sheet cake.

Shaded _____

Unshaded _____

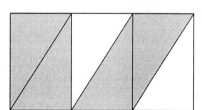

Shaded _____

Unshaded _____

Shaded _____

Unshaded _____

Shaded _____

Unshaded _____

2. Can you recognize equivalent fractions? Find the two figures from question #1 that represent equivalent fractions. Fill in the two blanks below to the left, to show the equivalence of two fractions that use different numbers to represent the same shaded part of the whole. Then, below to the right, do the same for the unshaded part of the whole.

Shaded: _____ = _____   Unshaded: _____ = _____

3. Do you know what a rational number is? Use complete sentences to explain to a friend how a rational number can be expressed as a fraction or a decimal.

_____

_____

_____

_____

4. Can you use the concept of ratio to make a comparison between two quantities? The table on the next page gives some data on the population of a certain mathematics class by race. There are a total of 36 students enrolled in this class. You will be asked to set up a ratio to compare the number of people of each race with the total number of students in the class. The ratio will be expressed as a fraction, decimal, and percent. Go to part *a* on the next page to get specific directions on how to fill in the table.

Race	Number of Students	Ratio: $\dfrac{\text{Number of Students}}{\text{Total in Class}}$	Decimal	Percent
Hispanic	6	$\dfrac{6}{36} = \dfrac{1}{6}$	0.167	16.7%
White	16			
Black	10			
Native American	1			
Asian	3			

a. Complete the third column of the table by finding the ratio of the number of each race of students to the total number of students in the class. Express each ratio as a fraction in reduced form.

b. Complete the fourth column of the table by converting each fraction in the third column to a decimal. Round your results to the thousandths place when necessary.

c. Complete the fifth column of the table by converting each decimal to a percent.

d. What information from the table tells you that 1 out of every 6 students is Hispanic?

_____

_____

e. Use the *fundamental principle of fractions* to show that $\dfrac{1}{6}$ and $\dfrac{6}{36}$ are equivalent fractions.

f. Show how to simplify $\dfrac{16}{36}$ to lowest terms by dividing the numerator and denominator by a common factor.

5. Do you know a way to determine if a fraction is close to 0, $\frac{1}{2}$, or 1? For example, a fraction is close to 0 if the numerator is small relative to the denominator, close to $\frac{1}{2}$ if the denominator is about twice the size of the numerator, and close to 1 if the numerator and denominator are almost equal in size.

   a. Complete each of the four fractions below by filling in the numerator or denominator with a positive integer that will make the value of the fraction close to 0 but not equal to 0.

   $$\frac{4}{} \qquad \frac{}{32} \qquad \frac{10}{} \qquad \frac{}{100}$$

   b. Complete each of the four fractions below by filling in the numerator or denominator with a positive integer that will make the value of the fraction close to $\frac{1}{2}$ but not equal to $\frac{1}{2}$.

   $$\frac{4}{} \qquad \frac{}{32} \qquad \frac{10}{} \qquad \frac{}{100}$$

   c. Complete each of the four fractions below by filling in the numerator or denominator with a positive integer that will make the value of the fraction close to 1 but not equal to 1.

   $$\frac{4}{} \qquad \frac{}{32} \qquad \frac{10}{} \qquad \frac{}{100}$$

6. Can you convert an improper fraction to a mixed number? Suppose you have 10 candy bars and wish to give an equal amount to 4 friends. How much candy should each friend receive? Set up the problem as an improper fraction, then express your answer as a mixed number in simplest form.

7. Do you know how to convert a mixed number to an improper fraction? Suppose you have 100 shares of stock in a company called WebTech, currently listed at $15\frac{3}{4}$ dollars per share. You want to figure out the total value of all your shares based on the current listing.

   a. Convert $15\frac{3}{4}$ into an improper fraction.

b. Find the total value of your 100 shares using the improper fraction found in part *a*. Show all work.

8. How do you add and subtract fractional expressions? Evaluate the following problems. Express your answers in simplest form.

a. $\dfrac{1}{16}+\dfrac{3}{16}+\dfrac{8}{16}$

b. $\dfrac{7}{20}+\dfrac{3}{5}$

c. $3\dfrac{5}{8}+1\dfrac{1}{2}$

d. $\dfrac{1}{4}+\dfrac{1}{3}$

e. $\dfrac{3}{4}-\dfrac{7}{8}$

f. $\dfrac{5}{6}-\dfrac{5}{9}$

g. $22\dfrac{7}{32}-18\dfrac{29}{64}$

h. $5\dfrac{3}{8}-2\dfrac{1}{6}-7\dfrac{5}{12}$

9. Can you work with rational numbers in decimal form? Suppose you are thinking of purchasing 10 gallons of gas at a price of 1.35\frac{9}{10}$ per gallon.

   a. If price per gallon can be expressed as $1.359, then what does the $\frac{9}{10}$ represent?

   _____

   _____

   b. What is the total cost for 10 gallons of gas? Show the calculation you need to perform and the answer.

   c. If the price per gallon includes a tax of $0.50, then what would the price of gas be without paying tax? Show the calculation you need to perform and give the answer in two forms: to the thousandths place and to the hundredths place with a fraction of a cent.

   d. If the price per gallon (1.35\frac{9}{10}$ or $1.359) increases by 5¢, then show how to find the new price. Express your answer in two forms as in part *c*.

10. Do you know how to find the reciprocal of a number? For example, find the reciprocal of the following expressions.

    a. $\frac{1}{10}$ *b.* $\frac{9}{16}$

    c. -62 *d.* $\frac{x}{y}$

11. What procedure is used to multiply two fractions? For example, show the process needed to evaluate the following expressions.

a. $\dfrac{7}{3} \cdot \dfrac{4}{5}$

b. $\dfrac{3}{20} \cdot \dfrac{5}{9}$

c. $2\dfrac{1}{4} \cdot \dfrac{8}{27}$

d. $\dfrac{3}{4} \cdot 24$

12. The following recipe for *Chewy Cocoa Brownies* will make 2 dozen brownies.

$1\dfrac{2}{3}$ cups granulated sugar $\dfrac{3}{4}$ cup baking cocoa

$\dfrac{3}{4}$ cup butter or margarine $\dfrac{1}{2}$ teaspoon baking powder

2 tablespoons water   2 large eggs

$1\dfrac{1}{3}$ cups all purpose flour $\dfrac{1}{4}$ teaspoon salt

2 teaspoons vanilla   Sifted powdered sugar

a. How can you use multiplication to adjust the recipe and make a double batch or 4 dozen brownies?

_____

b. Use the method you gave in part *a* to calculate the amount of each ingredient listed below.

- Granulated sugar

- Baking cocoa

- Baking powder

- All purpose flour

- Salt

13. What procedure is used to divide two fractions? For example, show the process needed to evaluate the following expressions.

a. $\dfrac{2}{3} \div \dfrac{1}{12}$

b. $\dfrac{6/7}{3/5}$

c. $\dfrac{5}{8} \div 3$

d. $1\dfrac{7}{8} \div 2\dfrac{11}{32}$

14. Can you tell whether a real number is rational or irrational? For example, state whether the following numbers are rational or irrational, and explain your reasoning.

a. $-2\dfrac{3}{8}$ _____

_____

b. $\sqrt[3]{27}$ _____

_____

c. $\dfrac{\pi}{2}$ _____

_____

d. $\sqrt{7}$ _____

_____

e. $49^{\frac{1}{2}}$ _____

_____

f.   0.625 _____

_____

15. If a plane is flying due south at 100 mph and the wind blows from the east at 50 mph, then the flight path of the plane will be to the southwest. See the figure below.

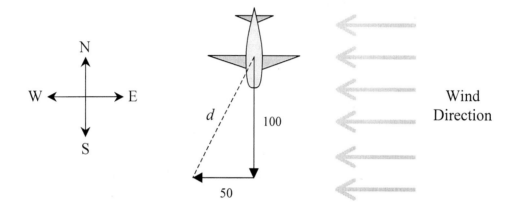

How far to the southwest will the plane travel after 1 hour? Round your answer to the nearest tenth of a mile. *Hint:* Since the directions south and west are at right angles, the plane's path of flight should be along hypotenuse *d*.

Chapter 3 Quiz

1. The fractions given below are close to either 0, $\frac{1}{2}$, or 1. Estimate which value that each fraction is closest to by using the following rules:

   - A fraction is close to 0 if the numerator is small when compared with the denominator.
   - A fraction is close to $\frac{1}{2}$ if the denominator is approximately two times as large as the numerator.
   - A fraction is close to 1 if the numerator and denominator are about equal.

   a. $\frac{4}{5}$ is close to _____   *b.* $\frac{1}{10}$ is close to _____

   c. $\frac{2}{23}$ is close to _____   *d.* $\frac{9}{17}$ is close to _____

   e. $\frac{45}{47}$ is close to _____   *f.* $\frac{5}{11}$ is close to _____

2. Suppose you have two recipes to make chocolate chip cookies. One recipe calls for $\frac{3}{4}$ cup of sugar and the other recommends $\frac{2}{3}$ cup of sugar. What is the difference in amounts of sugar for the two recipes?

3. Over the last 6 months, a teenager has grown $1\frac{1}{4}$ inches in height. If her previous height was $62\frac{1}{2}$ inches, then what is her new height?

4. The local school system has a policy that a student must live at least $1\frac{1}{2}$ miles from school to be eligible to ride on the school bus. In order to settle a dispute, the Vice Principal used his car to measure the distance from the high school to a certain house. Suppose the house missed the $1\frac{1}{2}$ mile cut off by $\frac{1}{16}$ of a mile. How far was the house from the high school? Express your answer as a mixed number and as a decimal rounded to the hundredths place.

5. The following recipe for *Chewy Cocoa Brownies* will make 2 dozen brownies.

$1\frac{2}{3}$ cups granulated sugar $\frac{3}{4}$ cup baking cocoa

$\frac{3}{4}$ cup butter or margarine $\frac{1}{2}$ teaspoon baking powder

2 tablespoons water   2 large eggs

$1\frac{1}{3}$ cups all purpose flour $\frac{1}{4}$ teaspoon salt

2 teaspoons vanilla   Sifted powdered sugar

  a. How can you use multiplication to adjust the recipe and make a half batch or 1 dozen brownies?

  _____

  b. Use the method you gave in part *a* to calculate the amount of each ingredient listed below.

   • Granulated sugar

   • Baking cocoa

   • Baking powder

- All purpose flour

- Salt

c. Suppose the only measuring cups available are $\frac{1}{4}$ cup, $\frac{1}{3}$ cup, $\frac{1}{2}$ cup, and 1 cup. Why would it be difficult to measure exact amounts of each ingredient needed to make a $\frac{1}{2}$ batch or 1 dozen brownies?

_____

_____

_____

6. It costs $1.25 to play a video game.

   a. How much will it cost to play the game 10 times?

   b. What is the maximum number of games you can play with $20?

7. Prove that the following statements are false.

   a. $\sqrt{36+64} = \sqrt{36} + \sqrt{64}$ *b.* $\sqrt{25-9} = \sqrt{25} - \sqrt{9}$

   c. $\sqrt{3} = 1.7$ *d.* $\sqrt{36} = 6^2$

8. Suppose you own a rectangular piece of land that measures $\frac{1}{4}$ mile on a side that is the length and $\frac{1}{8}$ mile on a side that is the width. See the figure below.

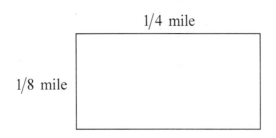

a. Find the area of the land (rectangle) by multiplying the length in miles times the width in miles to obtain a product in square miles (miles · miles $=$ miles²).

b. If one square mile equals 640 acres, then how many acres is this parcel of land?

c. Suppose you want to use 10 acres of the land to build a subdivision of new homes. The local government requires that any new housing construction to have at least $\frac{3}{4}$ acre of land to build on. It is estimated that 2 of the 10 acres must be set aside for access roads. If you want to build as many new homes as possible, then what is the maximum number of lots you can have in the subdivision? Show all work and explain your answer using complete sentences.

_____

_____

_____

9. The ancient Greeks were aware of a number called the *golden ratio* (see below). Some people believe the Greeks used the golden ratio to help construct architecture into shapes that were most pleasing to observe. The golden ratio is $\frac{1+\sqrt{5}}{2}$.

a. Since $\sqrt{5} \approx 2.2$, estimate the value of the golden ratio to the tenths place by substituting 2.2 in place of $\sqrt{5}$ and evaluating the above expression without the aid of a calculator.

b. Is $\sqrt{5}$ a rational or irrational number? Use complete sentences to support your answer with mathematical reasoning.

_____

_____

_____

10. Suppose you are on the 18th hole of your favorite golf course. See the figure below. The layout of this hole has most golfers hitting the ball 200 yards down the fairway, then the next shot is hit 150 yards at a right angle to the first drive. Although there are trees blocking any view of the flag (indicating the 18th hole), you know it is possible to hit a long drive over the trees to make the putting green in 1 stroke (shot).

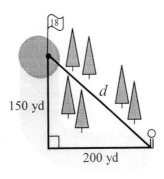

150 yd

d

200 yd

a. Use the Pythagorean theorem to estimate the distance you need to drive the ball across the trees to reach the putting green on the first shot.

b. The putting green is in the shape of a circle with a circumference of 90 yards. Find the diameter of the circular green to the nearest yard. _Hint_: diameter $= \dfrac{\text{circumference}}{\pi}$.

Cumulative Review Exercises: Chapters 1, 2, and 3

1. The numbers $\dfrac{9}{20} = 0.45$ and $\dfrac{11}{20} = 0.55$ are close to the number $\dfrac{1}{2} = 0.5$.

   a. Find a fraction that is closer to $\dfrac{1}{2}$ than $\dfrac{9}{20}$ but also less than $\dfrac{1}{2}$. Explain the reason why your fraction is closer.

   Fraction:

   _____

   _____

   b. Find a fraction that is closer to $\dfrac{1}{2}$ than $\dfrac{11}{20}$ but also greater than $\dfrac{1}{2}$. Explain the reason why your fraction is closer.

   Fraction:

   _____

   _____

2. A shoe store advertises that all their sneakers are $\dfrac{1}{3}$ off regular price. You are wondering how much it will cost to buy a pair of sneakers that are regularly $89.

   a. Calculate the discount by finding $\dfrac{1}{3}$ of $89. Round the discount to the nearest cent.

   b. What will the pair of sneakers cost before taxes are included?

   c. Suppose the tax rate is 5% of the price calculated in part *b*. Find the tax on the pair of sneakers, and round the tax to the nearest cent.

d. How much will the pair of sneakers cost after taxes are included?

3. Use the following three fractions: $\dfrac{11}{20}$, $\dfrac{5}{9}$, $\dfrac{6}{11}$ to answer the questions below.

a. Convert each fraction to decimal form.

b. State whether each number is a repeating decimal or terminating (ending) decimal and explain your reasoning.

_____

_____

_____

c. List each number in order from smallest to largest, then explain your reasoning.

Smallest: _____   Middle: _____   Largest: _____

_____

_____

_____

4. Why do we use exponential notation? What happens when we raise a number to a power? Let's examine these questions by looking at the number of ancestors you have. Consider your parents as 1 generation back, grandparents as 2 generations back, great grandparents as 3 generations, and so on. Complete the following table to gather some data. In columns 2, 3, and 4, express the number of ancestors from that generation using the different forms indicated. Then calculate the total ancestors you have going back each number of generations.

Generations Back	Ancestors (Repeated Multiplication)	Ancestors (Exponential Notation)	Ancestors (Integer Form)	Total Ancestors
1	2	2^1	2	2
2	$2 \cdot 2$	2^2	4	6
3	$2 \cdot 2 \cdot 2$			
4				
5				
6				
7				

a. Draw a tree diagram that shows all your ancestors going back 3 generations or to your great grandparents.

b. How many ancestors do you have from the tenth generation? Express your answer using the three forms used in the table.

c. How many ancestors do you have from the *n*th generation where *n* is any positive integer?

d. What is the total number of ancestors you have going back 10 generations?

    e. What is the total number of ancestors you have going back *n* generations?

5. Given the integers from 21 to 30, state whether each number is prime or composite. If it is prime, then explain why. If it is composite, then factor the number into the product of primes.

      21

                                                22

      23

                                                24

      25

                                                26

      27

                                                28

      29

                                                30

6. When is an integer a factor of another number? Answer the questions below without the aid of a calculator and explain your reasoning using complete sentences.

    a. Is 3 a factor of 561? _____

            _____

    b. Is 4 a factor of 3116? _____

            _____

    c. Is 5 a factor of 502? _____

            _____

    d. Is 6 a factor of $185,949,385 \cdot 6$? _____

            _____

e. Is 7 a factor of 7^3? _____

_____

f. Is 8 a factor of 2 + 8? _____

_____

g. Is 9 a factor of $\sqrt{9}$? _____

_____

7. Can you use place value clues to find a mystery integer? Read each clue in the first column and record the integer that it represents in the second column.

Place Value Clues	Mystery Integer
15 tens and 6 ones	
5 tens and 28 ones	
24 hundreds and 7 ones	
2 tens and 31 ones	
4 hundreds and 29 tens	
2 thousands and 11 hundreds and 55 ones	

8. Do not use a calculator or pencil and paper to perform the following calculations. Round each number so that you can estimate the answer mentally. Place the rounded numbers below each number, and then estimate the answer in your head. Record your total estimate to the right of the equal sign.

a.
$$312 \ + \ 675 \ + \ 290$$
$$\approx \underline{\hspace{1cm}} + \underline{\hspace{1cm}} + \underline{\hspace{1cm}} = \underline{\hspace{1cm}}$$

b.
$$7251 \ - \ 2863$$
$$\approx \underline{\hspace{1cm}} - \underline{\hspace{1cm}} = \underline{\hspace{1cm}}$$

c.
$$57 \ \cdot \ 811$$
$$\approx \underline{\hspace{1cm}} \cdot \underline{\hspace{1cm}} = \underline{\hspace{1cm}}$$

d.
$$3623 \ \div \ 59$$
$$\approx \underline{\hspace{1cm}} \div \underline{\hspace{1cm}} = \underline{\hspace{1cm}}$$

e.
$$5.25 \ \cdot \ 42.37$$
$$\approx \underline{\hspace{1cm}} \cdot \underline{\hspace{1cm}} = \underline{\hspace{1cm}}$$

f.
$$98\frac{15}{16} \ - \ 51\frac{1}{8}$$
$$\approx \underline{\hspace{1cm}} - \underline{\hspace{1cm}} = \underline{\hspace{1cm}}$$

9. Suppose you are traveling in a country that measures temperature in degree Celsius. The local weather bureau reports the current 9:00 a.m. temperature to be $-10°$ C. The report also says that the temperature will steadily rise $2\frac{1}{2}°$ C every hour for the next 4 hours.

   a. Complete the following chart to show the increase in temperature during half-hour intervals of time.

Time	Calculation Increase	Temperature (^{o}C)
9:00 a.m.		-10
9:30 a.m.	$-10 + 1\frac{1}{4}$	$-8\frac{3}{4}$
10:00 a.m.	$-8\frac{3}{4} + 1\frac{1}{4}$	
10:30 a.m.		
11:00 a.m.		
11:30 a.m.		
12:00 p.m.		
12:30 p.m.		
1:00 p.m.		

   b. Show how you could calculate the total rise in temperature from 9:00 a.m. to 1:00 p.m. using $2\frac{1}{2}°$ C and the operation of multiplication.

   c. If C is the temperature in degrees Celsius, and F is the temperature in degrees Fahrenheit, then the relationship between temperature scales is given by the following formula.

$$F = \frac{9}{5}C + 32$$

     • Convert the 9:00 a.m. temperature to degrees Fahrenheit.

- Convert the 11:00 a.m. temperature to degrees Fahrenheit.

- Convert the 1:00 p.m. temperature to degrees Fahrenheit.

10. Imagine you are considering a hike from the base of a hill to its peak. According to the map, the horizontal distance from the base to the peak is 10556 feet (almost 2 miles), while the elevation or vertical distance is 1325 feet (about $\frac{1}{4}$ mile). You will use the Pythagorean theorem to find the "slant distance" or hypotenuse, which is the real walking distance along the trail.

   a. Draw a picture that will help you visualize and solve the problem situation.

   b. Find the "slant distance" of the hike to the nearest foot.

Chapter 4

Percent, Rate, and Proportion

You learned in Chapter 3 that a *rational number* is the ratio of two integers or simply a fraction where the numerator and denominator are integer values (as long as the denominator is not 0). But all of these fractions can be expressed as decimal numbers that either repeat or come to an end (terminate). Also, each fraction and its equivalent decimal can be expressed as a percentage. Fractions, decimals, and percents—how are they the same? Why do you need three ways to look at one number? How do you know which form is best to use in a particular situation?

In Section 4.1, we will try to answer some of these questions as we explore the connections between the three forms: fraction, decimal, and percent.

The *percentage* is one of the most common ways to express information. Using a percent to describe information can clarify many situations. However, many people use percent to cloud what the numbers actually mean. You need to have number sense with respect to percentages because it is a popular form of communicating information in many everyday situations that affect our quality of life. In Section 4.2, you will examine some of the uses and abuses of percent.

The real world is full of *rates* such as the rate of pay, rate of speed, rate of exchange, rate of tax, and so on. In Section 4.3, you will investigate how these rates are calculated and what they mean to people's lives.

Finally, in Section 4.4, you will look at the concepts, procedures, and applications of *ratio* and *proportion*.

Section 4.1 Connections Between Fraction, Decimal, and Percent

Math Talk

Let's discuss the words **algebra** and **algebraic**. We can easily define *algebraic* as relating to algebra, but then what is *algebra*?

If you were going to describe what algebra means to the next person you see, what would you say? Many people would talk about formulas with letters substituted for numbers. Some might say that algebra is a collection of symbolic rules used to solve problems.

Simply stated, algebra is just a branch of mathematics that generalizes arithmetic by introducing variables to represent a range of numbers. For example, we know that order is not important when adding two numbers. We can show examples of this fact using specific numbers such as $3 + 2 = 2 + 3$. With algebra, we can let a and b represent any real numbers and write the general rule, $a + b = b + a$, also known as the commutative property of addition.

The power behind algebra is the ability to generalize, to make a statement that is true for all numbers in a set. Now let's look at how algebra can be useful in a daily context.

****

Suppose an employee of a large company works 20 hours each week at $10 an hour. Then the employee's weekly salary (not including deductions) can be calculated using arithmetic:

$$\$10 \cdot 20 = \$200$$

This employee knows that there are other employees making $10 an hour but who work anywhere from 10 to 50 hours per week. The weekly salary of any employee making $10 an hour depends on the number of hours worked. Since the hours worked changes for each employee, we let n be the variable representing hours worked. Then we can express the salary using an **algebraic expression**:

$$10 \cdot n$$

The company decides to set the hourly pay such that employees can make anywhere from $7 to $30 an hour. If we let r be a variable representing the pay rate in dollars per hour, then we have an even more general algebraic expression:

$$r \cdot n$$

This last algebraic expression can be entered into a spreadsheet program that calculates any employee's salary given the pay rate r and the number of hours worked n.

If we let s stand for the employees' salary, then we can use an **algebraic equation** to show the relationship between salary, pay rate, and number of hours worked: $s = r \cdot n$

The variables s, r, and n represent quantities that change. Exploring how these changing quantities are related is what algebra is all about.

In Discovery Adventure 1, you will investigate how comparing two numbers by division and then expressing this ratio as a percentage can reveal important information that might otherwise remain hidden.

Discovery Adventure 1: Shooting Hoops

Kristen and Brianna are good friends who play on the same basketball team. At the end of the season the coach compiled the following statistics on how accurate each team member was at shooting the ball through the hoop. The second column gives how many shots each team member made (ball through the hoop), and the third column lists the number of shots attempted.

Player	Shots Made	Shots Attempted
Kristen	157	312
Nancy	150	291
Shelly	145	317
Brianna	132	252
Cheryl	120	263
Pam	101	290
Monique	88	209
Jennifer	60	161
Stephanie	46	150
Teresa	39	95

a. What criterion did the coach use to order the list of basketball players?

_____

b. If you want to list the players according to who is the most accurate at making their shots, then what method would you use to order the players?

_____

c. For Kristen and Brianna, find the ratio of shots made to shots attempted and express this value as a fraction, decimal, and percent. Round the decimal to the hundredths place and convert this value to a percent (multiply by 100 and insert the percent symbol %).

Player	Made	Attempted	Fraction	Decimal	Percent
Kristen	157	312			
Brianna	132	252			

d. Which of the two friends is more accurate at shooting the ball through the hoop? Explain.

_____

_____

e. Go back to the original table above part *a* (page 267) and construct two additional columns to the right side. Label the fourth column **Fraction** and the fifth column **Decimal** as in part *c*. For each player, find the ratio of shots made to shots attempted. Then express this value as a fraction and as a decimal rounded to the thousandths place.

f. Based on the results from part *e*, create a new table listing the decimal output to the thousandths place in descending order from highest to lowest. In the third column, write each value as a fraction with a denominator of 100. Since *percent* means "divided by the hundred," the numerator is the percentage that the fraction represents. Record the shooting percentage in the last column using Kristen as a model.

Player	Decimal	Fraction	Percentage
Kristen	.503	$\dfrac{50.3}{100}$	50.3 %

g. Explain why it is necessary to round each decimal to the thousandths place instead of the hundredths place when listing the players in order of shooting accuracy. *Hint*: Compare Nancy to Brianna and Shelly to Cheryl. What would have happen if you rounded to the hundredths place?

_____

_____

_____

Feedback

If you round each decimal to the hundredths place, then both Nancy and Brianna had a shooting percentage of 52%. You can think of a 52% shooter as a basketball player that, on average, makes 52 out every 100 shots. In general, if a fraction has a denominator of 100, the numerator is considered the percent and can be denoted by the percent symbol %.

$$\frac{52}{100} = 52\%$$

If you think about a fraction as part of a whole, then 52 is the part, and 100 is the whole. So percents are the same as fractions that are standardized with a common denominator of 100. In this sense, you are using the percent symbol to take the place of "divided by 100." Therefore 52% can be read as "52 divided by 100."

It is important to round to the thousandths place to show that Brianna (52.4%) is a slightly more accurate shooter than Nancy (51.5%). Also, observe that Shelly (45.7%) is a slightly better shooter that Cheryl (45.6%).

Brush Up on Percentages

A **percentage** is a fraction with a denominator of 100. In Latin, the term *per centum* means "per 100". But *per* means "for each" or "for every". So *per centum* can translate to "for every 100". Therefore, 52% could be express as 52 for every 100. In Discovery Adventure 1, Nancy and Brianna should make an average of 52 shots for every 100 attempted.

Since a fraction bar implies division, the symbol for percent % can be replaced with "divided by 100." For example, if the variable x represents any real number, then

$$x\% = \frac{x}{100}$$

Letting $x = 25$, we have

$$25\% = \frac{25}{100} \quad \text{or simply} \quad \frac{1}{4}.$$

In the next Discovery Adventure, you have the opportunity to visualize the relationship between fraction, decimal, and percent using a 10-by-10 unit grid that represents an area of land.

Discovery Adventure 2: How Many Acres?

Suppose you own a 100-acre farm that is a 10 x 10 square equally divided up. Let each acre be represented by a small square on the grid below.

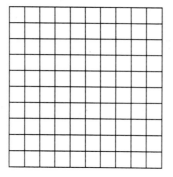

a.   What is the total number of rows on the grid?

b.   What is the total number of columns on the grid?

c.   Suppose that 30% of the farm is devoted to growing corn. How many acres (small squares) must be shaded to represent the land used for corn?

d.   How many rows must you shade to represent 30%?

e.   In the figure above, shade in the last three rows to represent the corn crop.

f.   What is the fraction that represents the ratio of corn rows to total rows?

$$\frac{\text{Corn rows}}{\text{Total rows}} =$$

g.   Express the fraction in part *f* in decimal form.

h.   What is the fraction that represents the ratio of all corn acres (small squares representing corn) to the total number of acres (total number of small squares)?

$$\frac{\text{Corn acres}}{\text{Total acres}} =$$

i.   Express the fraction in part *h* in decimal form.

j. The owner is thinking of selling part of his land to a developer. Give him a visual view of what it would look like to lose the following percentages of land by shading in the correct part of the whole.

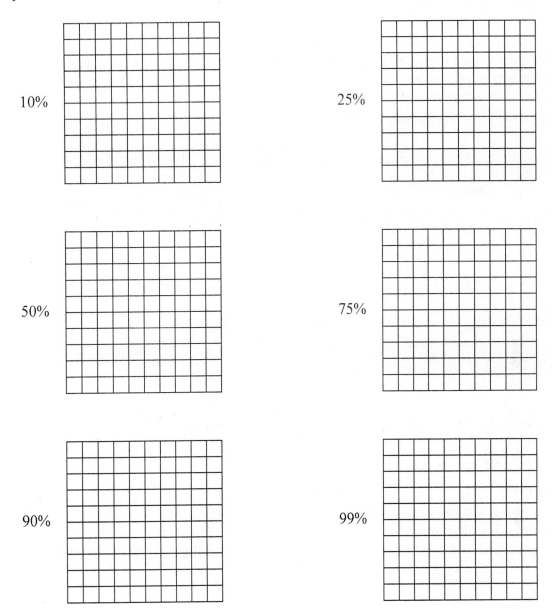

10%   25%

50%   75%

90%   99%

Feedback

The ratio of corn rows to total rows is three tenths, $\dfrac{3}{10}$, or as a decimal, 0.3. The ratio of each acre of corn to the total number of acres is thirty hundredths, $\dfrac{30}{100}$, or as a decimal, 0.30. Since $\dfrac{3}{10}$, 0.3, $\dfrac{30}{100}$, 0.30, and 30% are all equivalent forms of the same value, it is natural to ask, "Which form is best?" The answer is that it depends on the situation.

You need to be comfortable switching between different ways of expressing a real number.

Brush Up on Circle Graphs or Pie Charts

A *circle graph* or *pie chart* is a circular diagram that is divided into sectors, each of which represents a particular category. It can be used to display information that is divided into categories totaling to 100% and to compare the sizes of each category (sector). For example, consider the gross amount of a paycheck as the whole, with the categories as deductions and net pay.

Gross Pay	$2,179.01	100%
Categories	**Amount**	**Percent of Gross**
Federal Income Tax	$435.45	20%
Social Security Tax	$136.15	6.2%
Medicare Tax	$31.84	1.5%
State Income Tax	$115.49	5.3%
Net Pay	$1,460.08	67%

Since the distance around a circle measures 360°, you can find the number of degrees in each sector by multiplying its percent by 360°.

Federal Income Tax	20% of 360°	$.20 \cdot 360° = 72°$
Social Security Tax	6.2% of 360°	$.062 \cdot 360° = 22.32° \approx 22°$
Medicare Tax	1.5% of 360°	$.015 \cdot 360° = 5.4° \approx 5°$
State Income Tax	5.3% of 360°	$.053 \cdot 360° = 19.08° \approx 19°$
Net Pay	67% of 360°	$.67 \cdot 360° = 241.2° \approx 241°$

Refer to the figures below as we describe the construction.
- Draw a circle and mark its center.
- Draw a line that connects the circle to its center. This is called the *radius*.
- Place a protractor so that its center matches up with the circle's center and 0° lines up with the radius.
- To construct the Federal Income Tax sector, find 72° on the protractor and mark the circle. Draw a second line from the center to the 72° mark.
- To construct the Social Security Tax sector, move the protractor so that 0° lines up with the second line. Then measure 6.2%, make another mark, and draw a third line.
- Continue this process until all the categories appear and the circle graph is complete.

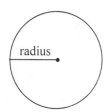
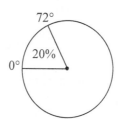
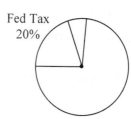

You need to be organized to keep track of your spending patterns, and just looking at the amount of each expense is not going to give you the big picture. To obtain a good financial overview, you need to look at the percent of money that is spent on individual items. To get this quick snapshot of your finances, you can build a circle graph. Let's investigate this process.

Discovery Adventure 3: Monthly Budget

It seems like every time you check your bank account there's never enough money to spend on fun stuff. You decide to put together a budget to figure out what percent of your total income is spent on necessary expenses. Suppose the net salary (take-home pay) for your household is $1652 per month. Fill in the following table to organize your information. Round results in the last 2 columns to the nearest percent.

Budget Item	Amount ($)	Fraction of Monthly Income	Calculation for Percent	Percent of Monthly Income
Rent	725	$\frac{725}{1652}$	$\frac{725}{1652} \cdot 100\%$	44%
Auto Loan	252			
Auto Fuel	40			
Food	95			
Electric Utility	116			
Phone Utility	90			
Savings	100			
Auto Insurance	98			

a. How much extra money do you have available to spend on fun stuff?

b. What percent of the monthly income is the amount in part *a*?

c. Combine some of the category items, so that you have 6 general categories: Utilities, Auto, Rent, Food, Savings, and Fun. Then complete a second table on the next page. Round the last column to the nearest percent.

Budget Item	Amount ($)	Fraction of Monthly Income	Calculation for Percent	Percent of Monthly Income
Rent	725	$\dfrac{725}{1652}$	$\dfrac{725}{1652} \cdot 100\%$	44%
Auto	390			
Food	95	$\dfrac{95}{1652}$	$\dfrac{95}{1652} \cdot 100\%$	6%
Utilities	206			
Savings	100	$\dfrac{100}{1652}$	$\dfrac{100}{1652} \cdot 100\%$	6%
Fun				
Total				

d. Let us construct a pie chart or circle graph using the percentage of monthly income for the 6 categories. Consider the entire area inside the circle to be the total monthly income, which is the whole or 100%. Divide the whole into 6 parts, making the size of each part's area relative to the percentage of total income. Be sure to label each piece with the category name and the corresponding percentage.

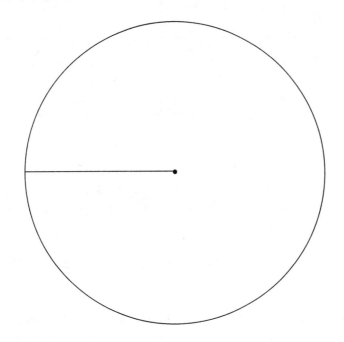

Feedback

In calculating the percent of monthly income for each budget item, you were asked to round to the nearest percent. For example, in the second table, the utilities' calculation for percent is expressed as

$$\frac{206}{1652} \cdot 100\% \approx 12.4697336\% \quad \text{or} \quad \text{about } 12\%.$$

Would it have been better to round to the tenths place or the hundredths place?

Tenths: 12.5%   Hundredths: 12.47%

The decision should be based on how accurate your results need to be. In this situation, you are investigating a monthly budget, so rounding to the nearest percent (ones place) presents the clearest snapshot of a person's finances. In this case, being more accurate would tend to cloud the picture of where the money is going. Unless you are told where to round, each problem must be evaluated on the degree of accuracy needed for that situation. Recall that in Discovery Adventure 1 you expressed a player's shooting percentage to the nearest tenth of a percent. This rounding was necessary to show which players were the most accurate shooters.

****

In summary, a circle graph or pie chart is a visual way to display a *distribution* of percentages that sum to 100%. The graph shows each category of the distribution as part of a whole, thereby allowing you to judge the relative size of each category.

We all know that there is always a sale going on somewhere and wherever there is a sale you are bound to find advertisements that express the information in percentages. Let's take a look at a situation in which understanding percentages can help clarify the problem.

▦ Discovery Adventure 4: It's on Sale!

After completing your budget, you know it will take at least 7 months to save enough money to afford a big screen TV. However, you just heard a radio advertisement that Slippery Sam's Electronic Depot has all big screen TV's on sale at 80% of their regular price. The ad claims that you don't need to make any payments for up to one year.

Upon arriving at the store, you notice the model you want has a sale price of $896 but no information on its regular price prior to the sale.

Use your calculator to go through the following guess and test strategy, where you are trying to guess 80% of what regular price equals the current sale price of $896. In short, 80% of what is 896? Make an initial guess, then take 80% of that guess. Record your results in the table on the next page and keep guessing until you zero-in on the correct answer. The first guess has been completed for you.

Guess	Test	Result	Conclusion
$1000	$0.80 \cdot 1000$	$800	Too low

Feedback

Although a guess and test strategy works just fine, there is a more direct way to find the answer. Let's look at the situation more carefully. First, taking a percent or fraction *of* something implies doing the operation of multiplication. For example, suppose your guess is represented by the variable *g*. Then the phrase "80% of *g* is $896" can be symbolized by the following equation:

$$0.80 \cdot g = 896.$$

Since the **inverse** operation of multiplication is division, we have

$$g = \frac{896}{0.80}$$
$$= 1120$$

To check your work, simply multiply the value for *g* by 80% or 0.80 to see if the result equals $896:

$$0.80 \cdot 1120 = 896.$$

The original equation above could also be symbolized by the following **equivalent equations**:

$$\frac{80}{100} \cdot g = 896 \qquad \text{or} \qquad \frac{8}{10} \cdot g = 896 \qquad \text{or even} \qquad \frac{4}{5} \cdot g = 896$$

Solving the last equation for g, we have

$$\frac{4}{5} \cdot g = 896$$

$$g = 896 \div \frac{4}{5} \qquad \text{inverse of multiplication is division}$$

$$= \frac{896}{1} \cdot \frac{5}{4} \qquad \text{division is multiplication by the reciprocal}$$

$$= \frac{4480}{4} \qquad \text{multiply}$$

$$= 1120 \qquad \text{simplify}$$

What we have done is use some **algebraic thinking** with the guess g as the variable or unknown number that we are trying to find.

****

Let's describe an organized method for solving equations like the one above. The variable can be isolated (alone on one side of the equal sign) if we undo or remove the operation of multiplication. Since 0.80 is being multiplied by g we perform the inverse (opposite) operation which is dividing both sides of the equality by 0.80.

$$0.80 \cdot g = 896$$

$$\frac{\cancel{0.80}\, g}{\cancel{0.80}} = \frac{896}{0.80}$$

$$1 \cdot g = 1120$$

$$g = 1120$$

This process can be described as solving an equation by **balancing** or making the same change on each side of the equation.

By performing the same operation on each side of the equal sign, we are applying one of the **properties of equality**. In other words, whatever you do to one side of the equation, you must do to the other side to keep things in balance. Here are a few rules you can apply to an equation without changing its solution.

Properties of Equality

- You can multiply or divide both sides of an equation by any real number except 0.

- You can add or subtract any real number to both sides of an equation.

Section Exercises: 4.1

1. In the table below are the final medal standings for the 1996 Summer Olympic games in Atlanta, Georgia. The top ten countries have been listed.

	Country	Gold	Silver	Bronze	Total
1	United States	44	32	25	101
2	Germany	20	18	27	65
3	Russia	26	21	16	63
4	China	16	22	12	50
5	Australia	9	9	23	41
6	France	15	7	15	37
7	Italy	13	10	12	35
8	South Korea	7	15	5	27
9	Cuba	9	8	8	25
10	Ukraine	9	2	12	23

a. What criterion is used to order the countries in the table?

_____

b. Do you think the standard of judgment used to order the countries is fair? Explain.

_____

_____

_____

_____

c. Mentally estimate what percentage of U.S. medals belong to each of the following categories. Record the result and explain your reasoning using complete sentences.

- Gold: _____

_____

- Silver: _____

_____

- Gold, silver, or bronze: _____

_____

- Platinum: _____

_____

d. Germany and Russia had a total count that was only two medals apart. However, the distribution of gold, silver, and bronze was not as close. Which of the two countries do you think had the best Olympic performance? Consider using percentages to help justify your answer.

_____

_____

_____

e. If you think that the given standings reflect the countries that performed the best in the 1996 Olympic games, explain why. Otherwise build new rankings and explain your method and why it is best.

_____

_____

_____

_____

New Rankings:

2. Decide which of the following phrases is the most accurate way to complete each sentence. Record the phrase in the proper place so that you have a true sentence for each part.

- 0%
- Fewer than 10%
- Approximately 25%
- Fewer than 50%
- Approximately 50%
- More than 50%
- Approximately 75%
- At least 90%
- 100%

a. _____ of people in the country are male.

b. _____ of female students at my college are taller than 5'9''.

c. _____ of students in my class are left-handed.

d. _____ of people in my town exercise at least 3 times a week.

e. _____ of students at my college work 10 hours or more.

f. _____ of people in my town have eaten some pizza in their life.

g. _____ of students at my college drink coffee each morning.

h. _____ of students in my class have blue eyes.

i. _____ of students in my class have brown hair.

j. _____ of students in my class have broken a bone in their body.

3. In each part below, 3 out of the 4 expressions are equivalent. Circle the expression that does not belong in the list, and explain your reasoning. Do not use a calculator except to check your answer.

a. 0.25 $\dfrac{1}{4}$ 25%   0.14

_____

_____

_____

b. $14 \cdot \dfrac{1}{2}$ 50% of 14   14% of 50 $(0.05)(14)$

_____

_____

_____

c.   0.275 $2\dfrac{3}{4}$ 275%   2.75

_____

_____

_____

d.   10% of 200   20% of 100   40% of 50   60% of 25

_____

_____

_____

4.   Use the grid of numbers on the next page as necessary to help estimate the percent of numbers from 1 to 100 that –

a.   are odd numbers.   **b.**   are divisible by 2 (multiples of 2).

c.   are prime numbers.   **d.**   are integers.

e.   have a first digit of 6.   **f.**   have a first or last digit of 3.

g.   are divisible by 4 (multiples of 4).   **h.**   have two digits that are both even.

i.   have two digits that add up to 14.   **j.**   are composite numbers.

1	2	3	4	5	6	7	8	9	10
11	12	13	14	15	16	17	18	19	20
21	22	23	24	25	26	27	28	29	30
31	32	33	34	35	36	37	38	39	40
41	42	43	44	45	46	47	48	49	50
51	52	53	54	55	56	57	58	59	60
61	62	63	64	65	66	67	68	69	70
71	72	73	74	75	76	77	78	79	80
81	82	83	84	85	86	87	88	89	90
91	92	93	94	95	96	97	98	99	100

5. The 1992 presidential election had some interesting data if we stop to consider percentages. The table below gives the final tally according to *The Kansas City Star* newspaper from November 5, 1992. Complete the table by finding the ratio of votes for a particular candidate to the total number of votes cast. Express your answer as a fraction, decimal, and percent.

Candidate	Votes	Ratio: votes to total votes cast		
		Fraction	Decimal	Percent
Clinton	43,728,375			
Bush	38,167,416			
Perot	19,237,247			

a. What percent of the total votes must a candidate receive to obtain a majority of the votes cast by the population?

b. Did a majority of voters in the country cast their ballot for Clinton?

c. If Perot had not been a candidate in the 1992 presidential race, how might this have changed the election?

_____

_____

_____

_____

d. Do you think that the presidential election process used in this United States is fair? Explain.

_____

_____

_____

_____

6. The following table organizes information on fatal occupational injuries for 1998 into 6 broad categories. The number of fatalities for each category is listed in column 2.

Fatal Occupational Injuries, 1998

Categories	Number	Percentage
Transportation Incidents	2,630	
Assault and Violent Acts	960	
Falls	702	
Contact with Objects and Equipment	941	
Exposure to Harmful Substance or Environments	572	
Fires and Explosions	205	
Other Events or Exposures	16	
Total	6,026	100%

Source: Bureau of Labor Statistics, U.S. Dept. of Labor

a. Complete the third column to find the fatality percentage for each category. What information is expressed in the percentages that the numbers in column 2 do not indicate?

_____

_____

_____

_____

b. Use the circular figure below to construct a circle graph or pie chart of the given information.

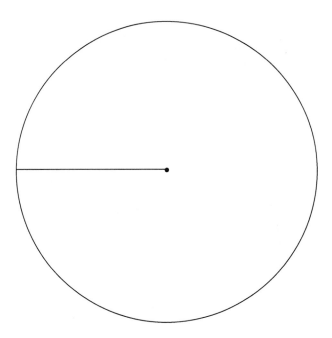

7. The table below gives information on employment and unemployment in the U.S. civilian labor force, for people 16 years of age and older, from 1994 to 1998. The employment and unemployment values are annual averages, in thousands. For example, the number of employed people in 1994 is 123,060 thousands, which is a little over 123 million.

Employed for 1994 $= 123,060 \cdot 1000 = 123,060,000$

Year	Employed	Unemployed	Unemployment Rate
1994	123,060	7,996	6.1%
1995	124,900	7,404	
1996	126,708	7,236	
1997	129,558	6,739	
1998	131,463	6,210	

Source: Bureau of Labor Statistics

Note: 1997 and 1998 are not strictly comparable with 1994-1996 because of revisions in population controls used in the household survey.

a. Complete the fourth column by finding the unemployment rate for each year from 1994-1998. The unemployment rate is calculated by dividing the number of unemployed by the total of employed and unemployed. For example,

$$\text{Unemployment rate for 1994} = \frac{7,996}{123,060 + 7,996} = \frac{7,996}{131,056} \approx .061 \quad \text{or} \quad 6.1\%$$

b. Suppose you want to calculate the employment rate for 1994. Show two different methods you could use to obtain the correct percentage of employed people. One method used should involve the unemployment rate.

8. The following bar graph shows U.S. car sales by vehicle size and type in 1998.

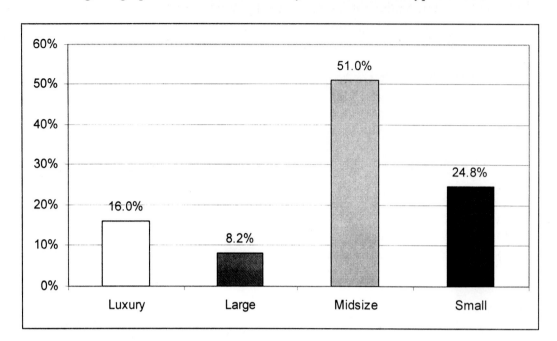

Convert the bar graph above to a circle graph below.

9. You go to a sporting goods store to find a pair of new sneakers. The advertisement displays the brand you want as "$99.95 sneakers now on sale for $79.95."

   a. What percent of the original price of $99.95 is the sale price of $79.95?

   b. What percent off the original price is the sale price? In other words, what are the percent savings when buying the sneakers on sale?

10. From 1997-2000 a crew of paleontologists have been digging ditches and moving dirt in the Patagonia region of Argentina to uncover a previously unknown dinosaur. The newly discovered dinosaur is about 10% bigger than Giganotosaurus, which was the world's largest predator, measuring 45 feet. What is the size of this newly found dinosaur?

11. Convert each percentage to a fraction and then a decimal.

   a. 100%   *b.* 0.05%

   c. 10.5%   *d.* 1%

   e. 0.1%   *f.* 150%

   g. 2000%   *h.* 5.2%

12. Convert each decimal to a percentage.

a. 0.75

b. 0.1

c. 0.035

d. 0.9075

e. 1.25

f. 5

13. Convert each fraction to a decimal and then write the value as a percentage. Round decimal to the thousandths place when necessary.

a. $\dfrac{1}{3}$

b. $\dfrac{5}{8}$

c. $\dfrac{6}{10}$

d. $\dfrac{1}{10000}$

e. $\dfrac{67}{25}$

f. $\dfrac{56}{127}$

14. Convert each percentage to a fraction and then simplify so that the fraction is in lowest terms.

a. 40%

b. $66\dfrac{2}{3}\%$

c. 120%

d. $\dfrac{3}{4}\%$

Section 4.2 Use and Misuse of Percent

Math Talk

When it comes to talking about percent, there is a bigger difference between the words *of* and *off* than just the additional letter *f*. If an item goes on sale for 25% **off** the original price, it is equivalent to saying that the sale price is 75% *of* the original price. For example, suppose that a shirt with a regular price of $38 goes on sale at 25% *off*. You might ask, "*Off* of what?" Well, let's assume it means "*off* the regular cost of $38." So you start out paying $38, but then subtract 25% *of* $38 from the regular cost of $38 to obtain the sale price.

For example, the statement

"Sale price is $38 minus 25% *of* $38"

translates to

$$\text{Sale Price} = 38 - 0.25 \cdot 38$$
$$= 38 - 9.50$$
$$= 28.50$$

There are two important pieces of information given in this calculation. First, you are saving $9.50 (25% *of* $38) when buying the shirt on sale. Second, the sale price of the shirt is $28.50.

But wait, if I take 25% *off* the regular price, doesn't that leave me paying 75% *of* the regular price? For example, the statement

"Sale price is 75% *of* 38"

translates to

$$\text{Sale Price} = 0.75 \cdot 38$$
$$= 28.50$$

Again, the sale price of the shirt is $28.50, but now we must add the 5% tax. The actual cost to the consumer is the sale price plus 5% *of* the sale price. For example, the statement

"Cost is $28.50 plus 5% of $28.50"

translates to

$$\text{Cost} = 28.50 + 0.05 \cdot 28.50$$
$$= 28.50 + 1.43$$
$$= 29.93$$

Note that the tax calculation $0.05 \cdot 28.5 = 1.425$ has been rounded to the nearest penny, $1.43. The cost that the consumer pays is $29.93. In calculating the cost, you follow the order of operations by multiplying and then adding. Can you think of a one-step calculation that gives the cost of the shirt to the consumer? *Hint*: Think about a value you can multiply by $28.50 to obtain the final cost of $29.93.

****

The first Discovery Adventure will explore how distributors complete a mark up (add a percentage amount to cost) on an item. Also, you will investigate how distributors complete a mark down (percent reduction in price) on an item that is going on sale.

Discovery Adventure 1: Best Buy

The college bookstore gets a certain graphing calculator model from a technology vendor at a wholesale cost of $70. The bookstore manager decides to mark up their cost by 25%.

a. Mentally estimate how much the bookstore will mark up the calculator cost.

b. Now compute 25% of 70 exactly.

c. After applying the mark up, how much will the bookstore sell the calculator for?

Suppose the calculator has not been selling well at the college bookstore because the local office superstore has it on sale. The superstore manager has an advertisement in the student newspaper saying that you can get the same calculator for $79, which is 30% off the regular price. For the next part of this Adventure, refer to the figure below.

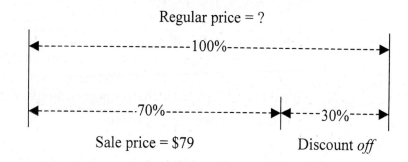

Regular price = ?

d. What was the regular price of the calculator at the superstore (before the sale)? Round your answer to the nearest cent. *Hint*: Use the figure above to help visualize how percent is being used in this problem.

e. To check your answer to part *d,* multiply by 0.70 or just 0.7. Do you obtain $79 exactly? Answer *yes* or *no* and explain why using complete sentences.

_____

_____

_____

_____

To stay competitive, the college bookstore begins advertising the same calculator on sale at 25% off the regular price of $87.50.

f. What is the bookstore's discount? Round the discount to the nearest cent.

g. What is the sale price at the bookstore?

h. At this point, which store is giving students the best buy? Explain your answer using complete sentences.

_____

_____

_____

i. Does it seem strange to you that the bookstore is marking up the wholesale cost ($70) by 25% to get a price of $87.50, and then taking 25% off that price ($87.50) to arrive at a sale price of $65.62? Complete all the calculations again and then explain why you don't end up with a sale price of $70.

_____

_____

_____

_____

j. The bookstore pays the wholesale cost ($70) for the calculator, and this value is greater than the sale price ($65.62) that they are charging the consumer. What do you think about the bookstore's strategy in trying to compete with the office superstore? What strategy would you recommend?

_____

_____

_____

_____

_____

_____

_____

k. If the state sales tax is 5% of the price, how much does a student end up paying the bookstore for the discounted calculator?

Feedback

At the bookstore, if you estimate the original price to be about $80, then 25% or $\frac{1}{4}$ of $80 gives an approximate mark up of $20. The number 80 is a convenient choice, because you can easily divide it into 4 equal parts. Since 80 is higher than the original price, you might guess a little less, about $18. The exact mark up is

$$0.25 \cdot 80 = \$17.50.$$

Therefore, the price of the calculator after the markup is calculated as follows:

$$\text{Bookstore's regular price} = \text{Wholesale cost} + \text{Markup}$$
$$= 70 + 17.50$$
$$= \$87.50$$

At the superstore, 30% off means that 70% of the regular price equals the advertised sale price of $79. For example,

$$70\% \text{ of Superstore's regular price} = \text{Sale Price}$$
$$0.70 \cdot \text{Superstore's regular price} = 79 \qquad (of \text{ implies multiplication})$$
$$\text{Superstore's regular price} = \frac{79}{0.70} \qquad \text{(inverse of multiplication is division)}$$
$$\approx \$112.86 \qquad \text{(round to the nearest cent)}$$

If you check the rounded result, you obtain

$$0.70 \cdot 112.86 = 79.002 \,.$$

Rounding the regular price means that we are using an approximation. Therefore, the check of your calculations cannot produce exact results. However, it is close enough to the exact value to have confidence in the work done.

The discount at the bookstore is

$$0.25 \cdot 87.50 \approx 21.88 \qquad \text{rounded to the nearest cent}\,.$$

So the sale price is calculated as follows:

$$\text{Sale Price} = \text{Regular Price} - \text{Discount}$$
$$= 87.50 - 21.88$$
$$= 65.62$$

The reason that a 25% mark up followed by a 25% discount does not bring you back to the wholesale cost ($70) is because 25% of $70 produces a mark up of $17.50. However, 25% of $87.50 produces a discount of $21.88, rounded to nearest cent. Since the discount is greater than the mark up, the sale price ($65.62) is less than the wholesale cost ($70).

Therefore, the bookstore is losing $4.38 on each calculator they sell. What is your strategy?

****

What happens when you increase a value (such as $100) by a percentage amount (say 5%), then increase the new value by another percentage amount (say 5% again)? Will this be equivalent to a 10% increase on the original value (of $100)?

To help answer these questions, begin the next Discovery Adventure where you will investigate the change in an employee's salary after 3 successive percent increases.

Discovery Adventure 2: Percents Don't Always Add Up

It's been two years working without a raise, but you just got the news that management has tentatively agreed to a new three-year contract. If the Union ratifies the contract, there will be a 3% increase for the first year, a 4% raise for the second year, and a 5% increase during the third year. You figure that by the third year you will have increased your original salary by 12%.

a. Do you agree or disagree with the last sentence above? Explain your reasoning using complete sentences.

_____

_____

_____

b. Suppose your current salary is $28,500 per year. If there is a breakdown in negotiations so that the contract is not signed, then your new salary will stay the same. In other words, your new salary is 100% of your former salary. Show how to calculate 100% of $28,500. *Hint*: Percent means "divided by 100," and the word *of* implies multiplication.

c. If the contract is ratified, then during the first year everyone will receive a 3% increase. This means getting 100% of your former salary ($28,500) plus a 3% increase. This can also be thought of as taking 103% of $28,500. What is your new salary during the first year of the new contract?

d. Using your answer to part *c*, what is your new salary during the second year of the contract, when you receive a 4% increase?

e. Using your answer to part *d*, what is your new salary during the third year of the contract, when you receive a 5% increase?

f. Now take the original salary of $28,500 plus 12% of the original salary to see how it compares with your answer to part *e*.

g. Can you explain why the three consecutive percent increases are not the same as a single percent increase that is the sum of the three?

_____

_____

_____

_____

Feedback

Assuming that the contract is ratified, we can look at one year at a time. During the first year of the new contract, there is a 3% increase on the old salary. For example,

New Salary = Old Salary + First Year Increase

New Salary = Old Salary + 3% of Old Salary

New Salary = $28,500 + 0.03 \cdot 28,500$

New Salary = $28,500 + 855$ ⇐ *First Increase*

New Salary = $29,355

At the start of the second year, the first year's salary becomes the old salary, and we have the following new salary calculation:

New Salary = Old Salary + Second Year Increase

New Salary = Old Salary + 4% of Old Salary

New Salary = $29,355 + 0.04 \cdot 29,355$

New Salary = $29,355 + 1174.20$ ⇐ *Second Increase*

New Salary = $30,529.20

At the start of the third year, the second year's salary becomes the old salary, and we have the following new salary calculation:

New Salary = Old Salary + Third Year Increase

New Salary = Old Salary + 5% of Old Salary

New Salary = $30,529.20 + 0.05 \cdot 30,529.20$

New Salary = $30,529.20 + 1526.46$ ⇐ *Third Increase*

New Salary = $32.055.66

$32,055.66 is the correct salary for the third year assuming that the contract is ratified and funded. Let's look at why the shortcut of adding percents 3%, 4%, and 5% to get 12% doesn't work if we want to calculate the new salary at the end of three years.

If we take the old (original) salary and increase it by 12%, we have the following new salary calculation:

$$\text{New Salary} = \text{Old Salary} + \text{Increase}$$
$$\text{New Salary} = \text{Old Salary} + 12\% \text{ of Old Salary}$$
$$\text{New Salary} = 28,500 + 0.12 \cdot 28,500$$
$$\text{New Salary} = 28,500 + 3420 \qquad \Leftarrow \textit{Single Increase}$$
$$\text{New Salary} = \$31,920$$

When taking 12% of \$28,500 we obtain an increase of \$3420, which brings your salary to \$31,920. However, applying a 3% increase in the first year adds \$855 to your old salary, giving you a new salary of \$29,355. So in the second year, when you apply a 4% increase (4% of \$29,355), you are not only taking 4% of \$28,500 but also 4% of \$855. The result is a \$1174.20 increase that brings your salary to \$30,529.20.

In the third year, when you apply a 5% increase (5% of \$30,529.20), you are not only taking 5% of \$28,500 but also 5% of \$855 (1st year raise) and 5% of \$1174.20 (2nd year raise). The result is a \$1526.46 increase that brings your salary to \$32,055.66. In effect, you are receiving a compound increase by continually getting an increase on the previous increase.

Therefore, a 3% increase the first year followed by a 4% increase the second year and a 5% increase the third year gives you more money than a 12% increase applied once.

$$\$855 + \$1174.20 + \$1526.46 > \$3420$$
$$\$3555.66 > \$3420$$

Percentages cannot be combined like real numbers. Finally, it should be noted that the method of calculation used (below left) could have been done using an alternative method (below right).

Old Salary + 3% of Old Salary

$$\text{Old Salary} + 3\% \text{ of Old Salary} \qquad = 100\% \text{ of Old Salary} + 3\% \text{ of Old Salary}$$
$$= 28,500 + 0.03 \cdot 28,500 \qquad\qquad = 103\% \text{ of Old Salary}$$
$$= \$29,355 \qquad\qquad\qquad\qquad\qquad = 1.03 \cdot 28,500$$
$$= \$29,355$$

> **Section Exercises: 4.2**

1. Refer to Discovery Adventure 2: Percents Don't Always Add Up as you work through the following parts.

    a. In the second year, the first year's salary ($29,355) becomes the old salary. Find the new salary for the second year by calculating 104% of the old salary.

    b. In the third year, the second year's salary ($30,529.20) becomes the old salary. Find the new salary for the third year by calculating 105% of the old salary.

    c. Why does the work you did in parts *a* and *b* produce the same answers as the previous work you did in Discovery Adventure 2?

    _____

    _____

    _____

2. Suppose the flyer for a large department store has the following advertisement.

    > 50% off
    > Entire Stock of Gold, Gemstone
    > And Sterling Silver Jewelry

    You decide to check the price of some of the advertised items to make sure they are actually 50% off the regular price. For each item listed, calculate the sale price based on 50% off the regular price. State whether or not the item's sale price is marked correctly.

    a. 14K Gold 1/2 Carat Diamond Solitaire Ring
    Sale $299.99   Regularly $599.99

    b. 10K Diamond Gold Pendants
    Sale $34.99   Regularly $81.99

    c. 14K Birthstone Earrings
           Sale $21.99   Regularly $52.99

    d. 14K Gold 3-Strand Rope Necklace
           Sale $99.99   Regularly $199.99

3. Complete the second row of each table below by finding the given percent of each value listed in the first row. Explain the pattern you see occurring in the second row. The percent of $50 has been completed and can be used as an example. Do not use a calculator!

a.

100% of	$50	$300	$2000	$40,000	$120,000
Equals	$50				

_____

_____

b.

10% of	$50	$300	$2000	$40,000	$120,000
Equals	$5				

_____

_____

c.

110% of	$50	$300	$2000	$40,000	$120,000
Equals	$55				

_____

_____

d.

200% of	$50	$300	$2000	$40,000	$120,000
Equals	$100				

e.

1% of	$50	$300	$2000	$40,000	$120,000
Equals	$0.50				

f.

0.5% of	$50	$300	$2000	$40,000	$120,000
Equals	$0.25				

g.

5% of	$50	$300	$2000	$40,000	$120,000
Equals	$2.50				

h.

50% of	$50	$300	$2000	$40,000	$120,000
Equals	$25				

i.

25% of	$50	$300	$2000	$40,000	$120,000
Equals	$12.50				

_____

_____

4. The following table presents 1990 census data on race for the United States. The source of the data is the Bureau of the Census, U.S. Department of Commerce.

Race	Number	Percent
All Persons	248,709,873	100.0
White	199,686,070	80.3
Black	29,986,060	12.1
American Indian, Eskimo, or Aleut	1,959,234	0.8
Asian-Pacific Islander	7,273,662	2.9
Other Race	9,804,847	3.9

a. Persons of Hispanic origin can be of any race. There are 22,354,059 persons of Hispanic origin from the total population of 248,709,873. Find the percent of the U.S. population that is of Hispanic origin.

b. About 1,959,234 individuals or 0.8% of the population identified themselves as Native American (American Indian, Eskimo, or Aleut.). What fraction of 1% is 0.8%?

c. American Indians make up 96% of the Native American population. How many American Indians are there in the U.S. population?

d. The 5 largest American Indian tribes are Cherokee (16.4% of American Indians), Navajo (11.7%), Chippewa (5.5%), Sioux (5.5%), and Choctaw (4.4%). Do the largest American Indian tribes listed above make up the majority (more than 50%) of all American Indian tribes? Use your answer from part *c* in completing the necessary calculations.

e. How many Cherokee are in the U.S. population (according to the 1990 data)?

f. If you **randomly** select 100 people from the U.S. population, how many do you expect to be black? *Hint: Randomly* means that every person in the population has the same chance of being selected.

g. If you randomly select 1000 people from the U.S. population, how many do you expect to be white?

5. Suppose a large department store prints the following advertisement.

> Now Through Election Day, Nov. 5
> SAVE
> 40%-60%
> When You Take An Extra 25% Off
> Prices Already Newly Reduced
> 25%-50%
> off original ticketed prices

a. The original price on a pair of pants was $110 at the above store. When prices are first reduced 25%–50%, the pants were on sale for $81.99. By what percent were the pants reduced during the first sale?

b. During the current pre-election day sale, you can take 25% off the $81.99 sale price. How much is the final cost to the consumer during this sale?

c. Suppose a competing store has the exact same pants, originally priced at $110. They are having one big sale where all pants are 50% off the original ticket price. What is the sale price of the pants at this store?

d. Which store gives the best buy? Why does a 25% off sale, followed by an extra 25% off sale, give different results than a 50% off sale?

_____

_____

_____

6. The following table presents 1990 census data on U.S. population by sex and age. The source of the data is the Bureau of the Census, U.S. Dept. of Commerce. As you work on the questions below, show all work and round your answer to the nearest tenth of a percent.

Total Population	**248,709,873**
SEX	
Male	121,239,418
Female	127,470,455
AGE	
Under 18 years	63,604,432
65 years and over	31,241,831

a. What percent of the U.S. population is male?

b. What percent of the U.S. population is female?

c. What percent of the U.S. population is under 18 years?

d. What percent of the U.S. population is 65 years and over?

e. What percent of the U.S. population is greater than or equal to 18 and less than 65?

f. Do we have enough information to calculate the percent of women that are 65 years and over? Use complete sentences to explain your answer.

_____

_____

_____

7. A medical screening test is a procedure that shows if a patient is likely to have a particular disease or illness. If a patient's test results are positive, then it is likely that the person has the disease or illness. However, since the test is not perfect, some people who test positive do not have the disease. Likewise, some people who test negative actually do have the disease or illness. Suppose a medical clinic gives 1200 rapid tests for strep throat during a particular week. Of the 1200 patients, 400 tested positive, but only 360 ended up being diagnosed as really having strep throat. Also, 80 people who tested negative on the rapid test were eventually diagnosed as having strep throat.

   a. Find the percentage of patients who tested positive on the rapid test.

   b. What percent of the patients testing positive ended up being diagnosed with strep throat?

   c. What percent of the patients testing positive ended up not being diagnosed with strep throat?

   d. Find the percentage of patients who tested negative on the rapid test.

   e. What percent of the patients testing negative on the rapid test ended up being diagnosed with strep throat?

8. Suppose researchers are working on a pill to improve memory. They hope to show that a student taking this pill will score higher on exams that require a good memory. Dr Quackenbush tests a large class on their recall of information presented during class lectures. Right before the exam each student is given a pill, but they do not know whether it is the memory pill or a "placebo." A placebo is a harmless pill containing no drugs. Here are the results:

Results of First Experiment

Type of Pill	Number Taking Exam	Number Successful at Passing Exam	Percent that Passed
Memory	60	35	
Placebo	25	13	

a. Complete the last column by calculating the percent of students who passed from each group.

b. Does it appear that the group given the smart pill was more successful at passing the exam? Explain.

_____

_____

The results make Dr Quackenbush think his pill is improving memory. To be sure, he decides to try the same experiment in a different class with more students. Here are the results:

Results of Second Experiment

Type of Pill	Number Taking Exam	Number Successful at Passing Exam	Percent that Passed
Memory	120	100	
Placebo	300	232	

c. Complete the last column by calculating the percent of students who passed the exam in each group.

d. Does it appear that the group given the memory pill was more successful at passing the exam? Explain.

_____

_____

Combine the data from both experiments on number of students taking the exam (second column) and the number of students passing the exam (third column). Put the totals in columns 2 and 3 of the table below. Do not combine the last columns on percent from the two previous tables.

Combined Data from Both Experiments

Type of Pill	Total Number Taking Exam	Total Successful at Passing Exam	Total Percent that Passed
Memory			
Placebo			

e. Now use the combined data in columns 2 and 3 above to calculate the total percent that passed from both classes. Record your results in the last column.

f. Using the combined data from both experiments, which group appears to be more successful at passing the exam? Explain.

_____

_____

g. Go back to the first two tables. In the last columns involving percent, add the percents and then divide the result by 2 for both the memory group and the placebo group. The results are the percentages averaged together for both groups.

h. What do the results of part g tell you about combining percents and finding the average?

_____

_____

_____

9. The average change in prices of consumer goods and services over time is called *inflation*. The consumer price index or CPI measures some of these changes. Let's take a look at the annual percent change in food items for the years 1989 to 1998 as measured by the CPI.

Year	1990	1991	1992	1993	1994	1995	1996	1997	1998
Percent Change	5.8	2.9	1.2	2.2	2.4	2.8	3.3	2.6	2.2
Cost of Food ($)									

a. Suppose a consumer went to the grocery store in 1989 and spent $100 on basic food items. Based on the CPI table above, how much would the consumer pay one year later, buying the same food items? Show all work and place the cost of food for 1990 in the table above.

b. Use the answer to part *a* to calculate how much the consumer would pay in 1991 for the same food items that originally cost $100 in 1989.

c. Continue filling in the third row for all the remaining years. Use the same process as in part *b* to complete your table. What is the cost in 1998 for the same bag of groceries that cost $100 in 1989?

10. Can you keep up with inflation? Suppose your salary increased by 2.5% every year after 1989. Take $100 dollars of your 1989 salary and explore how this value increases each year for the next nine years. For example, one year after 1989, every $100 from your salary increases by 2.5%. So the future value of $100 after one year is calculated as follows:

$$\text{Future value in } 1990 = 100 + 0.025 \cdot 100$$
$$= 100 + 2.50$$
$$= \$102.50$$

a. Find the future value of $100 in 1991 by increasing the 1990 value of $102.50 by 2.5%. Show all work below.

b. Continue the process of increasing the current value by 2.5% each year up to 1998. Record the results in the table below.

Year	1990	1991	1992	1993	1994	1995	1996	1997	1998
Percent Change	2.5	2.5	2.5	2.5	2.5	2.5	2.5	2.5	2.5
Future Value	102.50								

c. Compare the results of Section Exercise #9 (p. 305) with the work you did above, and then explain whether your salary earnings have kept up with the price of food.

_____

_____

_____

_____

Section 4.3 Rates and Percent Change

Math Talk

Before you investigate the first Discovery Adventure, a few words on terminology. If we think of a *ratio* as the comparison of two quantities, then a **rate** is just a special case of a ratio, where the two quantities have different units. For example,

- Suppose the speed limit on a highway is 65 mph. This is short for the rate, $\dfrac{65 \text{ miles}}{1 \text{ hour}}$. In other words, a car can travel at most 65 miles per hour on this particular highway.

- Bananas are on sale for $0.49 per pound. This can be expressed as the rate, $\dfrac{\$0.49}{1 \text{ pound}}$.

- In 1998, the United States had 566.4 violent crimes for every 100,000 inhabitants. This can be written as the rate, $\dfrac{566.4 \text{ violent crimes}}{100,000 \text{ inhabitants}}$.

Why were the first two examples given as "per 1 unit" and the last as "per 100,000 units?"

When comparing quantities, it is not necessary to get too focused on which term, ratio or rate, is the most appropriate to use. Many people use them interchangeably. Just remember that a ratio or rate implies that you are comparing two quantities.

A ratio or rate is used to compare one quantity to another. If we let the first quantity be x and the second be y, then the ratio of x to y or the rate of x to y can be denoted as follows:

$$x : y \quad \text{or} \quad \frac{x}{y}.$$

Be sure to include the units when expressing rates.

****

Note that the violent crime rate given above can be expressed in terms of different quantities of inhabitants. For example,

$$\frac{566.4 \div 10}{100,000 \div 10} = \frac{56.64 \text{ violent crimes}}{10,000 \text{ inhabitants}}$$

The above rate means that there are about 60 violent crimes for every 10,000 inhabitants.

$$\frac{566.4 \div 100}{100,000 \div 100} = \frac{5.664 \text{ violent crimes}}{1000 \text{ inhabitants}}$$

It also means that there are about 6 violent crimes for every 1000 inhabitants.

What would be the problem with expressing the violent crime rate in terms of every 100 inhabitants, 10 inhabitants, or 1 inhabitant?

_____

_____

_____

Suppose the violent crime rate is given as 0.005664 and you know the total U.S. population to be 270,296,000. Show how could you calculate the total number of violent crimes.

Discovery Adventure 1: Births and Deaths in Perspective

Often vital statistics about populations are given in terms of a rate per every 1000 people. To see why, let's examine 1996 data on the birth and death rates in both Canada and Haiti as compared with the world.

	Population (millions)	Birth Rate per 1000	Death Rate per 1000
World	5,607	25	9
Canada	29.1	14	7
Haiti	7	42	19

Source: World Almanac and Book of Health, 1996.

The first row of the table tells us that there are 5,607,000,000 people in the world and that in 1996, there were 25 births and 9 deaths for every thousand people in the world over 1 year.

a. Compare the birth rate of Canada with the birth rate of Haiti. Make a general statement comparing the two rates.

_____

_____

b. Compare the death rate of the world with the death rate of Haiti. Make a statement comparing the two rates.

_____

_____

c.   The world's birth and death rates are given as fractions and decimals below. Complete the table by entering the values for Canada and Haiti.

Country	Birth Rate Fraction	Birth Rate Decimal	Death Rate Fraction	Death Rate Decimal
World	$\dfrac{25}{1000}$	0.025	$\dfrac{9}{1000}$	0.009
Haiti				
Canada				

d.   The world's birth rate of $\dfrac{25}{1000}$ means that over a one-year period (in 1996) there were 25 births for every 1000 people in the world.

- How many births are there for every 100 people in the world? *Hint*: For the fraction $\dfrac{25}{1000}$, divide the numerator and denominator by 10.

- How many births are there for every 10 people in the world? *Hint*: For the fraction $\dfrac{25}{1000}$, divide the numerator and denominator by 100.

- How many births are there for every person in the world? *Hint*: For the fraction $\dfrac{25}{1000}$, divide the numerator and denominator by 1000.

e.   Use the information in part *d* to find the total number of births in the world during 1996.

f.   What was the total number of deaths in the world during 1996?

g. The excess of births over deaths is called the natural increase in the population. Find the natural increase in the world's population.

h. Find the rate of natural increase per 1000 people in the world using the following formula:

$$\frac{\text{natural increase in world population}}{\text{world population}} \div 1000$$

i. Explain what the rate from part *h* means in terms of world population growth.

_____

_____

_____

Feedback

The first things to establish when analyzing rates is what is being counted (births, deaths, marriages) and over what period of time (months, years, decades). When a rate is in fractional form, the numerator is the item being counted, and the denominator is the units (1000's, 100,000's) for the base population (people in the world, citizens of Canada, citizens of Haiti).

When first examining the population data, you might have noted that the birth rate in Haiti is 3 times that of Canada. In other words, during 1996, there were 3 times as many births for every 1000 people in Haiti as compared with every 1000 people in Canada.

In 1996, the number of births for every person in the world was 0.025. This means that for each person there were 0.025 births. While this rate does not seem to give useful information, it can be used in numerical calculations to find out other important information. For example, the total number of births in the world over 1 year can be expressed as

$$(\text{Birthrate Per 1 Person}) \cdot (\text{World Population}) = \text{Total World Births}$$
$$(0.025) \cdot (5,607,000,000) = 140,175,000$$

Whenever you express something per 1 unit, you can use this value in calculations that produce valuable information. For example, if Samantha's pay rate is $12.75 per hour and she works 24 hours per week, then her weekly earnings would be calculated as follows:

$$(\text{Pay rate per 1 hour}) \cdot (\text{Number of hours}) = \text{Earnings per week}$$
$$(\$12.75) \cdot (24) = \$306$$

The pay rate per hour ($12.75) is a value you can understand, but the birth rate per person is not. It is for this reason that the birth rate is expressed as per 1000 people.

$$(\text{Birth rate per person}) \cdot (1000) = \text{Birth rate per 1000 people}$$
$$(0.025) \cdot (1000) = 25$$

****

Now you will look at the birth rate and death rate of the United States population and how it has changed during the period from 1960 to 1997. You will investigate these rates using the following formula for percent change:

$$\text{Percent change} = \frac{\text{New value} - \text{Old value}}{\text{Old value}} \cdot 100$$

Discovery Adventure 2: Revealing Rates

Examine the following data from the National Center for Health Statistics, U.S. Dept. of Health and Human Services. Rates are given per 1000 people.

Year	Births Total number	Rate	Deaths Total number	Rate
1960	4,257,850	23.7	1,711,982	9.5
1970	3,731,386	18.4	1,921,031	9.5
1980	3,612,258	15.9	1,989,841	8.7
1990	4,158,212	16.7	2,148,463	8.6
1991	4,110,907	16.3	2,169,518	8.6
1992	4,065,014	15.9	2,175,613	8.5
1993	4,000,240	15.5	2,268,000	8.8
1994	3,952,767	15.2	2,278,994	8.8
1995	3,899,589	14.8	2,312,132	8.8
1996	3,891,494	14.7	2,314,690	8.7
1997	3,880,894	14.5	2,314,245	8.6

Suppose you want to know how the birth rate in 1980 compared to the birth rate in 1970. You could find the percent change using the formula just given:

$$\text{Percent change} = \frac{\text{New value} - \text{Old value}}{\text{Old value}} \cdot 100$$

$$= \frac{15.9 - 18.4}{18.4} \cdot 100$$

$$= \frac{-2.5}{18.4} \cdot 100$$

$$\approx -0.136 \cdot 100 = -13.6$$

The minus represents a 13.6 percent decrease in the birth rate. In other words, the number of births has decreased by 13.6%.

a. Find the percent change in the U. S. birth rate from 1980 to 1990, and then explain the trend in the number of births during this period.

_____

_____

_____

b. Find the percent change in the U. S. birth rate from 1990 to 1997, and then explain the trend in the number of births during this period.

_____

_____

_____

c. Find the percent change in the U. S. death rate from 1960 to 1970, and then explain the trend in the number of deaths during this period.

_____

_____

_____

d. How is it possible that more people died in 1970 than in 1960, yet the death rate stayed the same?

_____

_____

_____

e. Find the percent change in the U. S. death rate from 1970 to 1980, and then explain the trend in the number of deaths during this period.

_____

_____

_____

f. Complete the table below by filling in all the percent changes in birth rate and death rate over each period listed.

Years	Percent Change in Birth Rate	Percent Change in Death Rate
1960-70		
1970-80		
1980-90		
1990-97		

g. Use the table to explain the trend in the birth rate over the whole period from 1960-1997.

_____

_____

_____

_____

h. Use the table to explain the trend in the death rate over the whole period from 1960-1997.

_____

_____

_____

_____

i. When finding the percent change, why do we use the rate as "per 1000" instead of as "per the total number"?

_____

_____

_____

_____

Feedback

In using the percent change formula, you found the ratio of the change in rate (numerator) to the previous rate (denominator). Multiplying the ratio by 100 expresses the result as a percent increase (positive value) or percent decrease (negative value). For example, the percent change in the U.S. birth rate from 1980 to 1990 is calculated as follows:

$$\text{Percent change} = \frac{\text{New value} - \text{Old value}}{\text{Old value}}$$

$$= \frac{\text{Change in rate}}{\text{Previous rate}}$$

$$= \frac{16.7 - 15.9}{15.9}$$

$$= \frac{0.8}{15.9}$$

$$\approx 0.05 \quad \text{or} \quad 5\%$$

During the period from 1960 to 1970, the number of deaths increased by 209,049 while the percent change in the death rate remained the same (9.5 per 1000). This is not a surprising result if you consider that the U.S. population increased by 23,978,856 during the same period.

The rate per 1000 people is used to find the percent change in the birth and death rates because the total number would not take into account the rise in population over time.

****

Banks make money by using your money on things such as mortgages, personal loans, auto loans, and so on. If you deposit your money into an account that pays **interest**, then the bank is giving you something back for allowing them to use your money. In the next Discovery Adventure, you will look at how money can grow over time.

Discovery Adventure 3: Compound Interest

A bank account can earn interest over different periods of time (year, month, day, and so on). When that time arrives, the bank takes a percent of the total amount in the account, called the **principal**, and adds that value to the principal to produce a new principal. The process of adding interest to the principal for every new time period is called **compound interest**.

a. Suppose you invest $500 in a new account with a bank that pays an **annual interest rate** of 4.5% once every year. Let's see how that money would grow over 5 years if there were no deposits or withdrawals. Complete the table below following the pattern already started.

Year	Principal ($)	Interest ($)	Ending Balance ($)
1	500	$0.045 \cdot 500 = 22.50$	522.50
2	522.50		
3			
4			
5			

b. If you invest a larger amount, say $1000, in a new account with a bank that pays an annual interest rate of 4.5% compounded yearly, then show how that money would grow over 5 years if there were no deposits or withdrawals. Complete the table below following the pattern already started.

Year	Principal ($)	Interest ($)	Ending Balance ($)
1	1000	$0.045 \cdot 1000 = 45$	1045
2	1045		
3			
4			
5			

c. Now suppose you invest the same amount of $1000 in a new account with a different bank that pays an annual interest rate of 9% compounded yearly. Show how that money would grow over 5 years if there were no deposits or withdrawals. Complete the table below following the pattern already started.

Year	Principal ($)	Interest ($)	Ending Balance ($)
1	1000	$0.09 \cdot 1000 = 90$	1090
2	1090		
3			
4			
5			

d. If a 9% annual interest rate is compounded monthly, then 9% is broken up into 12 equal parts. What is the monthly interest rate when you apply 9% over a 12-month period? Show how you arrived at your answer.

e. Invest the same amount of $1000 in a new account with a bank that pays an annual interest rate of 9% compounded monthly. Complete the following table to show the monthly calculations over a one-year period.

Month	Principal ($)	Interest ($)	Ending Balance ($)
1	1000.00	$0.0075 \cdot 1000 = 7.50$	1007.50
2	1007.50		
3			
4			
5			
6			
7			
8			
9			
10			
11			
12			1093.81

f. Compare the ending balance when compounding monthly to the ending balance when compounding annually after one year. Explain why compounding with the same percent (9%), divided up $(9\%/12 = 0.75\%)$ and applied over shorter periods of time (months), increases the value of your investment over the same length of time (1 year).

_____

_____

_____

_____

g. Show how the $1000 investment in part *e* would continue to grow over 5 years compounding monthly, assuming that there were no deposits or withdrawals. Use your calculator to quickly do all monthly computations for each year, up to the 5th year, putting the final balance at the end of each year in the table below.

Year	Ending Balance ($)
1	1093.81
2	
3	
4	
5	

Feedback

Let's summarize your work on compound interest by first defining the terminology used.

Compound Interest Terminology

Principal – The current balance or total amount of money in your account.

Interest – A percent of the principal that is added to the current principal.

Rate of interest – The percentage used to calculate the interest.

Annual interest rate – The rate of interest each year.

In Discovery Adventure 3 (parts *a*, *b*, and *c*), you calculated the interest one time per year. For example, in part *c*, your bank gave an annual interest rate of 9% compound yearly. Therefore, 9% of your principal was added to the account each year. Here is the calculation for year 1:

$$\text{Balance after 1 year} = \text{Principal} + \text{Interest}$$
$$= \text{Principal} + \text{Rate} \cdot \text{Principal}$$
$$= 1000 + 0.09 \cdot 1000$$
$$= 1000 + 90$$
$$= 1090$$

When the interest ($90) is added to the principal ($1000), you obtain a new principal ($1090). The calculations for year 2 appear below:

$$\text{Balance after 2 years} = \text{Principal} + \text{Interest}$$
$$= \text{Principal} + \text{Rate} \cdot \text{Principal}$$
$$= 1090 + 0.09 \cdot 1090$$
$$= 1090 + 98.10$$
$$= 1188.10$$

After 2 years, the interest ($98.10) has increased because it is calculated on the original principal ($1000) plus the first year's interest ($90). The cycle will continue each year so that interest is always calculated on the current principal plus the previous interest. This process is called *compounding interest*.

In part *d*, the 9% annual interest rate is compounded monthly. The monthly interest rate when you apply 9% over 12 one-month periods is computed as follows:

$$\frac{0.09}{12} = 0.0075 \quad \text{or} \quad 0.75\% \text{ per month}$$

In part *e*, the interest is calculated 12 times using the monthly rate of 0.0075 or 0.75%. Since the interest is computed more often, the principal is able to grow to a larger amount ($1093.81) than if it was compounded yearly.

In general, the annual interest rate will produce a higher yield depending on the frequency of the compound period. However, it can be shown that the yield will not increase much when interest is compounded more often than that.

Section Exercises: 4.3

1. The following sentences describe different rates (comparison of two numbers with different units). In each part, read the words and then express the rate as a fraction with units. Reduce each fraction, when necessary, to a unit rate (a fraction with a denominator of 1).

   a. The car travels 150 miles in $2\frac{1}{2}$ hours.

   b. During the 150-mile trip, the car used 7.5 gallons of gas.

   c. The customer pays $11.85 to buy 3 pounds of turkey at the local deli.

   d. Last week a sales clerk received a paycheck with a gross pay of $307.50 for working a total of 30 hours.

   e. In 1999, Stephen paid $3348 in federal taxes on wages of $22,320. He wants to know the tax rate on his earnings for the year.

2. Recall Discovery Adventure 3: Compound Interest (pp. 315-317). In part *g*, we investigated how a $1000 investment would grow over 5 years when compounded monthly. What will happen to the $1000 investment if the interest is compounded more frequently?

   a. Suppose the interest is compounded daily, then what type of computations must be performed and how often will these computations be applied?

   _____

   _____

   _____

b. What do you think will happen to your investment with a daily compounding of interest? Explain.

_____

_____

_____

_____

3. In Discovery Adventure 3: Compound Interest part *c,* we showed that interest ($90) is calculated as the rate times the principal ($0.09 \cdot 1000$). Then summing the principal and interest ($\$1000 + \$90$) produced the ending balance ($1090). Here is an alternative way to proceed with the same problem:

$$\text{Principal} + \text{Interest} = 1 \cdot \text{Principal} + \text{Rate} \cdot \text{Principal}$$

$$= 1 \cdot 1000 + 0.09 \cdot 1000$$

$$= (1 + 0.09) \cdot 1000 \qquad \text{Distributive property}$$

$$= (1.09) \cdot 1000 \qquad \text{Add}$$

$$= 1090 \qquad \text{Multiply}$$

a. Use this alternative approach in the table below to find the same results as in part *c.*

Year	(1 + Rate) · Principal	Ending Balance ($)
0		1000
1	$(1.09) \cdot 1000$	1090
2	$(1.09) \cdot 1090$	
3		
4		
5		

b. Complete the following sentence.

At the end of each year, multiply the ending balance or current principal from the previous year by _____ to obtain the new ending balance or current principal.

c. The ending balance or current principal can be quickly computed on a calculator by entering the initial investment ($1000) and continually multiply by 1.09 each year. Complete the following table by expressing the calculation for ending balance using repeated multiplication and exponential notation.

Year	Repeated Multiplication	Exponential Notation
0	1000	1000
1	$1000 \cdot (1.09)$	$1000 \cdot (1.09)^1$
2	$1000 \cdot (1.09)(1.09)$	$1000 \cdot (1.09)^2$
3		
4		
5		

d. The compound interest formula that calculates the ending balance or current principal can be given as $P(1+r)^t$. Explain what the variables P, r, and t represent.

_____

_____

_____

e. While banks cannot pay high interest rates, stocks and bonds can. Use the formula from part d to find the future value of a $5000 investment after 10 years at an interest rate of 21% compounded yearly.

f. Find the future value of a $5000 investment after 10 years at an interest rate of 21% compounded monthly. You will have to make a slight adjustment to the formula in part d and to your calculation.

g. Find the future value of a $5000 investment after 10 years at an interest rate of 21% compounded daily. You will have to make a slight adjustment to the formula and your calculation.

4. In 1998, the United States had an estimated 3,944,046 births, 2,338,070 deaths, 2,244,000 marriages, and 1,135,000 divorces, all out of a total population of 270,298,524. Compute the following rates per 1000 population. (Source: National Center for Health Statistics, US Dept. of Health and Human Services.)

   a. Birth rate:

   b. Death rate:

   c. Marriage rate:

   d. Divorce rate:

5. Examine the following vital statistics in the U.S. obtained from the National Center for Health Statistics, US Dept. of Health and Human Services.

Category	1997 Total Number	1998 Total Number	1997 Rate per 1000	1998 Rate per 1000
Births	3,880,894	3,944,046	14.5	14.6
Deaths	2,314,245	2,338,070	8.647	8.650
Natural Increase				
Marriages	2,384,000	2,244,000	8.9	8.3

   a. *Natural increase* is the excess of births over deaths. Complete columns 2 and 3 in the "Natural Increase" row.

b. Use the 1998 U.S. population of 270,298,524 to find the natural increase rate per 1000 for 1998.

c. Find the percent change in the total number of births from 1997 to 1998.

d. Find the percent change in the birth rate from 1997 to 1998.

e. The answers to parts *a* and *b* have different meanings. Explain what each answer means and how they are different. *Hint:* The U.S. population increases each year.

_____

_____

_____

_____

_____

_____

f. There were 6% fewer marriages in 1998 than in 1997. Show the calculation you need to perform to arrive at this result.

g. The marriage rate for 1998 was 7% lower than in 1997. Show the calculation you need to perform to arrive at this result.

h. Explain how the percent change in the marriage rate (part *e*) can decrease more than the percent change in total number of marriages (part *d*) during the same period of time.

_____

_____

_____

_____

6. The New York City Police Department started an experiment in the early 1990s that stressed cleaning and fixing up neighborhoods, streets, parks, and subways as well as enforcing laws against street prostitution, drug dealing, graffiti, vandalism, and other "minor" crimes that affect quality of life. The following table appeared in a newspaper article on fighting crime.

Felonies in New York City
Population (1990): 7,322,564

Crime Category	1993	1996	Percent Change
Murder	1,927	984	
Rape*	2,255	2,883	
Robbery	85,892	49,306	
Assault	41,121	30,572	
Burglary	100,936	61,901	
Grand larceny	85,737	58,633	
Auto theft	111,618	59,440	
Total	429,486	263,719	

Source: KRT, New York City Police Dept.
*Increase attributed in part to increased reporting of the crime.

a. Complete the entries in the last column, which did appear in the newspaper article.

b. If we assume that the population of New York City remained about the same between 1993 and 1996, then what seems to have happened to the Big Apple during this three-year period?

_____

_____

_____

c. If there was an increase in the population between 1993 and 1996, then explain how the percent change in the last column is somewhat misleading.

_____

_____

_____

_____

d. Many crime-fighting experts think that this experimental policy of cleaning the urban landscape was essential in helping to reduce crime. Do you agree or disagree? Justify your answer.

_____

_____

_____

_____

e. What other factors would help to reduce crime in a big city such as New York? Justify your answer.

_____

_____

_____

_____

f. According to the newspaper article, Bryant Park went from a drug dealer hangout where 144 muggings occurred the year before the park was renovated to a tree-lined public area with only 1 mugging in the year after renovation was finished. What was the percent change in people being mugged over this period of time? Show all calculations.

7. The following data gives information on AIDS deaths and new AIDS cases in the U.S. from 1993-97. Fill in the third and fifth columns by finding the annual percent change in deaths and the percent change in new cases during this time period. Round each yearly change to the nearest tenth of a percent. Then answer the questions below.

Year	Deaths	Annual % Change in Deaths	New Cases	Annual % Change in New Cases
1993	44,108		102,082	
1994	48,110		77,092	
1995	47,858		70,839	
1996	34,557		66,398	
1997	14,185		58,254	

Source: Health, United States, 1999; HIV/AIDS Surveillance Report, Vol. 10, No. 2, covering through 1998; National Center for Health Statistics, U.S. Dept. of Health and Human Services.

a. Observe the annual percent change in deaths from 1993-97, and then explain the trend in the data during this time period.

_____

_____

_____

b. Observe the annual percent change in new cases from 1993-97, and then explain the trend in the data during this time period.

_____

_____

_____

c. From 1993-1994 there was a 9.1% increase in deaths and a 24.5% decrease in new cases of AIDS. Why do you think the number of deaths from AIDS went up at the same time that there was a big drop in new AIDS cases?

_____

_____

_____

d. During the period from 1994-1997 the number of deaths from AIDS dropped drastically. List what you think are the main reasons for this decrease. Explain.

_____

_____

_____

In Section Exercises #8–11, you will look at percent change in price and population. For example, suppose you go to a store and see a leather jacket on sale for $125. When you return to the same store one week later, you find that its price has been reduced to $100. The percent change in price is calculated as follows:

$$\text{Percent change} = \frac{\text{New price} - \text{Old price}}{\text{Old price}} \cdot 100$$

$$= \frac{100 - 125}{125} \cdot 100$$

$$= \frac{-25}{125} \cdot 100$$

$$= -0.20 \cdot 100$$

$$= -20$$

The leather jacket has been reduced 20% from the previous sale price.

8. According to the National Association of Realtors, the median (middle) price of existing single family homes changed from $121,800 in 1997 to $128,400 in 1998. Find the percent change in these home prices from 1997 to 1998. Show all work as in the example above. Round to the nearest tenth of a percent, and state your result using a complete sentence.

_____

9. According to the Census Bureau, the population of California was 23,667,764 in 1980 and 29,785,857 in 1990. Find the percent change in population from 1980 to 1990. Show all work. Round to the nearest tenth of a percent, and state your result using a complete sentence.

_____

10. According to the Census Bureau, the population of West Virginia was 1,950,186 in 1980 and 1,793,477 in 1990. Find the percent change in population from 1980 to 1990. Show all work. Round to the nearest tenth of a percent, and state your result using a complete sentence.

---

11. The Bureau of Labor Statistics uses the Consumer Price Index (CPI) to measure the average change in prices of selected goods and services needed for daily living. The CPI was 160.5 in 1997 and 163.0 in 1998. Find the percent change in the price level from 1997 to 1998. Show all work. Round to the nearest tenth of a percent, and state your result using a complete sentence.

Section 4.4 Ratio and Proportion

Math Talk

Let's talk about the words *ratio* and *proportion*. A **ratio** is the quotient of two quantities. Often we use a ratio to make a comparison between two quantities. For example, if there are 10 men and 20 women in your math class, then the ratio of women to men is written as

$$20 \text{ to } 10 \quad \text{or} \quad \frac{20}{10} \quad \text{or} \quad 20:10.$$

But this ratio can be reduced to the equivalent ratio,

$$2 \text{ to } 1 \quad \text{or} \quad \frac{2}{1} \quad \text{or} \quad 2:1.$$

This means for every 2 women there is 1 man in your class.

When you have two ratios that are equal, the equality is called a **proportion.** For example, in the math class considered above, the ratio of $\frac{20}{10}$ equals the ratio of $\frac{2}{1}$.

$$\frac{20}{10} = \frac{2}{1} \qquad \frac{20}{10} \text{ is proportional to } \frac{2}{1}$$

A proportion is the equality of two ratios. More formally, if a, b, c, and d are four related quantities such that the ratio of one pair $\frac{a}{b}$ equals the ratio of a second pair $\frac{c}{d}$, then the two pairs of quantities a, b and c, d are in proportion:

$$\frac{a}{b} = \frac{c}{d}$$

The same proportion can also be expressed using colon notation,

$$a:b::c:d$$

You can determine whether a proportion is true by checking to see if the cross products are equal.

$$\frac{a}{b} = \frac{c}{d} \quad \text{is true if} \quad a \cdot d = b \cdot c.$$

For example,

$$\frac{20}{10} = \frac{2}{1} \quad \text{is true because} \quad 20 \cdot 1 = 10 \cdot 2.$$

In the first Discovery Adventure, you will use proportional reasoning to investigate whether the height to base ratio of a ladder makes it safe to climb.

Discovery Adventure 1: The Safe Ratio?

Jim has decided to paint his house with help from his 10-year old son Mike. Before they begin the job, Jim explains that when setting up a ladder, a safe rule of thumb is to have a height-to-base ratio of 4 to 1. Mike nods his head, but he doesn't have a clue what his father is talking about.

a. In simplest terms, explain to Mike what a 4 to 1 ratio means in terms of setting up a ladder against the house.

_____

_____

_____

b. Mike's first attempt at setting up a ladder places the top 16 feet vertically off the ground and the bottom 2 feet horizontally away from the side of the house. Draw a picture of this situation below.

c. Do you think Mike has a safe height-to-base ratio for the ladder? If the placement is safe, explain why. Otherwise, state the possible dangers.

_____

_____

_____

_____

d. Before Mike attempts to climb the ladder, his father notices the placement and yells at Mike that he does not like his set-up. So Mike extends the ladder up and moves the bottom further out. The ladder is now positioned so that the top has the same vertical height of 16 feet, but the bottom is now 8 feet horizontally from the side of the house. Draw a picture of this situation.

e. Do you think Mike has a safe height-to-base ratio for the ladder? If the placement is safe, explain why. Otherwise, state the possible dangers.

_____

_____

_____

_____

f. Just as the bottom of the ladder starts to slip away from the house, Jim slams his shoe behind the bottom footing and grabs the ladder to stop the near accident. Dad decides he better model a safe ratio himself. So Jim lowers the ladder down a few rungs and places the top at the same vertical height of 16 feet, but the bottom is now 4 feet horizontally from the side of the house. Draw a picture of this situation.

g. Explain why the placement of the ladder in part *f* is safe.

_____

_____

_____

h. When the height-to-base ratio of 4 to 1 is expressed in fractional form $\frac{4}{1}$, what does the numerator and denominator tell you about the steepness (incline) of the ladder?

_____

_____

_____

Feedback

A ratio of four-to-one can be expressed in fractional form as $\frac{4}{1}$ or using colon notation as 4 : 1.

In the ladder situation, we can interpret this to mean that for every one foot of horizontal change there is 4 feet of vertical change or vice-versa. So, for every 4 feet you move the top of ladder up (vertically), you must move the bottom of the ladder 1-foot out (horizontally) away from the house to stay close to the safety standard.

The set-up Jim used (see Figure C on the next page) is safe because the following statement is true: "16 feet vertically to 4 feet horizontally is proportional to 4 feet vertically to 1 foot horizontally." For example,

$$\frac{16 \text{ ft.}}{4 \text{ ft.}} = \frac{4 \text{ ft.}}{1 \text{ ft.}}$$

The first placement was dangerous because a ladder ratio of $\frac{16}{2}$ can be reduced to the ratio of $\frac{8}{1}$. This ratio is too large and may cause the top of the ladder to fall backwards. You can say that $\frac{16}{2}$ is proportional to $\frac{8}{1}$ and write

$$\frac{16}{2} = \frac{8}{1}.$$

The second placement was dangerous because a ladder ratio of $\frac{16}{8}$ can be reduced to the ratio of $\frac{2}{1}$. This ratio is too small and may cause the bottom of the ladder to slip away from the house.

The proportional relationship between the 4 numbers is written as

$$\frac{16}{8} = \frac{2}{1}.$$

Figure A	**Figure B**	**Figure C**
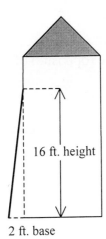	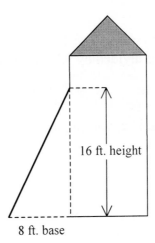	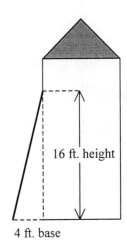
2 ft. base	8 ft. base	4 ft. base
Too steep, top might fall back.	Not steep enough, bottom might slip back and top slide down.	Safe set up, height to base ratio of 4 to 1.

In general, a ratio expressed as a vertical change over a horizontal change is known as the **slope** and can give us useful information on the steepness of a line.

$$\text{Slope} = \frac{\text{Vertical Change}}{\text{Horizontal Change}}$$

****

Recall that in Section 4.1 you explored solving an equation by *balancing* or making the same change on each side of the equation. Specifically, you were given the following rules.

Properties of Equality

- You can multiply or divide both sides of an equation by any real number except 0.

- You can add or subtract any real number to both sides of an equation.

Suppose you were asked to solve the following equation for the variable x.

$$\frac{x}{9} = \frac{5}{3}$$

The left side of the equal sign contains the expression $\frac{x}{9}$. The fraction bar implies what operation?

The expression $\frac{x}{9}$ translates to "a number divided by 9." What is the inverse (opposite) of dividing by 9?

To undo the division and isolate the variable x, you can multiply both sides by 9. For example,

$$\frac{x}{9} = \frac{5}{3}$$

$$9 \cdot \frac{x}{9} = \frac{5}{3} \cdot 9$$

$$\frac{\cancel{9}^{1}}{1} \cdot \frac{x}{\cancel{9}_{1}} = \frac{5}{\cancel{3}_{1}} \cdot \frac{\cancel{9}^{3}}{1}$$

$$x = 15$$

Another approach uses the fact that a proportion is true if the cross products are equal.

$$\frac{a}{b} = \frac{c}{d} \quad \text{is true if} \quad a \cdot d = b \cdot c$$

Let's use this approach to solve the example above.

$$\frac{x}{9} = \frac{5}{3} \quad \text{is true if} \quad x \cdot 3 = 9 \cdot 5$$

$$3x = 45$$

$$\frac{\cancel{3}^{1} x}{\cancel{3}_{1}} = \frac{45}{3}$$

$$x = 15$$

As another example, suppose you are given the following proportion.

$$\frac{5}{10} = \frac{4}{n}$$

If you want to solve for *n* (or find the value that can be substituted into *n* to make the equality a true statement), you can use the fact that a proportion is true if the cross products are equal.

$$5 \cdot n = 10 \cdot 4 \qquad \text{Set the cross products equal to each other.}$$

$$5n = 40 \qquad \text{Simplify.}$$

$$\frac{5n}{5} = \frac{40}{5} \qquad \text{Divide both sides of the equal sign by 5.}$$

$$n = 8 \qquad \text{Simplify.}$$

Also, you could start out by examining the original equation and use a guess and test strategy. Notice that the ratio $\frac{5}{10}$ on the left side of the equal sign can be reduced to $\frac{1}{2}$ so that the proportion can be expressed as follows:

$$\frac{1}{2} = \frac{4}{n}$$

So you are trying to find a value for *n* such that $\frac{4}{n}$ equals $\frac{1}{2}$. In other words, 4 divided by what number equals $\frac{1}{2}$? If the solution is not obvious by inspection, then proceed with the cross product method.

$$1 \cdot n = 2 \cdot 4$$

$$n = 8$$

As a check, substitute 8 for *n* in the original proportion.

$$\frac{5}{10} = \frac{4}{8} \qquad \text{Replace } n \text{ with its value, 8.}$$

Since the cross products are equal ($5 \cdot 8 = 40$ and $10 \cdot 4 = 40$), the proportion is true.

In the second Discovery Adventure, you will explore a situation in which one of the 4 quantities in a proportion is unknown. You will use the above techniques to solve this proportion for the unknown or variable.

Discovery Adventure 2: Capture-Tag-Recapture

Suppose in the course of their work, wildlife biologists want to estimate the number of fish in a lake. They use a procedure called capture-tag-recapture. This method involves catching a sample of fish in a big net, tagging each fish, and then releasing them back into the lake. After the fish are given enough time (several days) to mingle with the rest of the fish population, biologists make a second catch, taking note of the amount of fish having tags from the first catch.

The table below contains data on two species of fish: trout and bass. Let t be the total number of trout and b be the total number of bass in the lake.

Type	Total in Lake	Tagged in First Catch	Number in Second Catch	Recaptured from First Catch
Trout	t	217	106	12
Bass	b	236	335	17

a. For each type of fish, find the ratio of "tagged in first catch" to "total in lake," and place the results in the first row. Then find the ratios of "recaptured from first catch" to "number in second catch," and place the results in the second row.

	Trout Ratios	Bass Ratios
$\dfrac{\text{tagged in first catch}}{\text{total in lake}}$		
$\dfrac{\text{recaptured}}{\text{number in second catch}}$		

b. Assume that the ratio of "tagged in first catch" to "total in lake" is proportional to the ratio of "recaptured" to "number in second catch." Set up and solve a proportion that equates the two trout ratios.

$$\frac{\text{tagged in first catch}}{\text{total in lake}} = \frac{\text{recaptured}}{\text{number in second catch}}$$

c. Set up and solve a proportion that equates the two bass ratios.

d. On what other living creatures could you apply the capture-tag-recapture method for estimating wildlife populations? Explain why your choices are reasonable.

_____

_____

_____

e. Why do you think biologists wait a few days between the first and second catch?

_____

_____

_____

f. What would be the problem with making the second catch one year after the first catch?

_____

_____

_____

Feedback

To obtain a good estimate we must make sure that the creature being counted does not reproduce between the first and second capture. It is important that you wait long enough for the creatures to move and mix evenly throughout their environment. However, you do not want to wait too long because other factors like births, deaths, diseases, and changing environmental conditions may affect the population size.

Since it is usually impossible to count the exact number of living creatures within a wildlife population, the capture-tag-recapture sampling technique can be useful in estimating the size of a wildlife population in certain environments.

There are about 1917 trout and 4651 bass in the lake. These values can be obtained as follows:

$$\frac{217}{t} = \frac{12}{106}$$

$$217 \cdot 106 = t \cdot 12$$

$$23002 = 12t$$

$$\frac{23002}{12} = \frac{\cancel{12}\,t}{\cancel{12}}$$

$$1917 \approx t$$

$$\frac{236}{b} = \frac{17}{335}$$

$$236 \cdot 335 = b \cdot 17$$

$$79060 = 17b$$

$$\frac{79060}{17} = \frac{\cancel{17}\,b}{\cancel{17}}$$

$$4651 \approx b$$

In general, you may approximate the size of a wildlife population using the following proportion:

$$\frac{\text{Wildlife tagged in first sample}}{\text{Total wildlife in population}} = \frac{\text{Recaptured wildlife}}{\text{Wildlife in second sample}}$$

The equation for estimating wildlife populations indicates that the ratio of the number of tagged wildlife in the first sample to the total number of wildlife in the population is proportional to the ratio of the number of recaptured wildlife to the number of wildlife in the second sample.

****

Discovery Adventure 3: Alice in Waterland

Alice just received her first water bill from the town of Waterland. Alice thinks that the expected payment is a bit high, so she asks the Mr. Hatter for advice. He observes the following information from her bill.

Meter Readings in cubic feet		Consumption in cubic feet
Previous	**Current**	
196,300	205,500	9,200

Mr. Hatter tells Alice that she must convert the 9,200 ft^3 to gallons since he only understands volume measurements in gallons. Alice agrees, but she wants Mr. Hatter to be clear that 9,200 ft^3 is just another way to say 9,200 cubic feet and that it is the feet that is cubed, not the 9,200. She looks up the following conversion factor:

$$1 \text{ cubic foot} = 7.48 \text{ gallons}$$

a. Express the conversion factor above as a ratio (in fractional form) of gallons to cubic feet.

b. Let the consumption in gallons be represented by the variable *n*. Write a second ratio that compares the unknown amount of gallons to the known amount of cubic feet.

c. Set up and solve a proportion that equates the two ratios found in parts *a* and *b*. Make sure that you use the correct units in your set-up.

Mr. Hatter is now comfortable with the measurements in gallons. Unfortunately the table below has the block water usage in cubic feet. The first block, between 0 and 5000 cubic feet of water used, costs $1.80 per 100 cubic feet. The second block between 5000 and 10,000 cubic feet used cost $2.35 per 100 cubic feet, and so on.

Block water usage from (cubic feet) to	0– 5000	5000– 10,000	10,000– 20,000	20,000– 50,000
Water rates per 100 cubic feet	$1.80	$2.35	$2.45	$2.55

d. If Alice consumed 9,200 cubic feet of water, then what columns in the table will she need to use to figure out the total payment that must be made?

Let's first solve a proportion based on the first 5000 cubic feet that Alice used. Represent the unknown cost for the first 5000 cubic feet with the variable *x*.

e. Express the price of $1.80 per 100 cubic feet as your first ratio.

First Ratio:

f. Express the cost *x* for the first 5000 cubic feet used as your second ratio.

Second Ratio:

g. Set up and solve a proportion that equates the first ratio from part *e* to the second ratio from part *f*.

Now solve a proportion based on the remaining 4200 cubic feet that Alice used. Represent the unknown cost of the remaining 4200 cubic feet with the variable y.

h. Express the price of $2.35 per 100 cubic feet as your first ratio.

i. Express the cost y for the remaining 4200 cubic feet used as your second ratio.

j. Set up and solve a proportion that equates the first ratio from part h to the second ratio from part i.

k. Use your results from parts g and j to find the total payment Alice must make.

Feedback

To calculate the cost of the first 5000 cubic feet of water used, you need to solve the following proportion for the variable x.

$$\frac{\$1.80}{100 \text{ ft}^3} = \frac{x \text{ dollars}}{5000 \text{ ft}^3}$$

$$100 \cdot x = 1.80 \cdot 5000$$

$$100x = 9000$$

$$\frac{\overset{1}{\cancel{100}} x}{\underset{1}{\cancel{100}}} = \frac{\overset{90}{\cancel{9000}}}{\underset{1}{\cancel{100}}}$$

$$x = \$90$$

To calculate the next 4200 cubic feet cubic feet of water used, you need to solve the following proportion for the variable y.

$$\frac{\$2.35}{100 \text{ ft}^3} = \frac{x \text{ dollars}}{4200 \text{ ft}^3}$$

$$100 \cdot x = 2.35 \cdot 4200$$

$$100x = 9870$$

$$\frac{\overset{1}{\cancel{100}} x}{\underset{1}{\cancel{100}}} = \frac{\overset{987}{\cancel{9870}}}{\underset{10}{\cancel{100}}}$$

$$x = \$98.70$$

Summing x and y gives Alice's total water bill cost, $188.70. For example,

$$x + y = 90 + 98.70$$
$$= \$188.70$$

Section Exercises: 4.4

1. Let's return to the vital statistics from 1996 that you studied in Section 4.3. The statistics given in the table below involve proportional relationships. The following questions will have you construct and solve proportional equations involving one unknown.

	Population (millions)	Birth Rate per 1000	Death Rate per 1000
World	5,607	25	9
Canada	29.1	14	7
Haiti	7	42	19

Source: World Almanac and Book of Health

a. In 1996 there were 25 babies born per 1000 people in the world. Express the world birth rate as a ratio in fractional form.

b. Let n represent the number of babies born in 1996. Set up a second ratio based on the ratio of n babies per 5,607 million people (5,607,000,000 people) in the world.

c. Set up a proportion that equates the ratios in parts a and b. Then solve the proportion by setting the cross products equal to one another.

d. In a complete sentence, describe what the answer to part c means in terms of world births.

_____

_____

e. Find the number of deaths in the world during 1996 by completing a procedure similar to the work done in parts *a* through *c*.

f. What is the natural increase in the population of the world?

g. If the 4 years after 1996 have the exact same increase as in part *f*, then how many people will be on the planet earth by the end of the year 2000?

h. Part *g* assumes a constant increase during the 4 years. Suppose instead that the population is increasing at a faster and faster rate. What will this do to your estimate in part *g*?

_____

_____

2. When drugs are administered to patients, the amount is often calculated by the patient's weight. While lecturing, your math instructor is bit by the poisonous vampire ladybug. Quickly you recall from biology class that the only cure is the correct dose of Maximum Sulfate. You run to the lab to grab the bottle and return to class. The label says the safe dose is 20 mg (milligrams) per kg (kilogram) of body weight. Each member of the class gives an estimate of the instructor's weight. You average all the estimates and come out with 180 lbs(pounds).

a. If 1 kg is equivalent to 2.2 lbs, use ratios and proportions to figure out how much your instructor weighs in kilograms.

b. Use ratios and proportions to find the safe dose amount of Maximum Sulfate to give to your instructor.

3. Mike and Jim are taking a hike up Green Hills. On the way up, Mike observes a tall tree and wonders what its height is from the ground. Jim notices that both Mike and the tree are casting easy-to-measure shadows in the same direction. So he measures Mike's shadow to be 1½ meter and the shadow of the tree to be 4 meters. Jim explains to Mike that his height of 1 meters should be in proportion to the tree's height in meters.

    a. Assuming that both Mike and the tree are at right angles to the ground, draw two similar triangles labeling the length of each shadow and letting the variable *h* represent the height of the tree. *Hint:* Two triangles are **similar** when their corresponding angles are equal and the corresponding sides are proportional.

    b. Set up and solve the proportion that equates Mike's height-to-shadow ratio with the tree's height-to-shadow ratio.

4. Suppose you bought a new car eight months ago and now have 16,000 miles on it. At this rate, how many miles will you have driven the car by the end of the year?

5. At a pace of 8 minutes per mile, a runner burns off 120 calories a mile.

    a. How far would this runner have to run (at 8 minutes a mile) to burn off a 1,350-calorie meal?

    b. How many calories would the runner burn off if he ran a marathon race (26.2 miles)?

6. A certain company claims that its tablet "absorbs ten times its weight in stomach acid."

   a. If the tablet weighs 3 grams, how much acid can it absorb?

   b. Suppose you had a kilogram (1,000 grams) of excess acid in your stomach (unlikely, but just suppose). How many of these tablets would you have to take?

7. Going into the last day of the major league season, Babe Boggs and Kirby Lockett had identical batting records of 200 hits in 600 at bats. On the last day of the season, Boggs had 7 hits in 8 times at bat, while Lockett had 9 hits in 12 times at bat. Who won the batting title? Justify your answer in words. *Hint:* The best hitter is the one with the highest "hits to at bats" ratio.

   _____

   _____

   _____

8. Your workplace has finally agreed to budget some money to renovate the front entrance, so that it is accessible to wheelchairs. Suppose you are in charge of making sure the construction crew builds the ramp so that it rises at a gradual slope. According to disability laws, the maximum slope ratio is 1 to 12, meaning the ramp must rise 1 inch in height (vertically) for every 12 inches it runs in length (horizontally). The vertical distance from the ground to the building entrance is 54 inches.

   a. Express the maximum safe slope ratio as a fraction and in colon form.

b. Let the variable x represent the horizontal distance needed for the ramp. You have measured and verified that the vertical distance from the ground is 54 inches. Express the slope of the ramp as the ratio of rise over run. Include a picture of the proposed ramp.

c. Now setup and solve a proportion to find x, the horizontal distance (run) needed for the ramp to meet the maximum safe slope ratio.

d. Suppose there is enough available land in front of your building to increase the run of the ramp by 2¼ feet. What will your new slope ratio be, if expressed in terms of a 1-foot rise? Is this safer than the original design? Explain your answer in words.

Safety Analysis: _____

_____

_____

_____

9. Solve for the variable in each of the following proportions.

a. $\dfrac{x}{6} = \dfrac{2}{3}$

b. $\dfrac{7}{5} = \dfrac{14}{n}$

c. $\dfrac{16}{24} = \dfrac{a}{9}$

d. $\dfrac{10}{y} = \dfrac{40}{72}$

e. $\dfrac{b}{15} = \dfrac{16}{8}$

f. $\dfrac{32}{c} = \dfrac{5}{4}$

10. A popular summer vacation town has a year-round population of 4200 people. However, during the summer months, only 1 out of every 10 people in this town are year-round residents. What is the population of this town during the summer season?

Chapter 4 Summary

Key Terms

Section 4.1

- **Algebra** – A branch of mathematics that generalizes arithmetic by introducing variables to represent a range of numbers.
- **Algebraic** – Relating to algebra.
- **Algebraic Expression** – A combination of numbers, variables, and operations. For example,

$$x - 7, \quad 2\pi r, \quad \frac{n}{5}, \quad 12 + a$$

- **Algebraic Equation** – A mathematical statement that expresses the equality of two expressions, where at least one of the expressions involves a variable. For example,

$$x - 7 = 5, \quad \frac{n}{5} = \frac{3}{4}$$

- **Percentage** – A fraction with a denominator of 100 or part of 100. For example, 15 percent is $\frac{15}{100} = 15\%$. The percent symbol % means, "divided by one hundred."

- **Inverse** – The inverse operation can undo what the original operation performed. For example, the inverse of subtracting 7 is adding 7. Also, the inverse of dividing by 5 is multiplying by 5.

$$
\begin{aligned}
x - 7 &= 5 \\
x - 7 + 7 &= 5 + 7 \\
x + 0 &= 12 \\
x &= 12
\end{aligned}
$$

$$
\begin{aligned}
\frac{n}{5} &= \frac{3}{4} \\
5 \cdot \frac{n}{5} &= 5 \cdot \frac{3}{4} \\
\frac{\cancel{5}}{1} \cdot \frac{n}{\cancel{5}} &= \frac{5}{1} \cdot \frac{3}{4} \\
n &= \frac{15}{4}
\end{aligned}
$$

- **Equivalent Equations** – Equations have the same solution set.
- **Algebraic Thinking** – The process of thinking about the relationships between changing quantities.

Section 4.2

- **Off** – In certain contexts, the word *off* implies subtraction. For example, suppose Electronics Depot has all computers on sale at 20% off their regular price. You can calculate the sale price of a $1000 computer as follows.

$$\text{Sale price} = \text{Regular Price} - \text{Discount}$$
$$= 1000 - (0.20 \cdot 1000)$$
$$= 1000 - 200$$
$$= \$800$$

- **Randomly** – If you *randomly* select an item, then every item in the population has the same chance of being selected.

Section 4.3

- **Rate** – The comparison of two quantities having different units of measure. For example, if a jogger can run 3 miles in 30 minutes, then her rate of speed is expressed as follows.

$$\frac{3 \text{ miles}}{30 \text{ minutes}} = \frac{1 \text{ mile}}{10 \text{ minutes}} = \frac{0.1 \text{ mile}}{1 \text{ minute}}$$

- **Interest** – A percent of the principal that is added to the current principal.
- **Principal** – The current balance or total amount of money in your account.
- **Compound Interest** – The process of paying interest on the initial principal and all previous interest earned on the account.
- **Annual Interest Rate** – The rate of interest each year.

Section 4.4

- **Ratio** – A quotient used to compare one quantity to another. For example, a particular ice cream sandwich has a ratio of 60 fat calories to 180 total calories.

$$\frac{60 \text{ fat calories}}{180 \text{ total calories}}$$

Since the above fraction reduces to 1/3, you now know that 1 out of every 3 calories or 33% of the total calories comes from fat.

- **Proportion** – When you have two ratios that are equal, the equality is called a *proportion*. For example,

$$\frac{60}{180} = \frac{1}{3}$$

The above equality states that the ratio of 60 to 180 is proportional to the ratio of 1 to 3.

- **Slope** – A measure of steepness of a line using the ratio of vertical change over horizontal change.
- **Similar** – Two triangles are *similar* when their corresponding angles are equal and the corresponding sides are proportional.

****

Questions for Review

---

1. Fractions, decimals, percents, how are they the same? Let's examine a particular college course that has the following grading procedure.

   - Homework is $\frac{1}{8}$ of your final grade.

   - Quizzes are $\frac{1}{4}$ of your final grade.

   - Midterm Exam is $\frac{1}{4}$ of your final grade.

   - Final Exam is $\frac{3}{8}$ of your final grade.

   a. The table below lists the 4 grading categories and the total of all categories. Complete the table by expressing each grading category as a fraction, decimal, and percent of your final grade.

Category	Fraction	Decimal	Percent
Homework			
Quizzes			
Midterm Exam			
Final Exam			
Total			

   b. If Jessica had a 94% average on her homework, 88% average on her quizzes, 80% on the midterm exam, and 92% on the final exam, then her final grade in the above course would be calculated as follows:

   Final average = $\frac{1}{8}$ of HW + $\frac{1}{4}$ of Quizzes + $\frac{1}{4}$ of Midterm + $\frac{3}{8}$ of Final Exam

   $= 0.125 \cdot 94 + 0.25 \cdot 88 + 0.25 \cdot 80 + 0.375 \cdot 92$

   $= 11.75 + 22 + 20 + 34.5$

   $= 88.25\%$

   Use the model above to find Bill's final grade if he received a 76% average on homework, 85% average on Quizzes, 70% on the midterm exam, and 80% on the final exam.

2. How can you use money to visualize the concept of percent? *Percent* means "per 100" or "divided by 100." Since a dollar equals 100 cents and a cent is $\frac{1}{100}$ of a dollar, you can use money amounts to represent the concept of percent. For example, imagine different parts of a dollar such as a penny (1¢) is 1% of a dollar, a nickel (5¢) is 5% of a dollar, a dime (10¢) is 10% of a dollar, and a quarter (25¢) is 25% of a dollar.

For each percent given below, state the equivalent money amount.

a. 7%

b. 40%

c. 95%

d. 350%

e. 0.5%

3. Do you know how to construct a circle graph or pie chart? For example, suppose a certain college surveyed all its students on the question, "Do you drink alcohol at least once a week?" The following table gives the number of students answering *yes* or *no* according to gender.

Gender	Number of Responses	Do you drink alcohol at least once a week?	
		Yes	No
Female	2,346	41%	59%
Male	1,654	58%	42%

a. Construct a circle graph that illustrates the male use of alcohol at the college.

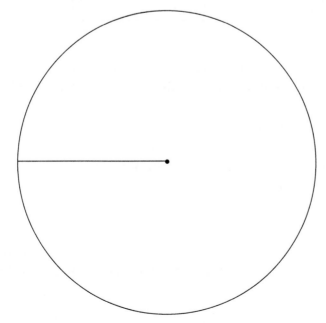

b. Construct a circle graph that illustrates the female use of alcohol at the college.

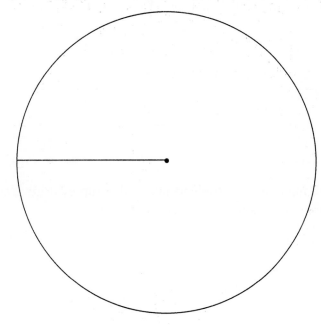

c. What percent of the college is female?

d. What percent of the college is male?

e. Calculate the total number of female students who drink alcohol at the college.

f. Calculate the total number of male students who drink alcohol at the college.

g. In parts *e* and *f,* you should have found that slightly more female students drink alcohol than male students at the college. How can this be true if the percent of males that drink alcohol is greater than the percent of females?

_____

_____

_____

_____

h. Did the majority (more than 50%) of students taking this survey drink alcohol? Show all work and explain your answer using a complete sentence.

_____

_____

_____

4. If you are given the check at a restaurant, can you calculate the tip mentally (in your head)? Suppose you decide to leave 10% of the check amount for fair service, 15% for good service, and 20% for excellent service. Finding 10% of a value is equivalent to multiplying that value by $\dfrac{10}{100}$ or 0.10, but this can be done mentally by moving the decimal point one place to the left. For example,

$$10\% \text{ of } \$66.40$$
$$0.10 \cdot 66.40 = \$6.64$$

Use the tipping method given above to answer the following questions.

a. If the check at a restaurant totals $46.80, then mentally determine the tip amount for service that is fair.

b. If the check at a restaurant totals $46.80, then mentally determine the tip amount for service that is good. *Hint:* $15\% = 10\% + 5\%$ and 5% is half of 10%.

c. If the check at a restaurant totals $46.80, then mentally determine the tip amount for service that is excellent. *Hint:* A 20% tip is twice a 10% tip, i.e., $20\% = 2 \cdot 10\%$.

5. How do you calculate a percent increase? For example, a dietician can determine a patient's energy or calorie needs by first finding the patient's Basal Energy Expenditure (BEE) or the minimum energy needed to sustain life in a resting person. Then, since people burn energy in their normal daily activities, you need to increase the BEE by a certain percentage based on their activity level.

Sedentary activity: Increase BEE by 30%
Moderate activity: Increase BEE by 40%
Strenuous activity: Increase BEE by 70%

If George has a BEE of 1822 calories, then calculate his energy or calorie needs for the three activity levels given above.

6. A clothing store has a policy of marking up all its merchandise by 25%.

   a. The store obtains a particular brand of dress shirt for the wholesale cost of $14. What will the price of the shirt be after the store does its mark up?

   b. Later the store puts the same dress shirt on sale by taking 25% off its regular price (found in part a.) What is the sale price?

   c. The cost of shirt was marked up by 25% and then that price was discounted by 25%. Explain why the sale price of this dress shirt (from part b) is not the same as the wholesale cost (from part a)?

   _____

   _____

   _____

7. If a quantity changes over time, do you know how to calculate the percent change? The following table presents data on median housing prices and median income by gender in the United States.

Year	Median Housing Price	Median Income	
		Men	Women
1997	$121,800	$35,248	$26,029
1998	$128,400	$36,252	$26,855

a. Calculate the percent change in housing prices from 1997 to 1998.

b. Calculate the percent change in income for men from 1997 to 1998.

c. Calculate the percent change in income for women from 1997 to 1998.

d. Based on the results from parts b and c, do you think women made any significant gains on men in terms of income?

_____

_____

_____

e. Have incomes kept up with housing prices? Use complete sentences in your answer.

_____

_____

_____

f. Set up a ratio that compares women's income to men's income in 1997. Calculate the ratio so that it is in decimal form.

g. What does this decimal value from part *f* mean in terms of income?

_____

_____

h. Set up a ratio that compares women's income to men's income in 1998. Calculate the ratio so that it is in decimal form.

i. Based on the results from parts *f* and *h*, do you think women made any significant gains on men in terms of income?

_____

_____

_____

8. State University has 120 full-time faculty and 360 part-time faculty.

a. What is the ratio of full-time faculty to part-time faculty?

b. Reduce the ratio found in part *a* to lowest terms and record the value below.

c. Set the ratio from part *a* equal to the ratio from part *b*. What mathematical term do we use to describe this equality?

9. Suppose the faculty union at State University (see Question #8) is holding an election for its officers (President, Vice President, Treasurer, etc.). Every full-time faculty member receives 1 whole vote, while each part-time faculty member receives $\frac{1}{4}$ of a whole vote.

a. Express $\frac{1}{4}$ as a decimal number and a percent.

b. How many part-time votes are needed to equal one full-time vote?

c. If all 360 part-time faculty vote in the election, then how many whole or full votes have been cast by the part-timers?

d. What is the total amount of whole votes, assuming all full-time and part-time faculty votes?

e. If every faculty member votes, what percent of the total votes are cast by the part-timers?

f. Suppose 90% of all part-timers and 20% of all full-timers voted for Candidate A for President. Who will win the election? Assume every faculty member votes and there are only two people running for President, Candidate A and Candidate B.

10. How can proportions be used to estimate future events? For example, a family moves into a new home and during the first 3 weeks uses 7350 gallons of water.

a. What is the ratio of gallons of water to number of days, during this 3-week period?

b. Let n be the amount of gallons used over a 1-year (365-day) period. Write a second ratio of gallons of water to number of days during a 1-year time frame.

c. Use the ratios from parts a and b to create an equality that assumes the use of water in the first 3 weeks as proportional to the water usage over 1 year. Then solve this proportion for n to estimate the amount of water the family will use over a year's time.

d. Check your answer to part c by showing that the cross products are equal.

Chapter 4 Quiz

1. Given the following 10 by 10 square grids, shade in the correct part of the whole to demonstrate how the following percentages can be visualized.

1%

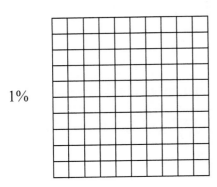

20%

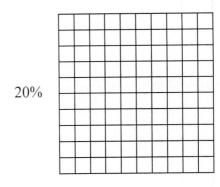

66%

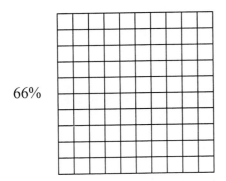

95%

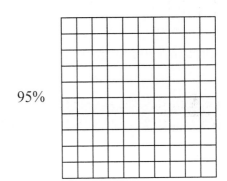

2. Fill in each blank with the correct value.

   a. 30% means 30 parts of _____, or 15 parts of _____, or 3 parts of _____.

   b. 75% means _____ divided by 100, or _____ divided by 20, or _____ divided by 4.

3. Find the number of geometric figures to shade in and complete the proportion so that a true statement is made.

   a. Shade in 25% of the circles and fill in the blank numerator to obtain a proportion that is true.

   $$\frac{25}{100} = \frac{}{12}$$

   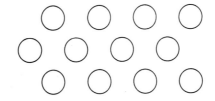

b. Shade in 10% of the squares and fill in the blank numerator to obtain a proportion that is true.

$$\frac{10}{100} = \frac{}{20}$$

c. Shade in 80% of the triangles and fill in the blank numerator to obtain a proportion that is true.

$$\frac{80}{100} = \frac{}{15}$$

4. Suppose Jane starts a nutritional plan of 2000 calories per day with 15% of calories from protein, 60% from carbohydrates, and 25% from fat. Find the number of calories Jane needs from protein, carbohydrates, and fat each day.

Protein:

Carbohydrates:

Fat:

5. Imagine you go to a bookstore that has all new hardcover books on sale at 20% off the regular price.

a. What is the sale price of a new hardcover book that regularly costs $30?

b. Suppose the store gives an extra 10% off the sale price to all college students. What would be the price of the book for any college student?

c. If the state sales tax is 5%, then what will be the final cost of the book to any college student?

6. Suppose you work for a company that offers you the following two options on how you can receive your annual raise in salary. Which option gives you the greatest increase in salary?

- An 8% increase at the end of 1 year or 12 months,
- A 4% increase after 6 months and then a second 4% increase after 6 more months.

Show all work and write your reasoning using complete sentences.

_____

_____

_____

7. Suppose you trade in your gas-guzzling vehicle, which receives 12 miles per gallon (mpg) for a small car that gets 45 miles per gallon.

   a. What is the percent change in mileage you receive from switching cars? Show all work and write your answer using a complete sentence.

_____

_____

   b. Previously you paid $60 per week for fuel to fill the tank of your gas-guzzling vehicle. Now you pay $15 per week to fill your small car. What is the percent change in fuel cost? Show all work and write your answer using a complete sentence.

_____

_____

8. Rates are often used when presenting data on events that occur in a population. For example, in 1998 there were 16,910 murders in the U.S., while the murder rate was 6.3 deaths per 100,000 people.

   a. Why do you think it's important to know the murder rate in addition to the total number of murders?

   _____

   _____

   _____

   b. Express the U.S. murder rate in fractional form.

   c. Let n represent the total population of the U.S in 1998. Set up a second ratio based on there being 16,910 murders per n people in the U.S.

   d. Set up and solve the proportion that equates the ratios in parts b and c.

9. Suppose half of a basketball game has been played and the team's best shooter Greg has made 5 out of the 10 shots attempted.

   a. If Greg misses his next 5 shots, what will happen to his shooting percentage? Complete the table by entering the ratio of shots made to shots attempted as a fraction in the third row, the decimal equivalent in the fourth row, and the shooting percentage in the fifth row.

Shots Made	5	5	5	5	5	5
Shots Attempted	10	11	12	13	14	15
Fraction	$\dfrac{5}{10}$					
Decimal	0.50					
Percent	50%					

b. Explain the trend in the data you developed in part *a*.

_____

_____

c. If Greg makes his next 5 shots, what will happen to his shooting percentage? Complete the table by entering the ratio of shots made to shots attempted as a fraction in the third row, the decimal equivalent in the fourth row, and the shooting percentage in the fifth row.

Shots Made	5	6	7	8	9	10
Shots Attempted	10	11	12	13	14	15
Fraction	$\dfrac{5}{10}$					
Decimal	0.50					
Percent	50%					

d. Explain the trend in the data you developed in part *c*.

_____

_____

10. Suppose you must examine a road map to find the distance between two cities. The map is drawn on a scale where 1 inch is equivalent to traveling 10 miles. If the cities are separated by 5.75 inches on the map, then use ratios and proportions to calculate the real distance between the two cities.

Chapter 5

Geometry and Measurement

To visualize and create useful objects of beauty, it is important to understand the fundamental concepts of plane and solid geometry. In this chapter, you will start to develop a spatial and measurement sense by working on concrete examples in familiar, everyday situations. You will also explore how exponential notation can be used to express the very large and very small numbers that naturally occur in the world around us.

In Section 5.1, you will explore problem situations that involve standardized units of the U.S. customary system and the metric system. Through estimation and measurement you will become comfortable working with metric units, doing conversions within the metric system, and converting between the U.S. and metric system.

In Section 5.2, you will investigate geometry that occurs on flat, two-dimensional surfaces called *planes*. Specifically, you will journey through Discovery Adventures involving the area and perimeter of plane figures. The rectangle is an example of an object of plane geometry. The two dimensions of the rectangle are length and width.

In Section 5.3, you will travel to the third dimension as you examine the properties and applications of solid geometry. Problems will focus on the volume and surface area of solid figures. The box is an example of a three-dimensional figure. If you take a rectangle and give it height, then you have added a third dimension to create the box.

In Section 5.4, you will work with problems containing very large and very small numbers and use an exponential notation called *scientific notation*. This convenient notation will make it easy to express these numbers and do calculations involving them.

Section 5.1 Estimation, Measurement, and Unit Analysis

Math Talk

A person's height can be measured in feet and inches, weight in pounds, and age in years. These terms that measure the quantity of an object are called **units**. Feet, inches, and pounds are examples of **standardized units** in the U.S. customary system. However, most countries use a set of standardized units called the metric system. For example, the metric system measures weight in kilograms (kg) and height in centimeters (cm).

Single terms like inches, pounds, kilograms, and centimeters are called **simple units**. If simple units are multiplied, divided, or raised to a power, then **compound units** are formed. For example, suppose you want to purchase a brand of coffee that is priced at $5 per pound. Since *per* means "divided by," this translates to

$$5\frac{\$}{\text{lb}} \text{ or } \frac{\$5}{1 \text{ lb}}.$$

In this case, the simple unit *dollars* is divided by the simple unit *pounds* to form the compound unit,

$$\frac{\text{dollars}}{\text{pound}} \quad \text{or} \quad \frac{\$}{\text{lb}}.$$

If you buy 2 pounds of the above coffee, the cost is calculated as follows:

$$2 \text{ lb} \cdot 5\frac{\$}{\text{lb}} = \frac{2 \cancel{\text{lb}}}{1} \cdot \frac{\$5}{\cancel{\text{lb}}} = \$10$$

The above calculation involves multiplying the simple unit *pounds* by the compound unit *dollars/pound*. Note how the same unit (pounds) in the numerator and denominator leads to a canceling of that unit, leaving the result in dollars.

Discovery Adventure 1: Body Fuel

To determine a person's energy or calorie needs, you need to find the Basal Energy Expenditure (*BEE*), which shows the minimum amount of energy needed by the body for basic life processes such as breathing, body temperature, gland functioning, heart activity, and circulation. The *BEE* is measured in calories using formulas for men and women that are based on weight, height, and age. For example, using the variables W for weight in kilograms (kg), H for height in centimeters (cm), and A for age in years, we have

Men:
$$BEE = 66 + (13.7 \cdot W) + (5 \cdot H) - (6.8 \cdot A)$$

Women:
$$BEE = 655 + (9.6 \cdot W) + (1.7 \cdot H) - (4.7 \cdot A)$$

a. Ask a friend to volunteer his/her weight, height, and age and record the results below.

Weight: Height: Age:

b. What type of unit conversions must be completed before applying the formula?

_____

_____

c. Use the fact that 1 kg = 2.2 lbs to convert your friend's weight from pounds to kilograms. Round your answer to the hundredths place.

d. Use the following facts, 1 ft = 12 in. and 1 in. = 2.54 cm, to convert your friend's height from feet and inches to total inches and then to centimeters. Round your answer to the hundredths place.

e. Substitute your friend's weight, height, and age into the appropriate *BEE* formula and calculate the number of calories needed to sustain your friend's life while at rest. Round to the nearest calorie.

f. The male *BEE* formula contains 4 terms: 66, $13.7W$, $5H$, and $6.8A$. Suppose 18-year Ben grows one inch over a 1-year period. Assuming his weight stays the same, which terms will be affected when calculating the change in his *BEE* during this time?

g. Without performing any calculations, explain how Ben's *BEE* will change.

_____

_____

h. Examine the two *BEE* formulas again and explain what happens to a person's energy needs as they get older. Assume the person's weight stays constant.

_____

_____

i. If your friend loses 20 pounds over the next 3 months, then what will the *BEE* indicate about his/her future energy needs?

_____

_____

j. The actual amount of calories a person needs depends on the *BEE* and an activity factor. Since people expend a certain amount of energy in their normal daily activities, you need to increase the *BEE* according to your activity level. For example, a person who is sedentary needs 30% more calories. Moderate activity needs 40% more, and strenuous activity needs 70% more. Calculate your friend's energy needs for each activity level.

Sedentary =

Moderate Activity =

Strenuous Activity =

Feedback

The first step before applying either *BEE* formula is to convert an individual's weight and height to the metric units of kilograms and centimeters. For weight, the conversion factor $1 \text{ kg} = 2.2 \text{ lbs}$, can be written as a ratio equal to 1 in the following two ways:

$$\frac{2.2 \text{ lb}}{1 \text{ kg}} = 1 \quad \text{or} \quad \frac{1 \text{ kg}}{2.2 \text{ lb}} = 1$$

Suppose James is a 43-year old man with height 5'11" and weight 180 pounds. To convert his weight to metric units, multiply 180 pounds by the ratio that will cancel pounds and leave kilograms.

$$180 \text{ lb} \cdot \frac{1 \text{ kg}}{2.2 \text{ lb}} = \frac{180 \text{ lb}}{1} \cdot \frac{1 \text{ kg}}{2.2 \text{ lb}}$$

$$= \frac{180 \text{ kg}}{2.2}$$

$$\approx 81.82 \text{ kg}$$

Another way you can convert pounds to kilograms involves solving a proportion (see Section 4.4 Ratio and Proportion). For example, letting x be the number of kilograms in 180 pounds, we have

$$\frac{2.2 \text{ lb}}{1 \text{ kg}} = \frac{180 \text{ lb}}{x \text{ kg}}$$

$$2.2 \cdot x = 1 \cdot 180 \qquad \text{Cross products must equal for proportion to be true.}$$

$$\frac{\overset{1}{\cancel{2.2}} \, x}{\underset{1}{\cancel{2.2}}} = \frac{180}{2.2} \qquad \text{Divide both sides by 2.2 to solve for } x.$$

$$x \approx 81.82 \text{ kg}$$

For height, you first need to express 5'11" in terms of inches only. Since $1 \text{ ft} = 12 \text{ in.}$, we have

$$5 \text{ ft} = 5 \cdot (1 \text{ ft}) = 5 \cdot (12 \text{ in.}) = 60 \text{ in.}$$

So,

$$5 \text{ ft } 11 \text{ in.} = 60 \text{ in.} + 11 \text{ in.} = 71 \text{ in.}$$

To convert inches to centimeters, the conversion factor, $1 \text{ in.} = 2.54 \text{ cm}$, can be written as a ratio equal to 1 in the following two ways:

$$\frac{1 \text{ in.}}{2.54 \text{ cm}} = 1 \quad \text{Or} \quad \frac{2.54 \text{ cm}}{1 \text{ in.}}$$

To convert James's height to metric units, multiply 71 inches by the ratio that will cancel inches and leave centimeters.

$$(71 \text{ in.}) \cdot \frac{2.54 \text{ cm}}{1 \text{ in.}} = \frac{71 \cancel{\text{ in.}}}{1} \cdot \frac{2.54 \text{ cm}}{1 \cancel{\text{ in.}}}$$

$$= 71 \cdot 2.54 \text{ cm}$$

$$= 180.34 \text{ cm}$$

With weight $W = 82.73$ kg, height $H = 180.34$ cm, and age $A = 43$ years, we can substitute these values into the *BEE* formula.

$$BEE = 66 + (13.7 \cdot W) + (5 \cdot H) - (6.8 \cdot A)$$

$$BEE = 66 + (13.7 \cdot 81.82) + (5 \cdot 180.34) - (6.8 \cdot 43)$$

$$BEE = 66 + 1120.934 + 901.7 - 292.4$$

$$BEE \approx 1796 \text{ calories}$$

Since the second ($13.7W$) and third ($5H$) terms are being added to the total, any increase in a person's weight or height will increase the total calories that person needs. Similarly, a decrease in weight or height will decrease the calories. The last term ($6.8A$) is subtracted from the total. This way, every time you have a birthday your BEE will decrease by 6.8 calories.

If James is moderately active, then you could calculate his caloric needs using either one of the following methods:

$$BEE + 40\% \text{ of } BEE = 1796 + 0.40 \cdot 1796 \qquad\qquad 140\% \text{ of } BEE = 1.40 \cdot 1796$$
$$= 1796 + 718.4 \qquad \text{Or} \qquad = 2514.4 \text{ calories}$$
$$= 2514.4 \text{ calories}$$

So James needs about 2514 calories per day based on his weight, height, and age. James knows that he has no control over his height and age but wonders whether his weight is at a healthy amount.

In the next Discovery Adventure, you will investigate how to find a person's *ideal body weight* using a rule. You will construct a table, look for patterns in the numbers, and develop a symbolic rule (or equation) to model the situation.

Discovery Adventure 2: Ideal Body Weight

There are tables available which claim to give a person's ideal body weight based on an individual's height. If you do not have access to any of these height/weight tables, then use the following rules to estimate ideal body weight.

Men – Use 106 pounds for the first 5 feet of height, plus 6 pounds for each inch over 5 feet.

Women – Use 100 pounds for the first 5 feet of height, plus 5 pounds for each inch over 5 feet.

a.   Use the appropriate rule to estimate your friend's ideal body weight.

b. Complete the following table for women between 5 feet and 5 feet 6 inches. Use the given rule to set up your calculation. Leave the last row, second column blank for now.

Height (feet and inches)	Rule of Thumb	Weight (pounds)
5' 0"	$100 + 5 \cdot 0$	100
5' 1"	$100 + 5 \cdot 1$	105
5' 2"	$100 + 5 \cdot 2$	
5' 3"		
5' 4"		
5' 5"		
5' 6"		
$\vdots$	$\vdots$	
5' n"		

Note: The 3 vertical dots in the second to last row mean that the above pattern continues on.

c. Observe the pattern in the **sequence** of calculations in the second column. Note the values that remain constant and the values that change. If n represents the number of inches over 5 feet, then use a variable expression to represent the rule for finding an ideal body weight for women. Place your result in the last row, second column and after the equal sign below.

Ideal Body Weight =

d. Use another variable expression to represent the rule for finding an ideal body weight for men. Again let n represent the number of inches over 5 feet.

e. Do you think that these rules can determine ideal body weight for everyone? If yes, tell why. Otherwise, explain why certain individuals are exceptions to the rule.

_____

_____

_____

f. Percent ideal body weight is the ratio of your current weight divided by your ideal body weight,

$$\text{Percent Ideal Body Weight} = \frac{\text{Current Weight}}{\text{Ideal Body Weight}} \cdot 100$$

Calculate your friend's percent ideal body weight above and explain what this value means in terms of having a healthy weight.

_____

_____

_____

_____

g. Assuming that the formula in part *f* gives accurate information, describe what a percentage over 100 would mean. Then describe what a percentage under 100 means.

_____

_____

_____

_____

Feedback

The rules for ideal body weight can be expressed as a formula or equation by letting *n* be the number of inches over 5 feet.

Women's ideal body weight $= 100 + 5n$ Men's ideal body weight $= 106 + 6n$

If your current weight is the same as your ideal body weight, then the percent ideal body weight will be 100%. Therefore, any percent greater than 100% represent the part of your weight that is more than your ideal weight. For example, if an individual's percent ideal body weight is 110%, then that person has 10% more body weight than the ideal amount. Similarly, any percent under 100% means the part of your weight that is under the ideal. For example, if an individual's percent ideal body weight is 90%, then that person has 10% less body weight than the ideal amount.

****

The metric system of measurement defines length, weight, and volume in a standardized method based on units that differ by factors of 10. The basic (standard) units we will examine appear in the table below.

Quantity Measured	Basic Unit	Symbol	U.S. System Equivalent
Length	meter	m	39.37 inches
Weight	gram	g	0.035 ounces
Volume	liter	L	1.06 quarts

In the next Discovery Adventure, you will explore how a prefix is used with a basic unit to show measurements that are larger or smaller than the basic unit.

Discovery Adventure 3: Going Metric

The following table gives prefixes that either increase or decrease the basic unit. The meaning of the prefix as compared to the basic unit is shown mathematically.

Prefix	Symbol	Compared to Basic Units	Prefix with Basic Units
milli	m	$\dfrac{1}{1000} = 0.001$	mm, mg, mL
centi	c	$\dfrac{1}{100} = 0.01$	cm, cg, cL
deci	d	$\dfrac{1}{10} = 0.1$	dm, dg, dL
None	Basic Unit	1	m, g, L
deka	da	10	dam, dag, daL
hecto	h	100	hm, hg, hL
kilo	k	1000	km, kg, kL

a. If we take the prefix *kilo* and combine it with the basic unit *gram*, what measurement unit do you obtain?

Full name: Abbreviation:

- How many grams are in a kilogram?

- How many kilograms are in a gram?

- How much does a 4 kg baby weigh in terms of grams?

- How many kilograms of coffee are in a coffee can labeled 311g?

b. If we take the prefix *centi* and combine it with the basic unit *meter*, what measurement unit do you obtain?

Full name: Abbreviation:

- How many meters are in a centimeter?

- How many centimeters are in a meter?

- How many meters are in a 20-cm ruler?

- How many millimeters are in a 20-cm ruler?

- How many centimeters are in a 200-m race?

- How many kilometers are in a 200-m race?

c. If we take the prefix *milli* and combine it with the basic unit *liter*, what measurement unit do you obtain?

Full name: Abbreviation:

- How many milliliters are in a liter?

- How many liters are in a milliliter?

d. If you look on a 12-ounce can of soda, there is the metric measurement of 355 mL. To see how a can of soda compares with a 2-liter bottle, you will first estimate and then convert between units.

- Estimate (no calculations) how many 355 mL cans of tonic are equivalent to one 2-liter bottle.

- Now convert 355 mL to liters.

- Amount of liters in 1 can: _____

e. How many soda cans have the same amount of tonic as in a 2-liter bottle? Round to the hundredths place.

Calculation:

Number of cans in a 2-liter bottle: _____

f. How many liters of tonic are in a 6-pack of 12-ounce cans? Round to the hundredths place.

Calculation:

Six Pack in Liters: _____

g. Suppose a 6-pack of tonic costs $1.99, and the same tonic in 2-liter bottles costs $1.79. Which purchase will give you the most tonic for your money? Round to the hundredths place. *Hint:* Find and compare the price per liter for each item.

Calculation(s):

Best Buy: _____

h. What is the cost per can of soda when buying a 6-pack? Round your answer to the nearest cent.

Calculation:

Six Pack Cost per Can: _____

i. What is the cost per can of soda when buying a 2-liter bottle? Round your answer to the nearest cent. *Hint:* Part *e* gives the number of cans that are equivalent to a 2-liter bottle.

Calculation:

2-Liter Bottle Cost per Can: _____

j. Suppose that 5 days a week you buy a can of soda from a vending machine for $0.75. How much would you save in a year if you only bought 6-packs from the store for $1.99 to satisfy your work-week soda fix?

Calculation(s):

Yearly Savings Buying 6-Packs: _____

Feedback

Let's try to visualize how you convert from one metric unit to another.

milli-	centi-	deci-	Base Unit	deka-	hecto-	kilo-
$\dfrac{1}{1000}$	$\dfrac{1}{100}$	$\dfrac{1}{10}$	1	10	100	1000

When converting from one unit to another, multiply or divide by a power of 10.

To convert from larger metric units to smaller ones, you multiply by 10 for each unit movement to the left. For example, to find out how many centimeters are in a 200 m race, we multiply 200 m by 10 twice because *centimeters* is two units to the left of *meters*.

$$200 \cdot 10 \cdot 10 = 200 \cdot 10^2$$
$$= 200 \cdot 100$$
$$= 20,000 \text{ cm}$$

To convert from smaller metric units to larger ones, you divide by 10 for each unit movement to the right. For example, to find out how many kilometers are in a 200 m race, divide 200 by 10 three times.

$$\frac{200}{10 \cdot 10 \cdot 10} = \frac{200}{10^3}$$
$$= \frac{200}{1000}$$
$$= 0.2 \text{ km}$$

Recall that multiplying by powers of 10 moves the decimal to the right and dividing by powers of 10 moves the decimal to the left. Therefore, multiplying by $10^2 = 100$ moves the decimal 2 places to the right and dividing by $10^3 = 1000$ moves the decimal 3 places to the left.

Any conversion can be expressed as a proportion. In the last example above, since 1 kilometer is equivalent to 1000 meters, we have the following conversion factors:

$$\frac{1 \text{ km}}{1000 \text{ m}} = 1 \quad \text{Or} \quad \frac{1000 \text{ m}}{1 \text{ km}} = 1$$

You can use either one of the last two ratios to convert meters to kilometers by setting up and solving a proportion. For example,

$$\frac{1 \text{ km}}{1000 \text{ m}} = \frac{x \text{ km}}{200 \text{ m}}$$ Like units must be in the same position on each side.

$$1 \cdot 200 = 1000 \cdot x$$ Cross products must be equal for proportion to be true.

$$\frac{200}{1000} = \frac{\cancel{1000}^{1} \, x}{\cancel{1000}_{1}}$$ Divide both sides by 1000 to solve for x.

$$0.2 = x$$

Another method uses the fact that the conversion factor written in ratio form is equal to 1. Since multiplying a number by 1 will not change the value, you can multiply 200 m by the ratio, $\frac{1 \text{ km}}{1000 \text{ m}}$. This will cancel meters and leave an equivalent amount in kilometers.

$$\frac{1 \text{ km}}{1000 \text{ m}} \cdot 200 \text{ m} = \frac{1 \text{ km}}{1000 \text{ m}} \cdot \frac{200 \text{ m}}{1}$$

$$= \frac{200 \text{ km}}{1000}$$

$$= 0.2 \text{ km}$$

We have explored conversions within the metric system in a number of ways. Now let's summarize by defining the different methods for converting 355 milliliters to liters.

Problem Solving Strategy: Converting within the Metric System

$\Rightarrow$ **Method 1: Moving the Decimal Point**

To convert from larger metric units to smaller ones, you multiply by 10 for each unit movement to the left. To convert from smaller metric units to larger ones, you divide by 10 for each unit movement to the right. So when converting 355 milliliters to liters, since milliliters are smaller than liters and 3 units away, we divide by $10^3 = 1000$. This has the effect of moving the decimal to the left three places.

$$355 \text{ mL} = \frac{355}{1000} \text{ L} = 0.355 \text{ L}$$

$\Rightarrow$ **Method 2: Using Proportions**

Write the ratio of the known quantity to the unknown quantity and use the conversion factor as a second ratio. Then equate these two ratios and solve the resulting proportion to find the unknown value. For example, the known quantity is 355 milliliters and the unknown quantity can be represented as x liters, giving us the ratio $\dfrac{355 \text{ mL}}{x \text{ L}}$. The conversion factor $1000 \text{ mL} = 1 \text{ L}$ can be expressed as the ratio $\dfrac{1000 \text{ mL}}{1 \text{ L}}$. Equating ratios produces a proportion we can solve as follows:

$$\frac{355 \text{ mL}}{x \text{ L}} = \frac{1000 \text{ mL}}{1 \text{ L}}$$

$355 \cdot 1 = x \cdot 1000$ Cross products must be equal for proportion to be true

$355 = 1000x$

$$\frac{355}{1000} = \frac{\cancel{1000}\,^1 \, x}{\cancel{1000}\,_1}$$ Divide both sides by 1000 to solve for x.

$0.355 = x$

$x = 0.355 \text{ L}$

(continued on next page)

$\Rightarrow$ **Method 3: Multiply to Cancel Units**

Multiply the known quantity by the conversion factor to cancel unwanted units. For example, to convert 355 milliliters to liters you can proceed as follows:

$$355 \text{ mL} \cdot \frac{1 \text{ L}}{1000 \text{ mL}} = \frac{355 \text{ mL}}{1} \cdot \frac{1 \text{ L}}{1000 \text{ mL}}$$

$$= \frac{355 \text{ L}}{1000}$$

$$= 0.355 \text{ L}$$

Section Exercises: 5.1

Questions 1–4 involve length measurements. The standard metric unit when measuring length is the meter (about 39.37 inches). Problem 1 requires a meter stick or metric tape measure. Problems 3 and 4 require a metric ruler that measures centimeters and millimeters.

1. List at least three everyday items that measure about 1 meter. You should choose things that are familiar and easy to visualize. For example, the length from the floor up to most doorknobs is approximately one meter.

   • _____

   • _____

   • _____

2. The most common unit for measuring lengths with many meters is the kilometer. The prefix *kilo* means thousand, so kilometer is 1000 meters. Take a look at the speedometer in your car and find kilometers per hour (km/hr) as well as miles per hour (mph). In a metric world, distance traveled is expressed in kilometers instead of miles. List at least three everyday items that measure about 1 kilometer. For example, my daily running route is a little over 3 miles, which is about 5 kilometers. I have each kilometer marked off for reference.

   • _____

   • _____

   • _____

3. For small measurements, you need a ruler that measures centimeters. Recall that a centimeter is $\dfrac{1}{100}$ of a meter, so you need 100 cm to equal 1 meter. List at least three everyday items that measure about 1 centimeter. For example, the fingernail on my index finger has a width of about 1-cm at its widest point.

   - _____

   - _____

   - _____

4. For really small measurements, you use millimeters (mm). A millimeter is the distance between each small tick mark on a centimeter ruler. There are 10 millimeters in every centimeter. This can be visualized on a metric ruler if you count the 10 tick marks between each centimeter mark. So 1 millimeter is $\dfrac{1}{10}$ of a centimeter. List at least three everyday items that measure about 1 mm. For example, the thickness of each one of my fingernails is about 1 mm.

   - _____

   - _____

   - _____

5. Suppose you have just enrolled as a student at Metric University (MU). You have a car available to travel the 12 kilometers between your apartment and the campus. The route you will take has a speed limit of 50 kilometers per hour (km/hr). At this speed, your car will average a mileage of 25 kilometers per gallon. Your first class each day starts at 8 a.m.

   a. Assuming you exercise regularly, would it be possible to walk from your apartment to MU during nice weather? Explain your answer using complete sentences.

   _____

   _____

   _____

b. Suppose you decide to travel to MU by car and want to get an idea of how long the trip will take at different speeds. Complete the table below using metric units. Round hours to the hundredths place and minutes to the tenths place. *Hint:* Use the following formula.

$$\text{Time} = \frac{\text{Distance}}{\text{Rate}}$$

Rate	Time	
km/hr	Hours	Minutes
10	1.2	72
20		
30		
40		
50		
60		
70		
80		

c. Every time you double your speed, what happens to the trip time? Justify your answer in words using complete sentences.

_____

_____

_____

d. If you are able to travel at an average speed of 120 km/hr, how long will it take to reach MU from your apartment?

e. Suppose your average walking pace is 5 km/hr. If it is a nice day and you decide to walk, how long will it take you to go from your apartment to the MU campus?

f. During your first 10 days of classes, your commute (one way) averages about 15 minutes. Approximately how many gallons of gas did your car use in commuting (both ways) over this 10-day period?

g. If your car has a 16-gallon fuel capacity and you only use the vehicle to drive back and forth to MU, how often will you have to refill the gas tank? Answer in complete sentences and explain your reasoning.

_____

_____

_____

h. What is the total distance that your car can travel on one tank of gas, assuming all the gas is used? Round your answer to the nearest kilometer.

i. Suppose that what you pay for gas is the foreign equivalent of $2.99 per gallon. What is the cost to fill an empty tank? Round your answer to the nearest cent.

j. What is the cost of gas per kilometer? Round your answer to the nearest cent.

k. Time for you to summarize your travel strategy. Explain when you will leave for school each morning, what your average speed will be, how often you will have to fill your tank, and about how much money ($) fuel will cost over a 15-week semester.

_____

_____

_____

_____

_____

_____

_____

Questions 6 and 7 involve measuring volume. The standard metric unit when measuring volume is the liter (L). One liter is equivalent to 1.06 quarts, which means that a liter and a quart are almost equivalent.

6.   List at least three everyday items that measure about one liter. For example, a bottle of spring water is one liter.

     •   _____

     •   _____

     •   _____

7.   Volume measurements less than 1 liter are made using milliliters (mL). A milliliter is $\frac{1}{1000}$ of a liter; there are 1000 milliliters in 1 liter. List some everyday items that weigh about 1 milliliter, 10 milliliters, and 100 milliliters. For example, I often administer liquid medication for my young children with droppers or hook spoons that have measuring marks from 1 mL to 5 mL, with 5 mL = 1 teaspoon (tsp.)

     1 milliliter: _____

     10 milliliters: _____

     100 milliliters: _____

Questions 8-10 involve measuring weight. The standard metric unit when measuring weight is the gram.

8.   One gram is equivalent to 0.035 ounce, which is approximately $\frac{4}{100}$ ounce or $\frac{1}{25}$ ounce. However, these values only tell you that a gram is a very small measurement as compared to an ounce. List some everyday items that weigh about 1 gram, 10 grams, and 100 grams.

     1 gram: _____

     10 grams: _____

     100 grams: _____

9. For objects that weigh 1000 grams or more, the kilogram (kg) is the preferred unit of measure. Since one kilogram is equivalent to about 2.2 pounds, most objects weighed in pounds in the U.S. would be weighed in kilograms almost anywhere else in the world. List some everyday items that weigh about 1 kilogram, 10 kilograms, and 100 kilograms.

   1 kilogram: _____

   10 kilograms: _____

   100 kilograms: _____

10. For items that weigh a fraction of a gram, the milligram (mg) is the most common unit of measure. A milligram is $\dfrac{1}{1000}$ of a gram; there are 1000 milligrams in 1 gram. List some everyday items that weigh about 1 milligram, 10 milligrams, and 100 milligrams.

   1 milligram: _____

   10 milligrams: _____

   100 milligrams: _____

11. Each year more than 300,000 people die from obesity-related health problems such as high blood pressure, coronary heart disease, cancer, and diabetes. This means that being overweight is the second leading cause of preventable death, right behind smoking. To help diagnose a weight problem, health professionals use the Body Mass Index or BMI, which is a measurement based on weight and height. BMI is defined as weight (in kilograms) divided by height (in meters) squared.

   a. Find your weight in kilograms (kg) using the conversion factor $1\,\text{kg} = 2.2046\,\text{lb}$. Round your answer to the hundredths place.

   b. Find your height in meters (m) using the conversion factor $1\,\text{m} = 39.37\,\text{in.}$. Round your answer to the hundredths place.

   c. Calculate your height (in meters) squared. *Hint:* Multiplying meters (m) by meters (m) gives the compound unit, meters squared (m^2) or square meters (sq. m). Round your answer to the hundredths place.

d. Find your BMI by taking your metric weight (from part *a*) divided by your metric height squared (from part *c*). Show all work below and express your BMI as a compound unit.

e. Let *w* represent weight in kilograms and *h* as height in meters. Use these variables to state a formula for finding BMI.

$$BMI =$$

f. Suppose you want to develop a BMI formula that uses pounds (lbs) and inches (in). When converting U.S. weight units to metric weight units as in part *a*, you can divide your weight *w* (in pounds) by 2.2046. Use a variable expression to represent this conversion.

g. When converting U.S. height units to metric weight units as in part *b*, you can divide your height *h* (in inches) by 39.37. Use a variable expression to represent this conversion.

h. Since BMI is defined as weight (in kilograms) divided by height (in meters) squared, the fractional expression from part *f* divided by the fractional expression from part *g* squared will produce a new formula based on pounds and inches. Take this new formula, shown below, and simplify it to an equivalent formula that would be easier to use.

$$\frac{\dfrac{w}{2.2046}}{\left(\dfrac{h}{39.37}\right)^2} =$$

i. Any BMI less than 25 indicates a healthy weight. A BMI of 25-29 indicates overweight, and a BMI of 30 or more indicates obesity. Calculate the BMI of the following individuals and state which of the three categories they are in. *Note:* Some very muscular people may have a high BMI without health risks.

- John: height 6'1" and weight 235 pounds.

- Jane: height 5'4" and weight 135 pounds.

- Frank: height 5'10" and weight 180 pounds.

12. Suppose you just returned from a trip overseas with $110 (U.S. dollars), 525 francs (currency for France), and 150 pounds (currency for United Kingdom).

   a. If you wanted to find the total amount of money left from your trip, what would you do? Explain your answer using complete sentences.

   _____

   _____

   _____

   _____

   b. Use the following exchange rates to convert your 525 francs and 150 pounds to U.S. dollars. Round to the nearest cent. *Hint:* Rates are based on annual average for 1999.

   $$1 \text{ dollar} = 5.8995 \text{ francs} \quad \text{And} \quad 1 \text{ dollar} = 1.6564 \text{ pounds}$$

   c. Since 1 U.S. dollar equals 5.8995 francs and 1 U.S. dollar equals 1.6554 pounds, write the equality that expresses the relationship between francs and pounds.

   d. Use the equality from part *c* to find the number of francs in 1 pound.

   e. Find the number of pounds in 1 franc.

   f. Express the total amount of money left from your trip in terms of pounds.

   g. Express the total amount of money left from your trip in terms of francs.

13. In the physical world, you can measure work using the compound unit *foot-pounds*. This unit equals the amount of work required in lifting a 1-pound weight vertically over a distance of 1 foot. See figure below.

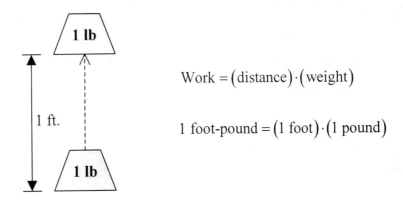

$$\text{Work} = (\text{distance}) \cdot (\text{weight})$$

$$1 \text{ foot-pound} = (1 \text{ foot}) \cdot (1 \text{ pound})$$

   a. How much work is required to lift a 5-pound weight a distance of 4 feet?

   b. How much work is required to lift a 10-pound weight a distance of 2 feet?

   c. How much work is required to lift a 2.5-pound weight a distance of 8 feet?

   d. During Phil's workout, his trainer claims that lifting a 100-pound barbell would require 300 foot-pounds of work. How many feet does Phil lift the barbell to do that much work?

   e. If a crane does 20,000 foot-pounds of work in lifting an object 50 feet, then how much does the object weigh?

Section 5.2 Plane Geometry: Area and Perimeter

Math Talk

When you hear the word *plane* in everyday conversation, it's usually in reference to an airplane. In math, a **plane** is a flat surface such as this page of paper you are reading. **Plane geometry** refers to the geometry of figures that have all their points lying on one plane. Some common plane figures are the circle, rectangle, and triangle.

 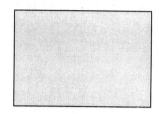 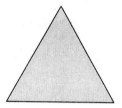

But plane figures can also be irregularly shaped objects. Imagine spilling some liquid on a piece of paper. It might have the following appearance:

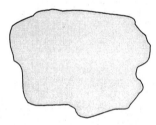

Every plane figure has the property that a line connecting any two of the figure's points must lie on its surface.

Two important concepts involving plane figures are *perimeter* and *area*. The **perimeter** of a plane figure is the distance around its border, and the **area** of a plane figure is the measure of the surface enclosed by its border.

****

In the first Discovery Adventure, you will begin your investigation of perimeter and area. The main focus of this adventure is how to measure the perimeter and area of a rectangle.

Discovery Adventure 1: Can a Foot Be Square?

Suppose you need to build a new kitchen floor with tiles that measure one square foot. After you decide to do the job, your mind begins to ask questions. What is a square foot? How many tiles should I purchase? Which side of the room is called the length, and which is the width?

A square has 4 sides that are equal in length, and in a square foot, that length must be one foot. Let's draw a picture of 1 square foot (not to scale) with the length of each side labeled.

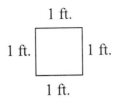

To really understand 1 square foot, stand up and look down. The floor space on the tile floor below you is about 1 square foot. Let's double that area by adding another square foot.

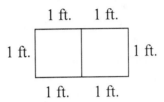

a. How many square feet of area are in the picture above?

b. What is the distance around the outside border of this area?

c. The area above will allow you and a friend to stand side by side. Let's continue to double the area by adding 2 more square feet. Label all the exterior sides of each square foot below as in the previous figure.

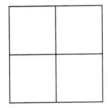

d. How many square feet of area are in the picture above?

e. What is the distance around the outside border of this area?

f. Let's continue to double the area by adding 4 more square feet. How many square feet of area are in the picture below?

g. What is the distance around the outside border of this area?

For each of the following rectangles, let's call the bottom or top edges the **length** and the left or right edges the **width**. Although some people think of the length as the longer edge and the width as the shorter edge, in reality the terms *length* and *width* are just used to distinguish between the edges of a rectangle that connect at a corner.

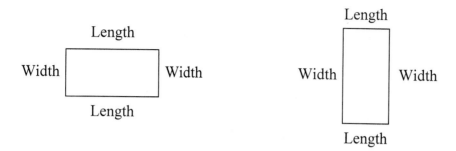

h. Record the length, width, area, and perimeter (distance around border) of the following rectangular figure. Be sure to include the units feet (ft) or square feet (ft^2) in your answers.

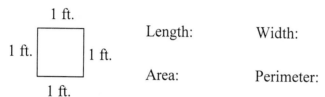

Length: Width:

Area: Perimeter:

i. Record the length, width, area, and perimeter of the following rectangular figure.

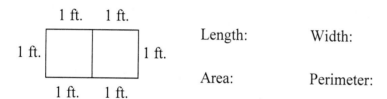

Length: Width:

Area: Perimeter:

j. Record the length, width, area, and perimeter of the entire rectangular figure below.

Length: Width:

Area: Perimeter:

k. Record the length, width, area, and perimeter of the entire rectangular figure below.

Length: Width:

Area: Perimeter:

l. Organize all your information by completing the following table.

Length (feet)	Width (feet)	Area (sq. ft.)	Length + Width (feet)	Perimeter (feet)

m. Compare the length and width of each rectangular region to its area. Look for patterns in the values and then suggest a possible formula for area in terms of length and width.

n. Compare the length and width of the rectangular region to its perimeter. Look for patterns in the values and then suggest a possible formula for perimeter in terms of length and width.

Feedback

The *area* of a rectangle is the surface enclosed by its boundary or border (sides or edges). Call the measure of either the bottom or top edge the *length* and the measure of either the left or right edge the *width*. With these 2 variables labeled, the area of a rectangle can be defined as follows:

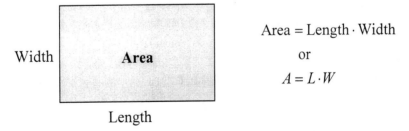

Area = Length · Width

or

$A = L \cdot W$

Width — Area — Length

For example, given 1 square inch $\left(1 \text{ in.}^2\right)$ 1 in.   1 in.

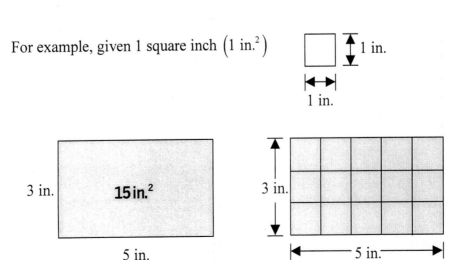

3 in.   **15 in.²**   5 in.

3 in.   5 in.

The *perimeter* of a rectangle is the distance around the four edges enclosing the rectangular region. Using length and width in describing the dimensions, the perimeter can be defined as follows:

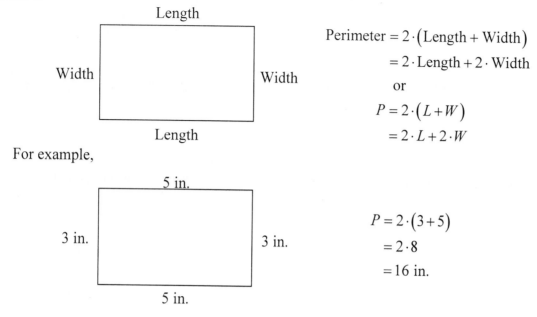

$$\text{Perimeter} = 2 \cdot (\text{Length} + \text{Width})$$
$$= 2 \cdot \text{Length} + 2 \cdot \text{Width}$$

or

$$P = 2 \cdot (L + W)$$
$$= 2 \cdot L + 2 \cdot W$$

For example,

$$P = 2 \cdot (3 + 5)$$
$$= 2 \cdot 8$$
$$= 16 \text{ in.}$$

Having investigated the concepts of area and perimeter, it's time for you to complete the job of laying down a new kitchen floor.

Discovery Adventure 2: A New Kitchen Floor

Suppose the dimensions of the kitchen are 8 ft by 10 ft, and each tile measures 1 square foot.

a. Draw a rectangular grid representing the kitchen floor to be tiled.

b. Find the area and perimeter of the kitchen. Show all work.

We can define the following variables for the rectangular kitchen floor:

L for length, W for width, A for area,   and P for perimeter.

c. What would be a formula for the area of a rectangle using the variables L, W, and A?

d. What would be a formula for the perimeter of a rectangle using the variables L, W, and P?

Feedback

Since each tile is 1 ft^2, you could find the area of the kitchen floor by counting the number of tiles and find the perimeter by counting the number of edges along its border. However, it would be more efficient to apply the formulas we have learned. For example,

$$A = L \cdot W$$
$$= (8 \text{ ft.}) \cdot (10 \text{ ft.})$$
$$= 80 \text{ ft.}^2$$

$$P = 2 \cdot (L + W)$$
$$= 2 \cdot (8 \text{ ft.} + 10 \text{ ft.})$$
$$= 2 \cdot 80 \text{ ft.}$$
$$= 160 \text{ ft.}$$

Note that even though we let the length $L = 8$ ft and the width $W = 10$ ft, it would have also been correct to let the length $L = 10$ ft and the width $W = 8$ ft. This would not change the results of either formula.

****

If you use the words **base** symbolized as b, and **height** symbolized as h, instead of length and width, then the definition of area can be written as follows:

Area of Rectangle $=$ base $\cdot$ height   or $A = b \cdot h$

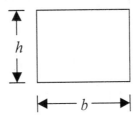

The area of a triangle can be found by forming a rectangle around it with twice the area of the triangle. Since the area of the rectangle is bh, then the area of the triangle must be half of that area or $\frac{1}{2} bh$.

$$\text{Area of a Triangle} = \frac{1}{2} \cdot \text{base} \cdot \text{height} \quad \text{or} \quad A = \frac{1}{2} \cdot b \cdot h$$

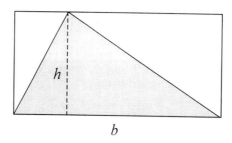

The area of any **polygon** (geometric figure with 3 or more sides) can be found by splitting the polygon into triangles and applying the area formula for a triangle to each 3-sided region.

For example, a **parallelogram** (4-sided geometric shape in which opposite sides are parallel) can be split along the diagonal d to form two triangles. See the figure below.

Parallelogram:

Area of a Parallelogram $= 2 \cdot \left(\text{Area of a Triangle}\right)$

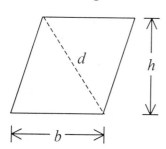

$$A = 2 \cdot \left(\frac{1}{2} \cdot b \cdot h\right)$$

$$A = \frac{\cancel{2}^{1}}{1} \cdot \frac{1}{\cancel{2}_{1}} \cdot b \cdot h$$

$$A = b \cdot h$$

Since the base b and the height h of each triangle are the same, we multiply the formula for the area of the triangle by 2.

What is the connection between the area of a parallelogram and the area of a rectangle? In fact, since a rectangle is a special parallelogram with four right angles, the area must be calculated using the same formula.

The **trapezoid** is a four-sided geometric shape with two parallel sides that do not have the same length. In the figure below, we combine a trapezoid with a copy of that same trapezoid flipped vertically.

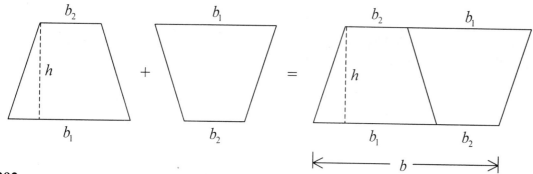

In the last part of the figure (furthest to the right), what familiar geometric object have we formed by arranging the two trapezoids in this manner? The answer is "a parallelogram."

Since the trapezoid is half the parallelogram, then the formula for finding its area must be half the formula of the parallelogram. Also, observe that the sum of the two trapezoid bases b_1 and b_2 equal the parallelogram's base b such that $b = b_1 + b_2$.

$$\text{Area of a Trapezoid} = \frac{1}{2} \cdot \left(\text{Area of a Parallelogram}\right)$$

$$A = \frac{1}{2} \cdot b \cdot h$$

$$A = \frac{1}{2} \cdot (b_1 + b_2) \cdot h \qquad \text{Replace } b \text{ with } b_1 + b_2$$

$$A = \frac{1}{2} \cdot h \cdot (b_1 + b_2) \qquad \text{Commutative Property of Multiplication}$$

In the next Discovery Adventure, you will explore how a rectangle can have different area measurements with the same perimeter. Your goal is to find the rectangle that gives the maximum area for a given fixed perimeter.

Discovery Adventure 3: A Rabbit House

Suppose you just obtained a rabbit and want to build a permanent home for your new pet. You have 14 feet of wire fencing available and want to build a rectangular enclosure that will give your rabbit the maximum amount of area to live in.

a. Draw a picture of one possible rectangle that has a perimeter of 14 feet. Label the diagram with the chosen dimensions (length and width).

b. Now draw a second picture similar to part *a* but use different dimensions.

c. Complete the table below to see all the possible rectangular areas that can be constructed with just whole numbers. The length, width, and perimeter should be in feet and the area in square feet (sq ft) or feet squared (ft^2).

Length L	Width W	Sum $L + W$	Perimeter $2 \cdot (L + W)$	Area $L \cdot W$
1	6	$1 + 6 = 7$	$2 \cdot (1 + 6) = 14$	$1 \cdot 6 = 6$
2				
3				
4				
5				
6				

d. As the length increases from 1 to 6 feet in steps of 1 foot, describe any patterns in how the area changes.

_____

_____

_____

e. If we consider only the whole numbers in the previous table, then what dimensions will give your pet rabbit the maximum amount of area to play in?

f. Suppose you let the length and width take on any real number values. Can you find dimensions that have a perimeter of 14 feet but have a larger area than your answer in part *e*? Explain.

_____

_____

_____

g. Complete the following table so you can focus on what happens when the length is between 3 and 4 feet.

Length (ft.)	Width (ft.)	Area (sq. ft.)
3.1		
3.2		
3.3		
3.4		
3.5		
3.6		
3.7		
3.8		
3.9		

h. What dimensions in the above table give the maximum area for your rabbit to live in?

i. What is the name of the special type of rectangle formed with the dimensions found in part *h*?

j. In this adventure, the perimeter was fixed at 14 feet. If the perimeter is fixed at any positive value, then will the square always have the largest area of all the possible rectangles you can construct? If yes, explain your reasoning and support your answer with a new example. Otherwise, give a counter example proving why this statement is false.

Feedback

The table you completed in part *c* should have shown that the area increases for lengths from 1 to 3 feet and then decreases for lengths from 4 to 6 feet. Note that rows 3 and 4, rows 2 and 5, and rows 1 and 6 have the same area because you are multiplying the same numbers in a different order.

Length L	Width W	Area $L \cdot W$
1	6	6
2	5	10
3	4	12
4	3	12
5	2	10
6	1	6

What happens between 3 and 4 feet? To help answer this question, you must construct a second table, which focuses on values between 3 and 4 feet.

Length (ft.)	Width (ft.)	Area (sq. ft.)	Symmetric Pattern
3.1	3.9	12.09	
3.2	3.8	12.16	
3.3	3.7	12.21	
3.4	3.6	12.24	
3.5	3.5	12.25	← Maximum
3.6	3.4	12.24	
3.7	3.3	12.21	
3.8	3.2	12.16	
3.9	3.1	12.09	

It is clear that the dimensions 3.5 ft. by 3.5 ft. produce a maximum area of 12.25 ft^2 because as the length increases or decreases by the same amount from 3.5, you obtain the same area. This is a **symmetric pattern**, which also occurs in the previous table, and shows that the length and width must be equal to obtain the maximum area. Hence, the special type of rectangle that gives a maximum area with a fixed perimeter is the square.

The following exercises will give you a chance to further investigate the concepts of perimeter and area as well as review the material just learned.

Section Exercises: 5.2

1. Suppose you own some property in the country and want to fence in a rectangular area for your new puppy, Buffy. Your veterinarian recommends at least 36 square meters of living space for Buffy. The type of fencing you want to purchase costs $10 per meter of length. How can you give Buffy 36 square meters of fenced-in area and keep the cost to a minimum?

    a. List the five ways you can factor 36 over the integers. One pair has been listed for you.

    $1 \cdot 36$, _____, _____, _____, _____.

    b. Use a centimeter ruler to draw four rectangles using the different factors you listed above as the dimensions, excluding $1 \cdot 36$. In your picture, 1 centimeter should be equivalent to 1- meter length of fencing. This will allow you to visualize a scaled-down version of some possible dog pens that have different perimeters but the same area. Careful construction should allow all 4 rectangles to appear in the space below.

c. Complete the following data table to explore all possible perimeters for rectangles with an area of 36 square meters and dimensions that are whole numbers.

Length (m)	Width (m)	Perimeter (m)	Total Cost ($)
1	36	74	740
2			
3			
4			
6			
9			
12			
18			
36			

d. What are the dimensions of the rectangular pen that minimizes the total cost of fencing in an area of $36 \, \text{m}^2$?

e. What is the minimum cost to build the rectangular pen?

f. Do you think it is possible to find dimensions that produce a smaller perimeter than the dimensions found in part d? Explain your reasoning using complete sentences.

_____

_____

_____

g. What is the name of the special type of rectangle formed with the dimensions found in part d?

h. In this exercise, the area was fixed at $36 \, \text{m}^2$. If the area is fixed at any positive value, then will the square always have the smallest perimeter of all possible rectangles you can construct? If yes, explain your reasoning and support your answer with a new example. Otherwise, give a counter example proving why this statement is false.

2. In Discovery Adventure 3, you have 14 feet of wire fencing available and want to build a rectangular enclosure that will give your pet rabbit the maximum amount of area to live in. Will building a pen in the shape of a circle instead of a square produce more or less area? *Hint:* You will need to use the following formulas for the area and circumference of a circle:

Area $= \pi \cdot (\text{radius})^2$ or $A = \pi \cdot r^2$

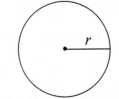

Circumference $= 2 \cdot \pi \cdot (\text{radius})$ or $C = 2 \cdot \pi \cdot r$

a. If you have 14 meters of wire fencing available to enclose the circumference (distance around a circle), what is the exact radius of the circle? *Hint:* Substitute 14 for C in the circumference formula and solve for radius r. Leave your answer as a fraction with π in the denominator.

b. What will the area of the circular garden be? Find the exact area A. Then approximate A by rounding your answer to the hundredths place.

c. How does the circle compare with the square in terms of maximizing the amount of area with a fixed perimeter?

_____

_____

_____

_____

d. What might be some problems with trying to build a circular pen?

_____

_____

_____

_____

399

3. Suppose the living room in your new house needs to be carpeted. The floor plan and dimensions are shown below. If the carpet to be put down costs $3 per square foot $\left(\$3/_{ft^2}\right)$, then how much will it cost to carpet the entire living room?

Hint: Partition the room into familiar geometric regions and find their area using known formulas. Then sum up the values of all these regions to obtain the total area.

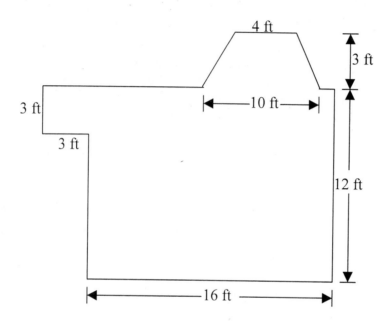

4. Suppose you are willing to devote an area of 120 square feet to building a rectangular deck with one side as the house. The side opposite the house, denoted as x, should measure between 8 ft and 15 ft. What are the best dimensions if you want to minimize the amount of lumber used along the 3 sides? Look at the figure below. *Hint:* You will not need lumber for the side along the house.

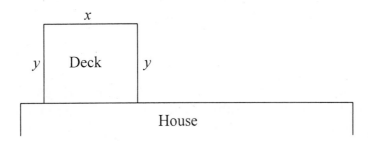

a. What would be a formula for the perimeter P of the deck in terms of sides x and y ?

b. Complete the table below by calculating sides y to nearest foot and then finding perimeter P using the formula from part *a.* *Hint:* The area is fixed at 120 ft^2 so that $x \cdot y = 120$.

x (feet)	y (feet)	P (feet)
8		
9		
10		
11		
12		
13		
14		
15		

c. Which dimensions from the above table will give you a perimeter that uses the least amount of lumber?

d. Explain why a square is not the best choice if you want to keep cost to a minimum?

_____

_____

_____

5. Suppose you plant a rectangular garden each year with one side as your backyard fence. The other three sides are to be enclosed with 24 feet of wire fencing. What would be the best dimensions to use if you want to maximize the area for a garden?

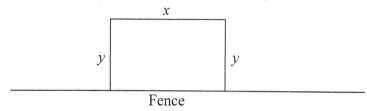

Fence

a. The distance around the 3 sides with fencing is called perimeter, which can be represented by the formula below. Substitute the given perimeter into this equation for P and then isolate the variable x by subtracting $2y$ from both sides of the equation.

$$P = x + 2y$$

b. Complete the following table to gather data on possible dimensions.

y (ft.)	x (ft.)	Area (sq. ft.)
3		
4		
5		
6		
7		
8		
9		

c. What dimensions, x by y, are needed for you to maximize your gardening area when using 24 ft of fencing on three sides?

d. What pattern in the table indicates that there is no need to investigate any further in our search for maximum area?

_____

_____

_____

6. Mario's Pizza Place is advertising three specials, each priced at $9.00.

> - Four small circular pizzas for $9.00 with diameter 16 cm.
>
> - Two medium circular pizzas for $9.00 with diameter 32 cm.
>
> - One large circular pizza for $9.00 with diameter 64 cm.

Explain which special is the better deal. Show all calculations needed in your analysis and use complete sentences to explain your answer. *Hint:* The formula for the area *A* of a circle with radius *r* and diameter *d* is given below.

$$A = \pi \cdot r^2 \quad \text{where} \quad r = \frac{d}{2}$$

_____

_____

_____

_____

_____

_____

_____

7. Suppose you have a picture of a pond near your house. The picture was taken from a plane flying directly above the pond. A 10-by-10 grid appears below. Each small square on the grid represents an area of 100 square yards.

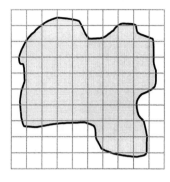

Scale: — 10 yd

☐ 100 yd²

a. Estimate the area of the pond and explain the procedure you used.

_____

_____

_____

b. Estimate the perimeter of the pond and explain the procedure you used.

_____

_____

_____

8. In the figure below, a circle has been constructed so that it fits inside a square.

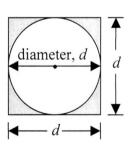

Area of the Square $= d \cdot d = d^2$

Area of the Circle $= \pi \cdot r^2 = \pi \cdot \left(\dfrac{d}{2}\right)^2 = \dfrac{\pi}{1} \cdot \dfrac{d^2}{4} = \dfrac{\pi}{4} \cdot d^2$

a. Compare the area of the circle to the area of the square. Use a percentage to estimate how much larger the square's area would be as compared to the circle's area.

b. The area of the circle is $\frac{\pi}{4} \cdot d^2$, but since the area of the square is d^2, then you can express the area of the circle in terms of the area of the square.

$$\text{Area of the Circle} = \frac{\pi}{4} \cdot \left(\text{Area of the square}\right)$$

Complete the sentence below by filling in the blank with the nearest percentage

The area of the circle is _____ of the area of the square.

c. In percentage terms, how much larger is the area of the square compared with the circle?

d. Estimate which geometric object has the largest perimeter—circle or square.
Hint: Perimeter is the distance around a geometric object. When the object is a circle, we usually call its perimeter the *circumference.*

e. Prove your answer to part *d* with the help of the following formulas. Explain your reasoning using complete sentences.

$$\text{Perimeter of the Square} = 4 \cdot d, \qquad \text{Circumference of the Circle} = 2 \cdot \pi \cdot r = 2 \cdot \pi \cdot \frac{d}{2} = \pi \cdot d$$

_____

_____

_____

9. Below you are given a number of squares, which are to be arranged into a rectangular shape.

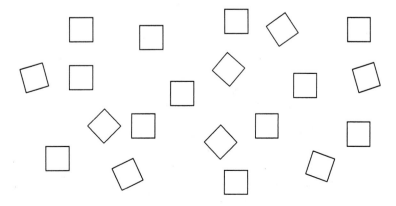

a. If each square represents 1 ft^2, then what is the area of any rectangular shape you can construct?

b. In the space below, please arrange the squares into a rectangular shape that has the smallest possible perimeter. Draw your own squares similar in size to the ones on the previous page.

c. What are the dimensions of the rectangle you constructed in part *b*? What is the perimeter?

d. Build another rectangle that has the same area as part *b* but a different perimeter.

e. Build another rectangle that has the same area as in parts *b* and *d* but with a different perimeter than the two previous constructions.

f. Imagine you have 35 squares that each measure 1 ft^2, which you want to arrange in a rectangular shape. What whole number dimensions will produce the smallest possible perimeter? *Hint:* It is not necessary to arrange the squares to answer the question.

g. Imagine you have 72 squares that each measure 1 ft^2, which you want to arrange in a rectangular shape. What whole number dimensions will produce the smallest possible perimeter?

h. Imagine you have *n* squares where *n* is any positive integer. What general procedure can you follow to find the dimensions of the rectangular shape that will produce the smallest possible perimeter?

_____

_____

_____

_____

10. Suppose you own a one-floor store located in the downtown business district. You plan on renting the store to a tenant at the cost of $2.25 per square foot. If the area has the dimensions given in the plane figure below, then what is the total cost required to rent this store? Show all work so that it is clear to the tenant how you arrived at the cost of rent.

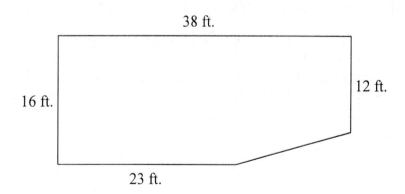

38 ft.

16 ft.

12 ft.

23 ft.

Section 5.3 Solid Geometry: Volume and Surface Area

Math Talk

Have you ever wondered about the fourth dimension? Does it exist? If so, what does it look like?

We live in a three-dimensional world where objects have length, width, and height. For example, the size or magnitude of a rectangular box can be measured using the length, width, and height of the box.

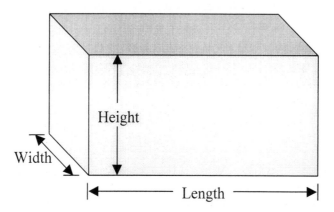

To understand higher dimensions, let's start by imagining a point in space. The point has no dimension. Now imagine moving the point so that the trace of motion is a line.

Point   A point can trace a line.

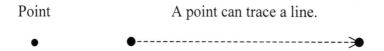

A *line* is a one-dimensional object that can be measured in inches (in), feet (ft), centimeters (cm), meters (m), and so on. If you move the line perpendicular to its position, then the trace of motion is a *rectangular plane*.

The line has length in units.   A line can trace a rectangle.

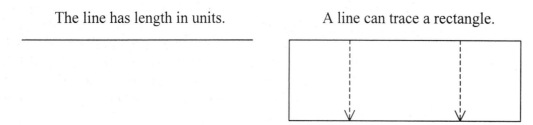

A *rectangle* is a two-dimensional object that can be measured in square inches (in^2), square feet (ft^2), square centimeters (cm^2), square meters (m^2), and so on. If you move the rectangular plane perpendicular to all its edges, then the trace of motion is a *rectangular solid*.

The rectangle has area in square units.

A rectangle can trace a rectangular solid.

Width

Length

The **rectangular solid** or box is a three dimensional object that can be measured in cubic inches (in^3), cubic feet (ft^3), cubic centimeters (cm^3), cubic meters (m^3), and so on. But what happens when you move the rectangular solid perpendicular to all its edges?

While it's difficult to imagine such an object given the necessary mathematical information, a computer can help you visualize a four-dimensional object. If the three-dimensional object is a cube (all edges having the same length), then its trace will produce something called a *hypercube*.

We will not consider any cases beyond the third dimension, but with the help of mathematics, some physicists have found that our universe might have ten dimensions. Unfortunately, seven of these dimensions are invisible to us without mathematics.

****

Time to experience something more concrete. In the first Discovery Adventure, you will construct one, two, and three-dimensional objects to get a better understanding of geometric forms. You will need a metric ruler to begin the adventure.

Discovery Adventure 1: Measuring in Three Dimensions

a. Draw a line with a length measuring 1 centimeter and label it 1 cm.

b. List at least three other units of length besides the centimeter.

_____

c. How would you measure a curved line such as your waist?

_____

_____

d. Is a line a one-, two-, or three-dimensional object? Explain.

_____

_____

e. Now draw a rectangle whose length and width measure 1 cm. Label your figure.

f. What is the name of a rectangle with length and width that are equal in measure?

g. What does a square unit of length, such as 1 cm^2, represent?

_____

_____

h. Is a square a one-, two-, or three-dimensional object? Explain.

_____

_____

i. Finally, draw a cube by adding 1 cm of height to the square you constructed earlier.

j. To measure a square, you need units of length and width. What do you need to measure a cube or any rectangular solid? Explain.

_____

_____

k. If a plane region (such as a square) is given height, we have a solid object in three-dimensional space (such as a cube.) The amount of space in a cube or any three-dimensional object is known as **volume**. How do you think volume is calculated? What type of unit would describe the volume of the cube you constructed in part *i*?

Formula for Volume =

Unit for Volume =

Feedback

If a plane region is given height, we have a solid object in three-dimensional space. When we add 1 cm of height to a square, a third dimension is introduced to give us a solid object called a **cube.** We can find the volume of the cube by multiplying the area of the square times the height of the cube.

$$\text{Volume of Cube} = (\text{Area of Square}) \cdot (\text{Height})$$
$$= (\text{Length}) \cdot (\text{Width}) \cdot (\text{Height})$$

But in a square the length and width have the same measure. Likewise, in a cube, the length, width, and height have the same measure. Therefore, if we refer to any of the cube's equal edges as the side, then the above formula translates as follows:

$$\text{Volume of Cube} = (\text{side}) \cdot (\text{side}) \cdot (\text{side})$$
$$= (\text{side})^3$$

Each side of the cube you constructed measures 1 centimeter. Hence, its volume is calculated as follows:

$$\text{Volume} = (1 \text{ cm}) \cdot (1 \text{ cm}) \cdot (1 \text{ cm})$$
$$= 1 \text{ cm}^3$$

So length measures one dimension in units such as cm. Area measures two dimensions in square units such as cm^2. Volume measures three dimensions in cubic units such as cm^3.

Observe the figure on the next page to visualize the concept of dimension.

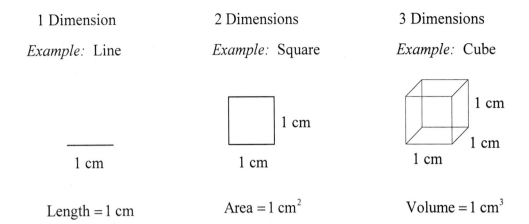

1 Dimension	2 Dimensions	3 Dimensions
Example: Line	*Example:* Square	*Example:* Cube

Length = 1 cm   Area = 1 cm^2 Volume = 1 cm^3

In Discovery Adventure 2, you will develop specific formulas for volume and surface area using three-dimensional figures called rectangular solids or more informally, boxes.

Discovery Adventure 2: Sugar Cubes

Suppose each of the little cubes (from Discovery Adventure 1) measuring 1 cm^3 is a sugar cube that you want to place in a box. The box measures 4 inches in length, 2 inches in width, and 3 inches in height. Consider the volume of the box to be the amount of 3-dimensional space within the box.

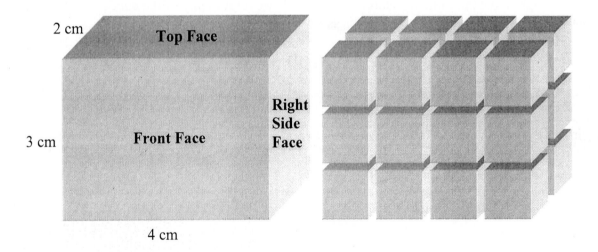

a. How many sugar cubes can fit inside the box?

b. Show how to calculate the volume of the box, and express your answer in cubic units.

c. The **surface area** of the box is the area of the entire surface, which encloses the 3-dimensional space inside the box. Assuming the box has a lid, how many rectangular faces cover its entire surface?

d. The front and back faces of the box should have the same area. Show how to calculate this area and the sum of both areas. Express your answers in square units.

Area of front face =

Area of front and back face =

e. The right and left side faces of the box should have the same area. Show how to calculate this area and the sum of both areas. Express your answers in square units.

Area of right side face =

Area of left and right side face =

f. The top and bottom faces of the box should have the same area. Show how to calculate this area and the sum of both areas. Express your answer in square units.

Area of top face =

Area of top and bottom face =

g. The total area of all 6 faces is the box's surface area. Express this area in square units.

h. Let the variables *L*, *W*, and *H* represent the length, width, and height of any rectangular solid like the box below. Use these variables to write a formula for finding the surface area of a rectangular solid (box). *Hint:* Observe the figure below and think about the calculations completed in parts *d* - *g*.

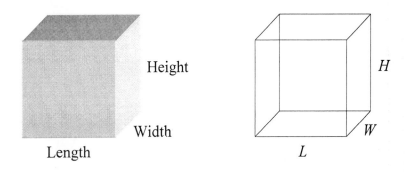

Surface Area =

Feedback

Since there are 24 sugar cubes in the box, the area must be 24 cm^3. This result can be obtained by counting the number of sugar cubes or finding the product of the length (3 cm), width (2 cm), and height (3 cm).

Formula for Volume of a Box

Given a rectangular solid or box of length L, width W, and height H, we can calculate the volume of the box using the following formula:

$$\text{Volume} = \text{Length} \cdot \text{Width} \cdot \text{Height}$$

For example, the volume of the box in Discovery Adventure 2 is
$V = (4 \text{ cm})(2 \text{ cm})(3 \text{ cm}) = 24 \text{ cm}^3$.

Since the area of the front and back faces are equal, we take two times the area of the front to calculate the area of both. In a similar fashion, we take two times the area of the right side to calculate the area of both the right and left sides. Also, we find two times the area of the top to calculate the area of the top and bottom sides. Then the *surface area* of the box (total area of all six faces) can be calculated as follows:

$$\text{Surface Area} = 2 \cdot (\text{Area of front}) + 2 \cdot (\text{Area of right side}) + 2 \cdot (\text{Area of top})$$
$$= 2 \cdot (4 \text{ cm} \cdot 2 \text{ cm}) + 2 \cdot (3 \text{ cm} \cdot 2 \text{ cm}) + 2 \cdot (4 \text{ cm} \cdot 3 \text{ cm})$$
$$= 2 \cdot 8 \text{ cm}^2 + 2 \cdot 6 \text{ cm}^2 + 2 \cdot 12 \text{ cm}^2$$
$$= 16 \text{ cm}^2 + 12 \text{ cm}^2 + 24 \text{ cm}^2$$
$$= 52 \text{ cm}^2$$

To generalize our work on surface area we give the following formula.

Formula for Surface Area of a Box

If the variables L, W, and H represent the length, width, and height of any rectangular solid or box, then the surface area can be calculated as follows:
$$\text{Surface Area} = 2 \cdot (L \cdot H) + 2 \cdot (W \cdot H) + 2(L \cdot W)$$

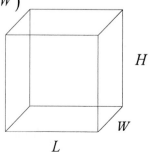

Section Exercises: 5.3

1. Suppose you have been invited to a friend's house for dinner and have promised to bring the dessert. How about some moist and chewy brownies? The recipe says that you'll need an 8-inch square pan, which will yield 16 brownies. If there are 8 people attending the dinner, then 16 brownies should be plenty as long as each brownie is big enough. Let's do some calculations to see exactly what the size of the brownies will be.

    a. Draw a square that represents a 2-dimensional view of the pan as you look straight down at it. Label the length of each side including the units.

    b. What is the area of the pan in square inches? Recall that the area of a rectangle is length times width.

    c. Now you know how many square-inch brownies you can have, but the recipe calls for 16 brownies. Go back to your two-dimensional square from part *a* and draw three equally spaced hash marks on each side. Then connect opposite side hash marks with straight lines such that you form a 4-by-4 square grid. If you cut the brownies along the grid lines, then how many brownies do you have for your dinner party?

    d. What is the length of a side of any brownie that you cut in part c?

    e. What is the area of each brownie?

f. Redraw the 4-by-4 grid you made in part *a*. Label the exterior edges of each brownie along the pan's perimeter (border) with the length found in part *d*. Do the edges along each side of the pan add up to 8 inches?

g. Suppose you decide to cut the brownies so that each person at the dinner receives one of equal size. Draw a picture of this situation labeling the length of each brownie's edge along the pan's perimeter. Assume the whole pan of brownies is to be given out.

h. What will be the dimensions and area of each person's brownie in part *g*? Be sure to include the units in your answers.

i. If the pan has a height of 2 inches, what will be the volume of each person's brownie? Be sure to include the units in your answer.

j. Show how to figure out the volume of the whole pan using the two procedures below.

- Calculate the sum of the volumes of all 8 brownies.

- Calculate the total volume using the dimensions of the pan.

2. While there are slight differences in the dimensions of different cereal boxes, most appear to have a similar shape. But why did cereal manufacturers choose this particular shape? Let's investigate the measurements of two different brands of cereal.

Cereal Name	Length (cm)	Width (cm)	Height (cm)	Volume (cm³)	Surface Area (cm²)
Frosted O's	19.5	6.5	29		
Apple Pops	19	6	27		

a. Find the volume of each box of cereal. Show all work below and place the results in the table above.

b. Find the surface area of each box of cereal. Show all work below and place the results in the table above.

c. If each box is completely filled with cereal, which brand provides the most cereal? Explain.

_____

_____

d. If both boxes are made from the same type of cardboard, which brand uses the most cardboard in making the box?

_____

_____

e. Suppose an employee suggests changing the dimensions of the two boxes to the values in the table below. Complete the table by finding the new volume and surface area of the proposed boxes.

Cereal Name	Length (cm)	Width (cm)	Height (cm)	Volume (cm³)	Surface Area (cm²)
Frosted O's	15.5	15.5	15.5		
Apple Pops	14.5	14.5	14.5		

f. Do you think that the manufacturer should make these changes? The employee claims that it will be cheaper to make the new boxes because less cardboard material is needed.

_____

_____

_____

3. In this exercise you will construct three open boxes (no lid) with different volumes from three blank sheets of paper with dimensions 21.6 cm by 27.9 cm (the standard 8½ in by 11 in paper). Follow the step-by-step procedure given below.

a. *Step #1*—From each of the four corner points (vertices), measure and mark 3 cm in the horizontal direction and 3 cm in the vertical direction.

Step #2—Use your ruler to draw 3 cm by 3 cm squares in each of the 4 corners.

Step #3—Use your scissors to cut out each 3 cm by 3cm square in each of the 4 corners.

Step #4—Fold up each of the sides to form an open box.

b. Repeat the steps in part *a*, except draw and cut out squares measuring 4 cm by 4 cm in each corner.

c. Repeat the steps in part *a*, except draw and cut out squares measuring 5 cm by 5 cm in each corner.

d. Estimate which box would have the largest volume. Explain.

_____

_____

e. Estimate which box would have the smallest surface area. Explain.

_____

_____

f. Find the volume and surface area of each box you constructed. Round volume to the nearest cubic centimeter, and round surface area to the nearest square centimeter. Organize your information in the table below. *Hint*: The length and width of each box will be smaller than the dimensions of the original paper because you cut out a square from each corner.

Length of Squares' Sides (cm)	Volume of Box (cm³)	Surface Area of Box (cm²)
3		
4		
5		

g. Which of the three boxes would you choose if you wanted to maximize the volume and minimize the surface area? Explain.

_____

_____

_____

4. Suppose you want to place your friend's birthday present in a box that measures 38 cm in length, 27.5 cm in width, and 10 cm in height. To make the box look special, you decide to wrap some ribbon around the box as shown below. How long must the ribbon measure to complete the wrap?

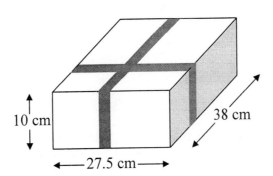

5. Suppose a 9 by 10 unit grid is drawn on a piece of cardboard, and then 9 square units are cut from each corner to produce the pattern as shown (below left). If you fold up the sides as pictured (below center), then a box in formed. Predict how many unit cubes (below right) are needed to fill in the 3-dimension space inside the box? Perform the calculation needed to obtain an exact answer.

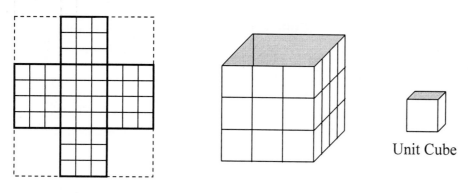

Unit Cube

Prediction:

Calculation:

Exact Answer:

6. Suppose you have a rectangular pool in your backyard with a base measuring 10 meters by 20 meters and a height of 3 meters. At the beginning of the summer, the pool is filled to capacity, but after a month of use, the depth of the water drops to 2.8 meters.

a. How many cubic meters of water are lost after the pool has been used for a month? Show all work.

b. If 1 cubic meter is equal to approximately 264 gallons, then how many gallons of water are lost after the pool has been used for a month?

c. Give some possible reasons for the loss of water.

_____

_____

7. Milk, orange juice and other liquids are sold in half-gallon containers. Suppose you want to measure the volume of a half-gallon container in metric units. Find an empty half-gallon container and cut off the top to form a box without a lid.

   a. Find the volume in cubic centimeters by measuring the length, width, and height of the box with a centimeter ruler.

      Length =   Width =   Height =   Volume =

   b. If a half-gallon is equivalent to 1.89 liters, then what is the volume of the container in milliliters (mL)?

   c. Should the answers to parts a and b be the same? Explain.

      _____

      _____

      _____

   d. What are the differences between a milliliter (mL) and a cubic centimeter (cm^3)?

      _____

      _____

      _____

8. Let's construct formulas for the volume and surface area of a right circular cylinder. Observe the diagram below and imagine that the rectangle is made of some bendable material. Recall the following formulas for area of a circle and area of a rectangle:

$$\text{Area of a Circle} = \pi \cdot (\text{radius})^2 \qquad\qquad \text{Area of a Rectangle} = \text{Length} \cdot \text{Width}$$

$$A = \pi \cdot r^2 \qquad\qquad\qquad\qquad A = L \cdot W$$

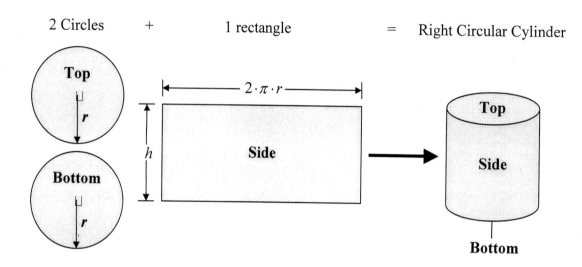

    a. Show how the areas of the circles and rectangle can be used to construct a formula for the surface area of the right circular cylinder. Your answer should be given in terms of the radius *r* and height *h*.

    b. Show that the volume of the right circular cylinder is the area of the base (bottom circle) multiplied by the cylinder's height (the distance between the top and bottom circles.) Your answer should be given in terms of the radius *r* and height *h*.

9. Canned food has the shape of a right circular cylinder, as in the figure below. The height and radius of "the can" determine the volume.

diameter

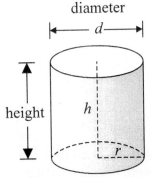

Right Circular Cylinder

$$\text{radius} = 1/2 \cdot (\text{diameter})$$

$$r = \frac{1}{2}d$$

$$\text{Volume} = \pi \cdot (\text{radius})^2 (\text{height})$$

$$= \pi \cdot r^2 \cdot h$$

Assuming that you like canned beans, which of the following sizes gives you more to eat?

• Canned beans with radius = 8 cm and height = 12 cm.

• Canned beans with radius = 12 cm and height = 8 cm.

Use the following concept to complete exercises 10 and 11.

> If two geometric objects have the same shape but different sizes, then the objects are **proportional** or **similar**. The **linear scaling factor** of two similar objects is the ratio of a length of some part of one object to the same part of the other object. For example, all the rectangular solids in the figure below are *similar*. The *linear scaling factors* when enlarging the first solid to obtain the second and third solids are 2 and 3, respectively.

10. Imagine a small room with the following dimensions: length 9 ft, width 6 ft, and height 8 ft. If we double each dimension, then we call this enlargement a linear scaling factor of 2. If we triple each dimension, then we call this enlargement factor a linear scaling factor of 3.

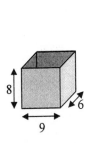

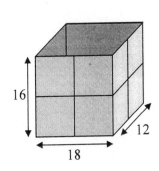

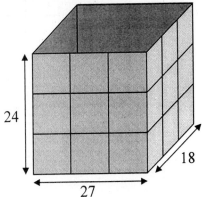

a. Suppose you change the size of the original room so that its length is 2 times as long, its width is 2 times as wide, and its height is 2 times as high. With a linear scaling factor of 2, how will the surface area and volume of the room change? In the space provided, list how the room's length, width, height, surface area, and volume will change as a result of a linear scaling factor of 2.

Length: _____   Width: _____   Height: _____

Surface Area: _____   Volume: _____

b. Suppose you change the size of the original room so that its length is 3 times as long, its width is 3 times as wide, and its height is 3 times as high. With a linear scaling factor of 3, how will the surface area and volume of the room change? In the space provided, list how the room's length, width, height, surface area, and volume will change as a result of a linear scaling factor of 3.

Length: _____   Width: _____   Height: _____

Surface Area: _____   Volume: _____

c. Now organize your information into a table that uses linear scaling factors from 1 to 6 in steps of 1. *Hint:* A linear scaling factor of 1 denotes the original room's dimensions.

Linear Scaling Factor	Length (ft)	Width (ft)	Height (ft)	Surface Area (ft²)	Volume (ft³)
1	9	6	8	348	432
2					
3					
4					
5					
6					

d. What happens to the surface area and volume as you increase the length, width, and height by larger linear scaling factors? Complete the table below to find out. *Hint*: Express each surface area and volume ratio as a power of the linear scaling factor.

Linear Scaling Factor	Surface Area	Surface Area Ratio $\left(\dfrac{\text{new surface area}}{\text{original surface area}}\right)$	Volume	Volume Ratio $\left(\dfrac{\text{new volume}}{\text{original volume}}\right)$
1	348		432	
2	1392	$\dfrac{1392}{348} = 4 = 2^2$	3456	$\dfrac{3456}{432} = 8 = 2^3$
3				
4				
5				
6				

e. Complete the following sentences by putting the correct answer in the blank space. For each sentence, the second blank indicates the exponential form of the answer in the first blank.

- If the linear scaling factor is 2, then the new room's enlarged surface area is _____ times or _____ the surface area of the original room.

- If the linear scaling factor is 2, then the new room's enlarged volume is _____ times or _____ the volume of the original room.

- If the linear scaling factor is 3, then the new room's enlarged surface area is _____ times or _____ the surface area of the original room.

- If the linear scaling factor is 3, then the new room's enlarged volume is _____ times or _____ the volume of the original room.

- In general, if the linear scaling factor is L, then the new object's enlarged surface area is _____ times the surface area of the original object.

- In general, if the linear scaling factor is L, then the new object's enlarged volume is _____ times the volume of the original object.

11. Suppose you work for a company that makes globes (of Earth). To produce a spherical globe, you need to make use of the following formula. *Hint:* The diagram is not to scale.

Volume of a Sphere

$$\text{Volume} = \frac{4}{3} \cdot \pi \cdot (\text{radius})^3$$

$$V = \frac{4}{3} \cdot \pi \cdot r^3$$

$r = 4.5$ inch $r = 6.75$ inch

a. What is the linear scaling factor when increasing the radius from 4.5 in. to 6.75 in.? *Hint:* Find the ratio of the radius of the second sphere to the radius of the first sphere.

b. What are the volumes of the spheres with radius 4.5 in. and 6.75?

c. Find the ratio of the volume of the second ($r = 6.75$) sphere to the volume of the first ($r = 4.5$) sphere.

d. Take the linear scaling factor from part *a* to the third power and then compare the result with the answer to part *c*. What does this tell you about the volume of a scaled-up sphere?

_____

_____

_____

_____

Section 5.4 Large Numbers, Small Numbers, and Scientific Notation

Math Talk

What type of numbers would you describe as *large*?

According to the U.S. Treasury Department, the federal **deficit** for the fiscal year of 1997 was $1,957,000,000. While this may seem to be a very big number, it pales in comparison to the U.S. public **debt** of $5,413,100,000,000 for the same fiscal year. A *deficit* occurs when the difference between the federal government's total outlays (spending) and total receipts (revenue) is a negative value. When this difference is positive, the country has a **surplus.** The *public debt* is the sum of all the federal deficits (−) and surpluses (+) since this country first started having a budget. Since there have been more budget deficit years than surplus years, the United States is in debt.

How would you describe the value of the federal deficit and public debt in words? Are these numbers better expressed in terms of millions, billions, or trillions of dollars? Technically, you could express them in any of these ways; however, the federal deficit for 1997 is best expressed in billions of dollars, and the public debt for 1997 in trillions of dollars.

What type of numbers would you describe as *small*?

All elements in this world are made up of small particles called *atoms*. These particles are so small that they can only be seen with the most powerful microscopes. Hydrogen, the smallest atom, has a diameter of about 0.0000000001 meters. Even though most people would consider
<u>9 zeros</u>
this length to be very small, the atom contains even smaller particles called *subatomic particles*. The three major subatomic particles are protons, electrons, and neutrons. The diameter of an electron is estimated to be less than 0.000000000001 meters. Having 11 zeros to the right of the
<u>11 zeros</u>
decimal point compared to 9 zeros means that a hydrogen atom is 100 times greater in length than an electron. So an atom is actually large when compared to a subatomic particle.

Therefore, large and small are relative terms. In other words, how large or small a number is depends on what value you are comparing it to. There is no definite way to determine where large numbers begin and small numbers end. When a number is large or small enough to require a long list of digits, then it is helpful to have a concise and consistent method for expressing that number.

****

In the first Discovery Adventure, you will investigate how powers of 10 can provide a solution for dealing with very large and very small numbers.

Discovery Adventure 1: Notation for Large and Small Numbers

A convenient way to express large and small numbers is to use powers of 10.

a. Complete the table below by writing each power of ten in expanded form. Then record the number of zeros for each expanded number.

Powers of 10	Expanded Form	Number of Zeros
10^0	1	0
10^1	10	1
10^2		
10^3		
10^4		
10^5		
10^6		

b. In each row, what is the connection between the exponent on 10 and the number of zeros in the expanded form? Explain.

_____

_____

_____

c. Express the numbers "one billion" and "one trillion" as decimal values in expanded form and as powers of 10.

Name of Number	Expanded Form	Powers of 10
One Billion		
One Trillion		

d. What happens if you multiply a nonzero integer value such as 7.0 by whole number powers of 10? Complete the table below by taking the exponential form from the first column and writing it in expanded form in the second column. In the third column, write the number of decimal places that the decimal point moves to the right when converting from exponential to expanded form.

Exponential Form	Expanded Form	Decimal Places Moved to the Right
7.0×10^0	7.0	0
7.0×10^1	70.0	1
7.0×10^2		
7.0×10^3		
7.0×10^4		
7.0×10^5		
7.0×10^6		

e. Repeat the work you did in part *d* using the number 7.235.

Exponential Form	Expanded Form	Decimal Places Moved to the Right
7.235×10^0	7.235	0
7.235×10^1	72.35	1
7.235×10^2		
7.235×10^3		
7.235×10^4		
7.235×10^5		
7.235×10^6		

f. Given the product of a number and a whole number power of 10, what general procedure can you follow to convert this exponential form into its equivalent expanded form?

_____

_____

_____

_____

g. Now explore the reciprocals of positive integer powers of 10 by completing the following table.

Reciprocals of Powers of 10	Expanded Form	Number of Zeros Including Ones Place
$1/10^1$	0.1	1
$1/10^2$	0.01	
$1/10^3$		
$1/10^4$		
$1/10^5$		
$1/10^6$		

h. In the second column of the table below, each value can be obtained by dividing the preceding value by 10. Complete the remainder of the second column by dividing the previous value by 10. State your result as a decimal number in expanded form.

Decreasing Powers of 10	Decimal Value
10^3	1000.0
10^2	100.0
10^1	10.0
10^0	1.0
10^{-1}	
10^{-2}	
10^{-3}	

i. The last three rows of part *h* should equal the first three rows of part *g*. Therefore,

$$10^{-1} = \frac{1}{10^1}$$

$$10^{-2} = \frac{1}{10^2}$$

$$10^{-3} = \frac{1}{10^3}$$

Based on the three equalities above, complete the following general statement:

If *n* is a positive integer power, then $10^{-n} =$

j. Complete both tables below in order to investigate the effect of multiplying by negative integer powers of 10. Convert the exponential form from the first column into its equivalent expanded form within the second column. In the last column, write the number of places that the decimal point has moved to the left after multiplying 7.0 and 7.235 by negative integer powers of 10.

Exponential Form	Expanded Form	Decimal Places Moved to the Left
7.0×10^{-1}	0.7	1
7.0×10^{-2}		
7.0×10^{-3}		
7.0×10^{-4}		
7.0×10^{-5}		
7.0×10^{-6}		

Exponential Form	Expanded Form	Decimal Places Moved to the Left
7.235×10^{-1}	0.7235	1
7.235×10^{-2}		
7.235×10^{-3}		
7.235×10^{-4}		
7.235×10^{-5}		
7.235×10^{-6}		

k. Given the product of a number and a negative integer power of 10, what general procedure can you follow to convert this exponential form into its equivalent expanded form?

_____

_____

_____

Feedback

If n is a positive integer, then the exponential expression 10^n represents a decimal number having n zeros between the first digit 1 and the decimal point.

$$10^n = 1,\underbrace{000,\ldots,000}_{n \text{ zeros}}.0$$

If you multiply a number by 10^n, where n is any whole number, then the decimal point moves n places to the right. For example, the U.S. public debt projected for the fiscal year of 2002 is given below in exponential and expanded forms.

$$6.3 \times 10^{12} = 6,\underbrace{300,000,000,000}_{12 \text{ places to the right}}.0$$

If you multiply a number by 10^n, where n is any negative integer, then the decimal point moves n places to the left. For example, the mass (in grams) of a hydrogen atom is given below in exponential and expanded forms.

$$1.673 \times 10^{-24} = 0.\underbrace{00000000000000000000000}_{24 \text{ places to the left}}1673$$

The exponential forms of the U.S. public debt and the mass of a hydrogen atom are examples of **scientific notation**.

Scientific Notation

A number is expressed in *scientific notation* when it is written as a number that is less than 10 and greater than or equal to 1 multiplied by an integer power of 10.

$$a \times 10^n, \quad \text{where } a \geq 1 \text{ and } a < 10, \text{ and } n \text{ is an integer.}$$

Scientific notation is a convenient way to represent very large numbers such as the U.S. public debt and very small numbers such as the mass of a hydrogen atom.

In expanded form, these numbers are not only difficult to understand, but they are also hard to use when completing calculations. To express these long numbers in scientific notation, follow the procedure given on the next page.

Converting a Number to Scientific Notation

To find the power of 10, expressed as n, count the number of places that the decimal point must be moved in order to obtain a number between 1 and 10. If the decimal point must be moved to the left, the exponent n is positive. If the decimal point must be moved to the right, the exponent n is negative. For example,

- To write the number 7,235,000,000 in scientific notation, move the decimal point 9 places to the left.

$$7,\underbrace{235,000,000}_{9 \text{ places to left}}.0 = 7.235 \times 10^9$$

- To write the number 0.0000007235 in scientific notation, move the decimal point 7 places to the right.

$$0.\underbrace{0000007}_{7 \text{ places to right}}235 = 7.235 \times 10^{-7}$$

To convert a number from scientific notation into a standard decimal number written in expanded form, you can follow one of the rules given below.

Convert From Scientific Notation to Expanded Form

- *Positive Exponents:*
  If the exponent is represented by n, you move the decimal point to the right n number of places. For example, to write the number 6.0025×10^{11} in expanded form, we move the decimal 11 places to the right.

$$6.0025 \times 10^{11} = 6\underbrace{00,250,000,000}_{11 \text{ places to right}}.$$

- *Negative Exponents*:
  With the exponent represented by n, move the decimal point to the left n number of places (the negative sign simply indicates that you move left). For example, to write the number 3.075×10^{-14} in expanded form, move the decimal 14 places to the left.

$$3.075 \times 10^{-14} = 0.\underbrace{00000000000003}_{14 \text{ places to left}}075$$

In the next Discovery Adventure, you will learn how to multiply and divide numbers written in exponential form. This will involve learning some short cuts for dealing with exponents.

Discovery Adventure 2: Rules for Exponents

Recall that exponential notation is a shortcut for repeated multiplication. For example,

$$10^3 = 10 \cdot 10 \cdot 10$$

a. Express 10^2 using repeated multiplication.

b. Express 10^5 using repeated multiplication.

c. How many tens are multiplied when finding the product, $10^2 \cdot 10^5$?

d. Represent the product $10^2 \cdot 10^5$ as "10 to a power".

$$10^2 \cdot 10^5 =$$

e. In the equation above, what is the relationship between the two exponents that occur to the left of the equal sign and the one exponent to the right? Explain using complete sentences.

_____

_____

_____

f. Generalize your results by completing the following rule. If a and b are positive integers, then

$$10^a \cdot 10^b =$$

g. In the quotient below, use the results from parts a and b to express the numerator and denominator using repeated multiplication.

$$\frac{10^5}{10^2} = \underline{\hspace{3cm}}$$

h. In your result to part g, cancel any common factors and express the simplified result as a power of 10. Record your answer to the right of the equal sign below.

$$\frac{10^5}{10^2} =$$

i. In the equation from part *h*, what is the relationship between the two exponents that occur to the left of the equal sign and the one exponent to the right? Explain using complete sentences.

_____

_____

_____

j. Generalize your results by completing the following rule. If *a* and *b* are positive integers, then

$$\frac{10^a}{10^b} =$$

Feedback

It appears that if you multiply powers of 10, then the short cut is to just add the exponents. For example,

$$10^2 \cdot 10^5 = \underbrace{(10 \cdot 10)}_{2 \text{ tens}} \cdot \underbrace{(10 \cdot 10 \cdot 10 \cdot 10 \cdot 10)}_{5 \text{ tens}} = 10^{2+5} = 10^7.$$
$$\underbrace{\hphantom{(10 \cdot 10) \cdot (10 \cdot 10 \cdot 10 \cdot 10 \cdot 10)}}_{2 \text{ tens} + 5 \text{ tens} = 7 \text{ tens}}$$

Rule for Multiplying Exponential Expressions

In general, given *a* and *b* are any positive integers, then

$$10^a \cdot 10^b = 10^{a+b}$$

In words, if the base (in this case, 10) is the same, then add the exponents ($a+b$).

If you divide powers of 10, then the short cut is to just subtract the exponents. For example,

$$\frac{10^5}{10^2} = \frac{\overset{1}{\cancel{10}} \cdot \overset{1}{\cancel{10}} \cdot 10 \cdot 10 \cdot 10}{\underset{1}{\cancel{10}} \cdot \underset{1}{\cancel{10}}} = 10^{5-2} = 10^3$$

Rule for Dividing Exponential Expressions

In general, given a and b are any positive integers, then

$$\frac{10^a}{10^b} = 10^{a-b}$$

In words, if the base (10) is the same, then subtract the exponents ($a-b$).

Discovery Adventure 3: Multiplying and Dividing Large and Small Numbers

Suppose you find out the following fact about the chemical element carbon:

- 1 carbon atom has a mass of 0.00000000000000000000001994 gram.

Hint: There are 23 zeros appearing in the number above, one to the left of the decimal point and 22 to the right of the decimal point.

a.   What mathematical operation can be performed to find the mass of 3250 carbon atoms?

b.   What mathematical operation can be performed to find the number of atoms in 0.625 gram of the element carbon?

c.   Explain why performing the operations in parts *a* and *b* would be a tedious task.

_____

_____

_____

_____

_____

436

d. Convert the following decimal numbers to scientific notation.

0.00000000000000000000001994 =

3250 =

0.625 =

e. Set up and perform the calculation needed to answer part *a*. Express the result in scientific notation and then in expanded form. *Hint*: First separate the coefficients (3.25 and 1.994) from the exponential terms (10^3 and 10^{-23}), and then multiply.

f. Set up and perform the calculation needed to answer part *b*. Express the result in scientific notation and then in expanded form. *Hint*: First separate the coefficients (6.25 and 1.994) from the exponential terms (10^{-1} and 10^{-23}), and then divide.

Feedback

It would be very tedious to complete any calculations using the mass of 1 carbon atom in expanded form. Therefore, the first step is to write all the numbers in scientific notation.

$$0.00000000000000000000001994 = 1.994 \times 10^{-23}$$

$$3250 = 3.25 \times 10^3$$

$$0.625 = 6.25 \times 10^{-1}$$

To find the mass of 3250 carbon atoms, we need to find the product of 3.25×10^3 and 1.994×10^{-23}. Since multiplication can be done in any order, we multiply the coefficients (3.25 and 1.994) and exponential terms (10^3 and 10^{-23}) separately.

$$\left(3.25 \times 10^3\right) \cdot \left(1.994 \times 10^{-23}\right) = \left(3.25 \cdot 1.994\right) \times \left(10^3 \cdot 10^{-23}\right) \quad \text{Separate the terms.}$$
$$= \left(6.4805\right) \times \left(10^{3+-23}\right) \quad \text{Add the exponents.}$$
$$= 6.4805 \times 10^{-20} \quad \text{Write in scientific notation.}$$

Therefore, the mass of 3250 carbon atoms is 0.000000000000000000064805 grams.

To find the number of atoms in 0.625 gram of carbon, we need to find the quotient of 6.25×10^{-1} and 1.994×10^{-23}. For convenience, we divide the coefficients (6.25 and 1.994) and exponential terms (10^{-1} and 10^{-23}) separately.

$$\frac{6.25 \times 10^{-1}}{1.994 \times 10^{-23}} = \frac{6.25}{1.994} \times \frac{10^{-1}}{10^{-23}} \quad \text{Separate terms.}$$
$$= 3.13440321 \times 10^{-1-(-23)} \quad \text{Subtract the exponents.}$$
$$= 3.13440321 \times 10^{22} \quad \text{Write in scientific notation.}$$

Therefore, 0.625 gram of carbon contains 31,344,032,100,000,000,000,000 atoms of carbon.

How do we add and subtract numbers in scientific notation? If you have a calculator that allows this type of notation, enter the calculation and have the machine compute the answer. The calculator might provide an answer in expanded form, which can then be changed to scientific notation, if desired.

It should also be noted that all the calculations involving multiplication and division could have been completed on a calculator. The important thing for you is to understand how scientific notation works and how it can be used to solve problems involving very large or very small numbers. As you work on the Section Exercises, you will become more comfortable with these ideas.

Section Exercises: 5.4

1. Each household has a budget, and so does the U.S. government. When the government's yearly expenditures (for administration and programs) are greater than its revenue (money collected from taxes), there is a federal budget deficit. If expenditures are less than revenue, there is a surplus. The following table gives the actual data on expenditures and revenue from the 1999 federal budget.

	Expanded Form	Scientific Notation
Revenue	$1,827,000,000,000	
Expenditures	$1,703,000,000,000	
Difference		

   a. Find the difference between the revenue and expenditures, and place the result in the last row of the second column. Was there a deficit or a surplus during 1999?

   _____

   b. Complete the last column by writing each value from the second column in scientific notation.

   c. Suppose you want to decrease the width of the second column to save space. Suggest a different way to list the numbers but still accurately display their value.

   _____

   _____

2. The national debt is a direct liability of the U. S. Government that represents the accumulated deficits in the government's budgets since the Revolutionary War. The federal debt held by the public was about 3.6 trillion dollars at the end of 1999.

   a. Write the federal debt in expanded form and in scientific notation.

   b. According to the Census Bureau, on August 1, 1999 there were an estimated 273 million people living in the United States. Suppose the U.S. Government wanted to pay off the entire public debt in 1999. If each member of the population pays an equal amount, then how much money would you owe the government? Show all work below.

c. If the government pays 5% annual interest on the national debt, then how much interest will they pay for the year 1999? Express your answer in expanded form and in scientific notation.

d. The revenue for 1999 was about 1,827 billion dollars. What percent of the revenue does interest make up? Express your answer in expanded form and in scientific notation.

3. Practice multiplying numbers expressed in scientific notation. Remember that to multiply exponential expressions with the same base, you add the exponents. Refer to the example below as needed.

e.g. $(3.7 \times 10^{19}) \cdot (6.2 \times 10^{-12}) = (3.7 \cdot 6.2) \times (10^{19} \cdot 10^{-12})$ Separate the terms.

$= 22.94 \times 10^{19+(-12)}$ Add the exponents.

$= \underset{2.294 \times 10^{1}}{\underline{22.94}} \times 10^{7}$ Write in scientific notation.

$= 2.294 \times 10^{8}$ Add the exponents.

a. $(3 \times 10^{5}) \cdot (2 \times 10^{-7})$

b. $(8.0 \times 10^{9}) \cdot (5.0 \times 10^{6})$

c. $(8.3 \times 10^{-8}) \cdot (2.5 \times 10^{-4})$

d. $(4.63 \times 10^{21}) \cdot (7.50 \times 10^{-8})$

4. Write your answers from Section Exercise #3 in expanded form.

   a.

   b.

   c.

   d.

5. Practice dividing numbers expressed in scientific notation. Remember that to divide exponential expressions with the same base, you subtract the exponents. Refer to the example below as needed.

$$\frac{1.8 \times 10^8}{5.0 \times 10^{12}} = \frac{1.8}{5.0} \times \frac{10^8}{10^{12}} \qquad \text{Separate the terms.}$$

$$= 0.36 \times 10^{8-12} \qquad \text{Subtract the exponents.}$$

$$= \underbrace{0.36}_{3.6 \times 10^{-1}} \times 10^{-4} \qquad \text{Write in scientific notation.}$$

$$= 3.6 \times 10^{-5} \qquad \text{Add the exponents.}$$

   a. $\dfrac{6.08 \times 10^{-5}}{1.9 \times 10^{-8}}$

   b. $\dfrac{2.21 \times 10^{12}}{6.5 \times 10^{14}}$

   c. $\dfrac{7.0 \times 10^4}{3.5 \times 10^{-9}}$

d. $\dfrac{10^{-16}}{1.3\times10^6}$ (*Hint*: $10^{-16}=1\times10^{-16}$)

6. Write your answers from Section Exercise #5 in expanded form.

    a.

    b.

    c.

    d.

7. The U.S. Federal Government obtains its revenues or receipts mostly from taxes. The following circle graph (or pie chart) shows the different sources that make up the estimated $2,019 billion in revenue that the government will receive during the fiscal year of 2001.

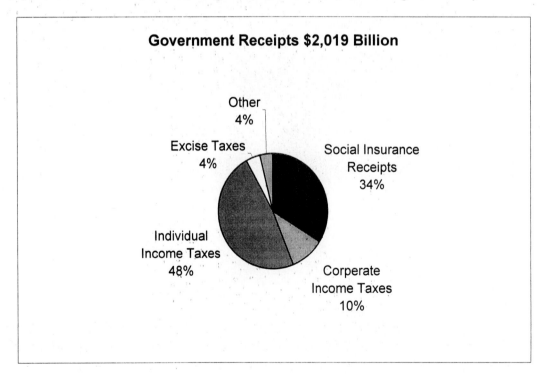

a. How much money does the U.S. Federal Government receive from Individual Income Taxes? State your answer as a decimal value in expanded form and in scientific notation. Show all work below.

b. It is estimated that the U.S. Federal Government will spend about $1.8 trillion in 2001. Explain whether the government can expect a surplus or a deficit.

_____

_____

8. During fiscal year of 2001, the U.S. Federal Government will spend an estimated $1,835 billion which can be divide into 9 categories as shown in the pie chart below.

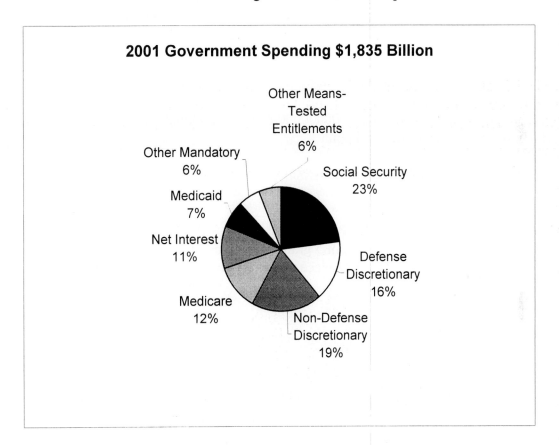

2001 Government Spending $1,835 Billion

a. How much money does the U.S. Federal Government spend on Social Security? State your answer as a decimal value in expanded form and in scientific notation. Show all work below.

b. Suppose the U.S. government is determined to eliminate the federal debt. If the government continues to have a surplus each year into the foreseeable future, then what category should shrink as a percent of the whole budget?

_____

_____

c. Suppose the percent of spending on Social Security and Medicare is expected to rise during 2002 and beyond. How will reducing the federal debt help assure that Social Security and Medicare will continue to have the necessary funding?

_____

_____

_____

9. One helium atom has a mass of 0.0000000000000000000000665 grams. *Hint:* There are 23 zeros to the right of the decimal point.

   a. Express this quantity in scientific notation.

   b. How many atoms are in a sample of 5 grams of helium? Express your answer in scientific notation, accurate to one place to the right of the decimal point.

10. Atoms contain smaller particles, known as subatomic particles, such as electrons, protons, and neutrons. The mass (in grams) of these three subatomic particles is given in the table below.

Particle	Mass
Electron	9.110×10^{-28}
Proton	1.673×10^{-24}
Neutron	1.675×10^{-24}

a. Explain how you write the mass of an electron and proton in expanded form. Do not write the expanded form, just explain the process that you need to complete.

_____

_____

_____

b. The mass of a neutron is a little larger than that of a proton. Find the difference in mass between the two subatomic particles.

c. Which particle has a larger mass, the neutron or the proton? Explain how you arrived at your answer.

_____

_____

_____

_____

d. Using your answer to part *c*, find out how many times larger this particle is as compared with the other smaller particle. *Hint*: Use division to find your answer.

Chapter 5 Summary

Key Terms

Section 5.1

- **Units** – Terms that measure the quantity of an object.
- **Standardized Units** – Inches and pounds are examples of standardized units in the U.S. customary system; centimeters (cm) and kilograms (kg) are examples from the Metric System.
- **Simple Units** – Single terms like inches, pounds, kilograms, and centimeters.
- **Compound Units** – Formed when simple units are multiplied, divided, or raised to a power. For example, distance in miles divided by time in hours gives us speed in miles/hour.
- **Sequence** – An ordered set of quantities or expressions.

Section 5.2

- **Plane** – A flat surface such as this page of paper.
- **Plane Geometry** – Refers to the geometry of figures that have all their points lying on one plane. Some common plane figures are the circle, rectangle and triangle.
- **Perimeter** – The distance around the border of a 2-dimensional geometric object. The perimeter of a rectangle is the distance around the four sides enclosing the rectangular region. Using length and width, perimeter can be defined as follows:

$$\text{Perimeter} = 2 \cdot \left(\text{Length} + \text{Width}\right)$$
$$= 2 \cdot \text{Length} + 2 \cdot \text{Width}$$

- **Area** – The area of a rectangle is the surface enclosed by its boundaries (sides or edges). With the measure of either the bottom or top side called *length* and the measure of either the left or right side called *width*, the area of a rectangle can be defined as follows:

$$\text{Area of Rectangle} = \text{Length} \cdot \text{Width}$$

- **Length/Width** –Terms used to distinguish between the different sides of a rectangle that connect at a corner. Unless all sides are equal (length = width), either the longer or shorter side can be defined as the length, then the remaining side will be the width.
- **Base/Height** – If the *base* is symbolized as b and *height* as h (instead of length and width), then the definition of area A of a rectangle can be written as follows:

$$\text{Area} = \text{Base} \cdot \text{Height} \quad \text{or} \quad A = b \cdot h$$

- **Polygon** – A geometric figure with 3 or more sides.
- **Parallelogram** – A 4-sided geometric shape in which opposite sides are parallel.
- **Trapezoid** – A 4-sided geometric shape with 2 parallel sides that do not have the same length.
- **Symmetric Pattern** – A pattern having the same arrangement on either side of a dividing line.

Section 5.3

- **Rectangular Solid** – A three-dimensional object that can be measured in cubic units.
- **Volume** – The measure of the space within a three-dimensional object. Given a rectangular solid or box of length L, width W, and height H, we can calculate the volume using the following formula:

$$Volume = Length \cdot Width \cdot Height$$

- **Cube** – A three-dimensional square with length, width, and height all the same number of units.
- **Surface Area** – The total area of all sides of a rectangular solid. Given a rectangular solid or box of length L, width W, and height H, we can calculate the surface area using the following formula:

$$Surface\ Area = 2 \cdot (L \cdot H) + 2 \cdot (W \cdot H) + 2 \cdot (L \cdot W)$$

- **Proportional or Similar** – Two geometric objects that have the same shape but different sizes.
- **Linear Scaling Factor** – The ratio of the length of one part of one object to that same part on another object.

Section 5.4

- **Deficit** – When the difference between total spending and total revenue is a negative value.
- **Debt** – When the financial balance is negative.
- **Surplus** – When the total revenue minus total spending is a positive value.
- **Scientific Notation** – A way to write a very large or very small number. A number that is greater than or equal to 1 and less than 10 multiplied by an integer power of 10 is a number written in scientific notation. Symbolically, $a \times 10^n$, where $a \geq 1$ and $a < 10$, and n is an integer.

****

Questions for Review

1. When do you need to convert from one set of units to another? For example, suppose Lisa is spending the academic year in France as an exchange student. While in France, she goes to a local doctor for a medical exam. The table below shows data on Lisa's office visit.

Height	170 centimeters (cm)
Weight	60 kilograms (km)
Body Temperature	37.5° Celsius
Time spent with patient	750 seconds
Charge for office visit	400 francs

   a. Use the conversion factor, 1 in. = 2.54 cm, to find Lisa's height in feet and inches.

b. Use the conversion factor, 1 kg = 2.2 lb, to find Lisa's weight in pounds.

c. Use the following formula to find Lisa's body temperature in degrees Fahrenheit.

$$Fahrenheit = \frac{9}{5} \cdot (Celsius) + 32$$

d. Find the time that Lisa spent in the doctor's office in minutes, and then in hours.

e. Use the conversion factor, 1 dollar = 5.8995 francs, to find the dollar amount that Lisa was charged for her office visit.

2. During Lisa's stay in France she decides to find out the daily cost for renting an automobile. The salesperson at U-Pay-Us Rental explains that their basic rental car costs 175 francs plus 1 franc per kilometer driven. To help Lisa understand, the salesperson begins to create and complete the table below.

Kilometers Driven	Calculation Rule	Cost of Rental
0	$175 + 1 \cdot 0$	175
25	$175 + 1 \cdot 25$	200
50	$175 + 1 \cdot 50$	
75		
100		
125		
150		
175		
200		
⋮	⋮	
k		

a. Complete the table, but leave the last row, second column blank for now.

b. Observe the pattern in the sequence of calculations within the second column. Note the values that remain constant and the values that change. If k represents the number of kilometers driven, then use a variable expression to represent the rule for finding the daily rental cost for the basic car. Place your result in the last row, second column and after the equal sign below.

Basic Car Cost =

c. The salesperson tells Lisa that the luxury rental car costs 250 francs plus 2 francs for each kilometer driven. If k represents the number of kilometers driven, then use a variable expression to represent the rule for finding the daily rental cost for the luxury car.

Luxury Car Cost =

d. If you drive the rental car a total of 70 km, then what will be the cost in francs to rent the basic car? What is the cost in francs to rent the luxury car?

e. Convert 70 km to miles. *Hint*: $1 \text{ mi} = 1.6 \text{ km}$.

f. Using the conversion factor, 1 dollar = 5.8995 francs, convert 245 francs to dollars, and 390 francs to dollars.

g. Summarize your findings by using a complete sentence to express how many miles you have driven and the cost in dollars of renting a basic or luxury car.

_____

_____

_____

_____

3. Do you understand the metric system and how to convert from one unit to another? Use the table below to help answer the following questions.

milli-	centi-	deci-	Basic Unit	deka-	hecto-	kilo-
$\dfrac{1}{1000}$	$\dfrac{1}{100}$	$\dfrac{1}{10}$	1	10	100	1000

a. When converting from one metric unit to another, the process involves multiplying or dividing by a power of 10. How do you know which operation to use? How do you know the correct power of 10 to use in your operation? Explain.

_____

_____

_____

_____

_____

b. How many liters are there in a 355mL (12 oz) can of tonic?

c. How many 355 mL cans of tonic are in a 2-liter bottle of the same brand of tonic?

d. Which of the following two items contains the most fluid? Show all work.

- A six-pack of 355 mL cans of tonic.

- A 2-liter bottle of tonic.

e. Suppose that a 355 mL can of tonic costs $0.75 and a 591mL bottle (20 oz) costs $1.25. Which is the best value? *Hint*: Find the unit cost of each item. In other words, what is the cost per 1 mL?

f. If a jogger runs 5 km, then how far has she traveled in meters?

g. If a sprinter runs 400 m, then how many kilometers has he run?

h. If an infant crawls 4 m, then how many millimeters did the baby move?

i. If an ant walks 50 cm, then how many millimeters did it walk?

j. Suppose you need to take 20 mg of a certain medication. How many grams did you take?

k. If you eat a bowl of ice cream that contains 40 grams of fat, then how many kilograms of fat have you consumed? How many milligrams of fat have you consumed?

4. Do you know how to find the perimeter and area of any polygon? For example,

Suppose you are considering the purchase of the following plot of land.

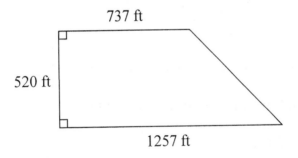

737 ft

520 ft

1257 ft

a. What is the perimeter? Show all work and include the proper units in your answer. *Hint*: Find the length of the unknown side by using the Pythagorean Theorem $\left(a^2 + b^2 = c^2\right)$.

b. What is the area? Show all work and include the proper compound units in your answer.

c. How many acres are contained within the plot? *Hint*: 1 acre = 43,560 square feet (ft^2).

5. How do you calculate the volume and surface area of a 3-dimensional object? For example, imagine that you own an in-ground pool in the shape of a rectangular solid. The pool measures 100 ft long by 50 ft wide by 10 ft deep.

a. Before filling the pool, you decide to paint the walls and bottom (5 faces). In the space below, draw three rectangles to represent one of the long sides, one of the short sides, and the bottom. Label the sides of these rectangles with the proper dimensions.

b. Find the total surface area of the pool's 5 faces. Show all work.

c. If one gallon of paint covers approximately 325 square feet, then how much paint will be needed to cover the 5 inside faces of the pool?

d. What is the volume of the pool?

 e. How many cubic feet of water will you need to fill the pool up to 6 inches from the top?

 f. How many gallons of water are in the answer to part *e*? *Hint*: 1 cubic foot = 7.48 gallons.

6. Suppose you own an above-ground pool that has the shape of a right circular cylinder. The pool measures 20 feet in diameter and 4 feet in depth.

 a. Draw a picture of the pool with its dimensions.

 b. What is the volume of the pool?
     Hint: Volume $= \pi \cdot (\text{radius})^2 \cdot (\text{height})$, $\text{radius} = 1/2 \cdot (\text{diameter})$

 c. How many cubic feet of water will you need to fill the pool up to 6 inches from the top?

d. How many gallons of water are needed in the answer to part *c*? *Hint*: 1 cubic foot = 7.48 gallons.

7. After buying the circular pool in Section Exercise #6, you realize that a cover will be needed for the top.

    a. If the diameter of the pool is 20 ft, then how many square feet (ft^2) do you need to cover the top area?

    b. One store sells the necessary cover size for $19.95, while a second store sells covers of the same quality for $0.06 per square foot. Which is the better deal? Show all work.

8. Do you understand the difference between higher dimensions?

    a. Write and picture a 1 –dimensional object. Clearly label the length of the object with its unit.

    b. Write and picture a 2-dimensional object. Clearly label the object including units, then find the perimeter and area of the object.

c. Write and picture a 3-dimensional object. Clearly label the object including units, then find the volume and surface area of the object.

9. Can you convert numbers from expanded form to scientific notation? For example, convert each of the following values to scientific notation.

   a. 3,500,000,000,000

   b. 1,096,000,000

   c. 0.0000002

   d. 0.000000000198

10. Can you convert numbers from scientific notation to expanded form? For example, convert each of the following values to expanded form.

    a. 2.03×10^5

    b. 4.9×10^{12}

    c. 1.0×10^{-14}

    d. 3.82×10^{-5}

11. Can you multiply and divide two numbers written in scientific notation? For example, perform the indicated operations.

    a. $\left(5.0 \times 10^6\right) \cdot \left(1.7 \times 10^9\right)$

    b. $\left(7.13 \times 10^{-6}\right) \cdot \left(3.45 \times 10^{17}\right)$

    c. $\dfrac{6.8 \times 10^{-6}}{3.4 \times 10^8}$

    d. $\left(1.69 \times 10^3\right) / \left(2.6 \times 10^5\right)$

Chapter 5 Quiz

1. In the metric system a prefix may be used with any basic unit to obtain measurements that are larger or smaller than that unit. Observe the table below, then answer the following questions.

milli-	centi-	deci-	Basic Unit	deka-	hecto-	kilo-
$\dfrac{1}{1000}$	$\dfrac{1}{100}$	$\dfrac{1}{10}$	1	10	100	1000

  a. What is the basic unit for each of the following types of measure?

  - Length

  - Mass and Weight

  - Volume

  b. Fill in the blanks to complete the following sentences.

  To convert from larger metric units to smaller ones, you _____ by 10 for each unit movement to the left. To convert from smaller metric units to larger ones, you _____ by 10 for each unit movement to the right.

2. If you run a 10-kilometer (km) race in 55 minutes, then what is your speed in miles per hour (mph)? Round to the hundredths place. *Hint*: $1 \text{ km} = 0.62 \text{ mi}$, $60 \text{ min} = 1 \text{ hr}$, and

  $$\text{Average Speed} = \frac{\text{Distance}}{\text{Time}}.$$

3. Without using any formulas, explain the difference between perimeter and area.

  _____

  _____

  _____

  _____

4. Suppose you plan on hiring a contractor to refinish the hardwood floors in the room pictured below.

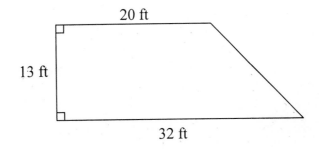

a. What is the perimeter? Show all work and express your answer with the proper units.

b. What is the area? Show all work and express your answer with the proper units.

c. If the contractor charges $2.75 per square foot, then what will be the cost to refinish the room?

5. Imagine an in-ground pool in the shape of a rectangular solid. The pool measures 60 meters long by 30 meters wide by 3 meters deep.

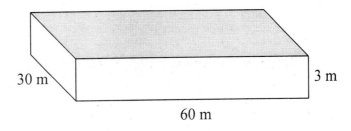

a. The surface area of the pool is made up of five rectangular faces: 2 long sides, 2 short sides, and 1 bottom. Draw three rectangles to represent one of the long sides, one of the short sides, and the bottom. Label the sides of these rectangles with the proper dimensions.

b. Find the surface area of the pool. *Hint*: What is the sum of the areas of all 5 faces?

c. Suppose you fill the pool so that the water line is 0.2 meters from the top. Find the volume of the pool up to the water line.

6. An engineer who is responsible for the maintenance of local roads needs to calculate how many tons of asphalt pavement to lay on a 2.3 mile stretch of roadway that is 30 feet wide. The asphalt has a thickness of $1\frac{1}{2}$ inches and weighs 160 pounds per cubic foot.

a. Suppose you want to calculate the volume of asphalt that is needed in cubic feet $\left(\text{ft}^3\right)$. What is the problem with using the units for length, width and height of the material?

_____

_____

_____

_____

b. Convert 2.3 miles to feet using the conversion factor, 1 mile = 5280 feet.

c. Convert $1\frac{1}{2}$ inch to feet using the conversion factor, 1 foot = 12 inches.

d. Use the results from parts *b* and *c* and the given width of the road to calculate the volume of the asphalt in cubic feet.

e. Using the answer from part *d* and the given information on weight, find the weight of the asphalt in pounds.

f. Convert your answer in part *e* to find the tons of asphalt being used.
Hint: 1 ton = 2000 pounds .

7. One hydrogen atom has a mass of 0.00000000000000000000001673 grams. *Hint:* There are 23 zeros to the right of the decimal point.

a. Express this quantity in scientific notation.

b. How many atoms are in a sample of 8 grams of hydrogen? Express your answer in scientific notation, accurate to two places to the right of the decimal point.

8. The atom has a diameter ranging from 0.1 to 0.5 nanometers. If 1 nanometer equals 1×10^{-9} meters, then what is the range of an atom's diameter in meters?

Chapter 6

Functional Relationships and Symbol Sense

Section 6.1 Numerical Relationships in Tables of Data
Section 6.2 Graphical Relationships in the Rectangular Coordinate System
Section 6.3 Symbolic Relationships in Equations

Chapter 6 introduces the concept of function from a numeric, graphic, symbolic, and verbal point of view. This is often called the "rule of four," because it provides four ways to look at any functional relationship. This chapter will also develop your symbol sense by building models of real world situations using tables, graphs, equations, and words.

In Section 6.1, the study of functions begins by exploring situations where one set of numbers has a dependent relationship with another set of numbers. Some of the concepts presented are independent and dependent variables, the basic input-output definition of function, function notation, and finding trends in tables of numbers by looking at rates of change.

In Section 6.2, graphing is introduced by plotting ordered pairs of data on a coordinate plane. This provides a visual way to illustrate the mathematical relationships that appear in tables of data. Discovery Adventures include the graphing of scatter and line plots, the discussion of domain and range, and the chance to make conclusions based on trends in graphs.

Section 6.3 provides the opportunity to develop symbolic rules or equations based on patterns in sets of data. The symbolic rules are used to answer questions involving substitution and then simplifying and solving one-variable equations using the properties of equality.

Section 6.1 Numerical Relationships in Tables of Data

Math Talk

Previously a *variable* was defined as a symbol, such as x or y, that represents an unknown member of a set of objects or numbers. In this section, we begin with a discussion about the words: **independent**, **dependent**, **input**, and **output**. In the study of mathematics, these words distinguish between two types of related variables: the **independent (input) variable** and the **dependent (output) variable**.

In our everyday world, the word *independent* can refer to someone or something that is not influenced by others or does not rely on anything to exist or function. For example, one of the goals of this course is to help you become an independent learner of mathematics. The opposite of independent is the word *dependent*, which means that there is a reliance on someone or something else in order to function. For example, students often depend on their instructors to guide them through any difficult material that they might be studying.

In mathematics, a variable in an equation is *independent* when its value determines the value of the other related variable, called the *dependent variable*. In other words, the dependent variable's value is determined by the value of the *independent variable*.

An example of this relationship is as follows. When a car is moving at a constant speed, the distance traveled depends on the amount of time the car has been moving. Since distance depends on time, distance is the dependent variable and time is the independent variable. We could reword this situation to say that the time spent in the moving car depends on how far the car traveled. In this sense, the dependent variable is time, and the independent variable is distance. So when we have a relationship between two variables, determining which variable is independent or dependent often depends on how you wish to look at the problem situation. The wording of the problem will usually make it clear which variable depends on the other. If you are unsure, pick out the two related variables, such as distance and time, and ask yourself which of the following two statements makes more sense in terms of the problem situation.

- Does the time that the car has moved depend on the distance traveled? Or,

- Does the distance traveled depend on how much time the car has been moving?

Another name for the independent variable is the *input variable*, and the dependent variable is the *output variable*. A value is entered into a rule as *input*, the rule is applied, and the resulting value becomes the *output*. For example, assume a car is moving at a constant speed of 60 mph. Enter 2 hours as the input. Then apply the rule, $\text{Distance} = \text{Rate} \cdot \text{Time}$, and determine the output or distance traveled.

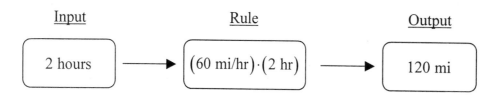

Now let's explore the relationship between independent (input) and dependent (output) variables further in the first Discovery Adventure.

Discovery Adventure 1: Tips vs. Sales

Desi works as a waitress at a local restaurant. She has been keeping a log of her sales in dollars and the total amount of money received in tips for each day on the job. Desi works on Monday, Wednesday, and Friday of each week and wants to see how her tips vary with total sales. The table below shows her last 3 weeks of work. Leave the last column blank for now.

Day	Date	Sales ($)	Tips ($)	Tips (% of sales)
Monday	7/3	695	140	
Wednesday	7/5	721	142	
Friday	7/7	1185	230	
Monday	7/10	702	136	
Wednesday	7/12	750	150	
Friday	7/14	1217	245	
Monday	7/17	690	131	
Wednesday	7/19	719	138	
Friday	7/21	1201	242	

a. What are the two related variables Desi wants to study in this problem situation?

b. Desi wants to predict the amount of money she will receive from tips based on her sales (in dollars). List one of the variables from part *a* as the independent variable and the other as the dependent variable. Use complete sentences to explain your answer.

_____

_____

_____

c. A **functional relationship** exists between two variables if for each value of the independent variable, there is exactly one corresponding value of the dependent variable. In other words, each input value has just one output value. Does a functional relationship exist in this problem situation? Explain.

_____

_____

_____

On Monday 7/3, the tips on sales of $695 were $140. These words can be expressed in symbols using **function notation**. For example,

$$T(695) = 140$$

The above notation is read as "T of 695 equals 140." What it means is that Desi can expect about $140 dollars in tips when she makes $695 in sales.

d. Complete the following mathematical statement by filling in the blank with the correct value.

$$T(719) =$$

e. Suppose we want to know the amount of sales you need to obtain $150 in tips. Find the amount of sales from the data in the table and then complete the following mathematical statement below, which expresses the same information using function notation.

$$T(\underline{\quad\quad}) = 150$$

f. Write a complete sentence that explains the following mathematical statement in words.

$$T(1217) = 245$$

_____

_____

g. Go back to the table and calculate the tips as a percent of sales. In the last column, write the percentage that Desi received in tips each day.

h. In general, what percentage can Desi expect to make in tips on any given workday?

_____

_____

i. Which workday allows Desi to make the most money in tips? Explain.

_____

_____

j. What is Desi's average pay (in tips) for each week during this three-week period? Show all work.

k. What is Desi's average pay (in tips) on Mondays during this three-week period? Show all work.

l. What is Desi's average pay (in tips) on Fridays during this three-week period? Show all work.

m. Suppose that on the next Friday Desi works, she has to cover two additional tables because one of the waitstaff has called in sick. The extra tables should bring her sales up to about $1500. Assuming this happens, complete the following statement.

$$T(1500) =$$

n. In words, describe a rule that will tell Desi the amount of money she will receive in tips based on the dollar amount of her sales.

_____

_____

Feedback

Sales and tips are variables that are expressed numerically in the form of a *table of values*. In this variable relationship, tips depend on sales, or tips are a function of sales. Therefore, sales is the independent (input) variable, and tips is the dependent (output) variable.

Let T represent daily tips in dollars and S represent the sales for that same day. Since tips T depends on sales S, you can express this relationship using function notation as

$$T(S).$$

This is read, "T of S," and it means that tips are a function of sales. $T(S)$ does not tell you to find the product of T and S! Although parentheses can imply multiplication, in this context they represent function notation. The independent variable, S, is always enclosed within parentheses. The variable T in front of the parentheses is the name of the function. In this case, T is also the dependent variable.

In the given table, each input value S produces just one output value T. This means that T is a function of S, or money obtained in tips is a function of the dollar amount of sales.

On most nights, tips are close to 20% of sales. On Wednesday 7/12, tips were exactly 20% of sales because $\dfrac{150}{750} = 0.20$ or 20% of $750 is $150. In function notation, this can be expressed as $T(750) = 150$. In words, "The tips on sales of $750 are $150."

It should be noted that the letter chosen as the name of the function does not have to be the same as the dependent variable. For example, we could have named our function f and written the functional relationship as

$$T = f(S)$$

T is still the dependent variable and S the independent variable, but now the name of the function is f. When T represents the dependent variable and the function name, we can make the following statement,

$$T = T(S).$$

In general, when a function is given numerically in the form of a table, each value associated with the independent variable matches up with exactly one value from the dependent variable. In other words, each input from the first set of numbers has one corresponding output from the second set of numbers.

If the table is presented vertically, then the independent (input) variable is usually the left column of numbers and the dependent (output) variable is the right column of numbers. For example,

Independent or Input Variable	Dependent or Output Variable
1 ⟶	3
2 ⟶	6
3 ⟶	9
4 ⟶	12

If the table is presented horizontally, then the independent (input) variable is usually the top row of numbers, and the dependent (output) variable is the bottom row of numbers. For example,

Independent or Input Variable	1	2	3	4
Dependent or Output Variable	4	8	12	16

In the next Discovery Adventure, you will develop a symbolic rule for a function. The rule will show the functional relationship between independent and dependent variables.
Can you determine the rules for the last two tables?

Discovery Adventure 2: Modeling Desi's Salary

Suppose that Desi will receive exactly 20% of her sales in tips and a weekly base salary of $70. Let's build a table to show how her total weekly pay depends on her sales per week.

Sales ($) x	Tips ($)	Base Salary ($)	Total Salary ($) y
2200	$0.20 \cdot 2200$	70	510
2300	$0.20 \cdot 2300$	70	530
2400			
2500			
2600			
2700			
2800			
2900			
3000			

a. Complete the table by following the pattern given in the first two rows.

b. Explain how tips are determined by sales.

_____

_____

c. Let the variable x represent possible sales in dollars and y the total salary in dollars. State which variable is the independent (input) variable and which is the dependent (output) variable. Explain how you arrived at your answers.

_____

_____

_____

d. Find a variable expression in terms of x that represents the dollar amount of tips that Desi will receive.

e. Explain how Desi's total salary is determined by sales.

_____

_____

f. Find a variable expression in terms of x that represents the total salary in dollars that Desi will receive.

g. Is y a function of x? In other words, does each input x (sales) have just one output y (total salary)? If yes, name your function f and record your expression from part f as the rule for your function $y = f(x) =$ rule in terms of x. Otherwise, state why this is not a functional relationship.

Yes, $y = f(x) =$

No, _____

_____

Feedback

Since tips are always 20% of sales, tips x depends on sales. This can be expressed symbolically as

$$0.20 \cdot x$$

Total salary is the amount you received in tips ($0.20 \cdot x$) plus your fixed base salary ($70). Therefore, total salary y depends on sales and can be expressed symbolically in terms of x.

$$y = 0.20 \cdot x + 70$$

The independent variable is x, and the dependent variable is y. Since each tip amount x produces just one total salary y we can say that y is a function of x. If we name the function f, then the relationship between x and y can be represented using function notation.

$$y = f(x) = 0.20 \cdot x + 70$$

This symbolic notation is read, "y equals f of x equals 0.20 times x plus 70" and means that y is a function of x that follows the rule,

$$\text{Total Salary} = \text{Tips} + \text{Base Salary}$$
$$\text{Total Salary} = 20\% \text{ of sales} + \$70$$

Functional notation has the advantage of allowing the user to express the input within parentheses. For example, you can enter an input of 2500 into the function named f, apply the rule, and calculate the output as follows.

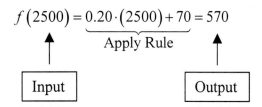

$$f(2500) = \underbrace{0.20 \cdot (2500) + 70}_{\text{Apply Rule}} = 570$$

Input   Output

Section Exercises: 6.1

1. Suppose you are looking to buy a house and want to know the minimum annual gross income needed to get a mortgage. If the lowest interest rate available is 8%, then the following table shows us the income needed for different loan amounts. The data assumes a 30-year loan and borrower's monthly payments that do not exceed 28% of gross income. Also, the data values do not include property taxes and insurance as part of the monthly payments.

Income ($)	Amount of Loan ($)
15,724	50,000
23,586	75,000
31,447	100,000
47,171	150,000
62,895	200,000

Source: National Association of Realtors

a. In this situation, a person's annual gross income is related to the maximum amount of loan needed to get a mortgage, assuming the interest rate of 8%. Does it make sense to think of the maximum possible mortgage loan as being a function of a person's income? Explain.

_____

_____

b. State which variable is independent and which is dependent. Explain your reasoning.

Independent variable: _____ Dependent variable: _____

_____

_____

c. If you can just afford a $50,000 dollar loan, then how much does your yearly income need to increase by to obtain a $75,000 loan. Show all work.

d. Use the table to approximate the income you need to obtain a $110,000 mortgage loan.

e. Let's examine how the amount you receive from a mortgage loan increases as the annual income increases by filling in the following table.

Income ($)	Change in Income ($)	Amount of Loan ($)	Change in Amount of Loan ($)
15,724		50,000	
23,586	7,862	75,000	25,000
31,447		100,000	
47,171		150,000	
62,895		200,000	

f. Based on your work in part e, how much yearly income would you need in order to receive a $125,000 loan? Show how you can get a nearly exact answer to this question.

g. Let M represent the largest mortgage you can get at different income levels. Complete the following mathematical statements using function notation.

$$M(31,447) =$$

$$M(\quad) = 150,000.$$

h. Explain what the following mathematical statement says in terms of salary and loan amount.

$$M(62,895) = 200,000$$

_____

_____

2. In this exercise, you will investigate median housing prices from 1990–1999. In the table below, the word *median* means the middle value of a set of numbers that are arranged in order from smallest to largest. Leave the last column blank for now.

Year of Sale	Median-Priced Existing Home	Annual Change in Median Price	
		Function Notation	Result
1990	$92,000		
1991	97,100	$P(1991) - P(1990)$	$5,100
1992	99,700		
1993	103,100		
1994	107,200		
1995	110,500		
1996	115,800		
1997	121,800		
1998	128,400		
1999	136,900		

a. Explain why the median price of a home is a function of the year of sale. Include in your explanation which variable is independent and which is dependent.

_____

_____

_____

b. Let t represent the year and m represent the median price of a home. From part *a*, you know that m is a function of t. If you call this function P, then function notation can be used to express the relationship as $m = P(t)$. How would you read this notation to a friend?

c. Use the data in the table to complete the following mathematical statements.

$P(1995) =$ _____ $P($_____$) = 115,800$

d. The change in the median price of a home from 1995 to 1996 can be expressed in function notation as follows.

$$P(1996) - P(1995) = 115,800 - 110,500$$
$$= \$5,300$$

Complete the last two columns in the table. When did the largest increase in median prices occur?

3. In this problem, the table used in Section Exercise #2 has been expanded to include more information.

Year	Median-Priced Existing Home	Average Mortgage Rate	Monthly Payment[1]
1990	$92,000	10.04%	$648
1991	97,100	9.30	642
1992	99,700	8.11	591
1993	103,100	7.16	558
1994	107,200	7.47	598
1995	110,500	7.85	639
1996	115,800	7.71	661
1997	121,800	7.68	693
1998	128,400	7.10	690
1999	136,900	7.26	748

([1]) Monthly Payment consists of principal and interest.

a. Each column in the table can be considered a variable. Monthly payment is a variable that directly depends on two other variables in the table. State these two independent variables and explain why monthly payment depends on them.

_____

_____

_____

b. Between 1991 and 1992, the median price of a home increased by $2,600, but the monthly payment decreased by $51. Explain why this occurred.

_____

_____

c. Between 1995 and 1996, average mortgage rates decreased, but the monthly payment increased. Explain why this occurred.

_____

_____

d. Suppose you want to further explore the topic of affording a house. Can you think of another variable that would determine whether a person could afford the monthly payment? Explain.

_____

_____

4. People who live in cold regions know that it's more than the actual temperature that determines how cold you feel. You lose heat from your body surface due to both temperature and wind. This means that wind speed can make you feel colder than the actual temperature.

Suppose the thermometer reads 20° Fahrenheit. The following wind chill table shows the relationship between wind speed (mph) and wind chill temperature (° F). For all questions below, assume a thermometer reading of 20° F. Leave the last column blank for now. *Note*: A more extensive table would have readings for many different temperatures.

Wind Speed (mph)	Wind Chill Temperature (°F)	Change in Wind Chill Temperature (°F)
calm (0 mph)	20	
5	16	–4
10	3	
15	–5	
20	–10	
25	–15	
30	–18	
35	–20	
40	–21	
45	–22	

Source: National Weather Service

a. If there is a 25-mph wind, then what is the wind chill temperature (° F)?

b. If we use T to represent wind chill temperature, show how the information in part *a*, can be expressed using functional notation. **Hint**: $T(\text{Wind Speed}) = \text{Wind Chill Temperature}$.

    c. Complete the following statement using function notation. When the actual temperature is 20°F, but the wind makes it feel like –10°F, then how fast in the wind blowing?

$$T(\underline{\hspace{1cm}}) = -10$$

    d. Explain what the following mathematical statement means in terms of the problem situation.

$$T(35) = -20$$

_____

_____

    e. Complete the last column in the table to find the change in wind chill temperature caused by a 5 mph increase in wind speed. The change in temperature due to a wind speed change from calm (0 mph) to 5 mph has been completed for you.

    f. Explain the trend in wind chill temperature as the wind increases in speed from calm (0 mph) to 45 mph in steps of 5 mph.

_____

_____

_____

    g. Between what two wind speeds do you find the greatest decrease in wind chill temperature?

    h. If wind speeds increase to 50 mph and higher, what effect do you think this has on wind chill temperature?

_____

_____

_____

5. Just as wind speed can make you feel colder than the actual temperature, relative humidity can make you feel hotter (or colder) than the actual temperature. The table on the next page is part of the Heat Index, which tells us how high humidity combined with high temperatures can affect the body's ability to cool itself. For example, if the actual temperature is 90°F and the relative humidity is 70%, then the 90°F thermometer temperature is going to feel like 106°F to the average person.

Note: The table just shows the apparent temperatures due to humidity for a thermometer reading of 90°F, whereas a more extensive table would have readings for many different temperatures.

Thermometer Reads 90°F	
Relative Humidity (%)	Apparent Temperature (°F)
0	83
10	85
20	87
30	90
40	93
50	96
60	100
70	106
80	113
90	122

Source: National Weather Service

a. If the variable *T* represents the apparent temperature that the body feels due to relative humidity, write a verbal translation of the following mathematical statement.

$$T(60) = 100$$

_____

_____

b. Use functional notation to express the following verbal statement in mathematical form. "If the actual temperature is 90°F, then a relative humidity of 70% will make the apparent temperature feel like 106° F."

c. As the relative humidity rises, the apparent temperature increases. But how would we describe this rise? Which statement below best describes how the apparent temperature is rising due to humidity? Circle your answer and justify it in words.
- As the relative humidity rises, the apparent temperature increases at a constant rate.
- As the relative humidity rises, the apparent temperature increases at an increasing rate.
- As the relative humidity rises, the apparent temperature increases at a decreasing rate.

_____

_____

d. What relative humidity value has no effect on how hot or cool our body feels? In other words, at what humidity level is the apparent temperature the same as the actual temperature of 90° F that is measured on the thermometer?

e. What happens if the relative humidity is less than the "no effect" point found in part *d*?

_____

f. What happens if the relative humidity is greater than the "no effect" point?

_____

6. When you work to earn an income, Uncle Sam (the Federal Government) asks for a percentage of your pay. The table below contains the 1999 income tax rates for different income levels. For example, suppose you have a taxable income of $100,000. The first $25,750 you earn is taxed at 15%, the next $36,700 ($62,450 - 25,750$) at 28%, and the final $37,550 ($100,000 - 62,450$) at 31%. So the total Federal tax on $100,000 would be calculated as $25,779:

$$0.15 \cdot (25,750) + 0.28 \cdot (36,700) + 0.31 \cdot (37,550) = 3862.50 + 10,276 + 11,640.50 = 25,779$$

Tax Rate	Taxable Income
15%	$0 to $25,750
28%	$25,751 to $62,450
31%	$62,451 to $130,250
36%	$130,251 to $283,150
39.6%	More than $283,150

a. Show how to calculate the tax that must be paid to the Federal Government on a taxable income of $200,000.

b. Construct a table for incomes from $0 to $25,000 in steps of $5000. Follow the pattern that has been started but leave the last row, second column blank for now.

Taxable Income	Tax Calculation	Tax Due
$0	$0.15 \cdot 0$	$0
$5000	$0.15 \cdot 5000$	
$10,000		
$15,000		
$20,000		
$25,000		
$\vdots$	$\vdots$	
x		

c. Let the independent variable, taxable income, be represented by x. Develop a rule for calculating tax in the 15% bracket ($0 to $25,750). Record this rule below and in the table as a variable expression in terms of x.

d. Let the dependent variable, tax due, be represented by y. Since tax due y is a function of taxable income x, you can express this relationship with function notation and the rule from part c.

$$y = f(x) =$$

e. Complete the mathematical statement below. Then describe how the statement reads, and express its meaning in terms of the problem situation.

$f(22,000) = \underline{\hspace{1.5cm}}$ reads $\underline{\hspace{5cm}}$ and means

_____

_____

477

7. To complete this problem, refer to the tax table in Section Exercise #6 as needed. Since the tax due on the first $25,750 of taxable income is always $3862.50 ($0.15 \cdot 25,750 = 3862.50$), this becomes a fixed part of the tax due for people earning between $25,751 and $62,450. The variable part for people in this bracket is the 28% of income over $25,750 that must be paid.

Taxable Income	Tax Calculation	Tax Due
$30,000	$3862.5 + 0.28 \cdot (30,000 - 25,750)$	$5052.50
$35,000	$3862.5 + 0.28 \cdot (35,000 - 25,750)$	
$40,000		
$45,000		
$50,000		
$55,000		
$60,000		
⋮	⋮	
x		

a. Construct a table that starts at $30,000 and goes up in steps of $5,000 until it reaches $60,000.

b. Observe the second column, which shows the tax calculation on different taxable incomes. Which values in each calculation stay the same and which change?

c. Let the independent variable, taxable income, be represented by x, where $x > 25,750$ and $x \le 62,450$ (the 28% bracket.) Develop a rule for calculating tax in the 28% bracket. Record this rule below and in the table as a variable expression in terms of x.

d. Let the dependent variable, tax due, be represented by y. Since tax due y is a function of taxable income x, express this relationship with function notation and the rule from part c.

$$y = f(x) =$$

e. Complete the mathematical statement below. Then describe how the statement reads and express its meaning in terms of the problem situation.

$f(53,000) = $ _____ reads _____ and means

_____

_____

8. The gravitational attraction of Earth is what gives all objects weight. However, the pull of gravity on the moon is 0.17 times what it is on Earth.

Earth Weight	Calculation	Moon Weight
1	$0.17 \cdot (1)$	0.17
2	$0.17 \cdot (2)$	0.34
3		
4		
5		
10		
50		
100		
$\vdots$	$\vdots$	
E		

a. Follow the pattern in the first two rows to complete the table above except for the last row, second column.

b. Is there a functional relationship between an object's weight on the moon and that same object's weight on Earth? Explain.

_____

_____

c. Let E represent an object's weight on Earth and M its weight on the moon. Write the rule that expresses M as a function of E.

$$M(E) =$$

d. Use function notation to express your weight on the moon.

e. Use a complete sentence to interpret the mathematical statement, $M(160) = 27.2$.

_____

_____

Use the following definitions to complete Section Exercises 9 and 10.

The **domain** of a function is the set of all possible values for the independent (input) variable. The **range** of a function is the set of all possible values for the dependent (output) variable. When a functional relationship exists between two variables, every value in the domain has one corresponding value in the range.

9. The following table presents data on new AIDS cases in the U.S. from 1985 to 1997. Look for trends in the data, but leave the last column blank for now.

Year	New Cases	Change in New Cases
1985	8,161	
1990	41,540	
1993	102,082	
1994	77,092	
1995	70,839	
1996	66,398	
1997	58,254	

(Source: The World Almanac 2000)

a. Explain why the number of new AIDS cases is a function of year.

_____

_____

b. List all the elements in the domain and range using the set notation given below.

Domain: { , , , , , , }

Range: { , , , , , , }

c. The independent variable is year, and the dependent variable is the number of new AIDS cases. Let x represent the year and y the number of new cases. Name your function f, and then use function notation to express y as a function of x.

   d. The change in the number of new AIDS cases between 1993 and 1994 can be expressed in function notation. Find this change and explain what the negative sign means in terms of the problem situation.

$$f(1994) - f(1993) =$$

   e. Use the procedure you followed in part *d* to complete the third column of the previous table. Then explain what this information means to the fight against AIDS.

   _____

   _____

   _____

   f. Estimate the number of new AIDS cases for 1998. Use function notation to describe your estimate.

10. In this exercise you will investigate some data from the Census Bureau on the aging U.S. population. The table below gives the number (in thousands) of people at age 65 and over and what percentage of the U.S. population they make up.

The Elderly Population (Age $\geq$ 65)

Year	Number (thousands)	Percent (% of U.S. population)
1900	3,080	4.1
1910	3,949	4.3
1920	4,933	4.7
1930	6,634	5.4
1940	9,019	6.8
1950	12,269	8.1
1960	16,560	9.2
1970	19,980	9.8
1980	25,550	11.3
1990	31,079	12.5

   a. In the second column, the number of elderly people is given in thousands. Express the number of elderly people in 1990 in expanded form and then in scientific notation.

b. Write a description of how the U.S. population has aged since the turn of the last century.

_____

_____

_____

c. If we analyze the percent of elderly people as a function of year, then find the set of values that make up the domain and the set of values that make up the range. List each set using the proper notation.

d. If the trend in this data continues, what major effects will it have on the country? What type of planning does the U.S. Government need to be doing?

_____

_____

_____

_____

_____

_____

_____

_____

_____

_____

_____

_____

Section 6.2 Graphical Relationships in the Rectangular Coordinate System

Math Talk

Let's talk about some words that are commonly used when constructing and analyzing graphs. We begin by introducing the **rectangular coordinate system** or **coordinate plane**.

The *coordinate plane* is built by drawing two perpendicular number lines called the **horizontal axis** and the **vertical axis** (see figure below). The horizontal axis indicates values of the independent (input) variable, and the vertical axis indicates the values of the dependent (output) variable. The point where the two axes intersect is called the **origin** and is labeled $(0, 0)$. The origin is our home base because it is the place to start when locating other points on the plane.

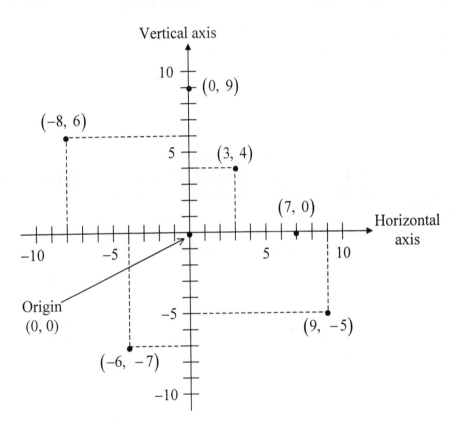

The points in the coordinate plane are **ordered pairs** that describe the location of each point by two numbers called the **horizontal** and **vertical coordinates**. For example, the ordered pair $(9, -5)$ has the number 9 as its horizontal coordinate and –5 as its vertical coordinate. This indicates that starting at the origin, you move 9 units to the right (positive direction), then 5 units down (negative direction).

The coordinate plane is split into four **quadrants** (see figure on next page), with quadrant I in the upper right corner and moving counterclockwise are quadrants II, III, and IV. Many of the problem situations you explore will focus on just the first quadrant where both coordinates are positive. Do you know why most applied problems only make use of quadrant I?

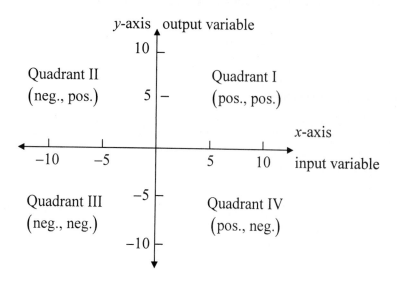

Suppose the input variable is represented by x and the output variable is represented by y. Then we have the following general form for an ordered pair, (x, y).

Each pair of x and y values are called **coordinates**, the **x-coordinate** and the **y-coordinate** respectively. The *x-coordinate* indicates horizontal (left or right) movement and the *y-coordinate* indicates vertical (up or down) movement. Horizontally we have positive values to the right of the origin and negative values to the left. Vertically, we have positive values upward from the origin and negative values downward. The horizontal axis or **x-axis** is where the independent variable (input or x) is placed, and the vertical axis or **y-axis** is where the dependent variable (output or y) is placed.

An ordered pair (x, y) can represent any point on the x-y plane. So the coordinates of an ordered pair are used to locate points on the x-y plane. See the figure below.

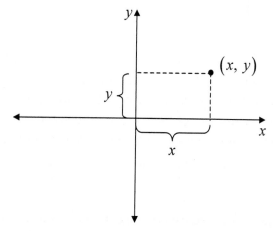

In the first Discovery Adventure, you will plot points, estimate coordinates, use ordered pairs and function notation, make predictions, and then describe trends based on wind chill data.

Discovery Adventure 1: Seeing the Wind's Effect on Temperature

The wind chill table below gives information on how an increase in wind speed can affect how cold you feel. The independent (input) variable is wind speed (mph) and the dependent (output) variable is wind chill temperature (°F).

Wind Speed (mph)	Calm	5	10	15	20	25	30	35	40	45
Wind Chill Temperature (°F)	20	16	3	−5	−10	−15	−18	−20	−21	−22

In the data above, each input value (wind speed) has one corresponding output value (wind chill temperature). These ordered pairs can be plotted on a grid with the independent variable along the horizontal axis and the dependent variable along the vertical axis.

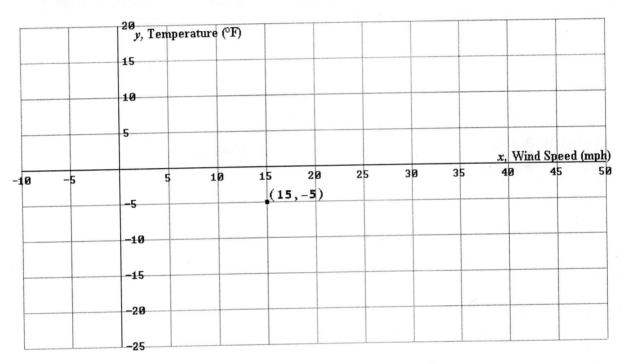

a. Plot each ordered pair from the table above as a point on the graph. For example, starting at the point where the horizontal and vertical lines intersect, the ordered pair $(15, -5)$ is located 15 units to the right and 5 units down. So if the first coordinate (number) from the ordered pair is positive you move right. If it is negative, you move left. From this new position, if the second coordinate (or number) from the ordered pair is positive, you move up. If it is negative, you move down.

b. Use the graph to estimate the wind chill temperature if the wind speed is 7 mph. Write your answer as an ordered pair, such as $(15, -5)$ and then use function notation, such as

$T(15) = -5$.

Ordered pair: (,   )   Function notation: $T($ $) =$

485

c. Use the graph to estimate the wind speed when the wind chill temperature is −8 °F. Write your answer as an ordered pair (input, output) and using function notation,

$T(\text{input}) = \text{output}$.

Ordered pair: (,   )   Function notation: $T($ $) =$

d. How much wind speed is necessary to send an actual 20°F thermometer reading to a temperature that feels like zero degrees? Write your answer as an ordered pair (input, output) and using function notation, $T(\text{input}) = \text{output}$.

Ordered pair: Function notation:

e. From the graph, what do you predict the wind chill temperature will be when the wind speed increases to more than 45 mph? Write your answer in words using a complete sentence.

_____

_____

f. How would you describe the trend of the graph as the wind speed goes from calm (0 mph) to 45 mph? Write your answer in words using complete sentences.

_____

_____

_____

_____

g. What are some advantages to using the graph instead of the table?

_____

_____

_____

h. What are some advantages to using the table instead of the graph?

_____

_____

_____

Feedback

A wind chill temperature of zero degrees Fahrenheit is reached when the wind speed is about 12 mph. This can be expressed as the ordered pair $(12, 0)$ or in function notation as $T(12) = 0$. Note that for any ordered pair, the value of the independent (input) variable is always the first coordinate and the value of the dependent (output) variable is the second coordinate. In function notation, the value of the independent (input) variable is always inside the parentheses and the dependent (output) variable is to the right of the equal sign.

When you draw a graph that displays two-variable data it is called a **scatter plot**. The trend of the function from 0 to 45 mph starts out with the temperature slowly decreasing from 0 mph (calm) to 5 mph. Then there is a large decrease in temperature between 5 and 10 mph. From 10 to 15 mph the decrease in temperature slows down again. From 15 to 25 mph there is a constant decrease in temperature. Finally, from 25 to 45 mph the temperature continues to decrease but at a slower and slower rate. When the wind speed increases to more than 45 mph we predict little change in wind chill temperature because the curve is decreasing at a decreasing rate.

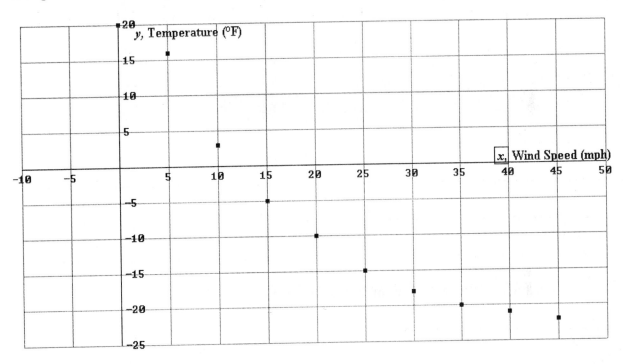

We do not expect any drastic changes in temperature at wind speeds that occur between data points. So, to predict what happens between data values, it is helpful to connect the points with line segments to form a **line plot**. (See the graph on the next page.)

To estimate the wind chill temperature if the wind speed is 7 mph, start at 7 on the horizontal axis and move vertically up until you reach the curve. Then move horizontally left to the vertical axis and estimate the temperature at this point.

To estimate the wind speed, if the wind chill temperature is –8 °F, start at –8 on the vertical axis and move horizontally right until you reach the curve. Then move vertically up to the horizontal axis and estimate the wind speed at this point.

A table and graph are two different ways to present the same data. A table has the advantage of letting you examine exact values and to calculate how one variable is changing with respect to the other. A graph shows the trend in the data and therefore provides the opportunity to make predictions.

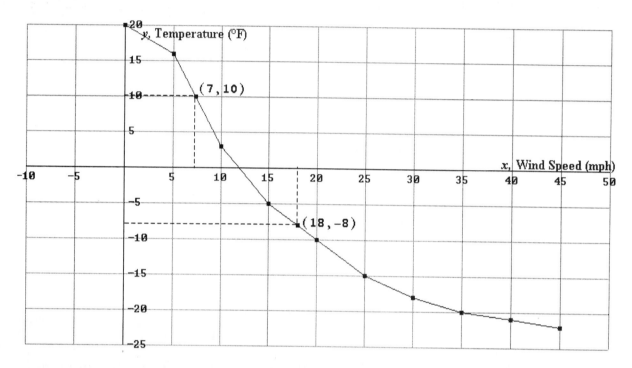

In the next Discovery Adventure, you will return to Discovery Adventure 2: Modeling Desi's Salary, which was explored in Section 6.1. You will be asked to use a function in symbolic form to create a table of values, and then graph the table to get a visual model of the situation.

Discovery Adventure 2: A Picture of Desi's Salary Model

Suppose Desi is given the following function, which is a model of her total weekly salary y depending on the amount of sales x she receives from waiting on tables.

$$y = f(x) = 0.20 \cdot x + 70$$

a. What are the independent (input) and dependent (output) variables in the function?

b. If you wish to graph this function on a coordinate plane, which axis will you use for the independent (input) variable? Which axis will you use for the dependent (output) variable?

c. Recall that the *domain* of a function is the set of all possible values for the independent (input) variable, and the *range* is the set of corresponding values for the dependent (output) variable. State the domain and range of the function called *f*. *Hint*: Consider what values are practical for the amount of sales *x*. There are many correct answers.

d. Based on the domain and range, what would be appropriate scales for the *x*-axis and *y*-axis?

e. Suppose Desi wants to know the total weekly salaries for any sales between $2000 and $3000 in steps of $200. Using function notation, find these salaries by substituting each sale into the function *f* for the input variable *x*. For example, $f(2000) = 0.20 \cdot (2000) + 70 = \$470$

f. Construct a table of values using the results of part *e*.

Sales ($) x	Total Weekly Salary ($) y
2000	
2200	
2400	
2600	
2800	
3000	

g. Graph each ordered pair from the table. Label each axis and connect the points with a line. *Note*: The jagged lines imply a break and so do not consider values before the first tick mark.

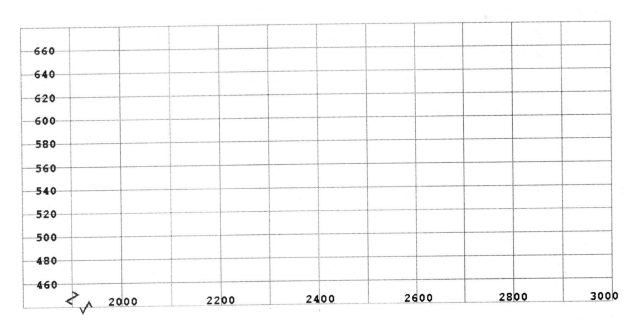

h. Your graph in part *g* should be a straight line that is increasing (moving upward from left to right). What does this type of graph tell you about Desi's salary as sales increase from $2000 to $3000?

_____

_____

_____

i. Complete the following sentences.

- As Desi's sales increase by $100, her salary _____.

- As Desi's sales increase by $50, her salary _____.

- As Desi's sales increase by $10, her salary _____.

- As Desi's sales increase by $1, her salary _____.

j. Observe the table and graph and explain why the ordered pairs produce a graph that is steadily increasing.

_____

_____

_____

Feedback

Since Desi's salary y depends on her sales x, the independent (input) variable x is on the horizontal axis or x-axis and the dependent (output) variable y is on the vertical axis or y-axis. The domain values are all possible amounts that Desi can reasonably expect in sales during any one workweek. Assuming Desi expects an amount between $2000 and $3000, then you can express her domain as $x \geq 2000$ and $x \leq 3000$.

Or alternatively as, $2000 \leq x \leq 3000$.

The range values are the corresponding salaries that match up with each sales amount in the domain. Since $f(2000) = 470$, $f(3000) = 670$, and salary increases as sales increase, then the range is any dollar value between $470 and $670. This can be expressed symbolically as

$$y \geq 470 \text{ and } y \leq 670$$

Or alternatively as, $470 \leq y \leq 670$.

There are other possible domains for this problem, depending on the amount of sales Desi can reasonably expect. For example, suppose Desi has never had weekly sales below $2400 and never above $2800. Using this information, her domain is

$$x \geq 2400 \text{ and } x \leq 2800 \quad \text{or alternatively,} \quad 2400 \leq x \leq 2800$$

The above domain would produce the following range.

$$y \geq 550 \text{ and } y \leq 630 \quad \text{or alternatively,} \quad 550 \leq y \leq 630$$

Finding the Domain

The key to finding the *domain* is seeing what values can possibly be substituted as input and knowing what values are practical or reasonable in the problem situation.

If a function is considered just from a mathematical viewpoint, then you can assume that the domain is all real numbers for which the function exists. If a function represents a real life relationship between two variables, then you also need to think about what input values make sense in terms of the real world situation.

The graph of Desi's salary function shows that as Desi's sales increase by a constant amount, her salary also increases by a constant amount. For example, every $200 increase in sales produces a $40 increase in salary. In general, a constant change in output with respect to a constant change in input will produce a graph that is a straight line.

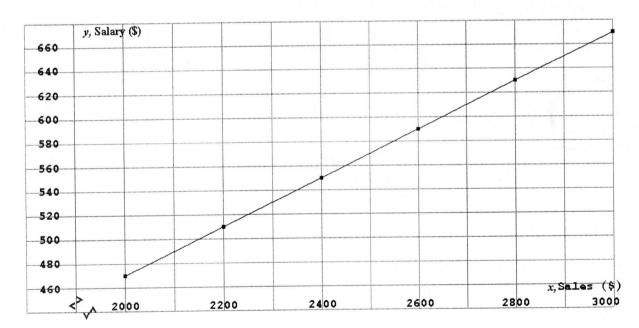

In the upcoming section exercises, you will have the opportunity to work with many different situations to give you experience in working with functions in graphical form.

Section Exercises: 6.2

1. Plot the following ordered pairs as points on the coordinate plane below. Label each point with the letter name given for each ordered pair.

    $A(0,-2)$, $B(3,2)$, $C(-4,7)$, $D(1,-6)$, $E(-5,-5)$, $F(6,0)$

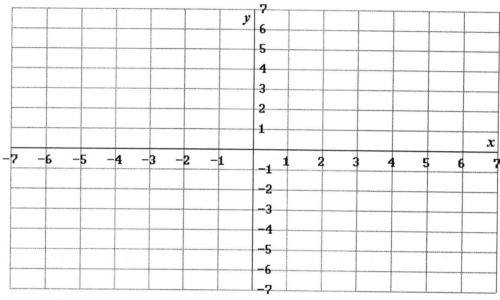

2. On the following coordinate plane, there are 6 points that are labeled with a letter. Write the ordered pair that indicates the coordinates of each point.

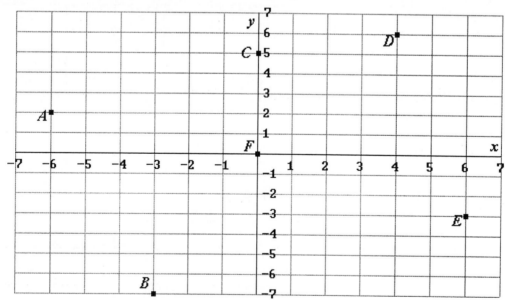

$A(\quad,\quad)$, $B(\quad,\quad)$, $C(\quad,\quad)$, $D(\quad,\quad)$, $E(\quad,\quad)$, $F(\quad,\quad)$

3. The following coordinate plane shows the graph of a function. The graph, called a *line plot*, indicates amount of pleasure travel by U.S. residents during the period of 1986-98. Each of the 13 data points is measured in millions of person-trips of 100 miles or more, one-way. The data points are connected to show the trend in travel volume during this period of time.

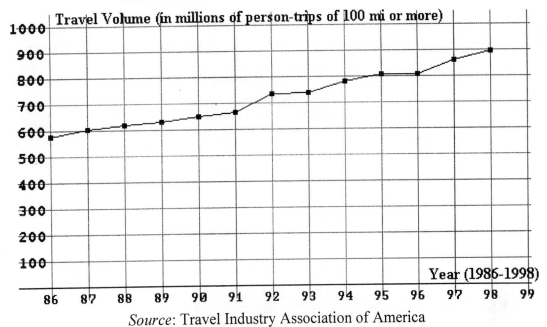

U.S. Resident Pleasure Travel Volume, 1986-98

Source: Travel Industry Association of America

a. What are the independent and dependent variables?

b. What are the units for the vertical axis?

c. What are the values of the domain?

d. Estimate the values of the range.

e. Describe the information that this function displays.

_____

_____

_____

f. 1996 was the only year when travel volume decreased from the preceding year. Can you think of any reason why this happened?

_____

_____

4. The following table of data shows the graph of a function. The table indicates the number of cellular telephone subscriptions during the period from December 1987 to December 1998.

Year	Number of Subscriptions
1987	1,230,855
1988	2,069,441
1989	3,508,944
1990	5,283,055
1991	7,557,148
1992	11,032,753
1993	16,009,461
1994	24,134,421
1995	33,785,661
1996	44,042,992
1997	55,312,293
1998	69,209,321

Source: CTIA Semi-Annual Wireless Survey

a. What are the independent and dependent variables?

b. Give a brief description of the domain without listing every element in the set.

c. Give a brief description of the range without listing every element in the set.

d. Write a description of this function. Include why the table represents a function.

_____

_____

_____

e. Plot each ordered pair from the data table in the coordinate plane below.

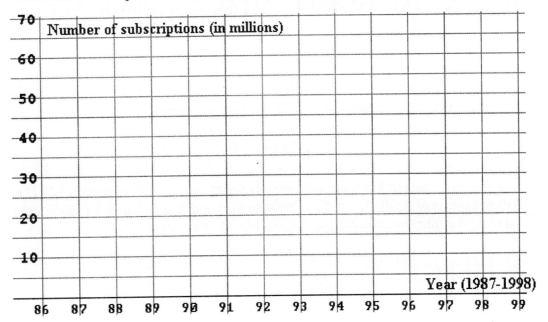

f. Connect the points with line segments to form a line plot of the data. Describe any trend in this data over the given period of time.

_____

_____

_____

g. Which one of the following statements would you use to describe the pattern in the graph? Circle the correct response and explain how the graph justifies your answer.

- During the years 1987-98, the total number of cellular telephone subscribers was increasing at a constant rate.

- During the years 1987-98, the total number of cellular telephone subscribers was increasing at an increasing rate.

- During the years 1987-98, the total number of cellular telephone subscribers was increasing at a decreasing rate.

h. Based on the given data, estimate the amount of cellular telephone subscribers in 1986. Justify your prediction.

5. Recall that in Discovery Adventure 2: A Picture of Desi's Salary Model, Desi was given the following model of her total weekly salary y as a function of the amount of sales x,

$$y = f(x) = 0.20 \cdot x + 70$$

Desi's best friend, Joy, waits on tables at a different restaurant that pays a higher weekly wage of $120, but the tips only average 18% of sales. Joy's salary function is

$$y = g(x) = 0.18 \cdot x + 120$$

a. Suppose Joy wants to know her total weekly salary for any sales between $2000 and $3000 in steps of $200. Using function notation, find these salaries by substituting each sale into the function g for the input variable x. For example,

$$g(2000) = 0.18 \cdot (2000) + 120 = 480$$

b. Construct a table of values using the results of part a.

Sales ($) x	Total Weekly Salary ($) y
2000	480
2200	
2400	
2600	
2800	
3000	

c. Graph each ordered pair from the table. Label each axis and connect the points with a line. Also, label the function line (or curve) as *g*.

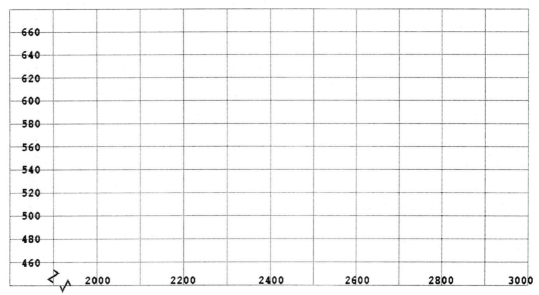

d. Graph Desi's function *f* on the same coordinate plane above.

e. If we are assuming that Desi and Joy produce the same amount of sales, then find the amount of sales for which they both will make the same salary.

f. Explain how the amount of sales determines which person (Desi or Joy) makes the most money each week.

_____

_____

_____

6. In each part below, you are told the location of a point in the coordinate plane. Indicate whether the *x*-coordinate (horizontal coordinate) and *y*-coordinate (vertical coordinate) are positive, negative, or zero. Explain your reasoning.

a. Quadrant I: _____

_____

_____

b. Quadrant II: _____

_____

_____

c. Quadrant III: _____

_____

_____

d. Quadrant IV: _____

_____

_____

e. The *x*-axis and to the right of the origin: _____

_____

_____

f. The *y*-axis and below the origin: _____

_____

_____

7. Suppose a survey was done on the amount of money people in the Boston and New York area are willing to pay for a round-trip ticket to do weekday travel between the two cities. The table below shows the quantity that a consumer would demand (be willing to buy) per day at different prices. Assume you want to study how demand depends on ticket price.

Price of Ticket ($)	Quantity Demanded (tickets)
25	10,000
50	9,000
75	8,000
100	7,000
125	6,000
150	5,000
175	4,000
200	3,000
225	2,000

a. Write a description of the independent and dependent variables.

b. Decide on a single letter to represent each variable and record your choice below.

c. In the space provided, construct a coordinate plane that will be suitable for graphing the data in the above table. Along each axis, write an appropriate scale and labels. The labels should include a brief description of the variable, the letter chosen to represent the variable, and the units of the variable. Plot the data points on your plane.

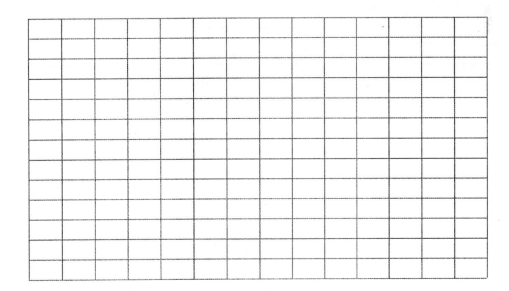

8. Refer to the table and graph from Section Exercise #7 to answer each part below.

    a. Connect the points to display the trend of the data. Then describe this trend in terms of ticket price and quantity demanded by consumers.

         _____

         _____

         _____

    b. Based on the survey data, if the price of a round-trip ticket was set at $250, estimate the quantity demanded by the consumers. Explain your reasoning.

         _____

         _____

         _____

    c. Why is it only necessary to show the first quadrant in the coordinate plane?

         _____

         _____

         _____

    d. What ticket price from the table would produce the highest revenue (income) for the airlines? Explain how you arrived at your answer.

         _____

         _____

         _____

9. The following graph presents a picture of the percent of total U.S. workers in farm occupations during the period from 1820 to 1980.

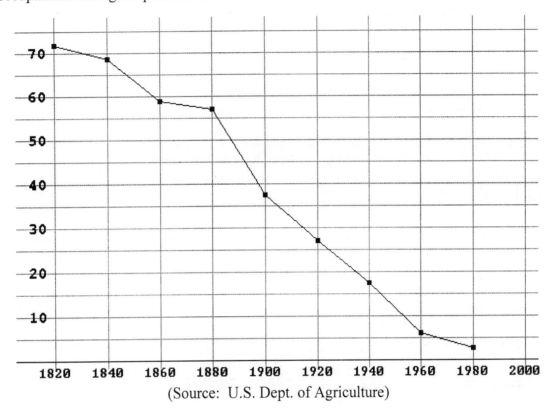

(Source: U.S. Dept. of Agriculture)

a. Estimate the percent of U.S. workers in farm occupations in the year 1880.

b. Complete the following table by estimating the percent of U.S. workers in farm occupations during the period from 1820-1980.

Year	Percent of U.S. Workers in Farm Occupations
1820	72
1840	
1860	
1880	
1900	
1920	
1940	
1960	
1980	

c. Describe how the percent of all U.S. workers in farm occupations has changed over this period of time.

_____

_____

_____

d. What 20-year time interval had the greatest drop in percent of workers in farm occupations? Explain the method you used to arrive at your answer.

_____

_____

_____

10. The following data shows the average fuel efficiency of all light vehicles (including cars, SUVs, minivans, vans, and light trucks) in miles per gallon (mpg) during the years 1975-99.

Year	All Light Vehicles (mpg)
1975	15.3
1980	22.5
1985	25.0
1990	25.2
1995	24.7
1999	23.8

(Source: Environmental Protection Agency)

a. Describe the independent and dependent variables. Explain your reasoning.

_____

_____

_____

b. Let the independent variable be x and the dependent variable be y. Explain why y is a function of x.

_____

_____

_____

c. Describe the domain and range for this data.

_____

_____

_____

d. Draw a scatter plot of the given data on the grid below. Be sure to use an *x*-scale and a *y*-scale that is suitable for the domain and range. Also, remember to clearly label each axis with a brief description of the variable, the letter chosen to represent the variable, and the units of the variable.

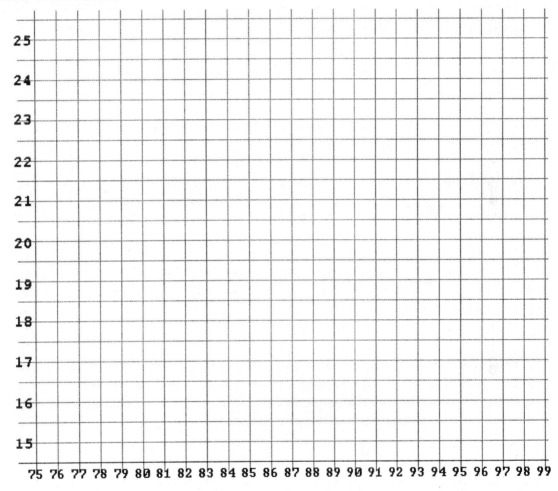

e. Describe the trend in fuel efficiency over the time period of 1975 to 1999. Explain why certain time intervals had increases in fuel efficiency and other time intervals had decreases.

_____

_____

_____

Section 6.3 Symbolic Relationships in Equations

Math Talk

We have defined a variable as a symbol, like x or y, that represents an unknown member of a set of objects or numbers. In conditional equations, a variable represents an unknown quantity whose values are to be found. Finding these values is called solving or evaluating the equation. The value(s) that satisfy the equation (make the equation a true statement) is its solution.

In Section 4.1, you learned about solving one-variable equations where it was necessary to use the **multiplication property of equality**.

Multiplication Property of Equality

You can multiply or divide both sides of an equation by any real number except 0.

In this section, you will also use the **addition property of equality**.

Addition Property of Equality

You can add or subtract any real number to both sides of an equation.

Let's take a look at solving an equation by **balancing** (using the properties of equality). First, an equation is *true* if the expression on one side of the equal sign has the same value as the expression on the opposite side. A true equation is like a balanced scale in that adding the same weight to both sides of the scale will maintain the balance.

Recall that in Section 2.1 we explored the process of solving a conditional equation for the variable by guessing. The word *conditional* means that the statement is true for only certain values of the variable. Those values are called the *solution*. For example, suppose you were asked to solve the following two conditional equations:

$$x + 12 = 5 \qquad \text{and} \qquad 2n - 3 = 6$$

How can we use the addition and multiplication properties of equality to solve these equations?

The goal is to obtain simpler equations and to ultimately isolate the variable on one side of the equal sign. The properties of equality can be applied to the equation without changing the solution. You want to express the equation in a simpler but equivalent form in which the answer is obvious.

For example, to solve $x + 12 = 5$ for the variable x, you need to apply a rule of equality that will eliminate the constant term, 12.

$$x + 12 = 5$$
$$x + 12 - 12 = 5 - 12 \qquad \text{Subtract 12 from both sides of the equation}$$
$$x = -7 \qquad \text{Simplify}$$

The key is to observe that the inverse (opposite) of adding 12 is subtracting 12. We subtract 12 from both sides to obtain an equivalent equation in the form, $x = \text{number}$. The solution is the number -7.

If the equation contains friendly numbers, then translate the equation into words and try to guess the solution by **inspection**. For example, $x + 2 = 5$ translates to "the sum of a number and 2 equals 5," or as a question, "what number added with 2 is five?" The solution is the number 3.

Now suppose we wish to solve $2n - 3 = 6$. How is this equation different from the last one we solved? What two numbers must be eliminated to isolate the variable n? First, you need to get the variable term $2n$ alone on one side of the equation. Consider what rule of equality you can apply to eliminate the constant term, 3. *Hint*: What is the inverse (opposite) of subtracting 3?

$$2n - 3 = 6$$
$$2n - 3 + 3 = 6 + 3$$
$$2n = 9$$

This translates into "the product of 2 and a number is 9" or as a question, "what number times 2 equals 9?" If you can mentally calculate the answer, then you are done. Otherwise you need to apply one more property of equality. *Hint*: What is the inverse (opposite) of multiplying by 2?

$$2n = 9$$

$$\frac{\cancel{2} \cdot n}{\cancel{2}} = \frac{9}{2}$$

$$n = \frac{9}{2} \quad \text{or} \quad 4\frac{1}{2} \quad \text{or} \quad 4.5$$

Let's check this solution by replacing n with $\dfrac{9}{2}$ in the original equation.

$$2n - 3 = 6$$

$$2 \cdot \frac{9}{2} - 3 = 6 \qquad \text{Replace } n \text{ with } \frac{9}{2}$$

$$\frac{\cancel{2}^{\,1}}{1} \cdot \frac{9}{\cancel{2}_{\,1}} - 3 = 6 \qquad \text{Cancel and multiply}$$

$$9 - 3 = 6 \qquad \text{Subtract}$$

$$6 = 6 \qquad \text{True, so the solution checks}$$

Let's solve two more equations, and then summarize what we have learned about solving conditional equations by the balancing method.

$\Rightarrow$ Solve: $18 - a = 19$

Solution: Isolate the variable term $-a$ by eliminating the constant term 18. The inverse of adding 18 is subtracting 18.

$$18 - a = 19$$

$$18 - a - 18 = 19 - 18 \qquad \text{Subtract 18 from both sides}$$

$$-a = 1 \qquad \text{Simplify. Note that } -a \text{ means } -1 \cdot a$$

$$\frac{\cancel{-1}^{\,1} \cdot a}{\cancel{-1}_{\,1}} = \frac{1}{-1} \qquad \text{The inverse of multiplying by } -1 \text{ is dividing by } -1$$

$$a = -1 \qquad \text{Cancel and simplify.}$$

$\Rightarrow$ Solve: $-13 = \dfrac{3}{4}x - 4$

Solution: Isolate the variable term, $\dfrac{3}{4}x$ by eliminating the constant term 4. The inverse of subtracting 4 is adding 4.

506

$$-13 = \frac{3}{4}x - 4$$

$$-13 + 4 = \frac{3}{4}x - 4 + 4 \qquad \text{Add 4 to both sides}$$

$$-9 = \frac{3}{4}x \qquad \text{Simplify. The inverse of multiplying by } \frac{3}{4} \text{ is dividing by } \frac{3}{4}$$

$$\frac{4}{3} \cdot -9 = \frac{4}{3} \cdot \frac{3}{4}x \qquad \text{Dividing both sides by } \frac{3}{4} \text{ is the same as multiplying both sides by } \frac{4}{3}$$

$$\frac{4}{3} \cdot \frac{-9}{1} = 1x \qquad \text{Cancel and Simplify}$$

$$-12 = x \qquad \text{Cancel and Simplify}$$

In general, solving an equation of the form $Ax + B = C$, where A, B, and C are real numbers, requires the following two steps:

1. Isolate the variable term Ax by applying the addition property of equality. This means adding or subtracting to eliminate the constant term B.

2. Isolate the variable x by applying the multiplication property of equality. This means multiplying or dividing to eliminate the coefficient A.

Note: The **coefficient** is the number being multiplied by the variable or simply the number in front of the variable.

Discovery Adventure 1: Maximum Heart Rate

The American Heart Association (AMA) recommends that the average person's heart rate stay between 50 to 75 percent of your maximum heart rate during exercise. Your maximum heart rate in beats per minute (bpm) can be estimated by subtracting your age from 220.

a. To understand the AMA's rule for maximum heart rate, finish building the table on the next page. Fill in all the rows up to age 50.

Age (years)	Rule	Maximum Heart Rate (bpm)
20	$220 - 20$	200
25		
30		
35		
40		
45		
50		
$\vdots$	$\vdots$	$\vdots$
a		H

b. In the last row, the independent variable, age is represented by the letter a. The dependent variable, maximum heart rate, is represented by H. Explain why H is a function of a.

_____

_____

c. Observe the patterns in the table. Then write the maximum heart rate rule in symbolic form in the last row of the table and below using function notation.

$$H(a) =$$

d. Using the symbolic rule from part c, find the maximum heart rate of a 28-year old person.

$$H(28) =$$

e. If a person's maximum heart rate is 188 bpm, what age would the AMA's rule predict? *Hint*: Substitute 188 for $H(a)$ in the function from part c and then solve the resulting equation for a by applying the properties of equality.

f. In part *d*, you substituted 28 for *a* and simplified the expression to obtain your answer. While in part *e*, you substituted 188 for $H(a)$ and solved for *a* to get your answer. How would you describe the difference between simplifying and solving?

_____

_____

_____

Feedback

Maximum heart rate *H* is a function of age *a* because for each input *a*, there is exactly one output *H*. This function is a rule in which you enter an age, subtract it from 220, and produce one maximum heart rate. Using function notation, you can write this rule as

$$H(a) = 220 - a$$

This rule predicts that a 28-year-old person has the following maximum heart rate:

$$H(28) = 220 - 28 = 192 \text{ bpm}$$

To *simplify* a numerical expression means to perform the necessary calculations to obtain the solution. In general, when you substitute a value for the independent variable, then you must simplify the resulting expression to obtain the corresponding value of the dependent variable.

If you are given a maximum heart rate of 188, then the age can be estimated by solving the following equation for *a*.

$188 = 220 - a$	
$188 - 220 = 220 - a - 220$	Subtract 220 from both sides to isolate $-a$
$-32 = -a$	Simplify
$(-1) \cdot (-32) = (-a) \cdot (-1)$	Multiply (or divide) both sides by -1 to change the signs
$32 = a$	Simplify
$a = 32$	Rewrite in form, *variable* = number

To *solve* many simple equations, you can apply the rules of equality until the variable is isolated on one side of the equal sign and/or the solution is obvious. In general, when you substitute a value for the dependent variable, then you must solve the resulting equation to obtain the corresponding value of the independent variable.

In the second Discovery Adventure, you will investigate a method for finding the heartbeat rate that a person should have during aerobic exercise. We will use a table to develop a symbolic rule for finding exercise heart rate as a function of the number of beats that occur during a 10-second pulse measurement.

Discovery Adventure 2: And The Beat Goes On

You can find your heartbeat rate during exercising by taking your pulse for 10 seconds when you take a break. Then multiply the number of beats by 6

a. What is the purpose of multiplying the number of beats by 6?

_____

_____

b. Construct a table showing the exercise heart rate, in beats per minute (bpm), for a ten-second pulse measurement of 22 beats, 23 beats, and so on up to 28 beats. The first row has been completed for you and can be used as a model.

Number (beats/10 sec.)	Rule	Exercise Heart Rate (beats/min.)
22	$6 \cdot 22$	132
23		
24		
25		
26		
27		
28		

c. In words, describe the process being followed in column 2.

_____

_____

d. Exercise heart rate is a function of the number of beats per 10 seconds. Suppose we call the input variable n, the output variable y, and the name of the function E, so that $y = E(n)$. Use these symbols to express the function in symbolic form.

$$y = E(n) =$$

e. Find the exercise heart rate when you count 29 beats during a 10-second pulse measurement. Use function notation when expressing your answer.

510

f. If a person's exercise heart rate is 126, then how many beats must have occurred during a 10-second pulse count? Find the number by setting up and solving the equation for *n*.

Feedback

The goal in the last Discovery Adventure was to develop a symbolic rule for finding a person's exercise heart rate, in beats per minute, using a ten-second-pulse reading. Since there are six 10-second time intervals in 1 minute (or 60 seconds), then we can multiply the number of beats in one 10-second interval by 6 to obtain the exercise heart rate in beats per minute. So the rule can be expressed as

$$y = E(n) = 6 \cdot n$$

If you count 29 beats during a 10-second pulse measurement, then the exercise heart rate can be expressed as follows,

$$y = E(29) = 6 \cdot 29 = 174 \text{ bpm}$$

If an exercise heart rate is 126, then you can find the number of beats that occurred in a 10-second interval by solving the following equation.

$$126 = 6 \cdot n$$

$$\frac{126}{6} = \frac{\overset{1}{\cancel{6}} \cdot n}{\underset{1}{\cancel{6}}} \qquad \text{Divide both sides by 6}$$

$$21 = n \qquad\qquad \text{Simplify}$$

$$n = 21 \qquad\qquad \text{Rewrite in form } variable = \text{number}$$

Discovery Adventure 3: Target Zone Heart Rate

Recall that the AMA recommends that the average person's heart rate stay between 50 and 75 percent of their maximum heart rate (MHR) during exercise. Let's develop a table that will display 50% and 75% of the maximum heart rate for ages 20 to 60 in steps of 10 years. This will produce a target zone heart rate (50-70% of MHR) for the listed ages.

Age (years)	MHR (bpm)	50% of MHR (bpm)	75% of MHR (bpm)
20	200	100	150
30	190		
40	180		
50	170		
60	160		

a. Complete the table by calculating 50% of the maximum heart rate in the third column and 75% of the maximum heart rate in the fourth column.

b. The formula for maximum heart rate H as a function of age a is $H(a) = 220 - a$.

Use this function to find two new functions, one for finding 50% of the maximum heart rate and the second for 75% of the maximum heart rate. Show all work.

c. Graph the two new functions found in part *b.* Lightly shade the area between the two lines to visualize the target zone heart rate (50-70% of MHR).

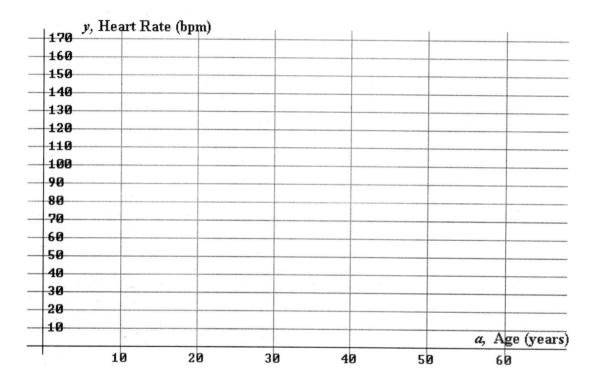

Feedback

The target zone heart rate gives you a range of values that the AMA believes the average person should target while doing aerobic exercise. The idea is that a sedentary person may want to start an exercise program near the 50-60% level and gradually increase to the 70-75% level. Athletes and people in top fiscal condition will work at even higher levels during exercise for cardiovascular conditioning. Therefore, any individual's target heart rate depends on the intensity level at which they wish to exercise.

The lower limit is given by 50% of the maximum heart rate, or 50% of $H(a)$. If we call this function L, then we can express a lower limit function as follows:

$$L(a) = 0.50 \cdot H(a) \qquad \text{50\% of maximum heart rate}$$
$$= 0.50(220 - a) \qquad \text{Multiply } 0.50 \text{ by MHR rule}$$
$$= 0.50 \cdot 220 - 0.50 \cdot a \qquad \text{Apply the distributive property}$$
$$= 110 - 0.50a \qquad \text{Simplify}$$

The upper limit is given by 75% of the maximum heart rate, or 75% of $H(a)$. If we call this function U, then we can express an upper limit function as follows:

$$U(a) = 0.75 \cdot H(a) \qquad \text{75\% of maximum heart rate}$$
$$= 0.75(220 - a) \qquad \text{Multiply } 0.75 \text{ by MHR rule}$$
$$= 0.75 \cdot 220 - 0.75 \cdot a \qquad \text{Apply distributive property}$$
$$= 165 - 0.75a \qquad \text{Simplify}$$

The lower limit function $L(a) = 110 - 0.50a$ and the upper limit function $U(a) = 165 - 0.75a$ are graphed on the following coordinate plane.

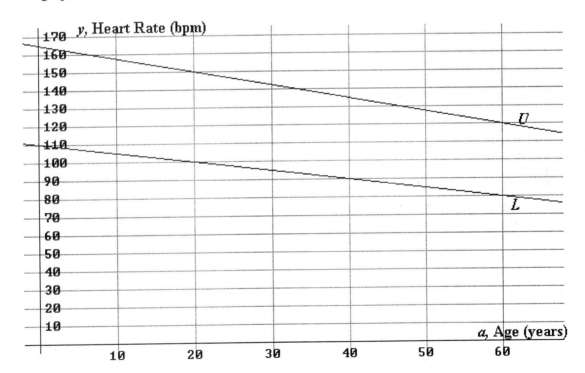

Section Exercises: 6.3

1. In Discovery Adventure 3: Target Zone Heart Rate, we established a zone using the lower limit function, $L(a) = 110 - 0.50a$ and the upper limit function, $U(a) = 165 - 0.75a$. These functions were developed using the formula for maximum heart rate H as a function of age a, $H(a) = 220 - a$.

   a. Suppose your physical condition allows you to exercise at the 70% level. In other words, your target heartbeat rate is 70% of your maximum heart rate. Create a function f to model this situation.

   $$y = f(a) =$$

   b. Use the model in part a to find the target heart rate y of a 33-year-old person.

   $$y = f(33) =$$

   c. Suppose another individual wants to obtain a 10-second pulse count of 23 while exercising. What is this person's target heart rate?

   d. Use the function developed in part a to set up and solve an equation to find the age of the individual in part c.

2. The following table gives the number of violent crimes per year in Safe City since 1990. So $t = 0$ is 1990, $t = 1$ is 1991, and so on.

Time (years since 1990)	0	1	2	3	4	5	6	7	8	9
Number of Violent crimes	100	90	80	70	60	50	40	30	20	10

   a. In words, explain any patterns you see in this data set.

   _____

   _____

   _____

b. Suppose we let t be the number of years since 1990 and C the number of violent crimes since 1990. Circle the function that models this situation and explain the reasoning for your choice.

i) $C(t) = 100 + 10 \cdot t$ ii) $C(t) = -10 \cdot t + 1$ iii) $C(t) = 100 - 10 \cdot t$ iv) $C(t) = t - 10$

_____

_____

_____

c. Verify that you chose the correct function in part b by finding $C(0)$, $C(1)$, and $C(2)$. Your results should match up with the first three values in row 2 of the table.

3. The following data gives the population of a town as a function of time (in years since 1980.) Let 1980 be year 0, 1985 be year 5, and so on.

Time (years since 1980)	0	5	10	15	20
Population	8,000	10,000	12,000	14,000	16,000

a. Explain how the population is changing over time.

_____

_____

_____

b. The data table shows how the population is changing every 5 years. Assuming the population always increases in a constant manner, complete the following sentence.

Every year since 1980 the population has _____ by _____.

c. Suppose the population is expected to increase at the same rate into the foreseeable future. Build a new table that will predict the population for the next 5 years after time 20 (year 2000). The population for the year 2001 has been recorded. Please fill in the population for the remaining years.

Time (years since 1980)	21	22	23	24	25
Population	16,400				

d. Let t represent the time since 1980 and P the population. Express the rule that gives P as a function of t. *Hint*: Your function needs to include a constant term that expresses the initial population in 1980 and a variable term that expresses the yearly increase.

$$P(t) =$$

e. Use the model you developed in part *d* to predict the population in 2010 (year 30). Show the input (using function notation), the rule (calculation), and the output (population).

f. In what year will the population be 19,200? Set up and solve an equation to answer this question.

4. The following function represents how the population P of Ghost Town has changed over time t in years since 1970. So $t = 0$ is 1970, $t = 1$ is 1971, and so on.

$$y = P(t) = 20,000 - 500 \cdot t$$

a. Find the initial population, $P(0)$.

$$P(0) =$$

b. In how many years will the population decrease to 5000? Set up and solve an equation to answer this question.

c. Complete the following table to determine how the population has changed every 5 years since 1970.

Time (years since 1970)	0	5	10	15	20	25	30
Population (in thousands)	20						

d. Graph the given function by plotting the ordered pairs from the above table, then connect the points with a straight line.

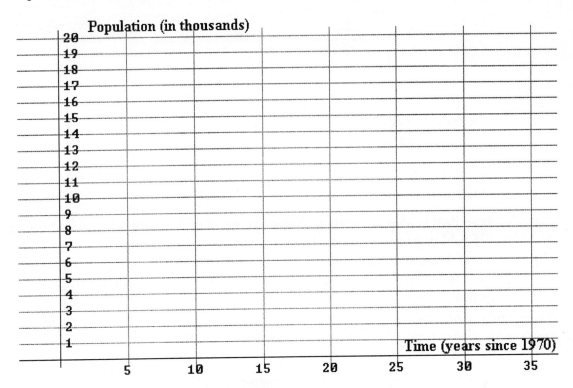

e. If the population continues to decline according to the given function rule, how long will it be before Ghost Town becomes a real ghost town (with a population of zero).

5. During the 1992 and 1996 Olympic games, Gail Deevers of the United States won the gold medal for finishing first in the 100-meter run. She ran at an average speed of about 9 meters per second.

a. Using the average speed given, complete the following table to show Gail's distance in meters every two seconds during a 100-meter run.

Time (seconds)	Distance Calculation	Distance (meters)
0		0
2	$9 \cdot 2$	18
4		
6		
8		
10		
12		

b. Let t be the time and G be Gail's distance from the official start line. Follow the pattern in column two and write the symbolic rule that gives G as a function of t.

$$G(t) =$$

c. Suppose Paul is able to maintain an average speed of 5 meters per second during a short run. If Paul is given a 40-meter head start, can he win a 100-meter race against Gail Deevers? Let's investigate by completing a table that has Paul begin the race 40 meters ahead of the official starting line and calculates his distance from the official starting line every two seconds.

Time (seconds)	Distance Calculation	Distance (meters)
0		40
2	$40 + 5 \cdot 2$	50
4	$40 + 5 \cdot 4$	
6		
8		
10		
12		

d. Let t be the time and P be Paul's distance from the official start line. Follow the pattern in the table above and write the symbolic rule that gives P as a function of t.

$$P(t) =$$

e. Based on the information from the two tables, when does Gail catch Paul during the race?

f. Based on the information from the two tables, who wins the race? Explain your reasoning.

_____

_____

_____

g. Set up and solve an equation that will give you the winning time. Round the time to the nearest hundredth of a second.

h. How far ahead was the winner when he or she crossed the finish line? Round the distance to the nearest tenth of a meter.

i. Set up and solve an equation that will give the time the second place runner crossed the finish line.

6. The coordinate plane below contains the graphs of the two functions from the 100-meter race in Section Exercise #5.

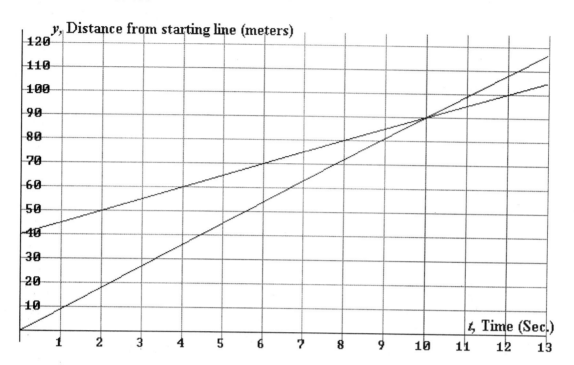

a. Label one line as Gail's function and the other as Paul's function in order to distinguish each runner's distance from the starting line as a function of time.

b. Use ordered pairs to label the points where the race starts for each runner.

c. Use an ordered pair to label the point where one runner catches up with the other.

d. Use an ordered pair to label the point where the winner crosses the finish line.

7. Suppose a third runner named Catia runs in the 100-meter race with Gail and Paul. The function given below represents her distance in meters from the starting line as a function of time in seconds.

$$y = C(t) = 30 + 6t$$

a. In what time does Catia finish the race?

b. List the order that each runner finishes the race.

   d. Assuming that the trend in the table continues, set up and solve an equation to find when Carl's income will reach $100,000.

10. Refer to the table in Section Exercise #8 as you complete this problem. Carl would like to develop an equation to model his expenditures E as a function of time t in years since 1996. So that, $t = 0$ is year 1996, $t = 1$ is year 1997, etc.

   a. Complete the following table by entering all the expenditures and then find the change in expenditures each year.

Time, t (years since 1996)	Expenditures, E ($)	Change in Expenditures ($)
0	28,500	
1		
2		
3		
4		

   b. Write a verbal rule that clearly describes how expenditures depend on time.

_____

_____

_____

   c. Write a symbolic rule that describes how E depends on t.

   d. Assuming that the trend in the table continues, set up and solve an equation to find when Carl's expenditures will reach $100,000.

Chapter 6 Summary

Key Terms

Section 6.1

- **Independent or Input Variable** – A variable in an equation is *independent* when its value determines the value of the other related variable, called the *dependent variable*.
- **Dependent or Output Variable** – The dependent variable's value is determined by the value of the *independent variable*.
- **Functional Relationship** – A *functional relationship* exists between two variables if for each value of the independent variable, there is exactly one corresponding value of the dependent variable. In other words, each input value has just one output value.
- **Function Notation** – If y is a function of x and you name the function f, then you can write

$$y = f(x)$$

which is read, "y equals f of x". This symbolizes that y depends on x. The independent variable or input is always inside the parentheses, and the name of the function comes before the parentheses.
- **Domain** – The set of all possible values for the independent (input) variable.
- **Range** – The set of all possible values for the dependent (output) variable.

Section 6.2

- **Rectangular Coordinate System** or **Coordinate Plane** – A system used to display points in a plane created by a horizontal and vertical axes that intersect at the origin.
- **Horizontal** and **Vertical Axes** – Horizontal and vertical lines used to locate a point in the coordinate plane.
- **Origin** – The point where the two axes intersect, labeled $(0, 0)$.
- **Ordered Pair** – Pair of numbers used to locate points in the coordinate plane.
- **Horizontal** and **Vertical Coordinates** – The location of any point (a, b) in the plane is determined by the two coordinates a and b. The first coordinate a (often called the x-coordinate) determines horizontal movement where positive values are to the right of the origin and negative values to the left. The second coordinate b (often called the y-coordinate) determines vertical movement, where positive values are above the origin and negative values are below the origin.
- **Quadrants** – Axes splits the plane into 4 quadrants where in the first quadrant, both quantities are positive. Then moving counterclockwise, we have the second, third, and fourth quadrants.
- **x-coordinate** – indicates horizontal (left or right) movement.
- **y-coordinate** – indicates vertical (up or down) movement.
- **x-axis** – Or horizontal axis, where the independent (input) variable is placed.
- **y-axis** – Or vertical axis, where the dependent (output) variable is placed.
- **Scatter Plot** – A graph that displays two-variable data as points on the coordinate plane.
- **Line Plot** – A *line plot* is formed when you connect the points of a scatter plot with line segments.

524

Section 6.3

- **Multiplication Property of Equality** – You can multiply or divide both sides of an equation by any real number except 0.
- **Addition Property of Equality** – You can add or subtract any real number to both sides of an equation.
- **Balancing** – Solving an equation by using the properties of equality.
- **Inspection** – When the solution to a problem is obtained by critically viewing a mathematical form, either through translating into words or turning the problem into a question.
- **Coefficient** – The number being multiplied by the variable or simply the number in front of the variable.

****

Questions for Review

1. When there is a relationship between two quantities (variables), can you find the independent and dependent variable?

   For example, suppose you are a travel agent who needs information on the amount of precipitation that occurs in the city of San Francisco during different times of the year. The following table gives the monthly normal precipitation in inches for San Francisco, CA. The months are numbered as January = 1, February = 2, and so on.

Month	1	2	3	4	5	6	7	8	9	10	11	12
Precip-itation	4.4	3.2	3.1	1.4	0.2	0.1	L	0.1	0.2	1.2	2.9	3.1

   Source: National Climatic Data Center
   (L = less than 0.05 inch)

   a. Describe the independent and dependent variable. Justify your answer.

   _____

   _____

   _____

   _____

   _____

   _____

525

b. Describe how precipitation changes throughout the year. What time periods during the year would be considered the city's wet season and dry season?

_____

_____

_____

2. Do you know when there is a functional relationship between two variables? Answer these questions to find out.

a. Referring to the situation in Question #1 (p. 525), is the amount of precipitation in San Francisco a function of the time of year (in months)? Explain.

_____

_____

_____

b. Complete the following sentence. We say that y is a function of x if _____

_____

3. Can you interpret and use function notation? Answer the following questions to find out.

Referring to Question #1 (p. 525), suppose we let the month of the year be represented by x, the amount of precipitation by y, and call the function P for precipitation. Then y is a function of x, which can be expressed as $y = P(x)$.

a. Complete the following mathematical statements.

- $P(11) =$

- $P(\underline{\hspace{1cm}}) = 1.4$

b. How do you read and interpret the following mathematical expression?
$$P(1) = 4.4$$

_____

_____

_____

4. Given a function, how do you find its domain and range?

For example, referring to Question #1 (p. 525), the domain is the set of all possible x values and the range is the corresponding y values.

   a. Use set notation to state the domain. Recall that set notation involves mathematically expressing each member of the set within braces.

   b. Use set notation to state the range.

5. Do you know how to graph two-variable data on the coordinate plane?

For example, referring to the data in Question #1 (p. 525), draw a scatter plot of all the ordered pairs contained in the given table of values. Then connect the points to form a line plot.

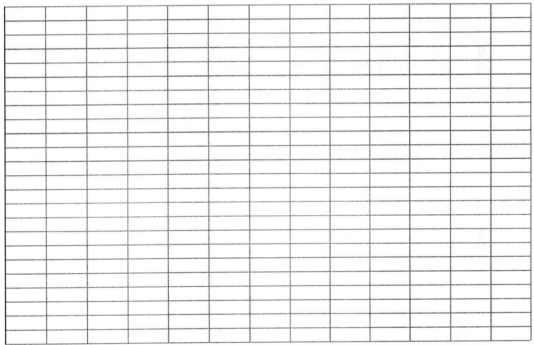

   a. During which 2 consecutive months is there the greatest decrease in precipitation? Explain your reasoning.

_____

_____

_____

b. During which 2 consecutive months is there the greatest increase in precipitation? Explain your reasoning.

_____

_____

_____

c. During which 5 consecutive months is there almost no change in precipitation? Explain your reasoning.

_____

_____

_____

6. The table below shows the amount of round-trip tickets between Boston and New York that the airlines are willing to supply (or sell) per day at different prices. Assume you want to study how the quantity supplied depends on ticket price.

Price of Ticket ($)	Quantity Supplied (tickets)
25	2000
50	3000
75	4000
100	5000
125	6000
150	7000
175	8000
200	9000
225	10,000

a. On the next page, draw a scatter plot of the data given in the table above. Along each axis, write an appropriate scale and labels. After plotting each point, connect successive points with a line segment to form a line plot.

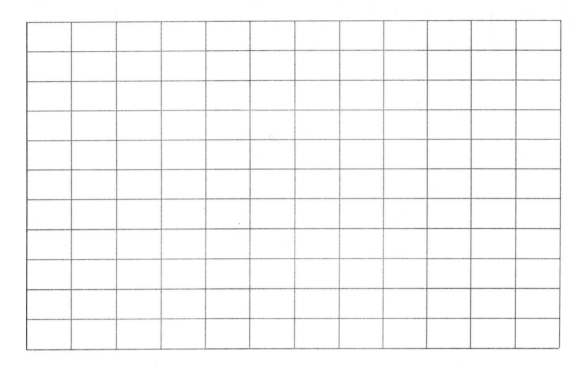

b. Describe what happens to the quantity of tickets that suppliers (airlines) are willing to sell as the price of a ticket increases.

_____

_____

_____

c. Describe what happens to the quantity of tickets that suppliers (airlines) are willing to sell as the price of a ticket decreases.

_____

_____

_____

d. On the coordinate plane in part *a*, graph the demand function data given in the table below. Label the demand function *D* and the supply function *S*. Assume this information comes from a survey on the amount of money people in the Boston and New York area are willing to pay for a round-trip ticket for weekday travel between the two cities. The table below shows the quantity a consumer will demand (be willing to buy) per day at different prices. Note that this is the same data that appears in Section Exercise #7, Section 6.2.

Price of Ticket ($)	Quantity Demanded (tickets)
25	10,000
50	9,000
75	8,000
100	7,000
125	6,000
150	5,000
175	4,000
200	3,000
225	2,000

e. An equilibrium price occurs when the quantity supplied equals the quantity demanded. Find this point on the graph and label it. In the space below, record the equilibrium ticket price and the quantity of tickets available at that price.

7. Refer to the tables and graphs from Question #6 to answer each part below. Suppose the airlines set the price of a round-trip ticket between Boston and New York at $175.

a. What will happen to the quantity of tickets that consumers are willing to buy?

_____

_____

_____

b. What will happen to the quantity of tickets that suppliers are willing to sell?

_____

_____

_____

c. How many extra tickets are available? How do you think the airlines will handle this surplus in tickets?

_____

_____

_____

8. Refer to the tables and graphs from Question #6 to answer each part below. Suppose the airlines set the price of a round-trip ticket between Boston and New York at $75.

a. What will happen to the quantity of tickets that consumers are willing to buy?

_____

_____

b. What will happen to the quantity of tickets that suppliers are willing to sell?

_____

_____

c. How many tickets are the airlines short of what the consumer is willing to buy? How do you think the airlines will handle this shortage in tickets?

_____

_____

_____

9. Are you able to develop an equation in two variables that symbolically shows the relationship between data values in a table?

For example, in the table on the next page, we have listed possible prices for a round trip ticket between Boston and New York, the quantity that consumers will demand at these prices, and the quantity that airlines will supply at these prices.

Price of Ticket ($)	Quantity Demanded (tickets)	Quantity Supplied (tickets)
25	10,000	2,000
50	9,000	3,000
75	8,000	4,000
100	7,000	5,000
125	6,000	6,000
150	5,000	7,000
175	4,000	8,000
200	3,000	9,000
225	2,000	10,000

a. Complete the following sentences to describe the trend in demand as the ticket price changes.

- As the price increases by $25, the quantity of tickets demanded by consumers will

  _____

- As the price increases by $1, the quantity of tickets demanded by consumers will

  _____

b. Based on the pattern in the data, what would be the quantity of tickets demanded by consumers if the price is $0. Although this would not happen, the answer will help you develop a demand rule by telling you the output when the input is zero.

c. Suppose *x* represents the price of a ticket, *y* represents the quantity demanded by consumers, and *D* is the name of the function. Use the results from parts *a* and *b* to develop an equation that models consumer demand as a function of price.

$$y = D(x) =$$

d. Complete the following sentences to describe the trend in supply as the ticket price changes.

- As the price increases by $25, the quantity of tickets supplied by the airlines will

  _____

- As the price increases by $1, the quantity of tickets supplied by the airlines will

_____

e. Based on the pattern in the data, what would be the quantity of tickets supplied by airlines if the price is $0? Although this would not happen, the answer will help you develop a supply rule by telling you the output when the input is zero.

f. Suppose x represents the price of a ticket, y represents the quantity supplied by the airlines, and S is the name of the function. Use the results from parts d and e to develop an equation that models supply as a function of price.

$$y = S(x) =$$

10. Suppose you are given a function in the form of an equation in two variables. Can you substitute a value for the independent variable and then simplify to find the value of the dependent variable? Can you substitute a value for the dependent variable and then solve to find the value of the independent variable?

For example, the supply and demand equations from Question #9 are given below. Use these functions to answer each part of this problem.

$$y = D(x) = 11,000 - 40x \quad \text{and} \quad y = S(x) = 1000 + 40x$$

a. Find the quantity demanded and the quantity supplied when the price of a ticket is set at $100.

b. If the quantity demanded is 5,000, then what is the price of a ticket?

c. If the quantity supplied is 3,000, then what is the price of a ticket?

Chapter 6 Quiz

1. The data table below gives the monthly normal temperatures for Des Moines, Iowa.

Month	1	2	3	4	5	6	7	8	9	10	11	12
Temperature	19	25	37	51	62	72	77	74	65	54	39	24

Source: National Climatic Data Center

   a. To examine how temperature varies each month throughout the year in Des Moines, describe the independent variable and the dependent variable.

   _____

   _____

   b. Is there a functional relationship between the independent and dependent variable? Explain your reasoning in a complete sentence.

   _____

   _____

   _____

c. Use the ordered pairs in the table to construct a scatter plot on the grid below. Then connect each point with a line segment to form a line plot. Be sure to include a scale and label for each axis.

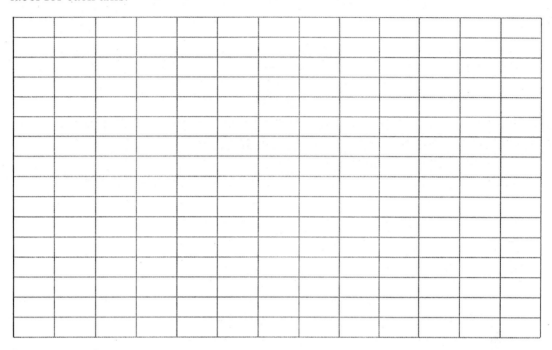

2. The manager of College Bookstore marks up the merchandise by 25%, meaning that the price of each item is 25% more than the cost to obtain it. In this situation, the price that a student pays for an item is a function of how much it costs the bookstore to obtain the item. The bookstore sells items that cost them up to $300 to obtain. Let the selling price be represented by y, the cost to the bookstore be represented by x, and the name of the function be P. Then we can use the notation, $y = P(x)$, to express y as a function of x.

a. What is the practical domain of this function based on the problem situation?

b. What is the corresponding range for this function?

c. Complete the following mathematical statement, and then write a complete sentence that explains its meaning in terms of the problem situation.

$$P(50) =$$

_____

_____

d. Complete the second column by applying the rule to each input x. Then calculate the corresponding output y and place the result in the third column.

Cost, x ($)	Rule	Selling Price, y ($)
50	$50 + 0.25 \cdot 50$	62.50
100		
150		
200		
250		
300		

e. Express the rule in the form of an equation in two variables, x and y.

3. The following graph shows the city of Boston's AIDS incidence rates (number of new cases per 100,000 population) by year from 1991 to 1998.

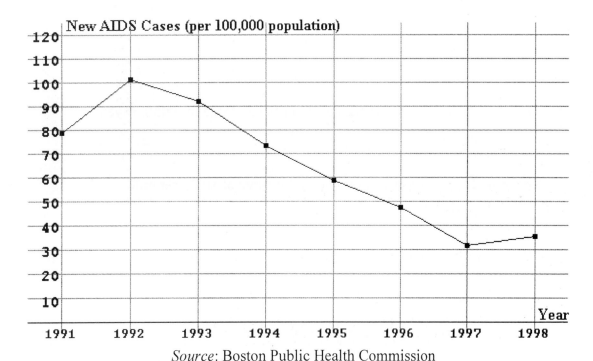

Source: Boston Public Health Commission

a. Estimate the number of new AIDS cases in the years 1991 and 1998 by completing the following statements.

$$A(1991) = \qquad \qquad A(1998) =$$

b. Estimate the change in Boston's AIDS incidence rates between 1991 and 1998 by completing the following statement. Explain what your answer means in terms of new AIDS cases. $A(1998) - A(1991) =$

_____

_____

c. In which two consecutive years did the AIDS incidence decrease the fastest? Explain your reasoning.

_____

_____

d. Find the year that there were 101.2 new AIDS cases per 100,000 population. Express your answer by completing the following statement.

$$A(\underline{\qquad}) = 101.2$$

4. Suppose you need to rent a car and have a choice of three rental dealers. You wish to find equations that represent the one-day rental cost C as a function of the number of miles driven m for each dealer in parts a, b, and c.

    a. The first dealer costs $25 per day and $0.30 per mile driven.

    b. The second dealer costs $45 per day and has no charge for miles driven.

    c. The third dealer charges just for mileage at a rate of $0.75 per mile.

    d. If you drive 70 miles, how much will the first dealer charge for a one-day rental?

    e. If you drive 70 miles, how much will the second dealer charge for a one-day rental?

    f. If you drive 70 miles, how much will the third dealer charge for a one-day rental?

    g. If the first dealer charges you $46, then how many miles did you drive during that one day?

    h. If the third dealer charges you $45, then how many miles did you drive during that one day?

Cumulative Review: Chapters 4, 5, and 6

1. The following table gives the population density of the states of Florida and Iowa from 1920 to 1990. The population density of a state is calculated as the ratio of the number of people that live in the state to the area of land within the state's border. The units for the table are people per square mile. This value indicates the (plane) space that the state has available for each resident.

State	1920	1960	1980	1990
Florida	17.7	91.5	180.0	239.6
Iowa	43.2	49.2	52.1	49.7

Source: Bureau of the Census

   a. Suppose we want to compare Florida's population density between 1920 and 1960. To make a comparison using subtraction, find the difference in population densities between 1960 and 1920. Explain what this value means in terms of the problem situation.

   _____

   _____

   _____

   b. To make a comparison using division, find the ratio of Florida's population density in 1960 to the density in 1920. Explain what this value means in terms of the problem situation.

   _____

   _____

   _____

   c. A third way to make a comparison is by using percentages. The percent difference or percent change in a quantity is calculated as follows.

$$\text{Percent Change} = \frac{\text{New value} - \text{Old value}}{\text{Old value}}$$

Find the percent change in the population density of Florida from 1920 to 1960. Then explain what this value means in terms of the problem situation.

_____

_____

_____

d. Complete the following table to get a better idea of the percent change in the population density of both Florida and Iowa over time.

Time period (years)	Percent Change in Population Density	
	Florida	Iowa
1920-60	4.17 or 417%	
1960-80		
1980-90		

e. Describe how Florida's population density has changed from 1920 to 1990. Explain the reasons for the change.

_____

_____

_____

_____

f. Describe how Iowa's population density has changed from 1920 to 1990. Explain the reasons for the change.

_____

_____

_____

_____

2. Suppose you want to plant a rectangular-shaped vegetable garden but need to protect it from your neighbor's wild kids. If you have 18 meters of wire fencing available to enclose the *perimeter*, what are some of the possible dimensions for the *area* of the garden?

a. Below are 3 possible garden areas where the width is given. Find the length for each rectangle and place your answer above the dashed line.

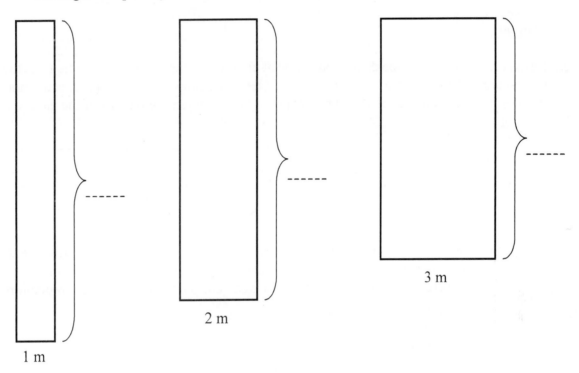

1 m   2 m   3 m

b. What is the sum of the length and width in each case above?

c. Knowing this sum, if the width is 4 meters, then what is the length?

d. Let the length be defined by the variable L, and the width by the variable W. We know that the length plus the width equals the sum found in part *b*. Use the value of that sum along with the variables L and W to write an equation involving length and width.

e. Use the addition (subtraction) property of equality to write the width in terms of the length. In other words, isolate W on one side of the equal sign and keep L on the other side with the value of the sum.

f. Complete the following table and observe the symmetrical pattern formed by the data.

Length, *L* (m)	1	2	3	4	5	6	7	8	9
Width, *W* (m)									
Area (sq. m)									

g. Based on the pattern of the data in part *f*, what are the dimensions of the pen that has the largest area? Explain your reasoning. *Hint*: The dimensions for maximum area are not listed in the table but can be found by analyzing the symmetrical pattern of the data.

_____

_____

_____

3. If you live in the Rocky Mountains of Colorado, the sound of silence you hear during the day might be interrupted by the chirping sound of the snow tree cricket during the evening. Biologists have gathered the following data on crickets' chirp rate at increasing temperatures.

Temperature (° Fahrenheit)	50	60	70	80
Number of chirps (per 15 sec.)	10	20	30	40

a. Complete the following sentence. As the temperature rises by 10 °F, the chirp rate…

_____

b. How does each chirp rate in the second row compare numerically with its associated temperature in the first row?

_____

_____

c. Choose appropriate one-letter variables to represent your two unknowns, chirp rate and temperature.

d. Use the information above to develop an equation that defines chirp rate in terms of temperature.

e. Verify that your equation models the problem situation by inputting each temperature from the table and seeing if you obtain the correct number of chirps.

f. Suppose you count 38 chirps during a 15-second interval. What should be the temperature according to your model? *Hint:* Use substitution and then apply the addition property of equality.

g. Predicting output values that correspond to input values that are between the given data is called *interpolation*. Use your model to complete this expanded table which has temperature readings every 5 °F.

Temperature (° Fahrenheit)	50	55	60	65	70	75	80
Number of chirps (per 15 sec.)	10		20		30		40

h. Predicting output values that correspond to input values that are beyond the given data is called *extrapolation*. Use your model to find the chirp rate for a temperature of 30 °F? 110 °F? Explain what these answers mean and whether you have confidence in them.

_____

_____

_____

i. Find the practical domain of this function and state your answer using either set notation or interval notation.

j. Now take the model you developed in part *d* and use the addition property of equality to write an equivalent equation that has the temperature variable isolated, so that temperature is written in terms of chirp rate.

k. Why would this new model be helpful in answering questions where the number of chirps is given and we want to find the temperature?

_____

_____

4. The following graph displays the number of cases of (intentional) gunshot wounds in Boston during the years 1994-1998.

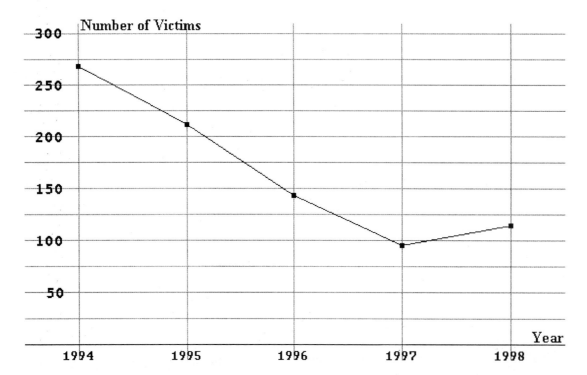

a. During which three consecutive years was there a decline in the number of intentional gunshot wounds from the previous year? Explain how the graph shows this information.

_____

_____

_____

b. In what year was there an increase in the number of intentional gunshot wounds from the previous year? Explain how the graph shows this information.

_____

_____

_____

c. Using function notation, give an estimate of the number of gunshot wounds in 1997 and 1998.

$$G(1997) = \qquad\qquad\qquad G(1998) =$$

d. Use the answers from part *c* to approximate the change in the number of gunshot wounds in 1998 from the previous year.

$$G(1998) - G(1997) =$$

e. Based on your answers to parts *c* and *d*, find the percent change in the number of gunshot wounds in 1998 from the previous year. Show all work.

f. In 1998, there were exactly 135 resident gunshot cases reported. Of these, 114 were "violence related" (as shown in the graph), indicating the intentional use of a gun to injure another person. What percentage of all gunshot wounds in 1998 was violence related?

5. Suppose you own a home with an old, in-grown pool in the back yard. The pool is falling apart and will be too expensive to fix, so you decide to fill it in with dirt at a cost of $8 per ton. The pool is a rectangular solid, so its volume can be calculated by the following formula.

$$\text{Volume} = \text{Length} \cdot \text{Width} \cdot \text{Height}$$

The figures below are a scale drawing of the pool's top view (looking down from above) and the pool's side view (imagine seeing the longer side from below the ground). The scale is

$$\frac{1}{4} \text{ in.} = 4 \text{ ft.}$$

Side View   Top View

a. Use a ruler to measure the length, width, and height of the pool in inches. Record the results below.

Length: Width: Height:

b. Use the scale and proportions to find the actual measurements for the length, width, and height of the pool in feet.

c. Find the volume of the pool.

d. Use the following information to help find the total cost to fill-in your pool with dirt.

- One cubic yard equals roughly 1.6 tons or 27 cubic feet.
- The cost to dump dirt is $8 per ton.

Chapter 7

Basic Concepts of Descriptive Statistics

Section 7.1 Organizing and Representing Data
Section 7.2 Summarizing Data by Measures of Center
Section 7.3 Summarizing Data by Measures of Spread

Chapter 7 will help develop an understanding of descriptive statistics. We will have the opportunity to organize, display, summarize, and then draw conclusions from interesting data sets. This chapter will also allow us to find measures of center and spread as useful summary statistics of data sets.

In Section 7.1, data is organized into frequency and relative frequency distributions. We will learn how to group the data into convenient class intervals to show the nature of the distribution. The frequency and relative frequency distributions are then pictured using bar graphs and histograms.

In Section 7.2, we will investigate three statistical measures of center: *mean*, *median*, and *mode*. Many of the problems will focus on which measure(s) of center are most representative of the data.

In Section 7.3, we will learn about measures of spread or dispersion to see how the values in a data set are scattered around the center. The Discovery Adventures explore such measures as the *range, standard deviation, lower and upper quartiles,* and the *interquartile range*. The *box plot* will be introduced as a graphical way to display five-number summary statistics.

Section 7.1 Organizing and Representing Data

Math Talk

Let's talk about the following statistical terms: *data, frequency distribution, relative frequency distribution, class intervals*, and *histogram*.

Data is a collection of factual information in the form of numbers or categories. For example, when you fill out a form that asks for your sex and age (in years), the former is categorical (female or male), and the latter is numerical (1, 2, 3, and so on up to the oldest individual still living.)

The word **frequency** is associated with how often something occurs. In statistics, the *frequency* is the number of items that occur in a given category. For example, in a class of 36 students there might be 2 students age 18 years, 3 students age 19 years, 5 students age 20 years, and so on. Also in the same class, there might be 20 women and 16 men.

A **frequency distribution** tells you the number of occurrences of each different data item, while the **relative frequency distribution** indicates the percent of times an item occurs compared to the total number of items.

If you have a large data set with many different items, then it is helpful to group the data into **class intervals** or categories. Each class is a range of values that is usually equal in length. For example, when considering the ages of 36 students, you could group the ages into class intervals of 14.5–19.5, 19.5–24.5, 24.5–29.5 and so on. The frequency distribution then becomes a table listing the number of data items in each class, and the relative frequency distribution is the percent of items in each class interval relative to the total number of items.

A **histogram** is a special type of bar graph where the bars are connected at common endpoints. The histogram is used to give a graphical picture of either the frequency or relative frequency distribution. The class intervals will appear along the horizontal axis, and the frequency or relative frequency will appear along the vertical axis. For example, here is the histogram of a frequency distribution that contains the ages of students in a class of 36.

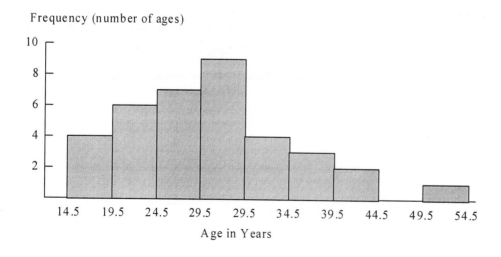

Discovery Adventure 1: Letter Grade Distribution

The grades from the last exam have just been presented to your class as follows:

B	B	C	F	A	B	D	C	C
B	C	D	A	C	C	B	B	D
C	A	D	B	A	C	F	C	B
F	C	B	C	C	B	D	D	C

The instructor does not look happy. How well do you think the class performed? How should the instructor interpret this data?

a. Suppose you want to organize this data to see what patterns these grades have. How would you group this data into different categories?

_____

_____

_____

b. Find the number of occurrences of each letter grade and record these values in the table below.

Grade	Frequency
A	
B	
C	
D	
F	

c. The table you constructed in part *b* is an example of a *frequency distribution*. It displays how often each of the different grades occurred. What part of the whole class received the letter grade A? Write your answer as a fraction, decimal, and percentage.

d. The answer to part *c* indicates how frequently the grade A occurs relative to all the recorded grades. Compute the *relative frequency* of each letter grade. Record the result first as a decimal value rounded to the thousandths place and then as a percentage.

Grade	Frequency	Relative Frequency (decimal and percent)
A		
B		
C		
D		
F		

e. What percent of the class received a C on the exam?

f. What percent of the class received a grade below C, meaning a D or F grade?

g. Does the instructor have reason to be concerned about class performance on this exam?

_____

_____

_____

Feedback

Organizing the data into a frequency distribution will let the instructor (and the class) know how many values (grades) are in each category (A, B, C, D, and F). This gives us a good indication of how the grades are distributed among the 5 categories. A quick scan of the table reveals that the two most popular grades are C and B in that order.

The relative frequency distribution displays the percentage (or fraction) of grades in each category. Specifically, we see the percentage (or fraction) of A's, the percentage of B's, the percentage of C's, and so on.

The *relative frequency* of a category is calculated by dividing the number of values (or frequencies) in a category by the total number of values in all categories. Or for short,

$$\text{Relative Frequency} = \frac{\text{Frequency}}{\text{Total Number}}$$

What might be of concern to the instructor (and the class) is the fact that one-quarter or 25% of the class earned a D or F on the exam.

$$\text{Relative Frequency of } D\text{s and } F\text{s} = \frac{\text{Frequency of } D\text{s and } F\text{s}}{\text{Total Number of Grades}} = \frac{9}{36} = \frac{1}{4} = 0.25 \quad \text{or} \quad 25\%$$

In the first Discovery Adventure, the data fell into one of five categories so it was natural to group the data as we did. However, if the data contains many different items, then we can group the data into class intervals of our own choosing. The next Discovery Adventure will ask you to group the data into equally-spaced classes (usually a range of values).

Discovery Adventure 2: Numerical Grade Distribution

In another class the instructor scores each exam using a numerical grade. Here is a list of scores from a recent exam:

57	81	96	88	63	82	77	75	99
68	90	84	95	72	75	66	83	59
81	92	75	87	78	79	70	62	56
68	73	77	81	93	62	61	87	76

a. Although classes do not have to be equally spaced, it often makes sense to adopt this approach. In the table below, each class interval has the same size. Complete the table by finding the number of scores that occur within each interval.

Class Interval (exam scores)	Frequency (number of scores)
50–59	
60–69	
70–79	
80–89	
90–99	

b. Find the number of data values by summing the frequencies in the second column.

c. Observe the way the class intervals are grouped. What type of information will this grouping give the instructor and the class?

_____

_____

_____

d. Create a relative frequency distribution by calculating the relative frequency of each class. Record your answer in the last column as a decimal value rounded to the thousandths place and as a percentage.

Class Interval (exam scores)	Frequency (number of scores)	Relative Frequency
50–59		
60–69		
70–79		
80–89		
90–99		

e. Use the information from part *d* to write a brief summary on how well the students performed on this exam.

_____

_____

_____

f. Suppose the instructor wants to assign letter grades that include plus and minus, A+, A, A–, B+, B, B–, C+, C, C–, D+, D, D–, and F. Construct a relative frequency distribution similar to part *d*, except choose class intervals that are nearly equal in size to fit this new type of grading method. *Hint*: Make each class interval a size that will include a range of 3–4 scores.

Letter Grade	Class Interval (exam scores)	Frequency (number of scores)	Relative Frequency
F			
D–			
D			
D+			
C–			
C			
C+			
B–			
B			
B+			
A–			
A			
A+			

Feedback

In the frequency distribution in part *a* and the relative frequency distribution in part *d,* we chose class intervals that covered a range of 10 scores. This makes sense if you want to see the distribution of scores grouped into the categories of A, B, C, D, and F. In this grade distribution, C is the grade that occurred most often with 11 scores. There are 15 scores above C and 10 scores below C. This is a useful distribution if you want to get a quick snapshot of how well the students did.

To obtain a more detailed distribution, we can increase the number of classes by decreasing the interval size to cover a range of 3-4 scores. This distribution has the advantage of making a distinction between the scores of say 88 (B+) and 81 (B–).

How you choose to group the data depends on how much detail you want to see. If you are not sure what size to make your classes, then experiment with different distributions until you find one that gives the most useful information. Often there are many choices that are equally good at representing the data set. Computers can make the selection process much easier by quickly showing you several distributions with different class sizes. Always try to make the class intervals equal or nearly equal in size unless it makes sense to proceed differently.

In the table below, we have one possible way to present the frequency distribution and the relative frequency distribution of part *f.*

Letter Grade	Class Interval (exam scores)	Frequency (number of scores)	Relative Frequency
F	56–59	3	0.083 or 8.3%
D–	60–62	3	0.083 or 8.3%
D	63–66	2	0.056 or 5.6%
D+	67–69	2	0.056 or 5.6%
C–	70–72	2	0.056 or 5.6%
C	73–76	5	0.139 or 13.9%
C+	77–79	4	0.111 or 11.1%
B–	80–82	4	0.111 or 11.1%
B	83–86	2	0.056 or 5.6%
B+	87–89	3	0.083 or 8.3%
A–	90–92	2	0.056 or 5.6%
A	93–96	3	0.083 or 8.3%
A+	97–99	1	0.028 or 2.8%

In the next Discovery Adventure, you will investigate some common ways to illustrate a frequency distribution or relative frequency distribution. These include the familiar bar graph, circle graph, and a new type of graph called a *histogram*. You will see that the histogram is a close relative to the bar graph. Discovery Adventure 3: Graphs, Graphs, and More Graphs

In Discovery Adventure 2, you first constructed a frequency distribution and a relative frequency distribution with five categories or class intervals for the numerical scores on an exam. See the table below. To visualize these distributions, we can construct a bar graph or a histogram. In both of these graphs, the category or classes are located along the horizontal axis and the frequency (or relative frequency) is shown along the vertical axis. A bar graph displays a separate bar for each class, and the histogram has classes that meet at a common endpoint so that the bars can be connected.

Class Interval (exam scores)	Frequency (number of scores)	Relative Frequency
50–59	3	0.083 or 8.3%
60–69	7	0.194 or 19.4%
70–79	11	0.306 or 30.6%
80–89	9	0.250 or 25%
90–99	6	0.167 or 16.7%

a. Finish constructing the bar graph below for the frequency distribution data. The horizontal scale and vertical scales are already in place. One bar appears completed below.

Frequency Distribution of Exam Scores

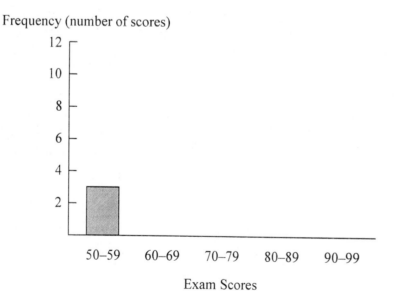

b. Now complete the bar graph below for the relative frequency distribution. You will have to roughly estimate the height of each bar.

Relative Frequency Distribution of Exam Scores

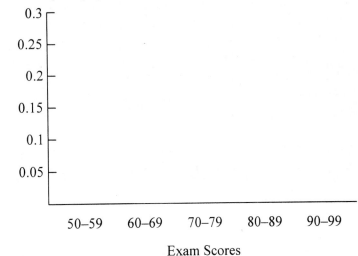

Relative Frequency (percent of scores)

0.3
0.25
0.2
0.15
0.1
0.05

50–59   60–69   70–79   80–89   90–99

Exam Scores

c. Explain how the shapes of the bar graphs for the frequency and relative frequency distribution compare.

_____

_____

d. To construct a histogram, you want consecutive class intervals to have a common endpoint that is (preferably) not equal to any of the data values. How would you change the current class intervals to build a histogram where the widths of the bars are equal? Record your results in the table below. *Hint*: Find the values that are halfway between each of the current class intervals.

Class Interval (exam scores)	Frequency (number of scores)	Relative Frequency

555

e. Complete the drawing of a histogram for the frequency and relative frequency distribution. The first two bars of the frequency distribution already appear and can be used as a model in completing both graphs.

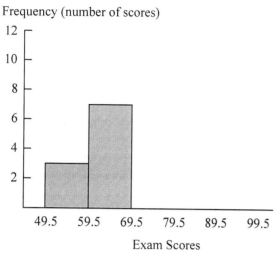

Frequency (number of scores)

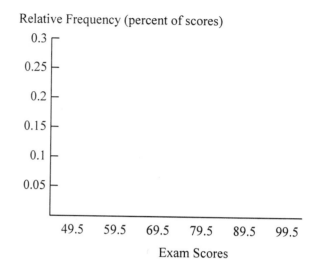

Relative Frequency (percent of scores)

Feedback

Bar graphs can be used for numerical and non-numerical data sets. For example, suppose the 36 students who took the exam in Discovery Adventures 2 and 3 were asked to record the color of their hair at the top of their exam. After collecting the exams, the instructor tabulated the following results:

Hair Color	Black	Blond	Brown	Red	Grey
Frequency	10	4	13	3	6

We cannot use a histogram for this data, but the bar graph given below works quite well.

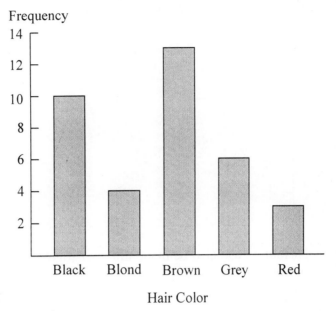

A histogram is another visual way to summarize numerical data such as the frequency distribution of exam scores shown below. In constructing the histogram, we chose common endpoints halfway between the original class intervals. For example, 59.5 is halfway between 59 and 60, 69.5 is halfway between 69 and 70, and so on.

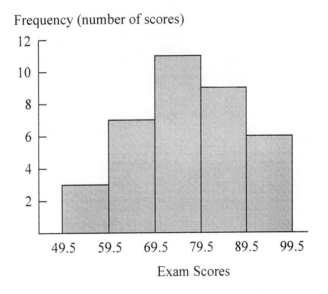

When analyzing a histogram you should try to describe its pattern in terms of shape, center, and spread. The above histogram is roughly symmetrical in shape, meaning there is a similar pattern on opposite sides of the highest bar or peak. If the symmetry was perfect and most real life data is not, then the shape would appear in a pattern like the graph below. The *center* of the above histogram occurs near the highest bar or peak. The *spread* of the histogram ranges from about 50 to 99.

In Sections 7.2 and 7.3, you will learn about center and spread in more detail.

Histogram for a Perfectly Symmetric Distribution

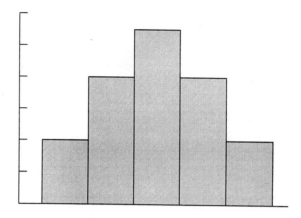

The relative frequency distribution can also be made into a histogram with the same general shape as the frequency distribution. For example, the relative frequency distribution for the exam scores appears below.

Relative Frequency (percent of scores)

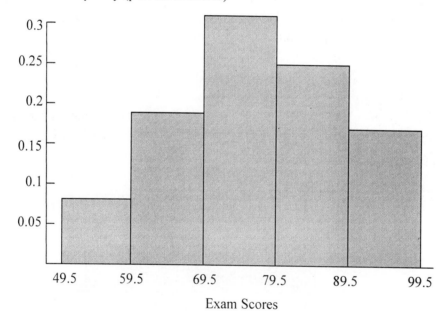

Exam Scores

Make sure to select your class intervals by choosing a size that will clearly display the shape of the data. Too many bars or too few bars will hide the true shape of the distribution.

Section Exercises: 7.1

1. The following data gives the number of students per computer in each academic year from the 1983-84 to the 1997-98 school years.

Academic Year	Students per Computer
1983-84	125
1984-85	75
1985-86	50
1986-87	37
1987-88	32
1988-89	25
1989-90	22
1990-91	20
1991-92	18
1992-93	16
1993-94	14
1994-95	10.5
1995-96	10
1996-97	7.8
1997-98	6.1

   a. Construct a bar graph that displays number of students per computer as a function of the academic year. Make sure to check that the graph is properly labeled.

b. How would you describe the trend in the number of students per computer during this 15-year period?

_____

_____

_____

c. What is your prediction for the number of students per computer during the 2004-5 academic year? Explain your reasoning.

_____

_____

_____

2. The table below shows the countries with athletes who have won the Olympic gold medal in the women's 200-meter run from 1948 to 1996.

Olympic Year	Country of Champions
1948	Netherlands
1952	Australia
1956	Australia
1960	United States
1964	United States
1968	Poland
1972	E. Germany
1976	E. Germany
1980	E. Germany
1984	United States
1988	United States
1992	United States
1996	France

a. Construct a frequency and relative frequency distribution for the above data.

   b. Use a bar graph to illustrate the frequency distribution.

   c. Use a bar graph to illustrate the relative frequency distribution.

3. The following table gives the average SAT scores in math by state for 1999. Note that the table includes all 50 states plus the District of Columbia.

AL	539		IL	539		MT	542		RI	492
AK	505		IN	487		NE	560		SC	469
AZ	523		IA	585		NV	512		SD	560
AR	536		KS	561		NH	510		TN	542
CA	509		KY	539		NJ	497		TX	490
CO	530		LA	534		NM	550		UT	555
CT	498		ME	493		NY	496		VT	497
DE	494		MD	505		NC	469		VA	498
DC	466		MA	499		ND	581		WA	515
FL	494		MI	534		OH	520		WV	515
GA	475		MN	550		OK	542		WI	554
HI	507		MS	536		OR	509		WY	537
ID	523		MO	538		PA	490			

a. Create 7 class intervals with equal widths of 20, starting at 460.5 and ending at 600.5. Then use the 7 intervals to construct a frequency and relative frequency distribution.

b. Draw a histogram of the frequency distribution in part *a*.

c. Draw a histogram of the relative frequency distribution in part *a*.

4. The following table gives the number of children born to each of the first 41 U.S. Presidents.

Washington	0	Buchanan	0	Coolidge	2
J. Adams	5	Lincoln	4	Hoover	2
Jefferson	6	A. Johnson	5	F. Roosevelt	6
Madison	0	Grant	4	Truman	1
Monroe	2	Hayes	8	Eisenhower	2
J.Q. Adams	4	Garfield	7	Kennedy	3
Jackson	0	Arthur	3	L.B. Johnson	2
Van Buren	4	Cleveland	5	Nixon	2
W. H. Harrison	10	B. Harrison	3	Ford	4
Tyler	14	McKinley	2	Carter	4
Polk	0	T. Roosevelt	6	Reagan	4
Taylor	6	Taft	3	Bush	6
Fillmore	2	Wilson	3	Clinton	1
Pierce	3	Harding	0		

Source: The World Almanac and Book of Facts

a. Construct a frequency and relative frequency distribution using the data above.

b. Draw a bar graph of the frequency distribution.

c. Draw a bar graph of the relative frequency distribution.

5. Suppose you did a survey of 35 female students that included information on their height and weight. The list below contains the weights of each student in the survey. In Section Exercises #8-10, you will examine the heights of these same students.

Weights of 35 female students

135	105	130	112	125	110	115
125	130	123	145	120	150	140
127	100	110	125	140	135	120
105	118	130	150	125	145	142
115	132	138	116	120	125	130

a. What percent of the weights were given as whole numbers with the ones digit ending in zero or five? Round your answer to the nearest percent.

b. Why did a large percentage of the female students give their weights as multiples of 5?

_____

_____

_____

c. Suppose you want to group the data so that each class interval has a width of 10 pounds. How can you choose interval endpoints that are not equal to any of the given weights?

_____

_____

_____

d. Although there are many ways to choose class intervals, start the first interval at 97.5 and end the last interval at 157.5. Record the class intervals in the first column of the table. Then complete the frequency and relative frequency distributions using 5 class intervals. *Hint:* The class intervals will have a width of more than 10 pounds.

Weight (pounds)	Frequency	Relative Frequency
97.5 –		
– 157.5		

e. Draw a histogram of the frequency distribution in part *d*.

f. Draw a histogram of the relative frequency distribution in part *d*.

6. Refer to the data in Section Exercise #5 (p. 564) to complete this problem. Suppose you want to see how the distributions in Section Exercise #5 would change according to the number of class intervals selected.

   a. If you want to have equal sized class intervals each with a width of 15 pounds, then how many intervals (bars) will your histogram contain?

   b. Construct a frequency and relative frequency distribution based on the information in part a. Begin the first interval at 97.5 and end the last interval at 157.5.

   c. If you want to have equal sized class intervals each with a width of 5 pounds, then how many intervals (bars) will your histogram contain?

   d. Construct a frequency and relative frequency distribution based on the information in part c. Begin the first interval at 97.5 and end the last interval at 157.5.

7. In this exercise, you will build two new histograms based on the relative frequency distributions of Section Exercise #6 (p. 566). Then you will examine and compare three histograms (the two in this problem and one from Section Exercise #5, part *f*, p. 565) that illustrate the same data but with different class intervals.

   a. Draw a histogram of the relative frequency distribution in Section Exercise #6, part *b*.

   b. Draw a histogram of the relative frequency distribution in Section Exercise #6, part *d*.

   c. Compare the two histograms above with the one in Section Exercise #5, part *f*. Order the three from most to least informative. Please explain your reasoning.

   _____

   _____

   _____

   _____

   _____

8. The table below contains the heights (in feet and inches) of the same 35 students you surveyed in Section Exercise #5 (p. 564). The heights are given in feet and inches, and 5' 4" means 5 feet and 4 inches tall.

Heights of 35 female students

5' 4"	5' 1"	5' 7"	5' 2"	5' 4"	5' 5"	5' 3"
5' 7"	5' 6"	5' 6"	5' 10"	5' 7"	5' 5"	5' 6"
5' 4"	5' 0"	5' 1"	5' 8"	5' 6"	5' 9"	5' 4"
5' 2"	5' 3"	5' 9"	5' 8"	5' 6"	5' 11"	5' 10"
5' 5"	5' 8"	5' 5"	5' 5"	5' 2"	5' 3"	5' 5"

a. Suppose you want to group the data so that each class interval has a width of 2 inches. How can you choose interval endpoints that are not equal to any of the given heights?

_____

_____

b. Although there are many ways to choose class intervals, start the first interval at 4' 11½" and end the last interval at 5' 11½". Record the class intervals in the first column of the table. Then complete the frequency and relative frequency distributions.

Height (feet and inches)	Frequency	Relative Frequency
4' 11½" –		
– 5' 11½"		

c. Draw a histogram of the frequency distribution in part *b*.

    d. Draw a histogram of the relative frequency distribution in part *b*.

9. Refer to the data in Section Exercise #8 (p. 568) when completing this problem. Suppose you want to see how the distributions in Section Exercise #8 would change using classes with smaller and larger widths.

    a. If you want to have equal-sized class intervals each with a width of 1 inch, then how many intervals (bars) will your histogram contain?

    b. Construct a frequency and relative frequency distribution based on the information in part *a*. Begin the first interval at 4' 11½" and end the last interval at 5' 11½".

    c. If you want to have equal-sized class intervals each with a width of 4 inches, then how many intervals (bars) will your histogram contain?

    d. Construct a frequency and relative frequency distribution based on the information in part *a.* Begin the first interval at 4' 11½" and end the last interval at 5' 11½".

10. In this exercise, you will build two new histograms based on the relative frequency distributions of Section Exercise #9 (pp. 569-570). Then you will examine and compare three histograms (the two in this problem and one from Section Exercise #8, part *d*, p. 569) that illustrate the same data but with different class intervals.

    a. Draw a histogram of the relative frequency distribution in Section Exercise #9, part *b*.

b. Draw a histogram of the relative frequency distribution in Section Exercise #9, part *d*.

c. Compare the two histograms above with the one in Section Exercise #5, part *f*, p. 565. Order the three from most to least informative. Please explain your reasoning.

_____

_____

_____

_____

_____

Section 7.2 Summarizing Data by Measures of Center

Math Talk

A statistical study is *observational* when certain characteristics of a group of items are observed or measured. Then each piece of data can be called an **observation**. For example, if you measure the weights of each student in your math class, then the values (weights) you record can be called *observations*. The number of observations is the number of values in the data set. It is helpful to summarize a set of data using measures of center and spread. In this section we will discuss the following statistical terms that describe center: *mean, median* and *mode*.

The *mean, median*, and *mode* are called measures of center because the data values tend to center about these particular numbers. But how do we measure such a number?

The **mean**, often called "the average" of a set of data, can be found by adding all the data values and dividing the result by the number of data values. For example, suppose we gather the following data: ages (in years) of a certain family of 5 people.

43	40	7	4	10

The sum of the 5 ages is 105. So the mean age is $\frac{105}{5} = 21$ years. Do the five ages tend to center about 21? The mean age tells us the age that each family member would be if the family's total living years were equally distributed among the 5 members. In this sense, the mean is the center of balance among all the family's ages. In other words the ages are evenly balanced about the mean.

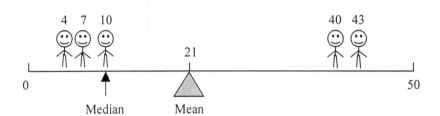

The **median** is the middle value of a set of data that is arranged in order from smallest to largest. If we arrange the ages of our family of five in order, the distribution appears as follows.

4	7	10	40	43

The median is 10 because half of the ages fall below it and half fall above it.

Neither the mean nor the median is a good representation of this data because the distribution of ages has two distinct groups (children and adults) whose ages are far apart.

Suppose we just consider the children's ages: 4, 7, and 10. What are the mean and median ages? In this case, both measures are good representations of the central tendency of the data.

The first Discovery Adventure involves the **mode**. Given a set of data, the *mode* is the value that occurs most often. If the data is grouped into class intervals, then the mode is the class interval or category that occurs most often.

Discovery Adventure 1: A Typical Item, The Mode

In Section 7.1, the example used in Math Talk focuses on the ages of students in a class of 36. Below is a list of each student's age.

21	20	30	35	25	19	57	44	28
45	42	22	18	33	24	27	30	34
48	19	32	26	20	31	19	33	38
31	25	41	28	30	36	27	39	23

a. Find the mode age or ages from the table of data above.

b. Complete the frequency distribution of the age data above. Then find the class interval mode, or the category of ages with the largest frequency.

Age (years)	Frequency
14.5 – 19.5	4
19.5 – 24.5	
24.5 – 29.5	
29.5 – 34.5	
34.5 – 39.5	
39.5 – 44.5	
44.5 – 49.5	
49.5 – 54.5	
54.5 – 59.5	

c. Explain why the class interval mode (from part *b*) is more representative of the center of the data than the mode age(s) from part *a*.

_____

_____

_____

Feedback

The age data is considered to be bimodal since there are two ages, 19 and 30, that occur most often. But having two modes that are 11 years apart is not very helpful in locating the central value. However, it is clear from the frequency distribution that the class interval with the greatest number of ages is 29.5 – 34.5. Therefore, student's in this group, ages 30 to 34, are more common than any of the other categories. This fact stands out very clearly when looking at the histogram for the frequency distribution.

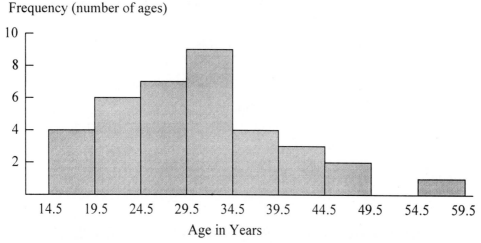

Hence, the mode is useful as a measure of the most common category in a data set. But if we are looking to describe the central or typical value of a data set with one number, then the summary statistics or the mean and median are usually better measures of center than the mode.

Before we define the mean, let's introduce some notation. Suppose we have a set of n data values denoted by

$$x_1, x_2, x_3, \ldots, x_n \quad \text{and read as, "x-one, x-two, x-three, and so on to x-n."}$$

The small, lower placed numbers are called *subscripts* and are used to distinguish between different data values. The data contains a certain number of observations, which can be arranged in a table.

Observation	1	2	3	...	n
Data Value	x_1	x_2	x_3	...	x_n

For example, suppose sleepless Sam keeps track of the number of hours of sleep he gets each night over a 6-day ($n = 6$) period.

Days of Week	1	2	3	4	5	6
Hours of Sleep	3	4	3	4	3	19

Then there are six observations ($n = 6$) of data: $x_1 = 3$, $x_2 = 4$, $x_3 = 3$, $x_4 = 4$, $x_5 = 3$, $x_6 = 19$.

574

Now, let's define the mean or arithmetic average.

The Mean (or Average)

The **mean** $\bar{x}$ of a set of data values x_1, x_2, x_3, ... , x_n is found by summing all the data and then dividing by the number of data values. That is

$$\text{The Mean} = \frac{\text{Sum of data}}{\text{Number of data values}} \quad \text{or} \quad \bar{x} = \frac{x_1 + x_2 + \cdots + x_n}{n}$$

In the previous example, sleepless Sam can find his mean hours of sleep by summing all the data (sleeping hours) and dividing the sum by the number of data values (6 days).

$$\begin{aligned}
\text{Mean hours of sleep} &= \frac{\text{Total hours of sleep}}{\text{Number of days}} \\
&= \frac{3+4+3+4+3+19}{6} \\
&= \frac{36}{6} \\
&= 6
\end{aligned}$$

Does this statistic ($\bar{x} = 6$ hours per day) seem representative of the entire set of observations ($x_1 = 3$, $x_2 = 4$, $x_3 = 3$, $x_4 = 4$, $x_5 = 3$, and $x_6 = 19$)?

In the next Discovery Adventure, you will explore the mean or arithmetic average of another set of data. Then later you will compare the mean with another common measure of center called the *median*.

Discovery Adventure 2: In Search of Average, The Mean

In Discovery Adventure 1, you were given the following ages of students in a class of 36.

21	20	30	35	25	19	57	44	28
45	42	22	18	33	24	27	30	34
48	19	32	26	20	31	19	33	38
31	25	41	28	30	36	27	39	23

a. What kind of data are you observing?

b. How many observations are in the table?

c.   ▦ Find the mean student age by summing all the observed data and dividing by the number of observations (data values). Please use a calculator and round your answer to the nearest year.

$$\bar{x} =$$

d.   Is the mean age a good statistical value to represent the center of the data being observed? Explain.

_____

_____

_____

e.   Suppose you are given the following frequency distribution (first and third columns of the table below), but do not have access to the actual, observed data (table of ages). How can you estimate the mean using only the information in this distribution? Try the following steps.

- Find a representative value for each class interval and record the value in column 2 of the table. For example, in the class 14.5 – 19.5, the midpoint is a good representative value.

$$\text{Midpoint of first class interval} = \frac{14.5+19.5}{2} = \frac{34}{2} = 17$$

- Find the product of the representative value and the frequency, then record this value in the last column.
- Sum all the values (products) in the last column.
- Divide this sum by the number of observations (data values). Record this value below.

Estimated Mean =

Age (years)	Representative Value (Midpoint)	Frequency	Product (Frequency) · (Midpoint)
14.5 – 19.5	17	4	$(17)\cdot(4) = 68$
19.5 – 24.5		6	
24.5 – 29.5		7	
29.5 – 34.5		9	
34.5 – 39.5		4	
39.5 – 44.5		3	
44.5 – 49.5		2	
49.5 – 54.5		0	
54.5 – 59.5		1	

f. Explain why the steps in part *e* can give a good estimate of the mean age.

_____

_____

_____

Feedback

The mean (average) student age can be calculated as follows.

$$\bar{x} = \frac{\text{Sum of Observations (Ages)}}{\text{Number of Observations (Ages)}}$$

$$= \frac{1100}{36}$$

$$= 30.\overline{5} \quad \text{or about 31 years}$$

Recall that in the Feedback after Discovery Adventure1, we concluded that the most typical group of ages is 30 to 34 years. Therefore, a mean age of 31 years seems like a good estimate of the center value in the data.

In part *e* you estimated the mean using the frequency distribution. This process involved finding a representative value (the midpoint) from each class interval and multiplying this value by the frequency. Then calculating the total of all the products and dividing this total by the number of values in the distribution (36).

$$\frac{4 \cdot 17 + 6 \cdot 22 + 7 \cdot 27 + 9 \cdot 32 + 4 \cdot 37 + 3 \cdot 42 + 2 \cdot 47 + 0 \cdot 52 + 1 \cdot 57}{36} = \frac{1102}{36} \approx 30.6$$

Note that the rounded answer of 30.6 is almost the same as the mean $30.\overline{5}$ calculated from all the original data.

So far you have learned that the mean represents the center of data by measuring the average value and the mode is the data value or class interval that occurs most frequently. Another common way to represent center is by measuring the value in the middle of the data called the *median*.

In the last Discovery Adventure you found the midpoint of a class interval by summing the endpoints and dividing by 2. For example, the midpoint of the class interval 14.5 – 19.5 is calculated as follows.

$$\text{Midpoint of first class interval} = \frac{14.5 + 19.5}{2} = \frac{34}{2} = 17$$

The median is the midpoint of a set of data, but we cannot find this data value by the method above because the process only works for finding the midpoint of an interval. Let's investigate how to find the median of a set of data in the third and last Discovery Adventure.

Discovery Adventure 3: In the Middle of Everything, The Median

Recall from Discovery Adventures 1 and 2 the age data from a class of 36 students. Suppose you randomly select 5 students from the class and record their ages in the table below.

<u>Data Table I, Unordered ($n = 5$, odd)</u>

23	25	20	57	25

a. Arrange the above data in order from smallest value to largest value.

<u>Data Table I, Ordered ($n = 5$, odd)</u>

b. Find the value in the middle of the ordered list and using an arrow label it the median.

c. Now suppose we randomly select one more student and add this person's age to data table I, thus creating a new data set given below. Note that the number of data points ($n = 6$) is now even.

<u>Data Table II, Unordered ($n = 6$, even)</u>

23	25	20	57	25	18

d. Arrange the above data in order from smallest value to largest value.

<u>Data Table II, Ordered ($n = 6$, even)</u>

e. Since the number of data points ($n = 6$) is even, there is no middle value. Select the two points nearest the middle and using an arrow label the line between these two numbers, "the middle." In the space below, find the average of these two middle values, this is the median of the second data set.

Feedback

In data table I, we had an odd amount of data, so the median is the middle value of the ordered set of data.

<u>Data Table I, Ordered</u> ($n = 5$, odd)

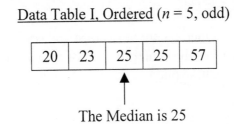

The Median is 25

In data table II, we have an even amount of data, so the median is the average of the two values (23 and 25) closest to the middle of the data.

<u>Data Table II, Ordered</u> ($n = 6$, even)

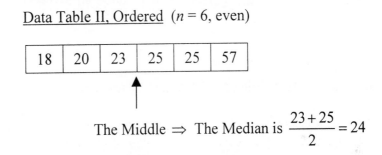

The Middle $\Rightarrow$ The Median is $\dfrac{23 + 25}{2} = 24$

The Median (or Middle)

Given an ordered set of n data values, we can find the middle using the formula $\dfrac{n+1}{2}$.

- If n is odd, the **median** is the middle value calculated with the above formula.

- If n is even, the **median** is the average of the two data values closest to the middle value calculated by the above formula.

579

The mean age for data table I is calculated as follows.

$$\overline{x} = \frac{20 + 23 + 25 + 25 + 57}{5} = \frac{150}{5} = 30 \text{ years}$$

Recall that the median age for this same data set is 25 years. Which summary statistic best describes the center of the data, the mean or the median? The answer to this question depends on the values in the data set and how we wish to use the information.

The last example shows how an extreme value(s) (a number that is much smaller or larger than most of the data) like 57 can have a big impact on the size of the mean. But the age of 57 does not influence the median. Therefore, the median is more representative of this data than the mean.

In many sets of data the mean and median are very close and sometimes equal. You will have to decide which measure best describes the center of a set of data values. Often it is appropriate to include both measures since you can explain in writing the reason for any difference in the statistics.

Section Exercises: 7.2

1. Suppose you work for a small company with a total of 8 employees including the President and Vice President of the firm. The salary of each of the 8 employees is given below.

| $32,000 | $45,000 | $120,000 | $100,000 | $40,000 | $42,000 | $45,000 | $42,000 |

a. Find the mode salary of the 8 employees and explain what it means in the problem situation.

_____

_____

_____

b. Find the mean salary of the 8 employees and explain what it means in the problem situation.

_____

_____

_____

c. Arrange the data in order from smallest to largest salary.

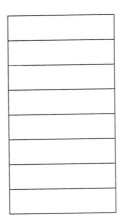

d. Find the median salary of all 8 employees and explain what it means in the problem situation.

_____

_____

2. In this problem you will analyze the measures of center found in Exercise 1 from some different viewpoints.

a. If you are the employee making $40,000 and feel you deserve a raise, then what measures of center if any will you present to the President to make your case? Explain.

_____

_____

_____

_____

b. If you are the President and need to keep company costs to a minimum, then what measures of center if any will you present to any employee (excluding the Vice President) looking for a raise? Explain.

_____

_____

_____

_____

c. If you are the Vice President and want to ask the President for a raise, then what measures of center (if any) will you present to the President to make your case? Explain.

_____

_____

_____

_____

3. Suppose your math instructor just handed back an exam to the class. To give the students an idea of how the class did as a whole, the following grade distribution is presented to the class.

Exam Score	Frequency
98	1
97	3
95	1
91	2
90	2
0	1

a. Find the mode and explain what this value tells you about the class performance on the exam.

_____

_____

_____

b. Find the median score on the exam. Show or explain how you arrived at your answer.

c. Find the mean score on the exam. Show or explain how you arrived at your answer.

d. Which of the three measures of center (if any) is the most representative of the data? Explain.

_____

_____

_____

_____

4. The following tables give the monthly normal temperatures of Philadelphia, PA and San Juan, PR. where January = 1, February = 2, and so on.

Philadelphia, PA

1	2	3	4	5	6	7	8	9	10	11	12
30	33	42	52	63	72	77	76	68	56	46	36

San Juan, PR

1	2	3	4	5	6	7	8	9	10	11	12
77	77	78	79	81	82	83	83	82	82	80	78

(*Source*: National Climatic Data Center)

a. Find Philadelphia's mean and median temperature over a 1-year period.

b. How do Philadelphia's 12 monthly normal temperatures compare with the measures of center found in part *a*?

_____

_____

_____

c. Find San Juan's mean and median temperature over a 1-year period.

d. How do San Juan's 12 monthly normal temperatures compare with the measures of center found in part *c*?

_____

_____

_____

5. Daniel just purchased a summer cottage in a resort town near the ocean. He plans on renting the cottage over a 10-week period to cover the yearly cost of his mortgage. The mortgage on this cottage (a second home) is $615 a month. Daniel needs to be careful not to charge too high a price since he has never rented the cottage before. To help decide what rental price to set, he obtained the following data on the weekly rent charged in ten other similar cottages nearby.

$750	$700	$725	$725	$750	$800	$675	$750	$775	$700

a. How much rent must Daniel charge per week to be able to use only rental income to pay his mortgage for 1 year? Remember that he is only able to rent the cottage for 10 weeks during the year.

b. Find the mean, median, and mode for this data.

c. Taking Daniel's best interest into consideration, suggest a weekly rental price for the cottage and explain your reasoning.

_____

_____

_____

_____

6. Suppose you are spending the month of July in a city that for the past 30 years has had a mean (average) temperature of 74° F in that month. During the first week of your stay in the city the local weather bureau has recorded the average daily temperatures (in degrees Fahrenheit) as follows.

62	60	63	62	65	61	98

a. Use the above data to find the mean and median temperature for this week.

b. Which of the two measures of center in part *a* is most representative of the temperature data during the first week in July? Explain.

_____

_____

_____

c. What needs to happen during the remaining 3 weeks of July for the mean monthly temperature to come close to the 30-year mean?

_____

_____

_____

d. By the end of July the average temperature for the month was 65° F. Use this value to find the mean temperature for July for the last 31 years.

7. Suppose you are given the following histogram for a frequency distribution on student scores for a particular exam.

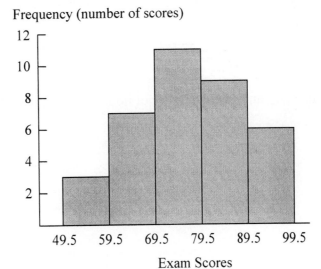

Frequency (number of scores)

Exam Scores

a. Complete the third column of the frequency distribution below, using the information in the given histogram. Then select a representative value for each class interval and record the value in column 2 of the table.

Age (years)	Representative Value	Frequency	Products
49.5 – 59.5	55		
59.5 – 69.5			
69.5 – 79.5			
79.5 – 89.5			
89.5 – 99.5			

b. In the fourth column, find and record the product of each representative value and its frequency.

c. Sum all the values (products) in the fourth column and divide this sum by the number of observations (data values).   Show all work in the space below.

d. Explain what the answer to part c means in terms of the problem situation.

_____

_____

_____

8. A survey of a fifth-grade class revealed the number of hours each child spent watching television on a typical school day.

3	2	4	1	0	2	3	5	4	7	12	3
1	2	3	5	6	0	1	0	4	3	2	4

   a. Find the mean, median, and mode number of hours a student watches television on a school day.

   b. Construct a frequency distribution for the given data set.

   c. Construct a histogram of the frequency distribution in part *b*.

   d. Which observation is the farthest away from the overall pattern?

e. What can you probably conclude about the data value found in part *d*?

_____

_____

_____

9. Recall Section Exercise #5 in Section 7.1 (p. 564) when you did a survey of 35 female students that included their height and weight. The list below contains the weights of each student in the survey. In Section Exercise #10, you will examine the heights of these same students.

Weights of 35 female students

135	105	130	112	125	110	115
125	130	123	145	120	150	140
127	100	110	125	140	135	120
105	118	130	150	125	145	142
115	132	138	116	120	125	130

a. Referring to parts *d* and *e* of Section Exercise #5, Section 7.1 (p. 565), find the class interval mode, or the category of weights with the largest frequency.

b. Order the data from the smallest value to largest value.

c. Show how to use a formula to find the middle of the data.

d. What is the median weight of the 35 female students?

e. Find the mean weight of the students.

10. The table below contains the heights in feet and inches of the same 35 students you surveyed in Section Exercise #9 (previous page). The heights are given in feet and inches, so 5' 4" means 5 feet and 4 inches tall.

Heights of 35 female students

5' 4"	5' 1"	5' 7"	5' 2"	5' 4"	5' 5"	5' 3"
5' 7"	5' 6"	5' 6"	5' 10"	5' 7"	5' 5"	5' 6"
5' 4"	5' 0"	5' 1"	5' 8"	5' 6"	5' 9"	5' 4"
5' 2"	5' 3"	5' 9"	5' 8"	5' 6"	5' 11"	5' 10"
5' 5"	5' 8"	5' 5"	5' 5"	5' 2"	5' 3"	5' 5"

a. Which measure of center requires you to convert the given heights from feet and inches to just inches? Complete this conversion, find the mean, and then convert the mean to feet and inches.

b. What is the median height of the 35 female students?

c. If a 5' 2" student wants to project her height as being close to the center of all heights, then which of the above measures is best? Explain.

_____

_____

_____

d. If a 5' 9" student wants to project her height as being close to the center of all heights, then which of the above measures is best? Explain.

_____

_____

Section 7.3 Summarizing Data by Measures of Spread

Math Talk

We have talked about different ways to measure the center of a data set, and now we will take a look at how the data is dispersed or spread. If we can represent the data in terms of center and spread, then we will have a useful summary. So let's talk about some terminology used in discussing how the values in a data set are scattered around the central value.

Consider the words: **spread**, **dispersion**, **variability**, and **deviation**. In everyday language, how would you define them? In statistics, all these terms refer to the location of data values about a measure of center (usually the mean or median.) For example, when discussing a set of data values, you might be asked to do the following:

- Describe the *spread* or *dispersion* of scores on the final exam.

- Find the **range** of scores and explain what this indicates about the *variability* of the data.

- Find each score's *deviation* from the mean.

The first task requires you to explain how the exam scores are distributed or scattered. Given the graph of a frequency distribution, you can describe the overall appearance of the exam scores. For instance, do some of the scores tend to cluster together? Are there any very high or very low scores?

The second task asks you to calculate the summary statistic called the *range* and explain what this number tells you about the exam scores. The *range* is the difference between the highest and lowest score. So it tells us the distance between the two extreme values.

The third task involves completing a series of calculations. Specifically, a score's deviation from the mean is simply the difference between the score and the mean.

In this section, you will learn how to calculate measures of spread such as the *range*, the *standard deviation*, the *lower and upper quartiles*, and the **interquartile range**. Do you know what *quartile* means? A quarter of something indicates one piece out of four total pieces. Informally, a quartile is one of the values that divide a distribution into four equal sized groups.

The quartiles and range are shown below for the set of integers from 0 to 100.

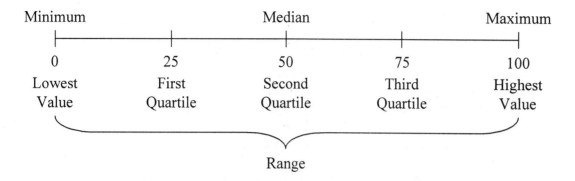

Before exploring the first Discovery Adventure, let's look at a few examples. Suppose we have a small class of 11 students who all receive a score of 85 on the first exam.

85	85	85	85	85	85	85	85	85	85	85

What number best represents the central value in this set of exam scores? How would you describe the spread of the data? The central value is 85 and the spread is 0. If we draw a histogram of this distribution it would be one tall bar.

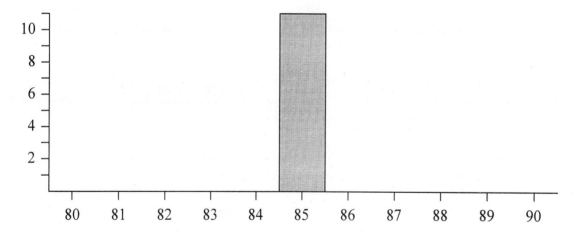

Suppose that on the second exam the scores were more spread out. Observe the second exam results in the table below.

85	84	85	84	87	81	88	86	85	82	86

If we arrange the scores in order from lowest to highest, then what numbers best describe the center and spread?

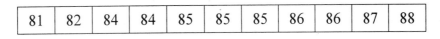

| 81 | 82 | 84 | 84 | 85 | 85 | 85 | 86 | 86 | 87 | 88 |

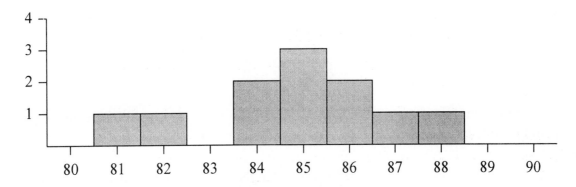

In the first Discovery Adventure, you will investigate the five-number summary (minimum, lower quartile, median, upper quartile, and maximum) for describing the center and spread of a set of data.

Discovery Adventure 1: Spread Out

Suppose the ($n = 11$) students in our previous example have just received back their third exam and want to compare their results, which are given in the table below.

| 78 | 86 | 94 | 59 | 82 | 97 | 66 | 88 | 85 | 90 | 72 |

a. Arrange the data in order from smallest to largest value.

b. Find the median score and label it *Med*. Recall that the formula $\dfrac{n+1}{2}$ can be used to locate the middle of the data set.

c. Use the space below to make an ordered list of the scores falling *below* the median score found in part *b*.

d. Find the median score from your low group in part *c*. This value is called the *lower quartile*. Go to the table in part *a* and label the lower quartile score as Q_1.

e. Use the space below to make an ordered list of the scores that are *above* the median score found in part *b*.

f. Find the median score from your high group in part *e*. This value is called the *upper quartile*. Go to the table in part *a* and label the upper quartile score as Q_3.

g. Go to the table in part *a* and find the lowest and highest score from the data set. Label the lowest score as *Min* for minimum value and the highest score as *Max* for maximum value.

h. Now record the exam score's five-number summary below.

Minimum: Lower quartile: Median: Upper quartile: Maximum:

Feedback

If we let the variable *x* represent any value in the exam score distribution, then the five-number summary can be symbolized as follows.

$$\min x = 59$$
$$Q_1 = 72$$
$$\text{Med} = 85$$
$$Q_3 = 90$$
$$\max x = 97$$

The minimum and maximum values are the lowest and highest values respectively in the data set. You know from past experience that the median represents the middle of a distribution. For instance, the exam score distribution has $n = 11$ data values, so the median value's location can be found as follows.

$$\text{Med} = \frac{n+1}{2} = \frac{11+1}{2} = \frac{12}{2} = 6$$

The sixth data value in the ordered list gives the median score of 85.

594

The lower quartile (or first quartile) tells you that one-quarter of the data occurs at or below this value. Similarly, the upper quartile (or third quartile) tells you that about one-quarter of the data occurs at or above this value. You could also say that about three-quarters of the data occurs at or below the upper quartile. So the quartiles give you information on the spread of the data.

Suppose one student was sick during the administration of the exam but scores 100 on the make-up. If we add another exam score to the distribution, then the data set will have $n = 12$ scores. Adding this value to the previous ordered list gives the following table.

Observation	1	2	3	4	5	6	7	8	9	10	11	12
Exam Score	59	66	72	78	82	85	86	88	90	94	97	100

$$Min \qquad\qquad Q_1 = 75 \qquad Med = 85.5 \qquad Q_3 = 92 \qquad\qquad Max$$

The minimum value remains 59, but the new maximum value is 100. The median of this data set is the score that lies halfway between observations 6 and 7.

$$Med = \frac{85+86}{2} = 85.5$$

There are six low scores below the median value of 85.5, so the lower quartile is the median of these scores, which lies halfway between observations 3 and 4. There are six high scores above the median value of 85.5, so the upper quartile is the median of these scores, which lies halfway between observations 9 and 10.

The calculations for the lower quartile and upper quartile are given below.

$$Q_1 = \frac{72+78}{2} = 75, \qquad\qquad Q_3 = \frac{90+94}{2} = 92$$

We can use the five-number summary to calculate two more summary statistics called the **range** and the **interquartile range** or IQR. These statistics are defined as follows.

The Range

The *range* measures the size of spread between the lowest and highest values in a data set. The range can be calculated as the difference between the maximum value and minimum value, or

$$Range = Max - Min$$

The Interquartile Range

The *interquartile range* measures the size of spread between the lower and upper quartiles. The IQR can be calculated as the difference between the upper quartile and lower quartile, or

$$IQR = Q_3 - Q_1$$

The five-number summary of the exam score's distribution is given below.

$$Min = 59 \qquad Q_1 = 75 \qquad Med = 85.5 \qquad Q_3 = 92 \qquad Max = 100$$

The range and interquartile range are calculated as

$$Range = 100 - 59 = 41 \qquad and \qquad IQR = 92 - 75 = 17$$

The graph that displays the five-number summary is called the **box plot** (or box and whiskers plot). For example, the box plot for the ($n = 12$) exam score distribution is illustrated below.

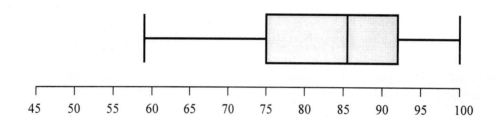

Box plots can be drawn either horizontally or vertically as long as an appropriate scale is included.

To analyze a box plot, start looking at the median line to find the middle of the data. The box shows the spread of the middle part of the data from the lower to upper quartile. The whiskers show the spread of the whole data set from minimum to maximum value.

Problem Solving Strategy: Building a Box Plot

1. Draw an appropriate scale that covers all the points in the distribution.

2. Construct a box from the lower quartile to the upper quartile.

3. Draw a vertical median line through the box.

4. Draw a vertical line at the minimum value and then draw a horizontal line between the lower quartile of the box and the minimum value.

5. Draw a vertical line at the maximum value and then draw a horizontal line between the upper quartile of the box and the maximum value.

The five-number summary uses the median as the measure of center and the quartiles and extreme values (max/min) as a measure of spread. However, when the mean is used as a measure of center, the **standard deviation** is used to measure spread. The standard deviation measures how far the data values are from their mean. Informally, we can think of the standard deviation as the average distance of the data from the mean.

Discovery Adventure 2: Deviating from the Mean

Suppose an instructor gave half the class a particular test named exam A and the other half a similar test called exam B. The class has 12 students, so 6 took exam A and 6 took exam B. The results are given in the table below.

Exam A	75	76	78	78	98	99
Exam B	77	81	82	85	87	92

a. Find the mean score for exam A.

b. Find the mean score for exam B.

c. What do the results of parts *a* and *b* indicate about the center and spread of each data set?

_____

_____

The difference between each score and the mean is called the *deviation* from the mean. The deviations tell you the directed distance between the mean and each data value.

d. Complete the table below by finding the deviations and squared deviations for each score on exam A. Then calculate the sum of the squared deviations in the last column, just under the last row.

Score	Deviation (score – mean)	Squared Deviation
75	$75 - 84 = -9$	$(-9)^2 = 81$

Sum =

e. Complete the table below by finding the deviations and squared deviations for each score on exam B. Then calculate the sum of the squared deviations in the last column, under the last row.

Score	Deviation (score – mean)	Squared Deviation
77	$77 - 84 = -7$	$(-7)^2 = 49$

Sum =

f. Compare the sum of the squared deviations for exams A and B. What does this tell you about the spread of each distribution?

_____

_____

_____

Parts *g* and *h* involve finding the standard deviation of each set of exam scores. There are two steps you must follow in calculating the standard deviation.

- First, divide the sum of the squared deviations by the number of data values minus 1.

$$\frac{\text{sum of squared deviations}}{n-1}$$

- Second, take the square root of the above result. The standard deviation is denoted by *s*.

$$s = \sqrt{\frac{\text{sum of squared deviations}}{n-1}}$$

g. Find the standard deviation of the set of scores from exam A.

h. Find the standard deviation of the set of scores from exam B.

i. Compare the standard deviations for exams A and B. What does this tell you about the spread of each distribution?

_____

_____

_____

Feedback

Did you notice that in both tables the sum of the deviations in column two was zero? The positive and negative deviations have the effect of canceling each other out. Thus, the sum of the deviations gives no useful information on the spread of the data. However, squaring each deviation gives positive values that must sum to a positive result. Therefore, the sum of the squared deviations tells us that the scores for exam A have greater spread or variability than exam B.

In the final formula for the standard deviation, we divide by $n-1$ rather than n. To find the average of the squared deviations you would divide by n, but it turns out that $n-1$ does a better job than n at measuring spread about the mean. Also, the square root compensates for the previous squaring and assures us that the standard deviation formula produces the same units as the data.

The standard deviations for exams A and B are calculated below.

Exam A: $\quad s = \sqrt{\dfrac{(75-84)^2 + (76-84)^2 + (78-84)^2 + (78-84)^2 + (98-84)^2 + (99-84)^2}{6-1}}$

Exam B: $\quad s = \sqrt{\dfrac{(77-84)^2 + (81-84)^2 + (82-84)^2 + (85-84)^2 + (87-84)^2 + (92-84)^2}{6-1}}$

These two calculations require a lot of number crunching and these data sets would not be considered large. Hence, computers or calculators with statistical ability are the usual choice to compute descriptive statistics. We define the standard deviation as follows.

The Standard Deviation

The *standard deviation* measures how far the data values are from their mean. It can be calculated by first finding the sum of the squared deviations divided by the number of data values minus 1, then taking the square root of this result. Using s to denote the standard deviation, we have

$$s = \sqrt{\frac{\text{sum of squared deviations}}{n-1}}$$

If the set of n data values are denoted as $x_1, x_2, x_3, \ldots, x_n$ and the mean is $\bar{x}$, then

$$s = \sqrt{\frac{(x_1 - \bar{x})^2 + (x_2 - \bar{x})^2 + (x_3 - \bar{x})^2 + \cdots + (x_n - \bar{x})^2}{n-1}}$$

In summary, the decision on how to measure the spread of any data set depends on your choice of central measure. If the median is the best measure of center, then the five-number summary should be used to measure center and spread. If the mean is the best measure of center, then the standard deviation should be used to measure spread. However, there are situations where all of these summary statistics should be used and other instances when none of them are useful. The more problems you work on, the easier it will be to decide what is best.

> ## Section Exercises: 7.3

1. The city of Boston has parking rates that are among the highest in the nation. The main reason parking garage operators can continue to increase rates is that the demand for parking is growing, and the supply of parking spaces is decreasing. The table below gives the first hour and daily rates at 22 garages located in downtown Boston.

Name of Garage or Lot	First Hour	Daily
First Federal Parking	$2.90	$9.65
Pier Sunpark	NA	$7
Boston Common Garage	$5	$20
Seaport Garage	$5	$21
Parcel 7 Garage	$5	$30
341 Newbury St.	$6	$18
Fansworth Street Garage	$7	$12
Dock Square Garage	$7	$24
Post Office Sq. Garage	$7.50	$29
Washington St.	$8	$18
101 Arch St.	$8	$22
Lafayette Garage	$8	$25
Center Plaza Garage	$9	$25
Downtown Crossing Garage	$9	$26
75 State St.	$9.50	$29
Ashburton Pl.	$10	$23
Boston Harbor Garage	$10	$25
Government Center Garage	$10	$25
149 Newbury St.	$10	$30
150 Federal St.	$10	$30
Kingston St.	$10	$28
Pi Alley Garage	$12	$30

(Source: The Boston Globe, August 4, 2000)

   a. ▦ Use a calculator or computer to find the mean and standard deviation of the first hour rates. *Hint:* NA means "not applicable" so don't include Pier Sunpark.

b. ▦ Use a calculator or computer to find the mean and standard deviation of the daily rates.

c. What do the two means and standard deviations tell you about center and spread of the first hour and daily parking rates?

_____

_____

_____

d. Find the five-number summary of the first hour rates.

e. What information does the five-number summary provide that is not available when using just the mean and standard deviation?

_____

_____

_____

2. Professor S. D. Mean has just finished grading twenty of his student exams. In this particular class, 10 students took exam X and 10 took exam Y.

Exam X	66	77	93	84	69	75	91	86	81	78
Exam Y	100	86	49	87	52	83	78	99	76	90

a. Find the mean and standard deviation of the set of scores from exam X.

b. Find the mean and standard deviation of the set of scores from exam Y.

c. Compare the mean and standard deviation of the exam X scores with the exam Y scores. What do these statistics tell you about the distribution of scores on each exam? Explain.

_____

_____

_____

_____

3. Recall in Section Exercise #4 of Section 7.2 (p. 584), the following tables were given on the monthly normal temperatures of Philadelphia, PA and San Juan, PR. where January = 1, February = 2, and so on. In that exercise, you calculated the mean and median temperatures of each city over a 1-year period. Use these means to help answer parts a and b.

Philadelphia, PA

1	2	3	4	5	6	7	8	9	10	11	12
30	33	42	52	63	72	77	76	68	56	46	36

San Juan, PR

1	2	3	4	5	6	7	8	9	10	11	12
77	77	78	79	81	82	83	83	82	82	80	78

(*Source*: National Climatic Data Center)

a. Find the standard deviation of Philadelphia's temperature data.

b. Find the standard deviation of San Juan's temperature data.

   c. Why is there such difference in the standard deviation of these two cities?

   _____

   _____

   _____

   _____

4. Refer to the temperature data in Section Exercise #3 (on the previous page) to complete the following parts.

   a. Find the five-number summary of the temperature data from each city.

   b. Calculate the range and the IQR (interquartile range) for each data set.

   c. What does the range and IQR tell you about the change in temperature between seasons in each city?

   _____

   _____

   _____

   d. Display each data set's five-number summary by creating two box plots on the same axis. Be sure that you label the scale along the axis. If your axis is horizontal, then one box plot should be directly above the other to compare the distribution's spread. If your axis is vertical, then place the box plots side by side.

5. Recall Section Exercise #5 from Section 7.2 (p. 585). Daniel just purchased a summer cottage in a resort town near the ocean. He plans on renting the cottage over a 10-week period to cover the yearly cost of his mortgage. The mortgage on this cottage (a second home) is $615 a month. Daniel needs to be careful not to charge too high a price since he has never rented the cottage before. To help decide what rental price to set, he has obtained data on the weekly rent charged in ten other similar cottages nearby.

$750	$700	$725	$725	$750	$800	$675	$750	$775	$700

  a. Find the five-number summary on the above data set.

  b. Calculate the range and the IQR (interquartile range) for the data set.

  c. What does the range and IQR tell you about the cottage rental market in this area?

  _____

  _____

  _____

  _____

  d. Display the data set's five-number summary by creating a box plot. Be sure that you label the scale along the axis.

6. Recall Section Exercise #3 from Section 7.1 (p. 561). The following table gives the 1999 average math SAT scores by state. Note that the table includes all 50 states plus the District of Columbia.

AL	539		IL	539		MT	542		RI	492
AK	505		IN	487		NE	560		SC	469
AZ	523		IA	585		NV	512		SD	560
AR	536		KS	561		NH	510		TN	542
CA	509		KY	539		NJ	497		TX	490
CO	530		LA	534		NM	550		UT	555
CT	498		ME	493		NY	496		VT	497
DE	494		MD	505		NC	469		VA	498
DC	466		MA	499		ND	581		WA	515
FL	494		MI	534		OH	520		WV	515
GA	475		MN	550		OK	542		WI	554
HI	507		MS	536		OR	509		WY	537
ID	523		MO	538		PA	490			

a. ▦ Use a computer or calculator with statistical capability to find the mean and standard deviation of the above data.

b. Explain what the mean and standard deviation tells you about 1999 math SAT scores.

_____

_____

_____

_____

c. In 1999, Connecticut had 80% of its high school graduates take the SAT, while Iowa had 5% of its high school graduates take the SAT. Do you think it is fair to compare the mean SAT scores of these two states? Explain.

_____

_____

_____

606

7. The histogram of a frequency distribution that contains ages of students in a class of 36 is given below. Suppose we wish to estimate the mean and standard deviation of this grouped data by first finding a representative value for each interval. The midpoint would be a good representative value for the given class intervals. For example, in the first interval, the midpoint is 17.

$$\frac{14.5+19.5}{2}=\frac{34}{2}=17$$

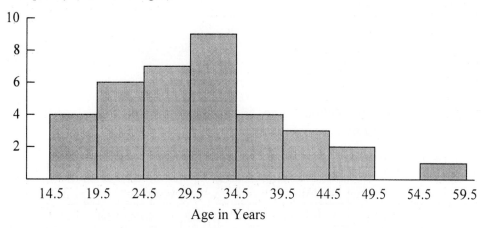

Frequency (number of ages)

Age in Years

a. Complete the following table by finding a representative value (midpoint) of each interval.

Class Interval (ages)	Representative Value	Frequency

b. Estimate the mean age of the above distribution. Round to the nearest year.

c. Estimate the standard deviation for the student age distribution. *Hint:* Include the frequency of each squared deviation in your calculation.

8. Recall Section Exercise #4 from Section 7.1 (p. 563). The following table gives the number of children for each of the first 41 U.S. Presidents.

Washington	0	Buchanan	0	Coolidge	2
J. Adams	5	Lincoln	4	Hoover	2
Jefferson	6	A. Johnson	5	F. Roosevelt	6
Madison	0	Grant	4	Truman	1
Monroe	2	Hayes	8	Eisenhower	2
J.Q. Adams	4	Garfield	7	Kennedy	3
Jackson	0	Arthur	3	L.B. Johnson	2
Van Buren	4	Cleveland	5	Nixon	2
W. H. Harrison	10	B. Harrison	3	Ford	4
Tyler	14	McKinley	2	Carter	4
Polk	0	T. Roosevelt	6	Reagan	4
Taylor	6	Taft	3	Bush	6
Fillmore	2	Wilson	3	Clinton	1
Pierce	3	Harding	0		

Source: The World Almanac and Book of Facts

a. Find the five-number summary on the above data set.

b. Calculate the range and the IQR (interquartile range) for the data set.

c. What does the range and IQR tell you about the number of children for each of the first 41 U.S. Presidents?

_____

_____

_____

_____

d. Display the data set's five-number summary by creating a box plot. Be sure that you label the scale along the axis.

9. The following tables give the monthly normal precipitation of Seattle, WA and Miami, FL. where January = 1, February = 2, and so on.

Seattle, WA

1	2	3	4	5	6	7	8	9	10	11	12
5.4	4.0	3.8	2.5	1.8	1.6	0.9	1.2	1.9	3.3	5.7	6.0

Miami, FL

1	2	3	4	5	6	7	8	9	10	11	12
2.0	2.1	2.4	2.9	6.2	9.3	5.7	7.6	7.6	5.6	2.7	1.8

(*Source*: National Climatic Data Center)

a. Find the mean monthly precipitation for a normal year in Seattle and Miami.

b. Find the standard deviation for monthly precipitation for a normal year in Seattle and Miami.

c. Based on the summary statistics in parts *a* and *b*, compare the precipitation for a normal year in Seattle and Miami.

_____

_____

_____

_____

_____

10. Refer to the situation in Section Exercise #9 (on the previous page) in completing the parts below.

a. Find the five-number summary for the monthly precipitation data for Seattle and Miami.

b. Calculate the range and the IQR (interquartile range) for the data set.

c. Do the summary statistics in parts *a* and *b* allow you to write a better comparative analysis than you did in Section Exercise #9, part *c*?

_____

_____

_____

_____

Chapter 7 Summary

Key Terms

Section 7.1

- **Data** – A collection of factual information in the form of numbers or categories.
- **Frequency** – The number of items that occur in a given category.
- **Frequency Distribution** – The number of occurrences of each different data item.
- **Relative Frequency Distribution** – The percent of times an item occurs compared to the total number of items. It is calculated as follows:

$$\text{Relative Frequency} = \frac{\text{Frequency}}{\text{Total Number}}$$

- **Class Intervals** – A *class* or *category* is a range of values that is usually equal in length. Large data sets can be grouped in classes to form frequency distributions and relative frequency distributions.
- **Histogram** – A special type of bar graph where the bars are connected at common endpoints. It is used to give a graphical picture of either the frequency or relative frequency distribution. The class intervals will appear along the horizontal axis, and the frequency or relative frequency will appear along the vertical axis.

Section 7.2

- **Observation** – A statistical study is *observational* when certain characteristics of a group of items is observed or measured. Then each piece of data can be called an *observation*. For example, if you measure the weights of each student in your math class, then the values (weights) you record can be called observations.
- **Mean** – Often called the *average* of a set of data. Calculate the *mean* by adding all the data and dividing the result by the number of data values.

$$\text{The Mean} = \frac{\text{Sum of data}}{\text{Number of data values}}$$

- **Median** – The middle value of a set of data that is arranged in order from smallest to largest. Given an ordered set of n data values, we can find the middle value using the formula $\frac{n+1}{2}$. If n is odd, the *median* is the middle value calculated with this formula. If n is even, the *median* is the average of the two data values closest to the middle value calculated by this formula.
- **Mode** – The value that occurs most often in a given set of data. If the data is grouped into class intervals, then the *mode* is the class interval that occurs most often.

Section 7.3

- **Spread** – Given a set of data, the *spread* of the data refers to how the data is distributed or scattered about the center value (mean or median).
- **Dispersion** – A measure of *dispersion* is the same as a measure of spread.
- **Variability** – A measure of *variability* is the same as a measure of spread (or dispersion).

611

- **Deviation** – Like spread, dispersion, and variability, *deviation* measures distance from the center. The deviations from the mean are calculated as the difference between each score and the mean.
- **Range** – The size of spread between the lowest and highest values in a data set. It can be calculated as the difference between the maximum value and minimum value.
- **Interquartile Range (IQR)** – The size of spread between the lower and upper quartiles. It can be calculated as the difference between the upper quartile and lower quartile.
- **Box Plot** – The graph that displays the five-number summary (maximum, minimum, median, upper quartile, lower quartile). Also called a *box and whiskers plot*.
- **Standard Deviation** – Measures how far the data values are from their mean. It can be calculated by first finding the sum of the squared deviations divided by the number of data values minus 1, then taking the square root of this result. Using s to denote the standard deviation,

$$s = \sqrt{\frac{\text{sum of squared deviations}}{n-1}}$$

****

Questions for Review

1. Do you know how to organize data into a frequency or relative frequency distribution? Can you draw a histogram for a frequency or relative frequency distribution?

    For example, the table below gives the monthly normal temperatures for Des Moines, Iowa.

Month	Jan	Feb	Mar	Apr	May	Jun	Jul	Aug	Sep	Oct	Nov	Dec
Temp.	19	25	37	51	62	72	77	74	65	54	39	24

(*Source*: National Climatic Data Center)

   a. Complete the frequency and relative frequency distribution that has been started below.

Class Interval (monthly temperatures)	Frequency (number of monthly temperatures)	Relative Frequency
9.5 – 19.5	1	0.083
19.5 – 29.5		
29.5 – 39.5		

b. Draw a histogram of the frequency distribution in part *a*.

c. Draw a histogram of the relative frequency distribution in part *a*.

d. Which class interval has the highest frequency of monthly temperatures? What is this measure of center called?

e. Explain what the frequency and relative frequency distributions tell you about monthly temperatures in Des Moines, Iowa.

_____

_____

_____

2. Another way to look at the distribution in Question #1 is to graph the normal monthly temperature for each month of the year using a bar graph.

a. Use the horizontal and vertical axis below to construct the bar graph described above. Be sure to label each axis and use an appropriate scale.

b. What type of information does the graph in part *a* show that is not available when examining the histograms in parts *a* and *c* of Question #1?

_____

_____

_____

3. Given a data set, can you find a value to describe the center of the data?
   For example, consider the data from Question #1 on normal monthly temperatures in Des Moines, Iowa. How can we find a central value in this data set? Answer this question by completing parts *a* and *b* below. Show all work.

   a. Find the mean monthly temperature during a typical year in Des Moines.

   b. Find the median monthly temperature during a typical year in Des Moines.

4. Given a data set, can you find a value to describe the spread of the data?
   For example, consider the data, from Question #1, on normal monthly temperatures in Des Moines, Iowa. How can we find a value or values to represent the spread of this data set? In other words, what are some measures of dispersion or variability that will give a good indication of how the data is scattered around the center? Answer this question by completing parts *a* and *b* below. Show all work.

   a. Find the five-number summary of normal monthly temperatures in Des Moines.

   b. Find the range of normal monthly temperatures in Des Moines. Now explain what this means in terms of the problem situation.

   _____

   _____

   c. Find the interquartile range of normal monthly temperatures in Des Moines. Now explain what this means in terms of the problem situation.

   _____

   _____

   _____

5. How do you decide what measures of center and spread to use when summarizing a set of data?

For example, the top ten movies in 1998 according to gross box-office sales are given below.

Title of Movie	Gross Sales (millions, $)
Titanic	488.2
Armageddon	201.6
Saving Private Ryan	190.8
There's Something About Mary	174.4
The Waterboy	147.9
Dr. Doolittle	144.2
Deep Impact	140.5
Godzilla	136.3
Rush Hour	136.1
Good Will Hunting	134.1

(*Source*: Variety, Feb.1 – Feb.7, 1999)

a. Find the mean and median gross sales of these top ten movies.

b. Compare the mean and median and explain any significant difference in their values.

_____

_____

_____

_____

c. Which measure of center is the most representative of the gross sales data for the top ten movies? Explain.

_____

_____

_____

d. Find the standard deviation of the gross sales data for the top ten movies.

e. Find the five-number summary of the above data set.

f. Which gives you more information about the center and spread of the gross sales data for the top ten movies: the five-number summary or the mean and standard deviation? Explain.

_____

_____

_____

_____

6. Suppose you remove the movie *Titanic* from the data and just consider the 9 remaining movies in the list from Question #5. How will the summary statistics on gross sales change from what you calculated in Question #5?

a. Find the mean and median gross sales of the remaining nine top movies.

b. How has the difference between mean and median values changed when comparing the top ten measures of center with the remaining nine measures of center? Explain.

_____

_____

_____

c. Find the standard deviation of the gross sales data for the remaining nine top movies.

d. How has the standard deviation changed when comparing the top ten data with the remaining nine data points? Explain.

_____

_____

_____

7. Suppose you remove the top three movies and just consider the seven remaining movies in the list from Question #5. How will the summary statistics on gross sales change from what you calculated in Question #6?

a. Find the mean and median gross income of the remaining seven top movies.

b. How has the difference between mean and median values changed when comparing your answers from part _a_ above with the answer from question #6, part _a_? Explain.

_____

_____

_____

c. Find the standard deviation of the gross sales data for the remaining seven top movies.

d. How has the standard deviation changed when comparing your answer in part _c_ above with the answer from Question #6, part _c_? Explain.

_____

_____

_____

Chapter 7 Quiz

1. Suppose a student named Kristy is taking an economics course and has received the following scores on the first four exams: 92, 95, 97, 96. Complete each part below and be sure to show the method necessary to calculate the following questions.

   a. Find Kristy's mean score from the first four exams.

   b. Find Kristy's median score from the first four exams.

   c. If Kristy receives a score of 100 on her fifth exam, what is her new mean score?

   d. If Kristy receives a score of 100 on her fifth exam, what is her new median score?

   e. If Kristy receives a score of 50 on her fifth exam, what is her new mean score?

   f. If Kristy receives a score of 50 on her fifth exam, what is her new median score?

   g. A score of 50 would be an unusually low score relative to the first 4 exams. Why can one unusual score have such a large effect on the mean but not on the median?

   _____

   _____

   _____

2. Suppose Kristy gets a score of 100 on her fifth exam so that her five scores are 92, 95, 97, 96, 100. Kristy's friend, Kevin had the same average as Kristy after 4 exams, but he received a score of 50 on his fifth exam. Kevin received a 96 on each of his first four exams.

   a. Find the standard deviation for Kristy's set of five exams.

   b. How do you think Kevin's standard deviation will compare with Kristy's? Do not complete any calculations, just think and explain.

   _____

   _____

   _____

3. Suppose 300 freshmen take an entrance exam to place them into the appropriate science course. The mean score for the exam is 75. At a later date, two freshmen take a similar make-up exam and receive scores of 98 and 96.

   a. Find the total points obtained by the 300 freshmen that initially took the exam. *Hint*: Substitute the proper values into the following formula, then solve for the remaining unknown.

   $$\text{Mean Exam Score} = \frac{\text{Total Points of all Exam Scores}}{\text{Total Number of Exam Scores}}$$

   b. Now find the mean exam score for all 302 freshmen (include the 2 additional make-ups.)

   c. The 2 make-up scores were very high relative to the original mean of the first 300 exams. What effect did the 98 and 96 have on the new mean score of all 302 exams? Explain.

   _____

   _____

   _____

4. The manager of a fast food restaurant has 22 employees working for her. The hourly pay rate for each employee is given below. The pay rate for each employee depends on the type of work, the amount of experience, and the individual's work ethic.

$9.25	$8.50	$9.25	$9.00	$8.50	$9.50	$8.00	$8.75
$9.00	$9.25	$8.75	$8.75	$10.00	$9.50	$8.50	$9.50
$9.00	$9.75	$9.00	$8.25	$9.00	$9.75	$9.25	$8.25

a. Complete the frequency and relative frequency distribution for each hourly pay rate. Round the relative frequencies to the thousandths place.

Hourly Pay Rate	Frequency	Relative Frequency
$8.00	1	0.042
$8.25	2	0.083
$8.50		

b. Finish drawing the bar graph of the frequency distribution from part *a*.

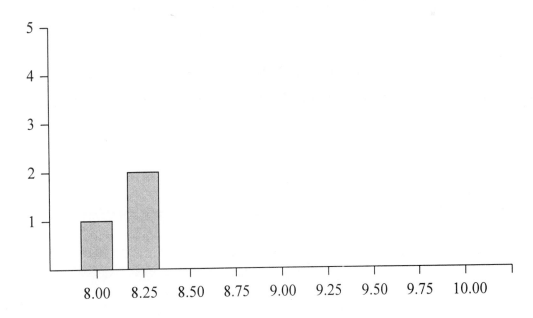

c. Find the midpoint of each class interval and record your answer in the second column. Then complete the frequency and relative frequency distribution of hourly pay rates using the class intervals given in the first row.

Hourly Pay Rate	Midpoint	Frequency	Relative Frequency
$7.88 – $8.62			
$8.62 – $9.38			
$9.38 – $10.12			

d. Finish drawing the histogram of the frequency distribution from part *c* above.

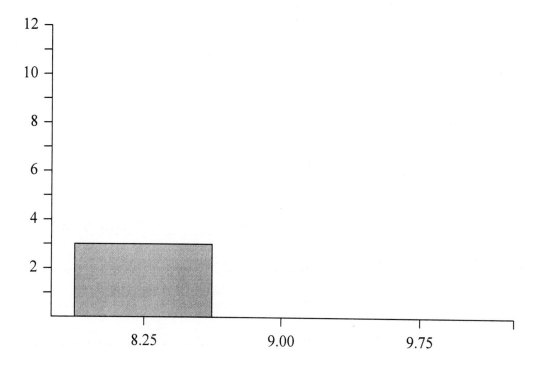

e. Observe the graphs in part *b* and part *d*. Which graph does the best job of representing the original data set of hourly pay rates? Explain.

_____

_____

_____

_____

5. In Quiz problem #4 (p. 621), you were given the hourly pay rate of 22 employees. Use that data to complete the following parts.

   a. Find the five-number summary of the data set.

   b. How is the five-number summary useful in describing the center and spread of the hourly pay rate data?

_____

_____

_____

_____

   c. Find the range of the data set.

   d. What does the range tell you about the hourly pay rate of the 22 employees?

_____

_____

_____

_____

   e. Find the interquartile range of the data set.

   f. What does the interquartile range tell you about the hourly pay rate of the 22 employees?

_____

_____

_____

_____

Chapter 8

Basic Concepts of Probability

Section 8.1 Probability Act I: A Classical Approach
Section 8.2 Probability Act II: An Empirical Approach

Chapter 8 presents the basic concepts of probability necessary to make predictions from sample data and determine the likelihood of chance events occurring. By the end of this chapter, you should understand the difference between classical and empirical probability.

In Section 8.1, we will introduce classical (or theoretical) probability by exploring situations that involve random events such as tossing a coin or rolling a pair of dice. We will assume throughout this chapter that the coin and dice are standard and not trick coins or dice. Topics explored in this section include randomness, the multiplication principle, conditional probability, and the probability of independent and dependent events.

In Section 8.2, we will introduce empirical or experimental probability by investigating situations that use simulations of experiments and sample data obtained at random from a population. This information will allow us to approximate probability by relative frequency. Topics explored include the law of large numbers, the complement of an event, and the relative frequency of a population versus a sample.

Section 8.1 Probability Act I: A Classical Approach

Math Talk

The Latin term *a priori* means "before the fact." When studying probability *a priori*, we are arriving at valid results prior to performing any observations or experiments. This approach is called **classical probability** or *theoretical probability*. But what is probability, and why should we study it?

Probability is the likelihood that a chance event will occur. For example, if a coin is tossed, what is the probability that it will land on heads? Since there are two possible outcomes (heads or tails) and only one of them is favorable (heads), there is a 1 in 2 chance of landing on heads when flipping a coin. This result could be expressed as a fraction, decimal, or percent as follows:

$$\text{Probability of landing on heads } = \frac{1}{2} \text{ or } 0.5 \text{ or } 50\%$$

Tossing a coin is a **random experiment** and the event of landing on heads is an outcome of that experiment. However, in this instance, we are calculating the probability without actually flipping the coin. The probability of the event (landing on heads) is being found *a priori* or prior to any coin-tossing experiment.

As we imagine tossing a coin, we are assuming the coin is **fair** meaning that it is equally likely to land on heads or tails after any toss. In this section, we can assume that all possible outcomes of an experiment are equally likely. In other words, every possible outcome has the same chance of happening.

Imagine we have 10 names written on separate pieces of paper and dropped in a hat. What does it mean to say that a name was drawn at **random** from the hat? In this context, *random* means that the paper has been mixed so that any of the 10 names has the same chance of being drawn. In general, all outcomes of a random experiment are equally likely to occur.

Classical Probability of an Event

If all outcomes of an experiment are equally likely to occur, then the probability of an event is the number of favorable outcomes (that result in the event occurring) divided by the number of possible outcomes.

$$\text{Probability an event} = \frac{\text{Number of favorable outcomes}}{\text{Number of possible outcomes}}$$

Letting E represent an event, the probability of an event can be denoted as $P(E)$. Or, we can write

$$P(E) = \frac{\text{Favorable}}{\text{Possible}}$$

The words *and*, *or*, and *not* are often used when finding the probability of an event. For example, your major area of study might have the following requirements:

- One course in math or science
- Freshman English I and Freshman English II
- Not less than 120 total credits

In the first bullet, the word *or* means that you could take either subject (math or science) or both to satisfy this requirement. The second bullet uses the word *and* to mean that both courses in English (Freshman English I and Freshman English II) must be taken. Finally, in the last bullet, *not* is used to mean that you cannot have less than 120 total credits if you want to graduate.

In general, given events E and F, we can use **and**, **or**, and **not** as follows:

- $P(E \text{ and } F)$: Denotes the probability that the event E **and** the event F both occur.
- $P(E \text{ or } F)$: Denotes the probability that the event E **or** the event F occurs **or** both occur.
- $P(\text{not } E)$: Denotes the probability that the event E does **not** occur.

In the Discovery Adventures for this section, you will use the classical approach to finding probabilities by applying the above formula to calculate the probability of an event *a priori*. The first adventure involves rolling one die.

Discovery Adventure 1: Rolling Die

Imagine rolling a single die (a cube with six faces numbered 1 to 6).

a. To use the classical probability formula, what assumptions must be made about the die?

_____

_____

b. How many outcomes are possible?

c. List the set of possible outcomes.

d. What is the probability of rolling a 5?

e. What is the probability of rolling a 5 or a 6?

f.   What is the probability of rolling an even number?

g.   What is the probability of rolling one of the following numbers: 1, 2, 3, 4, 5, or 6?

h.   Find $P(\text{number} = 7)$.

i.   Find $P(\text{number} > 3)$.

j.   Find $P(\text{number} \leq 2)$.

k.   Find $P(\text{number} \neq 3)$.

Feedback

The process of rolling a die has six possible outcomes: 1, 2, 3, 4, 5, or 6. We are assuming that the die is fair, meaning each of the six possible outcomes is equally likely to occur.

In part *d,* a favorable outcome is rolling a 5. Since there is one favorable outcome and six possible outcomes, we have

$$P(5) = \frac{\text{number of outcomes that result in 5}}{\text{number of possible outcomes}} = \frac{1}{6}$$

In part *e,* a favorable outcome is rolling a 5 or a 6. Since there are two favorable outcomes and six possible outcomes, we have

$$P(5 \text{ or } 6) = \frac{2}{6} = \frac{1}{3}$$

In part *f,* a favorable outcome is rolling an even number meaning 2, 4, or 6. Since there are three favorable outcomes and six possible outcomes, we have

$$P(\text{even}) = \frac{3}{6} = \frac{1}{2}$$

628

In part *g*, a favorable outcome is rolling one of the following numbers: 1, 2, 3, 4, 5, or 6. Since there are six favorable outcomes and six possible outcomes, we have

$$P(1 \text{ or } 2 \text{ or } 3 \text{ or } 4 \text{ or } 5 \text{ or } 6) = \frac{6}{6} = 1$$

Rolling one of the numbers: 1, 2, 3, 4, 5, or 6 must occur. Since, this event is certain to happen, it make sense that the probability is 1 or 100%.

In part *h*, there are no favorable outcomes because rolling a 7 is impossible. Therefore the probability of rolling a 7 is zero.

Our problem situation leads to the following facts about probability.

- $P(\text{event}) = 0$ indicates that an event cannot occur. In this case, there are no favorable outcomes.

- $P(\text{event}) = 1$ indicates that an event is certain to occur. In this case, every possible outcome is favorable.

- The probability of a particular event must be greater than or equal to zero and less than or equal to one. In symbols, we write $0 \leq P(\text{event}) \leq 1$.

The next Discovery Adventure will involve using a standard deck of playing cards. If you are not familiar with the rules of playing cards, then read the Brush Up feature below.

Brush Up on The Rules of Playing Cards

There are 52 cards in a standard deck of playing cards. The 52 cards are split up into four different "suits:" spades, hearts, diamonds, and clubs.

Each suit has 13 cards with ranks: 2, 3, 4, 5, 6, 7, 8, 9, 10, jack, queen, king, and ace (or 1). Since there are four suits, there are four cards of each rank. The jack, queen, and king are known as face cards.

There are 2 black colored suits (spades and clubs) and two red colored suits (hearts and diamonds).

Discovery Adventure 2: Pick a Card

Suppose you have deck of playing cards with one card selected at random. By *random*, we mean that any of the 52 cards has an equally likely chance of being drawn. Find the following probabilities for that one card.

a. What is the probability that the card drawn is an ace? $P(\text{ace}) =$

b. What is the probability that the card drawn is a jack or queen? $P(\text{jack or queen}) =$

c. What is the probability that the card drawn is a club? $P(\text{club}) =$

d. What is the probability that the card drawn is red? $P(\text{red}) =$

e. What is the probability that the card drawn is red or black? $P(\text{red or black}) =$

f. What is the probability that the card drawn is green? $P(\text{green}) =$

Feedback

There are 52 possible outcomes when selecting one card from a standard deck of playing cards. In part *a*, a favorable outcome includes an ace of spades, hearts, diamonds, or clubs. The probability of selecting an ace is calculated as follows.

$$P(\text{ace}) = \frac{\text{number of aces}}{\text{number of cards in deck}} = \frac{4}{52} = \frac{1}{13}$$

In part *b*, there are 8 possible outcomes since there are 4 jacks and 4 queens. The probability of selecting a jack or queen is

$$P(\text{jack or queen}) = \frac{8}{52} = \frac{2}{13}$$

In part *c*, there are 13 possible outcomes since each suit has 13 cards. The probability of selecting a club is

$$P(\text{club}) = \frac{13}{52} = \frac{1}{4}$$

In part *d*, there are 26 possible outcomes since there are two red suits, each with 13 cards. The probability of selecting a red card is

$$P(\text{red}) = \frac{26}{52} = \frac{1}{2}$$

In part *e*, there are 52 possible outcomes since all cards are red or black. The probability of selecting a red or black card is

$$P(\text{red or black}) = \frac{52}{52} = 1$$

In part *f*, there are 0 possible outcomes since there are only red and black suits. The probability of selecting a green card is

$$P(\text{green}) = \frac{0}{52} = 0$$

Earlier, in Math Talk, you considered the experiment of tossing a coin. There were only two possible outcomes, heads or tails. In the next Discovery Adventure, you will consider what happens when you toss a coin two consecutive times.

Discovery Adventure 3: Consecutive Flips

Suppose you flip a coin two consecutive times. Each flip can produce heads or tails. *Note*: A first flip of heads and second flip of tails should be considered as a different outcome than first flip of tails first and a second flip of heads.

a. How many outcomes are possible when you toss a coin two times in a row?

b. List all the possible outcomes denoting heads as H and tails as T.

c. What is the probability that you will toss one tails? *P*(exactly one tails) =

d. What is the probability that you will toss two heads? $P(\text{two heads}) =$

Feedback

In Discovery Adventure 3, if the first toss is heads, then the second toss could be heads or tails. Similarly, if the first toss is tails, then the second toss could be heads or tails.

Since each toss has two possible outcomes (H or T), two consecutive tosses must have $2 \cdot 2 = 4$ possible outcomes. This is an example of the **multiplication principle** which is defined on the next page.

Multiplication Principle

Suppose we have a sequence of two consecutive events. If the first event has m possible outcomes and the second event has n possible outcomes, then the sequence of two consecutive events has $m \cdot n$ possible outcomes.

In our example, the sequence of two consecutive events is tossing the coin two times in a row. The first toss has 2 possible outcomes and the second toss has 2 possible outcomes, implying that the sequence must have $2 \cdot 2 = 4$ possible outcomes. These 4 outcomes can be expressed as HH, HT, TH, and TT.

Since two of those outcomes contain exactly one tails result, we have

$$P(\text{exactly one tails}) = \frac{2}{4} = \frac{1}{2}$$

Also, since only one outcome contains two heads, we have

$$P(\text{two heads}) = \frac{1}{4}$$

Let's imagine another experiment: tossing a coin three consecutive times. Do you think the multiplication principle will hold for a sequence of three consecutive events?

Because there are 4 possible outcomes for two consecutive coin tosses and the third toss can be either heads or tails, we have 8 possible outcomes. This is consistent with the multiplication principle as shown below.

$$2 \cdot 2 \cdot 2 = 8$$

In general, the multiplication principle should hold for any sequence of events as long as each event is independent of all the others.

For example, suppose your job has a dress code for work. Listed below are items you own that would pass inspection at your work. How many possible ways can you arrange the pants, shirts, and shoes into different outfits to wear?

- Two pairs of pants
- Three shirts
- Two pairs of shoes

Since you are arranging each outfit from three groups of apparel (pants, shirts, and shoes), the total number of outfits is

$$2 \cdot 3 \cdot 2 = 12$$

You can visualize all the possibilities by using a tree diagram.

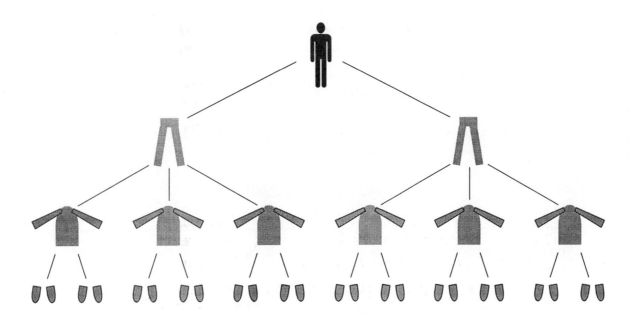

There are 2 ways to choose pants, and for each of those two ways, there are 3 ways to choose shirts. This means that there are $2 \cdot 3 = 6$ ways to choose pants and shirt. Then for each of the $2 \cdot 3 = 6$ ways to choose pants and shirt, there are 2 ways to choose shoes, so there are $2 \cdot 3 \cdot 2 = 12$ ways to choose an outfit. But would you consider all the outfits presentable to wear?

If you want to find all possible outfits, then selecting pants, shirts, and shoes are **independent events**. However, while there are 12 possible outfits to choose from, it is doubtful that all of them are suitable to wear together. For most of us, choosing a shirt depends on the selection of pants and vice-versa. The following definition will help you decide if certain events are independent of or dependent on each other.

Independent Events

Two events are *independent* if the outcome of one does not affect the outcome of the other. In general, events are independent if the occurrence or nonoccurrence of any one has no effect on any other.

The above definition is important because there is a convenient formula for calculating the probability of independent events occurring together (or consecutively).

Probability of Independent Events

If two independent events, A and B, have probabilities $P(A)$ and $P(B)$, then the probability that event A and B occur together (or consecutively) is

$$P(A \text{ and } B) = P(A) \cdot P(B)$$

This principle also applies to any number of independent events. For example, given independent events A, B, and C we have

$$P(A \text{ and } B \text{ and } C) = P(A) \cdot P(B) \cdot P(C)$$

Suppose you make three consecutive flips of a coin. Since flipping coins are independent events, the probability of flipping three heads can be calculated as follows:

$$P(Heads \text{ and } Heads \text{ and } Heads) = P(Heads) \cdot P(Heads) \cdot P(Heads)$$
$$= \frac{1}{2} \cdot \frac{1}{2} \cdot \frac{1}{2}$$
$$= \frac{1}{8}$$

Now suppose you want to know the probability of being dealt randomly two queens in succession from a deck of 52 cards. If you perform this experiment with replacement (first card is dealt, then placed back in the deck, and the deck is shuffled before the second card is dealt), then the dealing of each card is an independent event. Then you can apply the probability rule.

$$P(Queen \text{ and } Queen) = P(Queen) \cdot P(Queen)$$
$$= \frac{4}{52} \cdot \frac{4}{52}$$
$$= \frac{16}{2704} = \frac{1}{169}$$

However, if you deal two cards from a well-shuffled deck without replacement (first card is dealt, then the second card is dealt from the 51 remaining cards), then the second card is affected by the occurrence of the previous one. These events are dependent and the probability that you are dealt two queens in succession will be different from the calculation above.

The probability of getting a queen with the first card is the same as on the previous page, but the probability of getting a queen with the second card must account for only 51 cards remaining. Therefore, if the first card is a queen, only 3 queens remain. The probability of the second card being a queen, given that the first is a queen, is

$$P(queen \text{ given } queen \text{ on first card}) = \frac{3}{51}$$

Now the probability of being dealt two queens randomly in a row without replacement is

$$P(queen \text{ and } queen) = P(queen) \cdot P(queen \text{ given } queen \text{ on first card})$$

$$= \frac{4}{52} \cdot \frac{3}{51}$$

$$= \frac{12}{2652} = \frac{1}{221}$$

In general, we have the following rule for dependent events.

Probability of Dependent Events

Suppose two dependent events, E and F, have probabilities $P(E)$ and $P(F \mid E)$, read as "the probability of F given that E has already occurred." The probability that event E and F occur together (or consecutively) is

$$P(E \text{ and } F) = P(E) \cdot P(F \mid E)$$

In general, the probability that an event occurs, given that another event has already occurred is called **conditional probability**.

Conditional Probability

Conditional probability is the probability that an event will occur, given the condition that another event has already happened. Letting E and F be two events, the conditional probability that E will occur, given that F has already happened is denoted by

$$P(E \mid F)$$

and read "the probability of E given F". The vertical line stands for "given."

In the next Discovery Adventure, you will investigate the random experiment of throwing a pair of dice.

Discovery Adventure 4: Rolling Dice

Imagine you are playing a board game that requires rolling two dice to move around the board. Recall that a die is a cube with 6 faces numbering 1 through 6. In each part below, find the probability of rolling each sum with two dice.

a. Use the multiplication principle to calculate the number of possible outcomes for rolling two dice.

b. List all the possible outcomes of rolling two dice as ordered pairs in the table below. The first row has been done and serves as a model to complete the remaining ordered pairs. Note we have also included an outcome in the second row to make it clear that $(1, 2)$ and $(2, 1)$ are different outcomes.

$(1, 1)$	$(1, 2)$	$(1, 3)$	$(1, 4)$	$(1, 5)$	$(1, 6)$
$(2, 1)$					

c. Find the probability of rolling a sum of 8 with two dice.

$$P(\text{sum} = 8) =$$

d. Find the probability of rolling a sum of less than or equal to 3 with two dice.

$$P(\text{sum} \leq 3) =$$

e. Find the probability of rolling a sum of greater than 12 with two dice.

$$P(\text{sum} > 12) =$$

Feedback

When rolling a die, there are 6 possible outcomes. If you roll a pair of dice, it is the same as rolling a die two consecutive times. Therefore, there are $6 \cdot 6 = 36$ possible outcomes to rolling a pair of dice. So in part c of Discovery Adventure 4, the probability of rolling a sum of 8 is calculated as follows:

$$P(\text{sum} = 8) = \frac{\text{Number of outcomes resulting in 8}}{\text{Number of possible outcomes}} = \frac{5}{36}$$

In part d, there are three outcomes whose sum is less than or equal to 3. The outcomes are as follows.

$$(1,\ 1),\ (1,2),\ (2,1)$$

Hence, the probability is

$$P(\text{sum} \leq 3) = \frac{3}{36} = \frac{1}{12}$$

In part e, since there is no way to roll a pair of dice and obtain a sum greater than 12, the probability is zero.

Section Exercises: 8.1

1. Suppose 1000 raffle tickets are sold in a contest where the winner will receive a brand new car. One winning ticket will be selected at random from the 1000 tickets entered.

   a. What does the word *random* mean in the problem situation above?

   _____

   _____

   _____

   b. What is the probability of drawing a particular ticket?

   c. If Jason has purchased 50 of the 1000 tickets, then what is the probability that he has the winning ticket?

2. In Discovery Adventure 4, we looked at all possible outcomes for throwing two dice. Refer to the table of possible outcomes that you constructed (p. 636) to help answer the parts below.

   a. In part *c* of Discovery Adventure 4, you found the probability of rolling a sum of 8 with two dice. Find the probability of all other sums and organize your answers in the probability distribution table below.

Sum	2	3	4	5	6	7	8	9	10	11	12
Probability							$\dfrac{5}{36}$				

   b. If you add all the probabilities in the above distribution, what is the total probability?

   c. Explain how you could find the answer to part *b* without completing any calculations.

   _____

   _____

   _____

d. Suppose you are playing a game in which the goal is to guess the sum of rolling two dice. What sum should you guess to have the best chance of winning (guessing correctly)? Explain.

_____

_____

_____

3. Suppose you toss a coin and roll a die.

    a. Use the multiplication principle to calculate the number of possible outcomes for tossing a coin and rolling a die.

    b. Using the letters H and T to represent the heads and tails of the coin and the numbers 1, 2, 3, 4, 5, and 6 for the six faces of the die, list all possible outcomes.

    c. Find the probability of tossing tails _and_ rolling a six. $P(\text{tails and } 6) =$

    d. Find the probability of tossing tails _or_ rolling a six. $P(\text{tails or } 6) =$

    e. Find the probability of tossing tails _and_ rolling an odd number. $P(\text{tails and odd}) =$

    f. Find the probability of tossing tails _or_ rolling an odd number. $P(\text{tails or odd}) =$

    g. Find the probability of tossing heads _and_ tails. $P(\text{heads and tails}) =$

    h. Find the probability of tossing heads _or_ tails. $P(\text{heads or tails}) =$

4. Imagine you have a bag of hard candy that contains 9 cherries, 12 lemons, and 15 limes. Find the following probabilities assuming that you randomly select one piece of candy.

   a. $P(\text{cherry}) =$

   b. $P(\text{lemon}) =$

   c. $P(\text{lime}) =$

   d. $P(\text{not lemon}) =$

5. People who visit a casino often play a game of chance called *roulette*. The game involves a spin of the wheel, followed by a dropped ball, which randomly falls into one of 38 pockets. One pocket is marked zero, another double zero, and the remaining pockets are numbered from 1 to 36. The odd-numbered pockets from 1 to 35 are red, and the even-numbered pockets from 2 to 36 are black. The 2 remaining pockets are green. Find the following probabilities of the ball falling at random into the specified pocket.

   a. $P(\text{black}) =$

   b. $P(\text{double zero}) =$

   c. $P(\text{not green}) =$

   d. $P(\text{black and red}) =$

   e. $P(\text{black or red}) =$

   f.   What is the connection between parts *c* and *e*? Explain.

   _____

   _____

6. Suppose a couple wants to have three children. Assume that all possible outcomes are equally likely to occur.

   a. Letting G represent a girl and B a boy, construct a tree diagram to show the possible outcomes for a family of three children.

	First Child	Second Child	Third Child

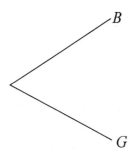

   b. List all the possible outcomes from having three children in the first row of the table below. In the second row, list the number of girls in each outcome.

Outcome	BBB							
Number of Girls	0							

   c. In the following table, complete the probability distribution for the number of girls that the couple might have. List each probability as a decimal number.

Event	0 Girls	1 Girl	2 Girls	3 Girls
Probability				

d. Construct a histogram of the distribution in part *c*.

7. Refer to Section Exercise #6 as you complete the following parts.

    a. If the couple has one child, then list the number of outcomes for 0 girls and 1 girl.

    b. If the couple has two children, then list the number of outcomes for 0 girls, 1 girl and 2 girls.

    c. If the couple has three children, then list the number of outcomes for 0 girls, 1 girl, 2 girls and 3 girls.

    d. The answers for *a*, *b*, and *c* are arranged below as rows 2, 3, and 4 of a triangle. Complete rows 1, 5, and 6 by following the numerical patterns in the triangle.

                                                    ___

    1 Child   1   1

    2 Children   1   2   1

    3 Children   1   3   3   1

    4 Children   ___   ___   ___   ___   ___

    5 Children ___   ___   ___   ___   ___   ___

e. Use the values for 4 children to find the following probabilities of each number of girls possible in a family with 4 children.

$P(G=0) =$ $P(G=1) =$ $P(G=2) =$ $P(G=3) =$ $P(G=4) =$

f. Use the values for 5 children to find the following probabilities in a family with 5 children.

What is the probability of having . . .

- Exactly 2 girls? $P(G=2) =$

- 2 or more girls? $P(G \geq 2) =$

8. Suppose you are in a class of 35 students that includes 10 business majors, 15 arts and sciences majors, 7 education majors, and 3 nursing majors.

a. If a student is selected at random from this class, what is the probability that the student is an education major?

b. If a student is selected at random from this class, what is the probability that the student is an arts and science major?

c. If a student is selected at random from this class, what is the probability that the student is not a nursing major?

d. If a student is selected at random from this class, what is the probability that the student is a business major or an arts and science major?

9. A college has 150 students participating in the band. The band is made up of 66 males and 84 females. Suppose a band member is selected at random.

a. What is the probability that the musician is a female?

b. What is the probability that the musician is a male?

c. What is the probability that the musician is a female or a male?

d. What is the probability that the musician is not a female or a male?

10. Suppose you are taking a True or False quiz that contains three questions. For each question, you have selected an answer randomly without reading the question.

a. Construct a tree diagram to show all the possible ways you could have answered the three questions.

b. List each outcome from part *a*, using T for a true answer and F for a false answer.

c. Complete the following distribution to show the probabilities of obtaining correct answers.

Number Correct	0	1	2	3
Probability				

d. What is the probability of getting all three questions correct?

e. What is the probability of getting two or more questions correct?

Section 8.2 Probability Act II: An Empirical Approach

Math Talk

In the last section, you investigated *classical probability*, which assumed that all outcomes of an experiment are equally likely to occur. For example, tossing a fair coin is an experiment that has two possible outcomes (heads or tails), and each outcome is equally likely to happen. The probability of heads is $\frac{1}{2}$ or 0.5, and the probability of tails is $\frac{1}{2}$ or 0.5. You calculate the classical probability as

$$P(\text{heads}) = \frac{\text{Number of favorable outcomes}}{\text{Number of possible outcomes}} = \frac{1}{2} = 0.5$$

In this case, you are calculating the probability *a priori*, before actually performing the experiment of tossing the coin. So if you toss a coin 100 times, should you expect it to land on heads 50 times?

The **empirical probability** of an event is found by observing the outcomes of an experiment that is repeated many times. It is calculated as

$$\text{Probability of an event} = \frac{\text{Number of times the event occurs}}{\text{Total number of times the experiment is repeated}}$$

For example, if you actually toss a coin 100 times and it lands on heads 45 times, then the empirical probability of obtaining heads is calculated as

$$P(\text{heads}) = \frac{\text{Number of heads}}{\text{Number of coin tosses}} = \frac{45}{100} = 0.45$$

This is an estimated probability based on the experiment being repeated again and again. Since the relative frequency of the event (landing on heads) is found by repeating the experiment (tossing the coin), the probability may change each time 100 coins are flipped. When approximating probability by relative frequency, the more times that the experiment is repeated, the closer the probability is to the actual probability of the event. This theory is known as the **Law of Large Numbers**.

Law of Large Numbers

The relative frequency of occurrence of an event approaches the actual or classical probability of that event as the number of observations (or experiments) gets larger and larger.

Empirical Probability of an Event

In general, if an experiment can be repeated, then the probability of an event is the proportion of occurrences of the event in the long run (after a very long number of repetitions). If an experiment is repeated n times and event E is observed to occur with frequency f times, then we have the following formula for calculating empirical probabilities:

$$\text{Probability of an event} = \frac{\text{Frequency of the event occurring}}{\text{Number of repetitions of the experiment}}$$

$$P(E) = \frac{f}{n}$$

Discovery Adventure 1: Quality Control

Suppose you are in charge of quality control at a plant that manufactures cell phones. As the phones come off the assembly line, they must be periodically checked for defects. You randomly select 200 cell phones for inspection and find that 5 have defects.

a. Construct a frequency and relative frequency distribution that shows the results of inspecting $n = 200$ phones for defects. State the relative frequency in both fraction and decimal form.

Cell Phone	Frequency f	Relative Frequency $\frac{f}{n}$
Defective		
Good		
Total		

b. If you randomly select a cell phone from the assembly line, then what is the probability that it is defective? What is the probability that the cell phone is good?

$$P(\text{defective}) = \qquad\qquad P(\text{good}) =$$

c. Why must the sum of the two probabilities in part *b* add up to 1?

_____

_____

d. If you symbolize the event of selecting a defect as D and the probability of that event occurring as $P(D)$, then how would you use the word *not* to represent the probability that the cell phone is good?

e. Explain why the relative frequencies of good and defective cell phones are not exact probabilities but approximate probabilities.

_____

_____

_____

_____

f. If you randomly selected $n = 400$ cell phones, do you expect the probabilities: $P(\text{defective})$ and $P(\text{good})$ to be the same as the results of part *b*? Explain.

_____

_____

_____

g. What will happen to all the previous calculations of relative frequencies if you continue to increase the size of n (number of phones inspected)?

_____

_____

_____

Feedback

The Discovery Adventure above is a good example of approximating probability by relative frequency. The experiment involves randomly choosing a cell phone from the assembly line for inspection. The two possible outcomes are that the cell phone was defective or not defective (good). You cannot find the probability of randomly selecting a defective cell phone by using the classical definition because the outcomes of the experiment are not equally likely. Instead, you repetitively performed the same experiment of inspecting a random cell phone from the assembly line.

The probability of selecting a defect could then be calculated using the empirical probability of an event E.

$$P(E) = \frac{f}{n}$$

$$P(\text{defective}) = \frac{5}{200} = \frac{1}{40} = 0.025$$

This means that about 1 out of every 40 cell phones coming off the assembly line are defective. As a percent you could say, the next randomly selected cell phone has a 2.5% chance of being defective.

The probability of not selecting a defective cell phone is equivalent to the probability that the randomly chosen phone is good.

$$P(\textit{not} \text{ defective}) = P(\text{good}) = \frac{195}{200} = \frac{39}{40} = 0.975$$

Therefore, you can state that 39 out of 40 phones being manufactured are good or 97.5 percent are not defective.

When symbolizing the event of selecting a defect as D and the probability of that event occurring as $P(D)$, then the probability that the cell phone is not defective or good can be expressed as

$$P(\textit{not } D) = 1 - P(D)$$
$$= 1 - 0.025$$
$$= 0.975$$

Complement of an Event

In general, for any event E, the event *not E* is called the *complement* of E. The probability of the complement of E is calculated using the following formula:

$$P(\textit{not } E) = 1 - P(E)$$

How can you rewrite this formula to state that the sum of the probabilities that event E occurs and does *not* occur is 1 or 100%?

$$P(E) + P(\textit{not } E) = 1$$

In Discovery Adventure 1, the random experiment inspected each cell phone for defects and the possible outcomes consisted of the phone being evaluated as good or defective. The 200 cell phones that were selected randomly are called the *sample* of the population of all cell phones manufactured at the plant. As the size of the sample increases, the law of large numbers says that the relative frequency approaches the actual or classical probability.

If it was possible to inspect every cell phone being manufactured at this plant, then calculating the relative frequency would produce the actual probability of any given phone being defective.

Defining Population and Sample

- A **population** is all the items we are interested in studying.
- A **sample** is part of a population.
- A **random sample** is a sample in which every item in the population has the same chance of being selected for the sample.
- A **sample space** for a random experiment is the set of all possible outcomes.

Relative Frequency of a Population vs. a Sample

In general, if given the entire population, then the relative frequency will calculate the actual or classical probability of an event. When a random sample is selected from the population, then the relative frequency is an approximation of the actual probability.

Discovery Adventure 2: Survey Says

Suppose a random sample of 1000 students from state colleges throughout the United States produced the following results on coffee consumption. Assume that one student is selected randomly from these 1000 students.

Cups of Coffee per day	Frequency	Relative Frequency
0	90	
1	220	
2	350	
3	170	
4	110	
5 or more	60	

a. Complete the table by finding the relative frequencies in the last column.

b. Does this situation allow you to use the classical approach to probability? Explain.

_____

_____

c. Find the probability that this student drinks coffee.

d. Find the probability that this student does not drink coffee.

e. Does the total sum of the probabilities in parts *c* and *d* equal 1? Explain.

_____

_____

f. Find the probability that this student drinks exactly two cups of coffee.

g. Find the probability that this student drinks two or more cups of coffee.

h. Find the complement of the event in part *g*.

Feedback

To use the ideas of classical probability, all the outcomes of an experiment must be equally likely to occur. In this situation the experiment is asking, how many cups of coffee a student consumes per day. The survey allows 6 possible outcomes in answering this question: 0, 1, 2, 3, 4, or 5 or more. Since all these outcomes are not equally likely we must take an empirical approach to computing probabilities of events.

The empirical approach to probability involves finding the relative frequency of each outcome. Recall that the relative frequency is calculated by dividing the frequency by the number of things in the sample. For example, the relative frequency that a student drinks exactly two cups of coffee is calculated as follows.

$$P(2 \text{ cups}) = \frac{350}{1000} = 0.35$$

Therefore, according to this survey, a little more than $\frac{1}{3}$ of state college students drink two cups of coffee per day.

If this experiment is repeated with another random sample of 1000 state college students, the empirical probabilities may be different. But the difference should be minimal, since the sample size is large.

The probability that a student drinks 2 or more cups of coffee can be computed by adding all the frequencies of drinking 2, 3, 4, and 5 or more cups and then dividing that total by 1000.

$$P(2 \text{ or more}) = \frac{350 + 170 + 110 + 60}{1000} = \frac{690}{1000} = 0.69$$

Another equivalent approach is to sum the relative frequencies of the last 4 outcomes in the table.

$$P(2 \text{ or more}) = P(2) + P(3) + P(4) + P(5 \text{ or more})$$
$$= \frac{350}{1000} + \frac{170}{1000} + \frac{110}{1000} + \frac{60}{1000}$$
$$= 0.35 + 0.17 + 0.11 + 0.06$$
$$= 0.69$$

So, based on this survey, about 70% of state college students drink 2 or more cups of coffee per day.

The complement of the event in part *g* is

$$P(not \text{ 2 or more}) = 1 - P(2 \text{ or more})$$
$$= 1 - 0.69$$
$$= 0.31$$

Therefore, about 30% of state college students drink less than two cups per day.

The exercises on the next page will allow you to further explore the ideas of empirical probability.

Section Exercises: 8.2

1. Match the numerical probability of the following events with the verbal statement that best describes it.

$$P(A) = 0, \quad P(B) = 0.05, \quad P(C) = 0.50, \quad P(D) = 0.95, \quad P(E) = 1$$

a. I am certain this event will happen.

b. There is a very slight chance that this event will occur.

c. This event has the same chance of happening as its complement.

d. There is a strong likelihood that this event will occur.

e. This event cannot occur under any circumstance.

2. Flip a coin 20 times and record the number of times that it lands on heads.

a. Are you certain to result in 10 heads? Explain.

_____

_____

_____

b. If you flip the same coin 200 times, would you expect the relative frequency of heads to be closer to the classical probability of obtaining heads *a priori*? Explain.

_____

_____

_____

3. The U.S. Bureau of the Census has made the following projections of total U.S. population by age for the year 2050. The total population is projected to be 393,929,000. (These projections are based on middle series data.)

Age (years)	Population	Relative Frequency
Under 5	27,106,000	
5–13	47,804,000	
14–17	21,207,000	
18–24	36,333,000	
25–34	49,365,000	
35–44	47,393,000	
45–54	43,494,000	
55–64	42,368,000	
65–84	60,636,000	
85–99	17,389,000	
100 and up	834,000	

a. Complete the table by finding the relative frequencies in the last column. Round to the thousandths place.

b. Imagine that one person is randomly selected from the U.S. population in the year 2050. What is the probability this person is 65 years or older?

c. Compare your answer to part b with the other relative frequencies in the table and then explain the importance of these projections in terms of preparing the country for the future.

_____

_____

_____

_____

_____

4. Suppose a survey was given to 100 randomly selected students at the local community college. The students were asked whether they are in favor or against a salary increase for the top administrators at the college. The results of responses by men and women to this question are given in the two-way classification table below.

	In Favor	Against
Women	10	50
Men	5	35

a. What does the number 10 (row 2/column2 cell) indicate about this problem situation?

_____

_____

_____

b. Each of the 4 cells contains a data value giving two characteristics. Explain what these two characteristics tell you about the problem situation?

_____

_____

_____

c. Insert the proper totals into the five new cells we have added to the previous table.

	In Favor	Against	Total
Women	10	50	
Men	5	35	
Total			

d. Find the probability that a randomly selected student is a man.

e. Find the probability that a randomly selected student is a woman.

f. Find the probability that a randomly selected student is in favor of the raises.

g. Find the probability that a randomly selected student is not in favor of the raises.

5. Let's take an in-depth look at the situation in Exercise 4. We will explore the concept of **conditional probability** as defined below.

Conditional Probability

Conditional probability is the probability that an event will occur, given the condition that another event has already happened. Letting E and F be two events, the conditional probability that E will occur, given that F has already happened is denoted by

$$P(E \mid F)$$

and read as "the probability of E given F". The vertical line stands for "given."

---

a. Place the results from Section Exercise #4, parts $d - g$, (previous page) along the bottom and right side of the table below. Note that we are representing "in favor" as event V, "against" as event A, women as event W, and men as event M.

	In Favor (V)	Against (A)	Total
Women (W)	10	50	
Men (M)	5	35	
Total			

$P(V) = \qquad P(A) =$

$P(W) =$

$P(M) =$

b. Next suppose we randomly select one male student from the 100 students in the sample. Find the probability that the student selected is in favor of the raises given that the student is a man. *Hint:* Since you know the student is a man, consider just the values in the second row labeled, "Male (M)."

$$P(V \mid M) =$$

c. Find the conditional probability that the student selected is in favor of the raises given that the student is a woman. *Hint:* Consider just the sample of women in row 1.

$$P(V \mid W) =$$

d. Although the overwhelming majority of students are against the raises, which gender has the higher proportion of students in favor of the raises?

655

6. Let's take another look at the situation in Section Exercise #4. This time you will investigate what to expect from the whole student body of 5000 students, based on the probabilities already found. In parts *a* – *d*, you only need to refer to Section Exercise #4 (p. 654). In parts *e* and *f*, you need to refer to Section Exercise #5 (p. 655).

   a. How many of the 5000 students do you expect to favor the raise?

   b. How many of the 5000 students do you expect to be against the raise?

   c. How many of the 5000 students do you expect to be women?

   d. How many of the 5000 students do you expect to be men?

   e. How many of the 5000 students do you expect to favor the raise given that the student is known to be a woman?

   f. How many of the 5000 students do you expect to favor the raise given that the student is known to be a man?

7. The table below gives the racial background of 100 students selected randomly at the local community college.

Race	Frequency	Relative Frequency
Native American	1	
Black	14	
White	72	
Asian	7	
Other	6	

   a. Complete the table by finding the relative frequencies in the last column.

b. What is the probability that a randomly selected student is black?

c. What is the probability that a randomly selected student is not white?

d. What is the probability that a randomly selected student is Asian or Native American?

8. According to the U.S. Bureau of Census, in 1998 there were about 34.5 million people living below the poverty level in United States out of a total population of about 270.3 million people.

   a. What is the probability that a randomly selected person in the U.S. is living below the poverty level?

   b. Of the total 34.5 million poor, 9.1 million are black. What is the probability that a randomly selected poor person is black?

   c. The total population of black people in 1998 was about 34.4 million. What is the probability that a randomly selected person in the U.S. is black?

   d. What is the probability that a randomly selected black person in the U.S. is poor?

   e. Explain why the result to part *d* is can be called conditional probability.

   _____

   _____

   _____

   _____

9. Two events are **mutually exclusive** if they cannot occur together. Suppose there are two students running for student president at Big State College. Suppose A represents an event that a student plans to trigger votes for candidate A in the election and B is the event that a student plans to get votes for candidate B.

a. Are events A and B mutually exclusive? Explain.

_____

_____

_____

One day before the election a poll was taken of 100 students asking which candidate they would vote for on Election Day. The results of the poll are given in the table below.

	Votes for A	Votes for B
Women (W)	35	25
Men (M)	18	22

b. Based on the poll, if a student from the college is selected at random, find the following probabilities.

$P(A) =$ $\qquad\qquad\qquad\qquad$ $P(B) =$

c. Based on the poll, if a female student is selected at random, find the following conditional probabilities.

$P(A|W) =$ $\qquad\qquad\qquad\qquad$ $P(B|W) =$

d. Based on the poll, if a male student is selected at random, find the following conditional probabilities.

$P(A|M) =$ $\qquad\qquad\qquad\qquad$ $P(B|M) =$

10. Suppose there are 200 men and 200 women that have full-time faculty positions at the local community college. Of these faculty members, there are 40 men and 10 women teaching in the math-science division

    a. What is the probability that a randomly selected full-time faculty member is a woman?

    b. What is the probability that a randomly selected full-time faculty member is a math-science division member?

    c. What is the probability that a randomly selected full-time faculty member (women only) is in the math-science division?

    d. What is the probability that a full-time faculty member (men only) selected at random is part of the math-science division?

    e. What is the probability that a full-time math-science division member selected at random is a woman?

Chapter 8 Summary

Key Terms

Section 8.1

- **Classical Probability** – Using probability theory to arrive at valid results prior to performing any observation or experiment.
- **Probability** – The likelihood that a chance event will occur.
- **Random Experiment** – The process of observing the outcome of a chance event.
- **Fair** – An experiment or game is *fair* if every possible outcome has the same chance of happening.
- **Random** – An item is selected at random from a collection if all the items in the collection have the same chance of being chosen.
- **Classical Probability of an Event** – If all outcomes are equally likely, then the probability of an event occurring can be calculated using the following formula:
$$\text{Probability an event} = \frac{\text{Number of favorable outcomes}}{\text{Number of possible outcomes}}$$
- **And** – The probability of events *E and F* indicates the chance of both events happening.
- **Or** – The probability of events *E or F* indicates the chance of either event happening or both.
- **Not** – The probability of *not E* indicates the chance that event *E* does not occur.
  Multiplication Principle – If a first event has *m* possible outcomes and a second event has *n* possible outcomes, then the sequence of both events has $m \cdot n$ possible outcomes.
- **Independent Events** – Two events are *independent* if the outcome of one does not affect the outcome of the other. In general, two events are independent if the occurrence or nonoccurrence of either one has no effect on the other.
- **Probability of Independent Events** – If two independent events, *A* and *B*, have probabilities $P(A)$ and $P(B)$, then the probability that event *A* and *B* occur together (or consecutively) is
$$P(A \text{ and } B) = P(A) \cdot P(B)$$
- **Probability of Dependent Events** – If two dependent events, *E* and *F*, have probabilities $P(E)$ and $P(F \mid E)$, read as "the probability of *F* given that *E* has already occurred," then the probability that event *E* and *F* occur together (or consecutively) is
$$P(E \text{ and } F) = P(E) \cdot P(F \mid E)$$
- **Conditional Probability** – The probability that an event will occur, given the condition that another event has already happened. Letting *E* and *F* be two events, the conditional probability that *E* will occur, given that *F* has already happened is denoted by
$$P(E \mid F)$$
and read, "the probability of *E* given *F*."

Section 8.2

- **Empirical Probability** – The *empirical probability* of an event is found by observing the outcomes of an experiment that is repeated many times. It is calculated as

$$\text{Probability of an event} = \frac{\text{Frequency of the event occurring}}{\text{Number of repetitions of the experiment}}$$

- **Law of Large Numbers** – The relative frequency of occurrence of an event approaches the actual or classical probability of that event as the number of observations (or experiments) gets larger and larger.

- **Complement of an Event** – In general, for any event E, the event *not E* is called the complement of E. The probability of the complement of E is calculated using the following formula.

$$P\left(not\ E\right) = 1 - P\left(E\right)$$

- **Population** – A *population* is all the items we are interested in studying.
- **Sample** – A *sample* is part of a population.
- **Random Sample** – A sample in which every item in the population has the same chance of being selected for the sample.
- **Sample Space** – The set of all possible outcomes for a random experiment.
- **Mutually Exclusive** – Two events are *mutually exclusive* if they cannot occur together.

****

Questions for Review

1. If asked to find the probability of an event, how do you decide whether to use a *classical* or *empirical* approach? For example, in each of the following situations, decide on the correct approach and apply this approach to answering the question.

   a. Suppose you buy a lottery ticket by selecting 6 different numbers between 1 and 49 and want to know the probability of matching the winning numbers that are picked at random by the State Lottery Commission. If you know that there are 14 million six number combinations that have the same chance of being picked, then find the probability of your ticket winning the lottery game.

b. Suppose there are 1000 families that live in your hometown. A random sample of 64 families in the town reveals that 36 have two children. If one family is selected at random from the 1000, then what is the probability the family has two children?

c. Suppose you are playing a board game that requires you to spin a wheel to decide how many spaces to move. The spinner has an equally likely chance of landing on any of the six positions numbered 1, 2, 3, 4, 5, and 6. If you spin the wheel, what is the probability that the spinner stops at the number 6 position?

d. Suppose a fast food restaurant has just introduced at new item called the "Monster Burger." Each customer who wants to order a burger can now choose between the regular burger and the monster burger. Yesterday the restaurant sold 1400 regular burgers and 600 monster burgers. If a random customer orders a burger from this restaurant, what is the probability that it will be the monster burger?

2. Can you find probabilities that involve the words, *and*, *or*, and *not*?

For example, imagine you must spin a wheel to move around a board game. The wheel has an equally likely chance of stopping on any of the 6 positions numbered 1, 2, 3, 4, 5, and 6. Find the following probabilities.

a. $P(2 \text{ or } 4) =$

b. $P(2 \text{ and } 4) =$

c. $P(\text{not } 2) =$

3. Do you know how to apply the multiplication principle?

For example, suppose you are invited to a wedding and have the following choices to make:

Appetizer: Clam Chowder or Caesar Salad

Main course: Chicken, Salmon, or Lasagna

Dessert: Mud Pie, Cheesecake, or Spumoni

a. How many possible ways can you choose an appetizer and main course?

b. How many possible ways can you choose an appetizer, main course, and dessert?

c. Construct a tree diagram that shows each 3-course meal that you can possibly select.

4. Can you decide if two events are independent of each other?

For example, in each situation below, state whether the two events are *independent* or *dependent* and explain your reasoning.

a. Suppose a card is dealt at random from a standard deck of 52 cards. The type of card is recorded and then replaced back in the deck. After the cards have been shuffled, another card is dealt at random from the same deck of 52 cards.

_____

_____

_____

b. Suppose we repeat the situation above without replacement. After the first card is dealt, it is not returned to the deck, and the second card is being dealt from the 51 remaining cards.

_____

_____

_____

5. Do you know how to find the probability of successive events? In other words, given events A and B, how do you find $P(A \text{ and } B)$?

For example, let's return to the two situations in Question #4. Suppose we want to know the probability of being dealt two aces in succession.

a. What is the probability of being dealt two successive aces with replacement? *Hint:* An experiment performed with replacement will result in independent events. If we name those events A and B, then $P(A \text{ and } B) = P(A) \cdot P(B)$.

b. What is the probability of being dealt two successive aces without replacement? *Hint:* An experiment performed without replacement will result in dependent events. If we name those dependent events A and B, then $P(A \text{ and } B) = P(A) \cdot P(B \mid A)$, where $P(B \mid A)$ means the conditional probability of B given that A has already occurred.

6. What important connection does the law of large numbers make between exact probability and relative frequencies? For example, suppose a major league baseball player has 130 hits in 520 times at bat.

a. Find the player's batting average which is calculated as the relative frequency of getting a hit each time,

$$\text{Probability of a hit} = \frac{\text{hits}}{\text{times at bat}}$$

b. A 0.25 batting average means the probability of getting a hit is $\frac{1}{4}$. Does this imply that the player will get 1 hit every 4 times at bat? Explain your reasoning using the law of large numbers.

_____

_____

_____

_____

7. How do you calculate the complement of an event?

   For example, in a college with 2000 students, a random sample of 100 students reveals that 60 think they receive too much homework, 30 think they receive a fair amount, and 10 think that they receive too little.

   a. If A is the event that a student believes they get too much homework, then write the complement of A using a complete sentence.

   _____

   _____

   _____

   b. What is the probability of A?

   c. What is the probability of the complement of A?

Chapter 8 Quiz

1. Suppose you are about to toss a coin two consecutive times.

    a. Draw a tree diagram that illustrates all the possible results of the two coin tosses.

    b. If we denote heads as H and tails as T, then use this notation to list all possible outcomes.

    c. What is the probability that both coins land on heads?

    d. In words, write the complement of the event in part *c*.

    e. What is the probability of the complement found in part *d*?

2. Suppose you toss a coin 100 times with the results given in the table below.

Outcomes	Frequency	Relative Frequency
Heads	42	
Tails	58	

    a. Complete the last column by finding the relative frequencies.

    b. The classical probability of tossing a fair coin and having it land on heads is 1/2 or 0.5. Why is this result different from the relative frequency of resulting in heads as in part *a*? Explain.

    _____

    _____

   c. What does the law of large numbers tell you about repeating this coin-tossing experiment a larger number of times? Explain using complete sentences.

_____

_____

_____

3. Instant Alert manufactures all of its pagers at plant *A* or plant *B*. Plant *A* manufactures 70% of the pagers and finds that 5% are defective. However, only 3% of the pagers manufactured at plant *B* are defective. Find all the probabilities in the tree diagram using the directions in parts *a* and *b* below.

   a. Let *A* and *B* be the events that a pager is manufactured at plants *A* and *B* respectively. Starting at the left side of the tree, fill in the probability that a pager selected at random came from plant *A*. Do the same with plant *B*.

   b. Let *D* and *N* be the events that a pager is defective and not defective respectively. Find the following conditional probabilities and place the results in the proper place in the tree diagram below.

- The probability that a randomly selected pager is defective given that it came from plant *A*.
- The probability that a randomly selected pager is not defective given that it came from plant *A*.
- The probability that a randomly selected pager is defective given that it came from plant *B*.
- The probability that a randomly selected pager is not defective given that it came from plant *B*.

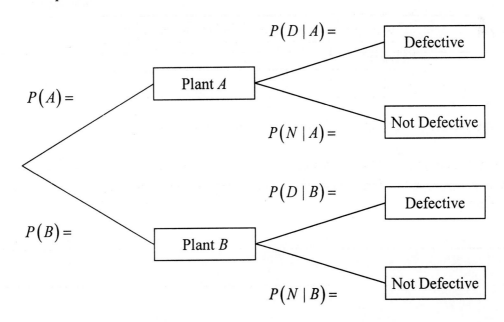

4. Now return to the last situation in Quiz problem #3 to calculate the probability of dependent events occurring together (or consecutively). Use the following formula to find the probability of the dependent events in parts $a - d$.

The probability that event E and F occur together (or consecutively) is

$$P(E \text{ and } F) = P(E) \cdot P(F \mid E)$$

a. Find the probability that a pager came from plant A and is defective.

$$P(A \text{ and } D) =$$

b. Find the probability that a pager came from plant A and is not defective.

$$P(A \text{ and } N) =$$

c. Find the probability that a pager came from plant B and is defective.

$$P(B \text{ and } D) =$$

d. Find the probability that a pager came from plant B and is not defective.

$$P(B \text{ and } N) =$$

e. Explain why the sum of all the probabilities in parts $a - d$ must add up to 1.

_____

_____

_____

Cumulative Review: Chapters 7 and 8

Many people who live on a particular street near the high school have complained to the local police that during school days from 2:45 to 3:00 p.m. motorists are going too fast along their street. The posted speed limit is 35 mph. The police attempt to verify this claim by having an officer record the speeds of vehicles with a laser gun during the above time frame. The results from a typical school day are given in the table below (in mph).

34	40	46	40	27	35	62	44	38	45	37
69	68	30	39	43	51	36	67	36	65	64
32	36	41	48	35	29	47	32	63	43	33

1. Complete the frequency and relative frequency distribution that has been started below.

Class Interval (speed in mph)	Frequency (vehicles)	Relative Frequency
24.5 – 29.5	2	0.06
29.5 – 34.5		
34.5 – 39.5		

2. Complete drawing the following histogram of the frequency distribution in Exercise #1.

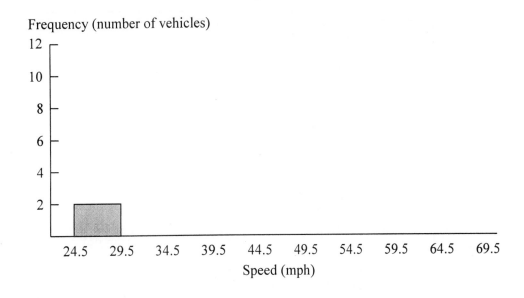

669

3. Complete drawing the following histogram of the relative frequency distribution in Exercise #1.

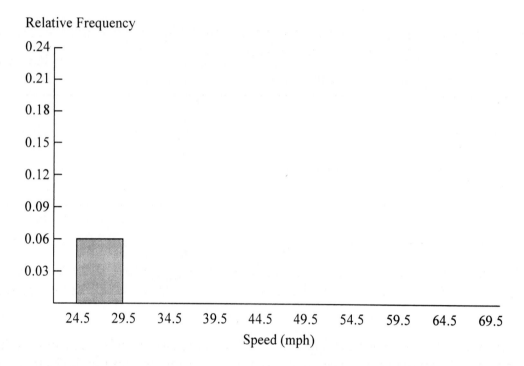

4. Explain what the frequency and relative frequency distributions tell you about the speed of vehicles along this certain street during the time immediately after school lets out.

_____

_____

_____

_____

5. Find the mean and standard deviation of the speed data.

6. Find the five-number summary of the speed data.

7. Find the range and the interquartile range of the speed data.

8. Which gives you more information about center and spread of the speed data: the mean and standard deviation, the five-number summary, or neither? Explain.

_____

_____

_____

_____

_____

9. Find the probability that a vehicle selected at random during a typical school day from 2:45 – 3:00 p.m. will be traveling at a speed that is within 5 mph of the speed limit (30 to 39 mph).

10. Find the probability that a vehicle selected at random during a typical school day from 2:45 – 3:00 p.m. will be traveling at a speed that is within 10 mph of the speed limit (25 to 44 mph).

11. Find the probability that a vehicle selected at random during a typical school day from 2:45 – 3:00 p.m. will be traveling at a speed between 60 and 70 mph.

12. Find the complement of the probability in Exercise #11 and explain what it means.

_____

_____

13. If you were the police officer writing a report to your superior on this situation, what would you say?

_____

_____

_____

_____

Section Exercises: 1.1

1 *a.* answers may vary
   b. 1 person gives 0 introductions
   c. 2 people give 1 introduction
   d. 3 people give 3 introductions
   e. 4 people give 6 introductions
   f. answers may vary
   g. answers may vary
   h. answers may vary

3 *a.* answers may vary
   b. answers may vary, but
         Deluxe package +1 8 x 10 + 7 Wallet
         =$50

5 *a.* 2160 calories
   b. 11
   c. 21

7 *a.*

No.	$perTok
1	$1.50
4	$1.25
10	$1.00
22	$0.91

   b. The 2nd option will provide the
         greatest income ($35)
   c. 16
   d. 10 tokens for $10.00

9 Yes, you will get $0.65 in change.

11 $\dfrac{\$100}{22} \approx \$4.55$ per person

Section Exercises: 1.2

1 *a.* Cumulative refers to the total of all
         people infected since HIV data first
         started being gathered in 1980.
   b. 4.7 million infected in 1995
   c. 4,700,000
   d. 700,000
   e. ≈ 2000 people per day
   f. 9,000,000,000
   g. 1000
   h. 9

   i. 6
   j. 999 million

3 *a.* 4 trillion dollars
   b. 9; 1,000,000,000
   c. 12; 1,000,000,000,000
   d. 1000
   e. $\approx \$20,000$

5 6 to 12 hours if each class is
   considered to be 1 hour

7 No

9 *a.* ≈ 27 square units
   b. ≈ 8 square units

Section Exercises: 1.3

1 *a.* answers may vary
   b.

Time	Whole #	Exp	Total
0	1	2^0	1
1	2	2^1	3
2	4	2^2	7
3	8	2^3	15
4	16	2^4	31
5	32	2^5	63
6	64	2^6	127
7	128	2^7	255

   c. 2^n
   d. Total knowing rumor = New
         friends hearing rumor + Previous'
         hour's total
   e. $2^{n+1} - 1$

3 answers may vary

5 Although $100,000 right now sounds
   nice, $2,097,152 is certainly worth a
   three week waiting period.

7 *a.* $3 \cdot \left(2 + 4^2\right)$
   b. $3 \cdot \left(2 + 4\right)^2$

c. $(3 \cdot 2 + 4)^2$

d. 22

9 Since $3^4 = 3 \cdot 3 \cdot 3 \cdot 3 = 81$ and
$4^3 = 4 \cdot 4 \cdot 4 = 64$, $3^4 \neq 4^3$.

11

1	1	1	1	1
2	4	8	16	32
3	9	27	81	243
4	16	64	256	1024
5	25	125	625	3125
6	36	216	1296	7776
7	49	343	2401	16807
8	64	512	4096	32768
9	81	729	6561	59049
10	100	1000	10000	100000

Chapter 1 Questions for Review

1 I. Read for understanding
II Plan a strategy
III Implement a strategy
IV Check and analyze your results
V Make conclusions and summarize them in writing.

3

Quantity	Total Cost
1	$19.95
2	$33.50
3	$48.50
4	$62.50
6	$88.50
12	$174.50

5 **a.** answers may vary, but some rounding is needed to find a quick estimate
b. $9.66
c. Estimation allows you to quickly decide if you have enough money, while exact answers let you know if the total cost at the register is correct.

7 **a.** an estimate
b. exact

9 yes, $2^4 = 4^2$

11 **a.** 2nd method is correct, multiply before adding
b. 2nd method is correct, fraction bar implies numerator and denominator must be simplified first.

Section Exercises: 2.1

1 **a.** 0
b. $a + 0 = a$
c. 1
d. $1 \cdot a = a$
d. zero and one

3

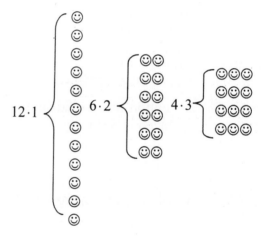

5 **a.** $60 = 2^2 \cdot 3 \cdot 5$
b. $150 = 2 \cdot 3 \cdot 5^2$

7 **a.** If you double the separate terms of a sum, it is the same as doubling the whole sum.
b. $2(x + 4) = 2x + 8$
c. a variable term cannot be combined with a constant

9 a.

$$4 \cdot (9 - 6) = 4 \cdot 9 - 4 \cdot 6$$
$$= 36 - 24$$
$$= 12$$

and

$$4 \cdot (9 - 6) = 4 \cdot (3)$$
$$= 12$$

b.

$$2 \cdot (7 - 3) = 2 \cdot 7 - 2 \cdot 3$$
$$= 14 - 6$$
$$= 8$$

and

$$2 \cdot (7 - 3) = 2 \cdot (4)$$
$$= 8$$

11 answers will vary

13 zero or five

Section Exercises: 2.2
1 a. charge: +4, Sum: $+7 + -3$
  b. charge: –1, Sum: $+3 + -4$
  c. answers may vary
  d. answers may vary

3 Add 0 using $\left({}^{+}3 + {}^{-}3 \right) = 0$
    Associative Property of Addition
    Simplify parentheses, add ${}^{+}2 + {}^{+}3 = {}^{+}5$
    Subtract, ${}^{-}3 - {}^{-}3 = 0$
    Add

5 a. $4500
  b. $3000
  c. $–1500
  d. cost is great than current revenue, so profit is negative
  e. 20
  f. $100
  g. demand for rentals might decrease
  h. $1500 short of goal

7 a. positive means weight gain and negative weight loss.

b.

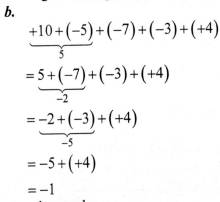

$$= 5 + (-7) + (-3) + (+4)$$

$$= -2 + (-3) + (+4)$$

$$= -5 + (+4)$$

$$= -1$$

c. –1 pound

9 a.

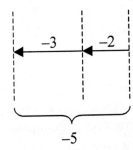

b. $-2 + (-3) = -5$

c. +2

11 5 feet above

13 the last bullet is incorrect

Section Exercises: 2.3
1 a. –30 **b.** 3 **c.** –28 **d.** –2 **e.** 36 **f.** –8
  g. 90 **h.** –24 **i.** –480 **j.** 540 **k.** 0

3 $12 \cdot \dfrac{1}{4} = 3$, $\;-15 \cdot \dfrac{1}{3} = -5$,

  $-25 \cdot \left(-\dfrac{1}{5} \right) = 5$, $\;16 \cdot \left(-\dfrac{1}{4} \right) = -4$,

  $0 \cdot 1 = 0$

5 a. $5^2 = (-5)^2 = 25$, even power produces positive value, but -5^2 means to square 5 and then apply the negative symbol giving -25

b. $5^2 = 5 \cdot 5 = 25$

$-5^2 = -(5 \cdot 5) = -25$

$(-5)^2 = (-5)(-5) = 25$

7 $a + (-b)$

9 answers may vary

11 a. $8 + 2 = 2 + 8 = 10$

b. $8 - 2 = 6; \quad 2 - 8 = -6$

c. $8 \cdot 2 = 2 \cdot 8 = 16$

d. $8 \div 2 = 4; \quad 2 \div 8 = \dfrac{2}{8} = \dfrac{1}{4}$

- The pairs in a and c produce the same answer.
- $a + b = b + a \qquad a \cdot b = b \cdot a$
- Commutative Property of Addition and Multiplication
- Subtraction. The answers are opposites.
  Division. The answers are reciprocals.

Chapter 2 Questions for Review

1 a. 1, 2, 3, 6, 9, 18

b. 1, 2, 4, 8, 16, 32, 64

3 They can be written as the product of primes in a unique way.

5 a. False, $4 - 6 = -2$

b. True, the product of any 2 natural numbers is also a natural number.

c. True, division by 0 does not produce a whole number.

7 a. $|-30| = 30 < |-40| = 40$

b. $|-25| = 25 > |15| = 15$

9

$-3 + 4 = 1$

$-3 + 3 = 0$

$-3 + 2 = -1$

$-3 + 1 = -2$

$-3 + 0 = -3$

$-3 + -1 = -4$

$-3 + -2 = -5$

$-3 + -3 = -6$

$-3 + -4 = -7$

11

$3 - 3 = 0$

$3 - 2 = 1$

$3 - 1 = 2$

$3 - 0 = 3$

$3 - {}^-1 = 4$

$3 - {}^-2 = 5$

$3 - {}^-3 = 6$

13

$-3 - 3 = -6$

$-3 - 2 = -5$

$-3 - 1 = -4$

$-3 - 0 = -3$

$-3 - {}^-1 = -2$

$-3 - {}^-2 = -1$

$-3 - {}^-3 = 0$

15 a. $7 \cdot 9 = 63, \quad 7 \cdot (-9) = -63,$

$-7 \cdot 9 = -63, \quad (-7)(-9) = 63$

b. $18/6 = 3, \quad 18/(-6) = -3,$

$-18/6 = -3, \quad (-18)/(-6) = 3$

Section Exercises: 3.1

1 *a.* $\dfrac{3}{7}, \dfrac{1}{5}, \dfrac{2}{5}, \dfrac{5}{11}$

    b. $\dfrac{3}{7}, \dfrac{1}{5}, \dfrac{5}{11}$

    c. $\dfrac{3}{7}, \dfrac{5}{11}$

    d. $\dfrac{3}{7}$

3 *a.* $\dfrac{1}{9}, \dfrac{2}{14}$

    b. $\dfrac{5}{9}, \dfrac{6}{13}, \dfrac{4}{9}, \dfrac{7}{12}, \dfrac{8}{14}$

    c. $\dfrac{11}{13}, \dfrac{10}{12}$

    d. answers may vary

    e. answers may vary

    f. answers may vary

    g. No

5 *a.* $-\dfrac{13}{7}; -1.9$

    b. Repeating, $1.\overline{857142}$

7 *a.* $\dfrac{1}{3} < \dfrac{1}{2}$

    b. $\dfrac{2}{4} < \dfrac{3}{5}$

    c. $\dfrac{3}{4} > \dfrac{2}{3}$

    d. $\dfrac{3}{6} = \dfrac{4}{8}$

    e. $\dfrac{4}{5} > \dfrac{5}{8}$

9 *a.* 8

    b. $\dfrac{24}{40}$

    c. 5

    d. $\dfrac{25}{40}$

    e. $\dfrac{25}{40} > \dfrac{24}{40}$

11 *a.* $\dfrac{10}{8} = \dfrac{5}{4} \dfrac{\$}{\text{gallon}}$

    b. 1.25 per gallon

    c. $15

Section Exercises: 3.2

1 *a.* $4\dfrac{3}{16}$

    b. $-2\dfrac{13}{16}$

    c. about $3600

    d. $20\dfrac{3}{32}$

    e. about $200,000

3 *a.* 1.4 or $1\dfrac{4}{10}$ or $1\dfrac{2}{5}$ pounds

    b. answers may vary

    c. answers may vary

    d. answers may vary

    e. answers may vary

    f. answers may vary

5 *a.* $1\dfrac{5}{8}$

    b. The correct nail size goes $1\dfrac{1}{8}$ inches into the second piece of wood with $\dfrac{1}{8}$ inch to spare. The other size nail measuring $1\dfrac{13}{16}$ inches will go all the way through both boards and have $\dfrac{1}{16}$ inch extra sticking out.

Selected Solutions to Odd-Numbered Exercises

7 *a.* 5 feet $6\frac{1}{4}$ inches

b. 5 feet $\frac{3}{4}$ inches

9 *a.* $\frac{7}{12}$ *b.* $\frac{3}{4}$ *c.* $\frac{45}{14}$ *d.* $-\frac{1}{18}$

e. $\frac{22}{15}$ *f.* $\frac{11}{8}$ *g.* $\frac{209}{210}$ *h.* $\frac{1}{12}$

i. $-\frac{1}{12}$ *j.* $\frac{19}{3}$ *k.* 6 *l.* $3\frac{1}{5}$

m. $-3\frac{1}{5}$ *n.* $1\frac{7}{12}$

11 *a.* $1.20

b. -0.13, -0.12, $0.40

d. 883.75 gallons

e. warm: $159.075; cold: $353.5

13 *a.* 2 hours per week

b. 17 minutes

c. 1 hour 30 minutes

d. 13 minutes

e. answers may vary

f. Rebecca puts in less hours and Gerry Jr. does more.

g. Answers may vary

Section Exercises: 3.3

1

Rate (mph)	Time (hours)	Change
10	20.6	
20	10.3	−10.3
30	6.9	−3.4
40	5.2	−1.7
50	4.1	−0.9
60	3.4	−0.7
70	2.9	−0.5
80	2.6	−0.3
90	2.3	−0.3

a. decreases

b. large decrease in travel time

c. small decrease in travel time

d. decreasing

3 *a.* false, *b.* true, *c.* true, *d.* false, *e.* false, *f.* false, *g.* true, *h.* true, *i.* false

5 *a.* 26.801; 95.023; 2459.438

b. 252.49; 23.86

c. 6.8; 1.2

7 *a.* 1; *b.* $1\frac{1}{4}$; *c.* $1\frac{1}{2}$; *d.* 375,000

9 This year 9 and last year 19

a. answers may vary

b.

Cost
$1.34
10.99
6.18
−1.24
0.96
0.31
1.51
10.82
$29.53

Section Exercises: 3.4

1 measurements may vary

a. The last two columns have values that are relatively close.

b. No, since you are measuring by hand there will be some error in your results.

3 *a.* $\sqrt{4}=2$ but $\sqrt{2}\approx1.7$

b. $\sqrt{6}=\sqrt{2\cdot3}=\sqrt{2}\cdot\sqrt{3}$

c. $\sqrt{16}-\sqrt{9}=4-3=1$

d. $\sqrt{100}-10=10-10=0$

678

5 answers may vary, but they should consider overall cost, environmental impact, and time to completion.

7 a.

1	$\sqrt[3]{1}$	1
8	$\sqrt[3]{8}$	2
27	$\sqrt[3]{27}$	3
64	$\sqrt[3]{64}$	4
125	$\sqrt[3]{125}$	5

b. The input n is the result of multiplying the output by itself three times.

c.

1	1^3	1
2	2^3	8
3	3^3	27
4	4^3	64
5	5^3	125

d.

2	$\sqrt[3]{2}$	1.260
3	$\sqrt[3]{3}$	1.442
4	$\sqrt[3]{4}$	1.587
10	$\sqrt[3]{10}$	2.154
100	$\sqrt[3]{100}$	4.641
1001	$\sqrt[3]{1001}$	10.003
10000	$\sqrt[3]{10000}$	21.544

e. answers may vary
f. output increases at a decreasing rate
g. no

9

$$\sqrt{1} = 1 \quad \text{because} \quad (1)^2 = 1$$
$$\sqrt{4} = 2 \quad \text{because} \quad (2)^2 = 4$$
$$\sqrt{9} = 3 \quad \text{because} \quad (3)^2 = 9$$

a. answers may vary, but between 1 and 2
b. answers may vary, but between 2 and 3

c. $\sqrt{2} \approx 1.41$, $\sqrt{3} \approx 1.73$, $\sqrt{5} \approx 2.24$ $\sqrt{6} \approx 2.45$, $\sqrt{7} \approx 2.65$, $\sqrt{8} \approx 2.83$

11 a. yes, **b.** yes, **c.** no **d.** yes

Chapter 3 Questions for Review

1 1st figure: $\frac{3}{4}$ shaded, $\frac{1}{4}$ unshaded

2nd figure: $\frac{2}{3}$ shaded, $\frac{1}{3}$ unshaded

3ed figure: $\frac{5}{8}$ shaded, $\frac{3}{8}$ unshaded

4th figure: $\frac{5}{8}$ shaded, $\frac{3}{8}$ unshaded

3 A rational number is the quotient of two integers and either a repeating or terminating decimal.

5 answers may vary

7 a. $\frac{63}{4}$, **b.** $1575

9 a. 9/10 of a cent, **b.** $13.59,

c. $0.859 = \$0.85\frac{9}{10}$,

d. $1.409 = 1.40\frac{9}{10}$

11 a. $\frac{28}{15}$, **b.** $\frac{1}{12}$, **c.** $\frac{2}{3}$, **d.** 18

13 a. 8, **b.** $\frac{10}{7}$, **c.** $\frac{5}{24}$, **d.** $\frac{4}{5}$

15 ≈ 111.8 miles

Section Exercises: 4.1

1   *a.*   Total number of medals
    b.   answers may vary
    c.   44% gold; 32% silver; 100% gold, silver or bronze; 0% platinum
    d.   answers may vary
    e.   answers may vary

3   *a.*   0.14
    b. $(0.05)(14)$
    c.   0.275
    d.   60% of 25

5.   Clinton:
$$\frac{43,728,375}{101,133,038} \approx 0.432 = 43.2\%$$

Bush: $\frac{38,167,416}{101,133,038} \approx 0.377 = 37.7\%$

Perot: $\frac{19,237,247}{101,133,038} \approx 0.190 = 19.0\%$

    a.   More than 50%
    b.   No
    c.   answers may vary
    d.   answers may vary

7   *a.*   1995 unemployment rate: 5.6%
        1996 unemployment rate: 5.4%
        1997 unemployment rate: 4.9%
        1998 unemployment rate: 4.5%
    b. $100\% - 6.1\% = 93.9\%$
$$\frac{123,060}{123,060 + 7996} \approx 0.939$$

9   *a.* ≈ 0.80 or 80%
    b. ≈ 0.20 or 20%

11 *a.* $\frac{100}{100} = 1$
    b. $\frac{0.05}{100} = 0.0005$
    c. $\frac{10.5}{100} = 0.105$

d. $\frac{1}{100} = 0.01$

e. $\frac{0.1}{100} = 0.001$

f. $\frac{150}{100} = 1.5$

g. $\frac{2000}{100} = 20$

h. $\frac{5.2}{100} = 0.052$

13 *a.* $0.\overline{3} = 33\frac{1}{3}\%$
    b. $0.625 = 62.5\%$
    c. $0.6 = 60\%$
    d. $0.0001 = 0.01\%$
    e. $2.68 = 268\%$
    f. $\approx 0.441 = 44.1\%$

Section Exercises: 4.2

1   *a.* $30,529.20
    b. $32,055.66
    c.   answers may vary

3   *a.* $300; $2000; $40,000; $120,000
    b. $30; $200; $4000; $12,000
    c. $330; $2200; $44,000; $132,000
    d. $600; $4000; $80,000; $240,000
    e. $3; $20; $400; $1200
    f. $1.50; $10; $200; $600
    g. $15; $100; $2000; $6000
    h. $150; $1000; $20,000; $60,000
    i. $75; $500; $10,000; $30,000

5   *a.* $\approx 25\%$
    b. $61.49
    c. $55
    d.   answers may vary

7 **a.** $33\frac{1}{3}\%$

b. 90%

c. 10%

d. $66\frac{2}{3}\%$

e. 10%

9 **a.** $105.80

b. $108.87

c. $128.38

Section Exercises: 4.3

1 **a.** $\dfrac{150 \text{ mi}}{2.5 \text{ hr}} = \dfrac{60 \text{ mi}}{1 \text{ hr}}$ or 60 mi/hr

b. $\dfrac{150 \text{ mi}}{7.5 \text{ gal}} = \dfrac{20 \text{ mi}}{1 \text{ gal}}$ or 20 mi/gal

c. $\dfrac{\$11.85}{3 \text{ lb}} = \dfrac{\$3.95}{1 \text{ lb}}$ or $3.95 \text{ \$/lb}$

d. $\dfrac{\$307.50}{30 \text{ hr}} = \dfrac{\$10.25}{1 \text{ hr}} = 10.25 \text{ \$/hr}$

e. $\dfrac{\$3348 \text{ tax}}{\$22,320 \text{ wage}} = \dfrac{\$0.15 \text{ tax}}{\$1 \text{ wage}}$

3 **a.** Ending balance year 2 = $1188.10

year 3 = $1295.03

year 4 = $1411.58

year 5 = $1538.62

b. 1.09

c. Year 3:
$$= 1000 \cdot (1.09)(1.09)(1.09)$$
$$= 1000 \cdot (1.09)^3$$

Year 4:
$$= 1000 \cdot (1.09)(1.09)(1.09)(1.09)$$
$$= 1000 \cdot (1.09)^4$$

Year 5:
$$= 1000 \cdot (1.09)(1.09)(1.09)(1.09)(1.09)$$
$$= 1000 \cdot (1.09)^5$$

d. P is the principal

r is the interest rate

t is the time

e. $5000(1 + 0.21)^{10} \approx \$33,637.50$

f. $5000\left(1 + \dfrac{0.21}{12}\right)^{10 \cdot 12} \approx \$40,095.92$

g. $5000\left(1 + \dfrac{0.21}{365}\right)^{10 \cdot 365} \approx \$40,806.20$

5 **a.** 1997 increase: 1,566,649

1998 increase: 1,605,976

b. $\dfrac{6}{1000}$

c. $\approx 0.016 = 1.6\%$

d. $\approx 0.007 = 0.7\%$

e. answers may vary

f. $\dfrac{2,244,000 - 2,384,000}{2,384,000} \approx -0.058$

g. $\dfrac{8.3 - 8.9}{8.9} \approx -0.067$

h. answers may vary

7 Annual % Change in Deaths:

1993-94: 9.1%

1994-95: –0.5%

1995-96: –27.8%

1996-97: –59.0%

Annual % Change in New Cases:

1993-94: –24.5%

1994-95: –8.1%

1995-96: –6.3%

1996-97: –12.3%

a. 1993-94 increased by about 9%. 1994-97 decreased by a larger amount each year

b. 1993-96 decreased by a smaller amount each year until 96-97 where the decrease was almost double the previous year

c. The deaths will be from previous year cases not new cases

d. Answers may vary

9 The population of California increased 25.8% from 1980-90

11 The CPI increased about 1.6% from 1997-98

Section Exercises: 4.4

1 *a.* $\dfrac{25}{1000}$

 b. $\dfrac{n}{5,607,000,000}$

 c. $\dfrac{n}{5,607,000,000} = \dfrac{25}{1000}$

 $n = 140,175,000$

 d. There were 140,175,000 babies born in 1996

 e. 50,463,000

 f. 89,712,000

 g. 6,055,560,000

 h. The part *g* estimate will need to be increased

3 *a.*

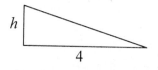

 b. $\dfrac{1}{1.5} = \dfrac{h}{4}$

 $h = 2\dfrac{2}{3}$ meters

5 *a.* 11.25 miles
 b. 3144 calories

7 Lockett won with .342 average compared with Bogg's .340

9 *a.* $x = 4$
 b. $n = 10$
 c. $a = 6$
 d. $y = 18$
 e. $b = 30$
 f. $c = 25.6$

Chapter 4 Questions for Review

1 *a.* Homework: $\dfrac{1}{8}$, 0.125, 12.5%

 Quizzes: $\dfrac{1}{4}$, 0.25, 25%

 Midterm: $\dfrac{1}{4}$, 0.25, 25%

 Final: $\dfrac{3}{8}$, 0.375, 37.5%

 Total: $\dfrac{8}{8}$, 1, 100%

 b. 78.25

3 *a.*

Yes
58%

No
42%

 b.

Yes
41%

No
59%

 c. ≈ 59%
 d. ≈ 41%
 e. ≈ 962
 f. ≈ 959

g. More female students at College

h. No, 48% drink alcohol

5 Sedentary: 546.6
Moderate: 728.8
Strenuous: 1275.4

7 a. ≈ 5.4%

  b. ≈ 2.8%

  c. ≈ 3.2%

  d. No, woman only made slight gains

  e. No, income increased by a smaller percentage than housing

  f. ≈ 0.74

  g. Women earn 74% of the income received by men

  h. ≈ 0.74

  i. No

9 a. 0.25 or 25%

  b. 4

  c. 90

  d. 210

  e. 43%

  f. Tie election between A and B

Section Exercises: 5.1

1 Answers may vary

3 Answers may vary

5 a. A kilometer is a little more than half a mile. It would be possible to walk but not many people would have the time.

  b.

Rate	Hours	Min.
10	1.2	72
20	0.6	36
30	0.4	24
40	0.3	18

50	0.24	14.4
60	0.2	12
70	0.17	10.3
80	0.15	9

  c. The time is cut in half. For example increasing the speed from 40 to 80 km/hr, decreases the time from 18 to 9 minutes.

  d. 6 minutes

  e. 2.4 hours or 2 hours 24 minutes

  f. 9.6 gallons

  g. $16.\overline{6}$ days or less.

  h. 400 km

  i. $47.84

  j. ≈ $0.12

  k. answers may vary

7 answers may vary

9 answers may vary

11 a.–d answers may vary

  e. $\dfrac{w}{h^2}$

  f. $\dfrac{w}{2.2046}$

  g. $\dfrac{h}{39.37}$

  h. $\dfrac{703 \cdot w}{h^2}$

  i. John: ≈ 31, obese
  Jane: ≈ 23, healthy
  Frank: ≈ 26 overweight

13 a. 20 foot-pounds

  b. 20 foot-pounds

  c. 20 foot-pounds

  d. 3 feet

  e. 400 pounds

Section Exercises: 5.2

1 a. 2·18, 3·12, 4·9, 6·6

  b. Draw pictures of four rectangles with measurements from part *a*

c.

L	W	P	TC
1	36	74	740
2	18	40	400
3	12	30	300
4	9	26	260
6	6	24	240
9	4	26	260
12	3	30	300
18	2	40	400
36	1	74	740

d. 6 m by 6 m

e. $240

f. No, based on the symmetric pattern in the table from part *c*

g. square

h. yes

3 $666

5 *a.* $x = 24 - 2y$

b.

y	x	A
3	18	54
4	16	64
5	14	70
6	12	72
7	10	70
8	8	64
9	6	54

c. 6 ft by 12 ft

d. symmetric pattern

7 *a.* ≈ 55 square yards

b. ≈ 33 yards

9 *a.* 20 ft^2

b.

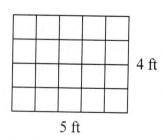

4 ft

5 ft

c. 5 ft by 4 ft; perimeter is 18 ft

d. 2 ft by 10 ft (below) or 1 ft by 20 ft

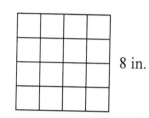

e. 2 ft by 10 ft or 1 ft by 20 ft

f. 5 ft by 7 ft

g. 8 ft by 9 ft

h. factors of *n* that are closest to forming a square

Section Exercises: 5.3

1 *a.*

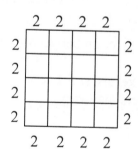

8 in.

8 in.

b. 64 square inches

c. 16 brownies

d. 2 inches

e. 4 square inches

f.

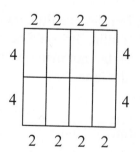

g.

684

h. 2 in. by 4 in. and area of 8 sq. in.

i. 16 cubic inches

j. $16+16+16+16+16+16+16+16$
$= 8 \cdot 16 = 128$ in.^{3}
Or 8 in.$\times$ 8 in.$\times$ 2 in. $= 128$ in.^{3}

3 d. box with 4 cm by 4 cm squares cut
e. box with 5 cm by 5 cm squares cut
f.

L	V	SA
3	1025	567
4	1083	539
5	1038	503

g. answers may vary

5 $3 \cdot 4 \cdot 3 = 36$ unit cubes

7 a. answers may vary
b. 1890 mL
c. No, different units are used
d. A milliliter is 1/1000 of a liter, the basic unit for measuring volume. A cubic centimeter is the product of 3 (centimeter) measurements of distance.

9 radius = 12 cm and height = 8 cm

11 a. 1.5
b. ≈ 381.7 in.^{3} and 1288.3 in.^{3}
c. ≈ 3.375
d. as the radius increases by a factor (1.5), the volume increases to the cube of that factor (3.375) times its original value

Section Exercises: 5.4

1 Revenue: 1.827×10^{12}
Expenditures: 1.703×10^{12}
Difference:
$124,000,000,000 = 1.24 \times 10^{11}$
a. surplus
b. above

c. delete 9 zeros and note that values are in billions of dollars

3 a. 6×10^{-2}
b. 4.0×10^{16}
c. 2.075×10^{-11}
d. 3.4725×10^{14}

5 a. 3.2×10^3
b. 3.4×10^{-3}
c. 2.0×10^{-5}
d. $\approx 7.69 \times 10^{-23}$

7 a. $969,120,000,000 = 9.6912 \times 10^{11}$
b. surplus of $2019-1800 = \$219$ billion

9 a. 6.65×10^{-24}
b. 7.5×10^{23}

Chapter 5 Questions for Review

1 a. $\approx 5'7"$
b. 132 lb
c. $99.5°$ F
d. 12.5 minutes or 1/5 hour
e. \$67.80

3 a. answers may vary
b. $\dfrac{355}{1000}$ L
c. ≈ 5.6 cans
d. a six-pack
e. bottle (20 oz)
f. 5000 meters
g. 0.4 km
h. 4000 mm
i. 500 mm
j. 0.02 g
k. 0.04 kg and 40,000 mg

5 a.

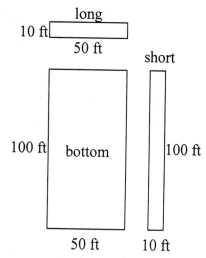

b. 8000 ft^2

c. ≈ 24.6, or about 25 gallons

d. 50,000 ft^3

e. 47,500 ft^3

f. 355,300 gallons

7 a. 314 ft^2

b. $19.95 cover

9 a. 3.5×10^{12}

b. 1.096×10^9

c. 2×10^{-7}

d. 1.98×10^{-10}

11 a. 8.5×10^{15}

b. $24.5985 \times 10^{11} = 2.45985 \times 10^{12}$

c. 2×10^{-14}

d. $0.65 \times 10^{-2} = 6.5 \times 10^{-3}$

Section Exercises: 6.1

1 a. Yes, monthly payments depend on income.

b. Independent: income
Dependent: loan amount

c. $7862

d. answers may vary from $33,000 to $36,000

e. Changes given in following table

Income	Loan Amount
7862	25,000
7861	25,000
15,724	50,000
15,724	50,000

f. $\approx \$39,309$

g. 100,000; 47,171

h. a $62,895 income allows a loan of up to $200,000

3 a. mortgage rate and housing price

b. mortgage rate decrease more than offset the housing price increase

c. small decrease in mortgage rate does not offset the large increase in median-priced housing

d. income, but answers may vary

5 a. 60% humidity makes a temperature of 90°F feel like 100°F

b. $T(70) = 106$

c. increases at an increasing rate

d. 30%

e. apparent temperature is cooler than the actual temperature

f. apparent temperature is warmer than the actual temperature

7 a.

Income	Tax
$35,000	$6452.50
$40,000	$7852.50
$45,000	$9252.50
$50,000	$10,652.50
$55,000	$12,052.50
$60,000	$13,452.50

b. only income changes

c. $3862.5 + 0.28 \cdot (x - 25,750)$

d. $= 3862.5 + 0.28 \cdot (x - 25,750)$

e. 11,492.50; f of 53,000 equals 11,492.50; income of $53,000 requires $11,492 in taxes

9 *a.* each year has just one number of new cases

b.
$$\{1985,1990,1993,1994,1995,1996,1997\}$$
$$\left\{\begin{array}{l}8161,41540,102082,77092,70839,\\66398,58254\end{array}\right\}$$

c. $y = f(x)$

d. −24,990; negative sign means a decrease in new cases

e. answers may vary, but the change in new cases dropped each year after 1993

f. answers may vary

Section Exercises: 6.2

1

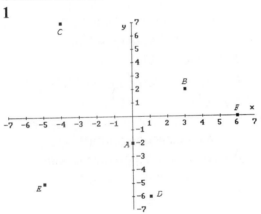

3 *a.* independent: year; dependent: travel volume

b. millions of person trips of 100 mi or more

c. $\left\{\begin{array}{l}1986,1987,1988,1989,1990,\\1991,1992,1993,1994,1995,\\1996,1997,1998\end{array}\right\}$

d. $\approx \left\{\begin{array}{l}580,600,615,625,650,675,740,\\745,790,810,805,870,895\end{array}\right\}$

e. a steady rise in travel volume over the years 1986-98

f. answers may vary

5 *a. and b.*

$$g(2200) = 0.18 \cdot (2200) + 120 = 516$$
$$g(2400) = 0.18 \cdot (2400) + 120 = 552$$
$$g(2600) = 0.18 \cdot (2600) + 120 = 588$$
$$g(2800) = 0.18 \cdot (2800) + 120 = 624$$
$$g(3000) = 0.18 \cdot (3000) + 120 = 660$$

c. and d.

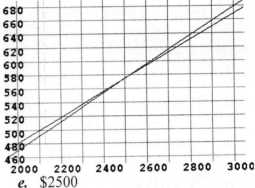

e. $2500

f. For sales greater than 2500 Joy makes more money and sales less than 2500 Desi makes more money.

7 *a.* independent: price of ticket; dependent: quantity demanded

b. answers may vary

c.

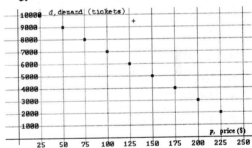

9 *a.* $\approx 3\%$

b.

1840	≈ 68
1860	≈ 59
1880	≈ 57
1900	≈ 37
1920	≈ 27
1940	≈ 18
1960	≈ 6
1980	≈ 3

c. decreased from $\approx 72\%$ to $\approx 3\%$

d. 1880-1900 about a 20% drop

Section Exercises: 6.3

1 *a.* $f(a) = 154 - 0.70a$

   b. $f(33) \approx 131$ bpm

   c. 138 bmp

   d. $a \approx 23$ years

3 *a.* Population is increasing by 2000 people every 5 years.

   b. increased by 400

   c.

22	23	24	25
16,800	17,200	17,600	18,000

   d. $P(t) = 8000 + 400t$

   e. $P(30) = 20,000$

   f. 28 years or 2008

5 *a.*

4	$9 \cdot 4$	36
6	$9 \cdot 6$	54
8	$9 \cdot 8$	72
10	$9 \cdot 10$	90
12	$9 \cdot 12$	108

   b. $G(t) = 9t$

   c.

4	$40 + 5 \cdot 4$	60
6	$40 + 5 \cdot 6$	70
8	$40 + 5 \cdot 8$	80
10	$40 + 5 \cdot 10$	90
12	$40 + 5 \cdot 12$	100

   d. $P(t) = 40 + 5t$

   e. 10 seconds

f. Gail wins in less than 12 seconds

g. $t \approx 11.11$

h. 4.45 meters

i. $t = 12$ seconds

7 *a.* $t \approx 11.67$ seconds

   b. 1) Gail, 2) Catia, 3) Paul

   c. answers may vary

   d. answers may vary

9 *a.* the change is 2000 each year

   b. Income starts at $30,000 ($t = 0$) and increases $2000 per year.

   c. $I(t) = 30,000 + 2000t$

   d. $t = 35$ or the year 2026

Chapter 6 Questions for Review

1 *a.* the month (independent) determines the amount of precipitation (dependent)

   b. winter is wet and summer is dry

3 *a.* $P(11) = 2.9$; $P(4) = 1.4$

   b. "P of one equals 4.4" means the precipitation in the 1st month is normally around 4.4 inches

5

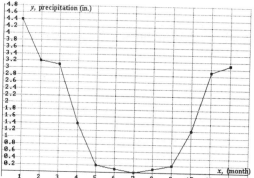

   a. between month 3 (March) and 4 (April) the steepest drop occurs

   b. between month 10 (Oct.) and 11 (Nov.) the steepest rise occurs

   c. month 5 (May) through 9 (Sept.) the line plot is nearly flat

7 *a.* demand will decrease to 4000

   b. supply will increase to 8000

c. 4000; airlines will probably lower
the price to unload the extras

9 *a.* decrease by 1000; decrease by 40

   b. 11,000

   c. $D(x) = 11,000 - 40x$

   d. increase by 1000; increase by 40

   e. 1000

   f. $S(x) = 1000 + 40x$

Section Exercises: 7.1

1 *a.*

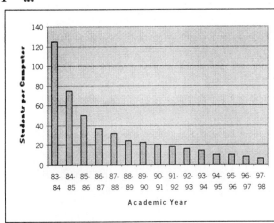

b. decreased each year

c. answers may vary, but around 5

3 *a.*

Class Int.	Frequency	Rel. Freq.
460.5-480.5	4	0.078
480.5-500.5	13	0.255
500.5-520.5	10	0.196
520.5-540.5	12	0.235
540.5-560.5	9	0.176
560.5-580.5	1	0.020
580.5-600.5	2	0.039

b.

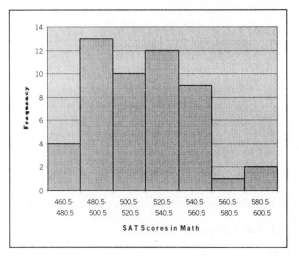

c.

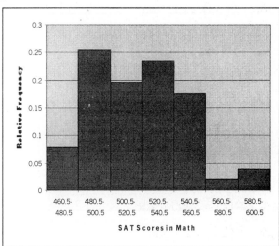

5 *a.* 77%

   b. answers may vary

   c. Start at 0.5 lb below least weight,
so 1st interval is 99.5-109.5.

   d.

Weight	Frequency	Rel. Freq.
97.5-109.5	3	0.086
109.5-121.5	10	0.286
121.5-133.5	12	0.343
133.5-145.5	8	0.229
145.5-157.5	2	0.057

e.

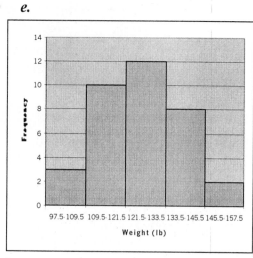

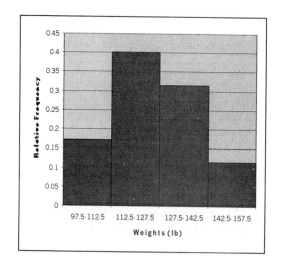

f.

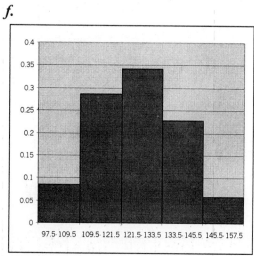

b.

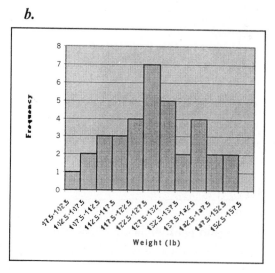

7 *a.*

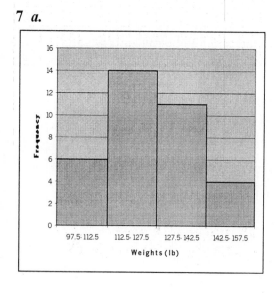

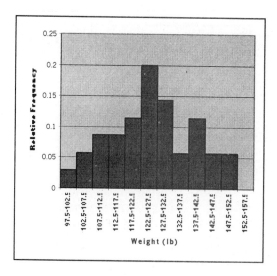

c. answers may vary

9 *a.* 12

b.

Height	Freq.	Rel. Freq.
4'11½"-5'½"	1	0.029
5'½"-5'1½"	2	0.057
5'1½"-5'2½"	3	0.086
5'2½"-5'3½"	3	0.086
5'3½"-5'4½"	4	0.114
5'4½"-5'5½"	6	0.171
5'5½"-5'6½"	5	0.143
5'6½"-5'7½"	3	0.086
5'7½"-5'8½"	3	0.086
5'8½"-5'9½"	2	0.057
5'9½"-5'10½"	2	0.057
5'10½"-5'11½"	1	0.029

c. 3

d.

Height	Freq.	Rel. Freq.
4'11½"-5'3½"	9	0.257
5'3½"-5'7½"	18	0.514
5'7½"-5'11½"	8	0.229

Section Exercises: 7.2

1 *a.* $42,000 and $45,000 are the salaries that occur most often

b. $\bar{x} = \$58,250$ is the average salary

c.

1	32,000
2	40,000
3	42,000
4	42,000
5	45,000
6	45,000
7	100,000
8	120,000

d. $43,500 is average of the two middle (4th and 5th) salaries

3 *a.* 97 is the most common grade

b. 93 is the average of the two middle (5th and 6th) scores in the ordered data set

c.

$$\frac{1 \cdot 98 + 3 \cdot 97 + 1 \cdot 95 + 2 \cdot 91 + 2 \cdot 90 + 1 \cdot 0}{10} = 84.6$$

d. answers may vary, but the median and mode are not influenced by the extreme score of 0

5 *a.* at least $738

b. mean: $735, median: $737.50, mode: $750

c. answers may vary

7 *a. and b.*

Rep Val.	Freq.	Prod.
55	3	165
65	7	455
75	11	825
85	9	765
95	6	570

c.

$$\frac{165 + 455 + 825 + 765 + 570}{36} \approx 77$$

d. a score of 77 is the estimated mean for the exam

9 *a.* 121.5–133.5

b.

100	105	105	110	110	112	115
115	116	118	120	120	120	123
125	125	125	125	125	127	130
130	130	130	132	135	135	138
140	140	142	145	145	150	150

c. $\dfrac{35+1}{2} = \dfrac{36}{2} = 18$

d 125

e. ≈ 126

Section Exercises: 7.3

1 *a.* mean $\bar{x} \approx \$8.04$ and standard deviation $\approx \$2.27$

b. mean $\bar{x} \approx \$23.03$ and standard deviation $\approx \$6.68$

c. 1ˢᵗ hour rates are centered at $8 and vary about $2.25 from the center. Day rates are centered at $23 and vary about $6.70 from the center.

d. $Min = 2.9$, $Q_1 = 6.5$, $Med = 8$, $Q_3 = 10$, $Max = 12$

e. The difference between max and min values and between upper and lower quartiles.

3 *a.* ≈ 17.0

b. ≈ 2.3

c. answers may vary but Philadelphia's temperatures vary more as the seasons change

5 *a.* $Min = 675$, $Q_1 = 700$, $Med = 737.5$ $Q_3 = 750$, $Max = 800$

b. range $= 125$ and $IOR = 50$

c. Big difference, $125 between *Max* and *Min*, but only $50 between the upper and lower quartile.

d.

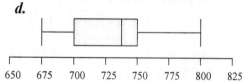

| 650 | 675 | 700 | 725 | 750 | 775 | 800 | 825 |

7 *a.*

Age	Rep	Freq
14.5-19.5	17	4
19.5-24.5	22	6
24.5-29.5	27	7
29.5-34.5	32	9
34.5-39.5	37	4
39.5-44.5	42	3
44.5-49.5	47	2
49.5-54.5	52	0
54.5-59.5	57	1

b. ≈ 31

c. ≈ 9.4

9 *a.* Seattle: $\bar{x} \approx 3.2$, Miami: $\bar{x} \approx 4.7$

b. Seattle: ≈ 1.8, Miami: ≈ 2.6

c. Miami averages 1.5 inches more precipitation per month than Seattle. Also, Miami's monthly temperature varies more throughout the year.

Chapter 7 Questions for Review

1 *a.*

Temp	Freq	Rel Freq
9.5-19.5	1	0.083
19.5-29.5	2	0.167
29.5-39.5	2	0.167
39.5-49.5	0	0
49.5-59.5	2	0.167
59.5-69.5	2	0.167
69.5-79.5	3	0.25

b.

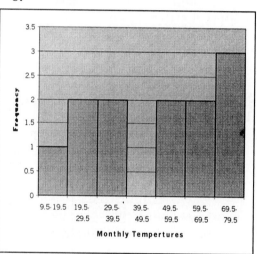

c.

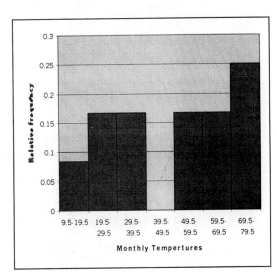

d. 69.5–79.5; mode

e. answers may vary but no month has normal temperatures in the forties (39.5–49.5)

3 *a.* $\bar{x} \approx 50$

b. $Med = 52.5$

5 *a.* $\bar{x} \approx 189.4$ million, $Med = 146.05$ million

b. The mean is about 43 million larger than the median due to one extreme value ($488.2 million) which only effects the mean.

c. Answers may vary, but the median is not influenced by Titanic's unusually high gross sales.

d. ≈ 107.8 million

e. $Min = 134.1$, $Q_1 = 136.3$, $Med = 146.05$, $Q_3 = 190.8$, $Max = 488.2$

f. Five-number summary

7 *a.* $\bar{x} \approx 144.8$, $Med = 140.5$

b. The difference has decreased from 12 million to 4.3 million.

c. ≈ 13.9

c. decreased by 11.9 million

Section Exercises: 8.1

1 *a.* Random means each ticket is equally likely to be selected.

b. $1/1000 = 0.001$

c. $50/1000 = 1/20 = 0.05$

3 *a.* $2 \cdot 6 = 12$

b. H1, H2, H3, H4, H5, H6, T1, T2, T3, T4, T5, T6

c. $1/12 = 0.08\overline{3}$

d. $7/12 = 0.58\overline{3}$

e. $3/12 = 1/4 = 0.25$

f. $9/12 = 3/4 = 0.75$

g. 0

h. 1

5 *a.* $18/38 \approx 0.474$

b. $1/38 \approx 0.026$

c. $36/38 \approx 0.947$

d. 0

e. $36/38 \approx 0.947$

f. "not green" is the same as "black or red"

7 *a.* zero girls: 1, one girl: 1

b. zero girls: 1, one girl: 2, two girls: 1

c. zero girls: 1, one girl: 3, two girls: 3, three girls: 1

d. row one: 1
row five: 1 4 6 4 1
row six: 1 5 10 10 5 1

e. $P(G = 0) = 1/16 = 0.0625$,
$P(G = 1) = 4/16 = 1/4 = 0.25$,
$P(G = 2) = 6/16 = 3/8 = 0.375$,
$P(G = 3) = 4/16 = 1/4 = 0.25$
$P(G = 4) = 1/16 = 0.0625$

f. $P(G = 2) = 10/32 = 5/16 = 0.3125$
$P(G \geq 2) = 26/32 = 13/16 = 0.8125$

9 a. $84/150 = 0.56$

 b. $66/150 = 0.44$

 c. 1

 d. 0

Section Exercises: 8.2

1 a. $P(E) = 1$

 b. $P(B) = 0.05$

 c. $P(C) = 0.50$

 d. $P(D) = 0.95$

 e. $P(A) = 0$

3 a.

Age	Rel. Freq.
− 5	≈ 0.069
5-13	≈ 0.121
14-17	≈ 0.054
18-24	≈ 0.092
25-34	≈ 0.125
35-44	≈ 0.120
45-54	≈ 0.110
55-64	≈ 0.108
65-84	≈ 0.154
85-99	≈ 0.044
100 +	≈ 0.002

 b. 0.20

 c. answers may vary

5 a.

	V	A	T	P
W	10	50	60	0.60
M	5	35	40	0.40
T	15	85	100	
P	0.15	0.85		

 b. $5/40 = 1/8 = 0.125$

 c. $10/60 = 1/6 = 0.1\overline{6}$

 d. women

7 a.

Race	Rel. Freq.
Nat. Am.	0.01
Black	0.14

White	0.72
Asian	0.07
Other	0.06

 b. 0.14 or 14%

 c. 0.28 or 28%

 d. 0.08 or 8%

9 a. Yes, a student campaigning to get votes for A will not simultaneously campaign for B.

 b. $P(A) = 53/100 = 0.53$,

 $P(B) = 47/100 = 0.47$

 c. $P(A|W) = 35/60 = 0.58\overline{3}$,

 $P(B|W) = 25/60 = 0.41\overline{6}$

 d. $P(A|M) = 18/40 = 0.45$,

 $P(B|M) = 22/40 = 0.55$

Chapter 8 Questions for Review

1 a. classical,

$$P(win) = \frac{1}{14,000,000} \approx 0.00000007$$

 b. empirical, $36/64 = 0.5625$

 c. classical, $1/6 = 0.1\overline{6}$

 e. empirical, $600/2000 = 0.30$

3 a. $2 \cdot 3 = 6$

 b. $2 \cdot 3 \cdot 3 = 18$

 c.

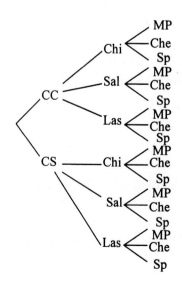

5 **a.** $\dfrac{4}{52} \cdot \dfrac{4}{52} \approx 0.0059$

   b. $\dfrac{4}{52} \cdot \dfrac{3}{51} \approx 0.0045$

7 **a.** Students believe they do not receive too much homework.

   b. $P(A) = 60/100 = 0.60$

   c. $P(\text{not } A) = 0.40$